THE
SCOTTISH WAR OF
INDEPENDENCE

THE
SCOTTISH WAR OF
INDEPENDENCE

EVAN MACLEOD BARRON

BARNES
& NOBLE
BOOKS
NEW YORK

First published in 1914

This edition published by Barnes & Noble, Inc.

1997 Barnes & Noble Books

ISBN 0-76070-328-0

Printed and bound in the United States of America

97 98 99 00 01 M 9 8 7 6 5 4 3 2

QF

INTRODUCTION

In this book I claim to have presented for the first time an accurate and understandable narrative of the Scottish War of Independence. No period in the history of Scotland has hitherto been so misrepresented as this, no period has suffered so much from the carelessness and partisanship of historical writers, and no period has been treated with less of that impartial and inquiring spirit which is supposed to be the perquisite of the historian. Of the truth of these assertions abundant evidence will be found in the following pages.

It is, perhaps, impossible for any writer, be he Scottish or English, to approach the study of the Scottish War of Independence without some bias, conscious or unconscious, in favour of his own country. In the following pages I have done my best to be impartial, but none the less I frankly confess that I write as a Scotsman and as a Highlander, and that, accordingly, my sympathies are, naturally and rightly, Scottish and Highland. I use the latter phrase advisedly, for the Highlands have for so long been treated with such ignorance, neglect, and, I regret to say, contempt by Scottish historians, that I have found it necessary to emphasize, in a manner which some people may resent, the part played by the Highlands and the rest of Celtic Scotland in the War of Independence. I would simply ask such readers to remember that I am " up against " the accepted theories and beliefs of centuries, and that the true blame for any seemingly undue emphasis on things Highland and things Celtic in these pages lies at the door of those modern historians who have used the reputation which is theirs to perpetuate a view of Scottish history which is altogether fallacious and misleading. I would ask them to realise that the history of Scotland is not the history of the southern counties which the kingdom of the Scots added to itself by conquest and annexation, but the history of the whole land and people of Scotland.

The facts which I have elucidated in the following pages, and the conclusions drawn from these facts, completely revolutionise the history of the War of Independence, and, if I may say so without egotism, throw a new and vivid light on the whole history of Scotland. For the first time the tale of the part played in the War of Independence by Celtic Scotland, and especially by the north—that is all Scotland north of a line drawn from a little north of Renfrew on the Clyde to Bo'ness on the Forth, practically the line of Antonine's Wall—is told in its entirety and placed in its true perspective; and I venture to say it will come as a revelation even to those who imagined that they were thoroughly acquainted with the history of the War of Independence. In short I may say that I claim to have proved beyond the possibility of doubt that the War of Independence was the achievement of Celtic Scotland, and especially of the northern part of Celtic Scotland, and that Teutonic Scotland—Lothian—had neither lot nor part in the Scots' long struggle for freedom. If I am right then the history of the twenty most critical years in the history of Scotland has been revolutionised and rewritten; and as my claim is, therefore, a high one I trust no one will be so wanting in the critical or the historical faculty as to pass judgment upon it without first considering carefully the evidence I have adduced in the following pages.

It will be noticed that part of this book is devoted

to a consideration of the actions and the motives of the Bruces during the twenty years which preceded the slaying of the Red Comyn in 1306. I venture to claim that in it I have cleared the memory of King Robert Bruce of most of the charges which have been brought against him, and for the first time placed his actions and his motives in their true light—a light which contrasts very favourably indeed with that in which he has hitherto appeared in the pages of Scottish history. It is peculiarly appropriate that this vindication of the character of Scotland's patriot king should be forthcoming in the year which witnesses the sex-centenary of his crowning triumph of Bannockburn.

I should, perhaps, add that this book is based almost entirely on contemporary or fourteenth-century authorities —documents, chronicles, charters, letters, despatches, and so on—and that in its compilation I have had the advantage of consultation with several of the leading Celtic and Scottish scholars of the day. I should also explain that in order to avoid overloading my pages with references, I have not thought it necessary, save in a few instances, to give volume and page references to chronicles or histories mentioned in the text. It will be noticed also that I rarely give a volume, page, or number reference to Rymer's *Foedera*. The reason is that three separate editions of *Foedera* are in existence, and as I was compelled to consult sometimes one and sometimes another of these the varying references would have been confusing. Moreover, the very complete chronological *Syllabus of Rymer's Foedera* in the Rolls Series makes volume, page, or number reference unnecessary. All the reader requires to do is to turn up in the Syllabus the document referred to, under its date, and he will find a synopsis of its contents and a reference to the precise place where the full text may be found in each of the editions.

It is only fair to say that the bulk of the following pages appeared weekly in the columns of the *Inverness Courier* during the past eighteen or twenty months. They have, however, been revised, altered, and rearranged for this book, and a considerable amount of new matter has been added. I should also say that the quotations from *Scalacronica* and the *Chronicle of Lanercost* are taken from Sir Herbert Maxwell's admirable translations of these two valuable chronicles, and that the edition of Barbour's *Bruce* which I have used is that so excellently edited by Mr. W. M. Mackenzie and published in 1909. It is far and away the most scholarly edition of *The Bruce* at present in print.

I also desire to acknowledge my indebtedness to a volume published as long ago as 1858 by the late Dr. James Taylor, Elgin, viz., *Edward I in the North of Scotland*. It is a marvel of learning, skill, and care, and throws much light on the history of the period.

I cannot conclude this Introduction without expressing my deep gratitude to all—and they have been many—who have assisted me in the compilation and production of this book. I desire especially to acknowledge my indebtedness to the following :

To the Curators of the Advocates' Library, Edinburgh, for placing the resources of the library at my service, and to Mr. W. K. Dickson, LL.D., Keeper of the Library, and his assistants, Mr. George Stronach and Mr. W. Maxwell Cooper, for the unfailing courtesy and consideration which they extended to me during the many months I spent in the library ; to Mr. P. J. Anderson, the learned and courteous Librarian of Aberdeen University ; to Professor Hume Brown for much welcome advice and encouragement ; to Mr. John Buchan for kind and much appreciated assistance ; to my old and esteemed teacher, Mr. Thomas Cockburn, for reading the MS. and giving me the benefit of his advice on certain matters; to my friend Mr. William Dunbar, Advocate; to Mr. R. K. Hannay, of the Register House, for his help in elucidating a knotty problem; to my friend Mr. Cyril Lely for much invaluable assistance in connection with the printing and the proof-reading of this book; to Mr. W. Rae Macdonald for information in regard to matters relating to seals and coats-of-arms and for the replica of the seal which appears on the cover; to Mr. William Mackay, LL.D., for helpful criticism and the loan of valuable books; to Mr. John Minto, Keeper of the Signet Library; to my friend Mr. W. B. G. Minto, Aberdeen; to my friend Mr. Charles L. Riach, Advocate; and to my friend, and one-time instructor, Mr. W. J. Watson, LL.D., for giving me frequently and generously the benefit of his unrivalled knowledge of the Celtic language, literature, race, and history, and extending to me much valued assistance in other ways. I desire also to acknowledge the invaluable help I have received in a thousand ways from my father and my brother, and to express my obligation to Mrs. Ritchie for the full and adequate Index which completes the book.

26th May 1914.

LIST OF ABBREVIATED REFERENCES

BAIN.—Bain's *Calendar of Documents relating to Scotland.*

B. P.—*The Scots Peerage,* edited by Sir James Balfour Paul.

CHRONICLES.—*Chronicles of the Reigns of Edward I and Edward II.* (Rolls Series).

ITINERARY.—Gough's *Itinerary of Edward I, 1272-1307.* Vol. II. No page references are given in footnotes, as the Itinerary is arranged chronologically.

PALGRAVE.—Palgrave's *Documents and Records illustrating the History of Scotland.*

REGISTRUM MAGNI SIGILLI.—Vol. I., 1912 edition. Edited by J. Maitland Thomson.

STEVENSON.—Stevenson's *Documents illustrative of the History of Scotland, 1286-1306.*

VITA EDWARDI SECUNDI.—*Chronicles* (see above), Vol. II.

CONTENTS

CHAPTER I

SCOTLAND AT THE OUTBREAK OF THE WAR OF INDEPENDENCE

CHAPTER II

THE HISTORICAL BACKGROUND

CHAPTER III

THE BEGINNINGS OF THE STRUGGLE

CONTENTS XV

CHAPTER X

THE TRUTH ABOUT THE BRUCES (1286–1292)

CHAPTER XI

THE TRUTH ABOUT THE BRUCES (1292–1298)

CHAPTER XII

THE TRUTH ABOUT THE BRUCES. SOME ELEMENTARY CONSIDERATIONS

CHAPTER XIII

THE BRUCES AND THE COMYNS
(1298–1304)

CHAPTER XIV

BRUCE AND LAMBERTON

CHAPTER XV

WILLIAM WALLACE AND ROBERT BRUCE

b

CHAPTER XVI

THE SLAYING OF THE RED COMYN

CHAPTER XVII

THE NORTH FROM 1297–1304

CHAPTER XVIII

HOW THE ENGLISH FARED IN MORAY IN 1304

CHAPTER XIX

BRUCE'S BID FOR A KINGDOM

CONTENTS

CHAPTER XX

BRUCE'S ADHERENTS IN 1306

CHAPTER XXI

BEFORE AND AFTER METHVEN

CHAPTER XXII

THE MYSTERY OF THE ISLAND OF RATHLIN

CHAPTER XXIII

Some Problems of 1307

CHAPTER XXIV

Reconstruction of Events from September 1306 to September 1307

CHAPTER XXV

Bruce and the Earl of Ross

CONTENTS

CHAPTER XXVI

CAMPAIGN IN MORAY AND ROSS (1307)

CHAPTER XXVII

THE CAMPAIGN IN ABERDEENSHIRE (1307–8)

CHAPTER XXVIII

THE HERSCHIP OF BUCHAN

CHAPTER XXIX

THE CONQUEST OF ARGYLL

CHAPTER XXX

NOVEMBER 1308 TO MARCH 1309

CHAPTER XXXI

THE CONQUEST OF GALLOWAY

CHAPTER XXXII

BRUCE'S FIRST PARLIAMENT

CONTENTS

CONTENTS

CHAPTER XXXIX

BANNOCKBURN : THE FIRST PHASE

CHAPTER XL

BANNOCKBURN : THE SECOND PHASE

CHAPTER XLI

THE END OF THE WAR

CHAPTER XLII

CONCLUSION

MAP AND PLANS

The
Scottish War of Independence

A Critical Study

CHAPTER I

SCOTLAND AT THE OUTBREAK OF THE WAR OF INDEPENDENCE

EARLY in the year 1296 occurred the first overt act of war in the long struggle between Scotland and England, a struggle provoked by the overmastering ambition of Edward I of England. In October 1295, John Balliol, Scotland's vassal king, goaded at last into action by the constant and humiliating interference of Edward I in the affairs of Scotland, renounced the allegiance which had been extorted from him, and began to prepare for the war which he knew was now inevitable. In March 1296 the Scottish army invaded England by the western march, and laid waste the north-western counties as far as Hexham. This invasion was doubtless precipitated by the knowledge that Edward I, with a mighty army, was approaching the Scottish border by the east coast, and he in fact entered Scotland two days after the Scots had entered England. Berwick, the largest and wealthiest town in Scotland, was immediately invested, was captured by assault after a brief siege, and given up to a three days' sack and massacre, the horrors of which were long remembered, and have left a stain on the memory of the English king which nothing will ever wash away. Fresh from the massacre of Berwick, Edward advanced to Dunbar, and there on 27th April he inflicted on the

A

Scots a great defeat, dispersing their army with much slaughter, and capturing their leaders and the flower of their nobility and knighthood.   Thence he marched in triumph through Scotland as far as Elgin, pressing forward, as the Lanercost chronicler has it, "with kingly courage into the region of the unstable inhabitants of Moray, whither you will not find in the ancient records that any one had penetrated since Arthur."   On his way thither he received, on 7th July 1296, at Stracathro in Kincardine, the surrender of John Balliol and the renunciation of his throne.

Elgin was reached by way of Aberdeen, Fyvie, Turriff, Banff, Cullen, and the Enzie on 26th July,[1] and there Edward remained till the 29th, on which day, a Sunday, he set out on his return journey, proceeding by way of Rothes, Arndilly, and the castle of Galval, a stronghold of Sir Andrew de Moravia, and through the valley of the Fiddoch, Balvenie, Mortlach, and the Cabrach to Kildrummy, a seat of the Earl of Mar.[2] From Kildrummy he continued his southward march by way of Kincardine O'Neil, Kincardine in the Mearns, Brechin, Arbroath, Dundee, and the Carse o' Gowrie to Perth, and thence by way of Scone, Lindores, Dunfermline, Stirling, Linlithgow, and Edinburgh to Berwick, which he reached on 22nd August.[3]   During his triumphal progress Edward received the submission and the homage of two thousand of the leading men of the land, nobles, knights, clergy, landholders, and burgesses, and at a Parliament at Berwick on 28th August these again swore fealty, together with the whole community of Scotland, whatever that may mean.[4]   This is the famous transaction, which is recorded in the " Ragman Rolls," which were compiled at the time from the original homages to which the seals of the granters were attached.

All Scotland now seemed prostrate at Edward's feet. Dunbar had deprived the country of her natural leaders ; the surrender of John Balliol and Edward's march to

---

[1] Itinerary.   [2] Ibid.   [3] Ibid.   [4] Bain, ii. 193, &c.

Elgin had emphasized the feeling of helplessness which Dunbar had begotten, and had brought home to the mind of the whole country a sense of Edward's power; all the great men of Scotland, with hardly an exception, had sworn fealty to the conqueror; and finally, throughout the length and breadth of the kingdom, the castles were held for England and were garrisoned by Edward's men. Even in the districts beyond Elgin, whither Edward himself had not penetrated, the power of England had made itself felt, and the castles of Inverness, Nairn, Forres, Urquhart, Dingwall, and Cromarty, the castles which were the outward and visible sign of the authority of the kingdom of Scotland in the north, were in English hands.[1] Good cause had Edward for believing that his dream was at last realised, and that Britain was his from sea to sea.

His satisfaction, however, was short-lived. The very ease and completeness of his triumph in 1296 should have warned him that it was a triumph only on the surface. He had caught Scotland stunned and dazed by the debacle of Dunbar; and by the rapidity of his march through the country and the display of his might he had brought her people to their knees before they had time to recover from their stupefaction or take steps to remedy the disasters which had fallen on them. But their spirit was not broken. It was simply temporarily demoralised, and as soon as they had had a little breathing space, recovery, quick and certain, set in. For Scotland, in spite of the evident disbelief of many modern authorities, was at the close of the thirteenth century a nation in every sense of the word. She had a national consciousness and a national sentiment. Patriotism, though perhaps not quite patriotism in the modern meaning of the word, was by no means so "rudimentary" as Mr. Andrew Lang and other writers would have us believe. Neither patriotism, nor a love of independence, nor a hatred of England and English domination, sprang full-blooded into life as a result of the War of Independence. They were, on

---

[1] See various entries, Bain, ii., and Stevenson, ii.

the contrary, the causes which really lay at the root of
that war, as any intelligent reading of the history of
Scotland in the centuries prior to 1300 must make clear.
Hatred of England was not, it is true, prior to the War
of Independence, so deep or so personal as it afterwards
became. But hatred of a kind there certainly was, a
hatred begotten partly of distrust, partly of suspicion,
and partly of dislike. During the thirteenth century the
feeling is, perhaps, not so evident as in earlier centuries,
but it is apparent none the less.

The vast majority of the Scottish people, it must
never be forgotten, were in the thirteenth century Celtic
in race, language, and sentiment. Even the nobility were
by no means so entirely Anglicised or Normanised as is
generally believed, while the legend that the whole seaboard of the east coast from Berwick to Inverness was
inhabited by English-speaking strangers of English race
is a legend and nothing else. Even the so-called English burghs are largely the figment of too vivid imagina-
tions. Such burghs as existed were few in number and
small in size, while their population was, in Scotland
north of the Forth, with one or two exceptions, far more
Celtic than Teutonic. As a matter of fact, moreover,
the Teutonic element in the burghs north of Forth was
not English to any appreciable extent. It was Fleming
almost entirely, which is a very different thing. That
is to say, the ancestors of the burgesses of foreign name
did not come as a rule either from England or by way
of England. They came, most of them, direct from the
Continent. They had, therefore, neither knowledge of
nor sympathy with England, and as most of them married
Celtic wives, their descendants were, as a rule, almost as
Celtic as the Celts in spite of their foreign names. A
modern analogy may be found to-day in the case of the
British citizen who goes to the United States. He
marries and rears a family, and these children, British
born and bred as their parent or both their parents may
be, are as American in sympathy and outlook as the
purest born citizen of the United States. This is within

the personal knowledge of every reader of these pages. The British immigrant, in spite of ties of race, blood, and language, does not absorb the American. The American instead absorbs him or at the very least his family.

Now, in Scotland in the early Middle Ages this was even more true. The Fleming merchant-trader came to a land with which he had no ties of blood, sympathy, or language. He came to exploit it, but found it a good and pleasant land, and so stayed. Are we to believe that throughout the centuries he married and intermarried with people of his own race only, and so remained an alien amid an unfriendly population? The idea is preposterous, yet it is the idea which is at the bottom of much that is written concerning the so-called Teutonic element in Scotland. There is only one town in the whole of Celtic Scotland, that is in all Scotland outside Lothian, to whose people the term foreign can with any degree of truth be applied in the thirteenth century. That town is Aberdeen, and the curious thing is that right down the centuries the true son of Aberdeen has maintained certain characteristics of his own, so much so that even to-day the typical Aberdonian is different from his fellow-Scots elsewhere.

For this there are excellent historic reasons. Aberdeen is the one town in Scotland outside Lothian which was founded by, or at least sprang into importance because of a large settlement of foreigners. These foreigners were Flemings, and throughout the Middle Ages the population of Aberdeen remained very largely Fleming or of Flemish extraction. For that there were two main reasons. To Aberdeen the Flemings had come in much greater numbers than to any other place north of the Forth, and between Aberdeen and the Low Countries there was constant communication. Aberdeen too, served an extensive district, a district which was rich in the staple products of the period. Thus she grew rapidly in size and importance, and as she occupied, on the Aberdeenshire seaboard, a position extremely favourable for carrying on a Continental trade, and as the bulk of her trade was with the Low Countries, she frequently received accessions to her population from her kinsmen across the water. Her burgesses in consequence, both on account of their size as a community, and the coming and going between them and the Low Countries, did not intermarry with the Celts of the surrounding districts to any appreciable extent, as did their kinsmen elsewhere, but married women of their own race and reared their children in the midst of a community preponderatingly Fleming by descent. That is why, for at least six hundred years, Aberdeen was not only regarded by the surrounding districts as more or less an alien community, but actually was such in very many ways. But Aberdeen was not an English community. It had no English sympathies. It was, indeed, not only an integral part of the kingdom of Scotland, but was almost more Scottish than the Scots in its dislike of the English and its hatred of English domination; and, as we shall see in the course of our narrative, its burgesses were actively engaged on the side of the patriots during the long struggle with England.

It is high time, indeed, that the English myth in Scottish history was exploded once and for all. The only people of English blood who are found in any numbers in Scotland are the people of Lothian. And they, it must never be forgotten in the study of Scottish history, and especially in the study of early Scottish history, became part of the kingdom of Scotland by conquest.[1] The tradition of that conquest has survived among the Celts even to our own day, and we may be very sure, therefore, that in the thirteenth century, less than 300 years after the event, it was a very potent memory. Moreover, all recent research goes to show that in the thirteenth century the language of the bulk of the people of all Scotland outside Lothian was Celtic. In the districts to the south as well as

[1] See Robertson's *Scotland under her Early Kings*, Hume Brown's *History of Scotland*, &c., &c.

to the north of the Forth and Clyde, Celtic, save in
Lothian, was the popular tongue.

Now it will be made clear in the following pages
that it was precisely the English-speaking counties, that
is to say Lothian, which were the last to throw off the
English yoke, and while this may be partly explained by
their proximity to England it is not by any means either
the whole or a sufficient explanation. On the other
hand Celtic Scotland not only bore the brunt of the
struggle for independence, but raised the standard of
revolt time and again, and ranged itself on the side of
many a desperate forlorn hope when the English-speaking counties were content to look on passively or submit
quiescently.

There were, of course, English-speakers in Celtic
Scotland. English, after all, was the language of com-
merce, and English after the conquest of Lothian, and
by means of the later efforts of the English wife of
Malcolm Canmore, and Malcolm Canmore's successors,
became also, until it was superseded by Norman-French,
the language of the Court. But though it spread into
Celtic Scotland its progress was slow, and those who
spoke it a comparatively small proportion of the population even in the thirteenth century. It is a gross exaggeration to write, as is far too frequently done, of a sort
of peaceful English conquest of Celtic Scotland in the
eleventh, twelfth, and thirteenth centuries. The influx
of English fugitives after the Norman Conquest was
nothing like so great as is too often imagined, and they
certainly did not settle in Celtic Scotland in any considerable numbers. The English-speakers in Celtic
Scotland were, in the main, Celts or Flemings or people
of mixed Celtic and Flemish descent, who either acquired
English themselves, for reasons of business or State, or
inherited it from their ancestors who had acquired it for
similar reasons. But the important thing to realise and
to remember is that the presence of the English language
in Celtic Scotland was not due to the same causes as its
presence in Lothian, and that practically all those in

Celtic Scotland who spoke English in the thirteenth century, spoke Gaelic as well. There was, therefore, this very important distinction between Lothian and the rest of Scotland. The English-speakers in Celtic Scotland were, with very few exceptions, not English in race or sentiment. When not Celts they were as much a part of the ancient Celtic kingdom as the Celts themselves, and when the struggle with England came they were just as forward and just as eager to throw off the English yoke as the most ardent Celt of them all. In this they formed a striking contrast to those who spoke the English tongue in Lothian.

I do not mean by that last sentence that the inhabitants of the English-speaking counties proved disloyal to the kingdom of Scotland. On the contrary, at the beginning of the war they fought as desperately against England as any of their fellow-subjects, as their defence of Berwick shows. But their antagonism to England was neither so traditional nor so deep-rooted as was that of Celtic Scotland, while between them and their neighbours across the border were many ties of language and blood, which the long peace between the two countries undoubtedly cemented. Thus there was not in these counties the same undying detestation of English domination that there was elsewhere in Scotland ; and so we find, as the war drags on, that the resistance gradually grows less, until at last, during the first seven or eight years of Bruce's reign, it is practically non-existent. Of course the fact that these counties lay in close proximity to the English border, and would therefore often be the first to feel the weight of England's hand, was an important factor in their attitude, but while that is so we must not let it blind us to the fact that community of language and race also played a part. The neighbouring Celtic counties to the west and south were just as easily accessible from England as was Lothian—how often was Scotland invaded by the western march ?—yet, until the blood-feud begotten by the death of Comyn ranged part of them against Bruce, they bore a great share in the struggle for independence, while even after 1306, and in spite of the blood-feud, their efforts and their sacrifices on behalf of the national cause were much greater than those of the neighbouring counties of Lothian.

As late as August 1313 the whole of the English-speaking counties were in the hands of England. There were English garrisons in Berwick, Roxburgh, Edinburgh, Dunbar, Linlithgow, Yester, Dirleton, Luffenok, Jedburgh, Cavers, Livingston, and perhaps Selkirk; and English sheriffs still ruled in Berwick, Roxburgh, Edinburgh, Haddington, and Linlithgow. Beyond these only the isolated castles of Stirling and Bothwell were held for England in all the rest of Scotland. These are hard facts which cannot be explained away.[1] To put my whole contention on this point briefly, the English-speaking counties were eager to remain part of Scotland, but they were not moved by the same deep-rooted antipathy to English domination as was the rest of Scotland. Their resistance was therefore less prolonged. They reconciled themselves to English rule, accepting it as an accomplished, though an unpleasant, fact, and they were slow to join in the desperate efforts which were made by Celtic Scotland to cast it off. All of which emphasizes the difference in race and in sentiment between them and the rest of Scotland, and points irresistibly to the conclusion that, had the latter been animated by the same spirit as the former, the independence of Scotland would never have been won.

There remains the question of the magnates of the realm, those knights and nobles who are usually held up to us as overwhelmingly English or Anglo-Norman in race, language, tradition, and sentiment. That this is also an exaggerated conception I endeavour to show on a subsequent page. Meanwhile, it will suffice to say that the old Celtic nobility was at the end of the thirteenth century by no means extinct, that many Celtic knights

[1] See various entries in Bain's *Calendar, Rotuli Scotiae,* &c. See also Chapter XXXVII.

and nobles are numbered among the so-called Anglo-Normans quite erroneously, and that in the old Celtic kingdom a much larger number of men of knightly rank fought on the side of the patriotic cause than has hitherto been imagined. Their names will be found in a later chapter.

The question of Norman organisation is quite another matter. For the moment we are dealing with the question of nationality, but it may at once be said that while nationality was at the bottom of the resistance to England, it was the Norman capacity for organisation which made that resistance effective, and, in the end, triumphant. My point, meantime, is that it is altogether erroneous to regard the feudal aristocracy of Scotland as Anglo-Norman in race or sentiment. Some of them, of course, were; but the majority, at the close of the thirteenth century, were Anglo-Norman only in their culture. They were in every other respect more Celtic than English or Norman, and therein lies the explanation of much that seems mysterious in their actions during the War of Independence.

Finally, a quotation from two English chroniclers, one of the period and one a little later, will point the moral of my whole argument on this question of nationality and patriotism. Says the Lanercost chronicler, writing of Bruce's campaigns down to the beginning of 1312 : " In all these aforesaid campaigns the Scots were so divided among themselves that sometimes the father was on the Scottish side and the son on the English, and vice versa ; also one brother might be with the Scots and another with the English ; yea, even the same individual be first with one party and then with the other. But all those who were with the English were merely feigning, either because it was the stronger party, or in order to save the lands they possessed in England ; *for their hearts were always with their own people, although their persons might not be so.*" (The italics are mine.) The other quotation is from Knighton. It is a thing to be remarked, says he, " that the whole followers of the nobility attached themselves to Wallace ; and that although the persons of

their lords were with the king in England, their heart
was with Wallace, who found his army reinforced by so
immense a multitude of the Scots that the community of
the land obeyed him as their leader and prince." It must
be admitted that either of these quotations, especially
when it is remembered that they come from Englishmen,
is difficult to reconcile with the view that in Scotland at
the close of the thirteenth century there was neither
homogeneity, patriotism, nor a sense of nationality.

To sum up, my whole contention on this matter is
that Scotland at the death of Alexander III was a nation
in a fuller sense of the meaning of that term than has
been conceded by any of our modern historians. Its
organisation was modelled on Anglo-Norman lines, and
that fact, together with a misreading of authorities, and
an inability to shake off the influence of certain writers
of the English school, has led the majority of Scottish
historians to assume that the nation itself had become,
by the close of the thirteenth century, largely Anglicised
or Normanised. It is impossible, in the space at my disposal, to go into that question at length; but I have
shown that there is good reason for believing that, far
from being Anglicised, in any sense of the word, the vast
majority of the people of Scotland outside Lothian were
Celtic in race, in speech, and in sentiment. The national
sentiment of the country was, undoubtedly, largely Celtic
in its inspiration; and it is this fact which explains the
otherwise inexplicable strength of the resistance to England of a people who have too long been supposed to
have possessed neither national consciousness nor national
cohesion, and who have too long been assumed to have
been largely English in race, language, and sentiment.
For it is a fact beyond question that throughout the early
history of the land that is now called Scotland the Celt
loved not the Saxon, and down to the death of Alexander
III disliked, distrusted, and despised him. These things
were part of the heritage of that Celtic kingdom which
for centuries had known England as its deadliest foe,
which had wrested by force of arms a large territory from

England, which had ever to be on its guard against English aggression, which had seen English influences remodelling its institutions in a way which it disliked and frequently took up arms against, and which, even in the comparatively peaceful years of the thirteenth century, had witnessed and had resented English efforts to obtain by guile that voice in the affairs of Scotland which it coveted, but which, it had failed to obtain by force. The national sentiment of all Scotland outside Lothian was, in a word, traditionally and instinctively anti-English; while Lothian, long before the death of Alexander III, had been so thoroughly absorbed in the kingdom of Scotland that her people were an integral part of the Scottish nation and considered themselves as such, though they were not moved by the same inherent distrust and dislike of England as were the inhabitants of the rest of Scotland. It was, therefore, the national sentiment of the kingdom of Scotland, a sentiment mainly Celtic in its origin and its inspiration, which lay at the root of the resistance to England, which inspired rising after rising against seemingly hopeless odds, which, in spite of crushing defeat and cruel repression, filled the ranks of the patriots again and again, and which finally brought Scotland safely through the fiery furnace of the War of Independence.[1]

---

[1] Among the various authorities on which the statements as to the Celts and the distribution of Gaelic are founded may be mentioned, *Transactions of Gaelic Society of Inverness*, *Records of Inverness*, vol. i. (*New Spalding Club*), *Old Statistical Account*, Robertson's *Scotland under her Early Kings*, Skene's *Celtic Scotland*, the *Book of Buchan*, Bain's *Calendar*, Stevenson's *Documents*, various books on Place-names, &c., &c.

CHAPTER II

THE HISTORICAL BACKGROUND OF THE WAR OF INDEPENDENCE

At the very outset of our study of the history of the War of Independence it is necessary, though it should not be necessary, to remind ourselves that we must keep constantly in view the fact that we are dealing with a period so remote and so different from that in which we live, as the closing years of the thirteenth century and the opening years of the fourteenth. The reminder is necessary, because a fact so essential to the true elucidation and understanding of the history of the War of Independence is sometimes more often forgotten than remembered, and that by people from whom we have a right to expect better things. This lack of perspective, if I may call it so, is seen most frequently in the very important matter of dates. It is absolutely impossible to arrive at anything like a true reconstruction of the War of Independence unless we get our dates right; yet time and again events are misunderstood, and all manner of historical difficulties are created, by errors and confusion in regard to dates. These errors, in many cases, would not have occurred, and much confusion would in consequence have been avoided, had a fact of the first importance to the historical writer been constantly kept in view, the fact, namely, that the historical background of the period under notice must never be lost sight of. It is almost incredible that any historical writer should neglect a matter so manifestly important, but it is a lamentable fact, none the less, that very frequently he does, and it will be made abundantly evident in the following pages that the period of the War of Independence has been particularly unfortunate in this respect.

What, then, is the historical background which is of such importance to the history of the War of Independence? It may be stated in a single sentence—the whole conditions of the country and the times. It will be well, however, to elaborate this a little. It is constantly forgotten by historians of the period that Scotland was in the fourteenth century, and by Scotland I mean the land itself, not the people, a very wild country. Thick forests of large extent were common in most parts of the kingdom. Huge wastes of moor, moss, bog, and water abounded. Roads in the modern conception of the word there were none, tracks of the roughest description providing the sole means of communication by land. Rivers were wide, deep, and swift-running, and could be crossed only by ford or ferry, bridges being exceedingly few and far between. And, finally, the climate was considerably colder, wetter, and harsher than it is in the twentieth century. Civilisation, moreover, had not as yet addressed itself to the means of overcoming these natural disadvantages. Journeys by land were undertaken on horse or on foot, by sea in small vessels ill-equipped for the manifold perils of man and weather. Moreover, the great forests, the vast wastes, the rugged hillsides, and the wild defiles of the mountains, made brigandage easy and the life of the outlaw attractive to desperate men. So communication was at all times slow and arduous, and the way of the traveller beset by many perils.

It is this matter of communication which, for our special purpose, is of supreme importance. If we lose sight of it, we shall never solve many of the riddles of the War of Independence. In a country such as we have described communication must plainly, under the most favourable circumstances, have been slow. The traveller, too, must, for his own protection, have ridden in company or fully armed. The progress of a company could, in the circumstances of the time, have seldom exceeded fifteen to twenty miles a day, and might well have been a good deal less. The rate of progress of a single traveller, or of a knight with a mounted escort, could not have been much greater, for it must be remembered that the military horses of the period were not graceful Arab steeds, light of build and fleet of foot, but strongly built animals, capable of carrying the weight of a knight in full armour, and of braving the rigours of mediæval warfare. In the course of our narrative we shall come across many instances of the time actually taken by parties, large and small, in traversing various distances, but meantime a single example, taken from a reign subsequent to our period, will suffice.

In 1336 Edward III set out for Blair Athol on his famous ride to the relief of the Countess of Athol, who was being besieged by the third Andrew de Moray in the castle of Lochindorb. His entire force was mounted, the time was the month of June, when the weather was likely to be favourable, and when the days at least were long and the nights short; and Edward pressed forward in such haste and with such vigour that, when he reached his destination, his horses had suffered greatly, many having died, and those which survived being much emaciated. Yet he took four days to traverse the sixty to seventy miles which lie between Blair Athol and Lochindorb.[1]

The weather and the season of the year of course played an extremely important part in the speed with which a man could travel in the fourteenth century, and this is a matter which must also be borne in mind. As a general rule it may be laid down that a knight, mounted and travelling in haste, could, in the height of summer, cover the journey from Inverness to Berwick in ten days to a fortnight, and the journey from Berwick to London in about the same period. A messenger, therefore, from Perth to London would take nearly three weeks, and from Inverness to London nearly a month. But that was only in the summer months. In winter and spring it was a very different matter. Then not only were the days short and the nights long, the

[1] Bain's *The Edwards in Scotland*, p. 89.

weather bad, the roads worse, and the rivers often impassable, but fodder for horses was very difficult to get, was often, in fact, quite unobtainable. Accordingly, it may be said that, as a rule, the journey from Inverness to London for fully six months of the year would occupy at the very least two months, and often a good deal more, and that from Berwick to London not less than three or four weeks. Barbour, in describing Bruce's alleged ride from London to Lochmaben in January 1306, says he accomplished it in fifteen days "riding day and night," which he plainly regards as a feat of no ordinary kind. We may also note that the sea was seldom used as a means of communication. Nearly every knight and every messenger of whatever degree, of whose method of travelling any record remains, accomplished the journey from Scotland to England, and vice versa, by land.

A comparison with a much later period will bring out the difficulty of communication even more clearly. Says Mr. Grey Graham, in his *Social Life in Scotland in the Eighteenth Century*: "The highways were tracks of mire in wet weather and marshes in winter, till the frost had made them sheets of ice, covered with drifted snow. When rain fell, the flat ground became lakes with islands of stone, and the declivities became cataracts. Even towns were connected only by pack-roads, on which horses stumbled perilously along . . . over unenclosed land and moorland, where after rain it was difficult to trace any beaten track."

And again, "As to travelling to far-off London, the obstacles were too great for poor persons, too perilous for nervous persons, to undertake the expedition. It was expensive, it was tedious, it was adventurous. . . . In fact to travel that road," that is from London to Edinburgh, "spending fourteen days on the way," in a closed bodied carriage and six horses, "cost two gentlemen in 1725 the sum of thirty pounds sterling." And these fourteen days, it may be added, were the last fourteen days of May. If conditions were such as late as the eighteenth century we can easily imagine what they must have been in the thirteenth and fourteenth centuries.

If these facts are kept in view in studying the history of the War of Independence, many pitfalls will be avoided and many grave misconceptions as to the character and the progress of the war removed. In particular it will be recognised that it is not only erroneous but stupid to apply to an occurrence in Scotland the date of the English document which mentions it. Yet this is very frequently done with results which are often ridiculous in the extreme. For example, it is a matter of the most common occurrence for a writer to assert that such and such a castle north of the Forth was in the hands of the English on, say, 15th December in a certain year because on that day orders were issued in London regarding it. Presumably the constable of the castle had on that very day communicated with London by some sort of mediæval telegraph of which we know nothing! The only intelligent treatment of such a record is, of course, to regard it simply as an indication that on the date when news of the castle was last despatched it was still in the hands of England; and it is in endeavouring to arrive at the date of that despatch that all the conditions of the country and the time must be kept in view. And so with most of the English documents on which our knowledge of events in Scotland depends. Each must be read in the light of all the conditions and circumstances of the time. It is necessary to emphasize this fact, both for the reason that disregard of it in the past has led to all manner of confusion, and because in the following pages attention will be directed to it repeatedly.

B

CHAPTER III

THE BEGINNINGS OF THE STRUGGLE

It is usually assumed, and frequently stated in histories of Scotland, that the rising of the Scots which is placed in May 1297 was due to the oppression of the officials whom Edward had set over Scotland. That view is entirely erroneous. The acts of oppression of which the English officials were undoubtedly guilty may in some cases have been the occasion of revolt, but they were certainly not the cause. The cause, as we have seen in the first chapter, lay very much deeper, and it is indeed somewhat extraordinary that any Scottish historian should have thought it necessary to ascribe the risings of 1297 to any cause so superficial as the behaviour of Edward's officials. The whole history of Scotland prior to 1297 shows the Scots to have been a warlike and independent race, ready always to resort to arms in defence of what they deemed their freedom or their rights. In 1296 they had been overcome for the moment by the completeness of the disaster at Dunbar, and by Edward's subsequent march through the kingdom, but it requires only a cursory acquaintance with their previous history to know that that seeming triumph could only have been of the most transient nature, and that on the very first opportunity the whole country would be up in arms. The history of Scotland prior to the year 1297 has been written in vain, if it is seriously contended that there would have been no rising against the domination of England in 1297 and subsequent years had it not been for extraneous causes such as the oppression of English officials.

The materials which exist for reconstructing the history of the months which elapsed between Edward's return to England in September 1296 and the first notice of a revolt in Scotland on a large scale, are unfortunately very scanty. So scanty indeed are they that most writers have contented themselves with beginning the tale of the renewal of the War of Independence with the attack of Douglas and Wallace on the English justiciar at Scone in May 1297. The fact of the matter, however, is that the war was renewed almost as soon as Edward was over the border, though perhaps it did not at that time assume dimensions sufficient to alarm Edward. In the beginning it naturally took the form of widely separated local risings, and a more or less serious state of disorder in districts which were not strongly held by English garrisons. These ebullitions, however, did not at once assume dangerous proportions, for the simple reasons that for some months they were unconnected with one another, and were not properly organised, the coming of winter naturally making communication between the different parts of the country difficult, while the fact that the natural leaders of the people were prisoners in England made organised rebellion, or rebellion on a large scale, at first well-nigh impossible.

In spite of these drawbacks, however, risings throughout the winter of 1296–97 there were. Although there is no historic confirmation of the tales of the deeds of Wallace during this period there can be little doubt that they have some basis in fact, for they merely reflect a condition of things which was common to the greater part of Scotland during these months. The first proof of the truth of this is found in the order which the English king issued, on 9th April 1297,[1] to "his faithful lieges of Argyll and Ross," commanding them to consult with and aid "his chosen and faithful Alexander of the Isles" in putting an end to disorders in these parts. "For certain malefactors and disturbers of our peace," runs the order, "who wander through divers places in these parts, and commit murders, burn-

[1] *Rotuli Scotiae*, i. 40, and Note at end of chapter.

ings, and other injuries against our peace, do you seek from day to day and do not rest until they are arrested and placed in safe custody." The date of this order is, as remarked, 9th April, which means of course that news of widespread trouble in Argyll and Ross had been despatched to Edward not later than the end of February. From another document[1] we know that one of the personages concerned in these troubles was Alexander of Argyll, and the document we have quoted shows that the disorders were not confined to one district, and were on a fairly considerable scale. But if the disturbances in Argyll and Ross were sufficiently serious in February to warrant the despatch of a report concerning them to Edward, it is clear that they had not suddenly sprung into prominence in a single day. They must, in fact, have been going on for a considerable period, and have eventually reached a point at which Edward's officials on the spot felt incapable of dealing with them. Which means, in other words, that throughout the whole winter of 1296–97 Argyll and Ross were, to put it at its lowest, in an extremely disturbed state, if not in actual revolt. And Argyll and Ross at that time covered the whole of the west of Scotland from the Firth of Clyde to Loch Broom.

What is true of Argyll and Ross is true of the greater part of Scotland outside Lothian. The fact that no records exist of a nature similar to that relating to Argyll and Ross is no evidence to the contrary, for a glance at the various Calendars of Documents of the period will show that extremely few documents relating to the affairs of Scotland between September 1296 and July 1297 have survived. The fact, however, that, as we shall see presently, all Scotland outside Lothian was in open rebellion by the month of May 1297 is sufficient proof of its condition in the preceding months.

The evidence for the widespread nature of the state of revolt which existed in May 1297 is plain and unmistakable. On 4th June[2] Edward, far away in Canter-

---

[1] Stevenson, ii. 187, &c.   [2] *Ibid.*, 170.

bury, issued a series of orders for the suppression of the insurrection in Scotland. " Since there are many persons," it begins, " who disturb the peace and quietness of our kingdom and make divers meetings, conventicles, and conspiracies in very many parts (*in pluribus locis*) of the land of Scotland, both within our liberties and without, and perpetrate depredations, homicides, burnings, robberies, rapines, and other evils in divers manners," therefore these orders are issued. Plainly, therefore, all these things had occurred long before the beginning of May, else had Edward's officers not been able to forward him, not later than the middle of that month, despatches which contained reports of risings in widely separated districts.

Now, the exact terms of the sentence which, eight years later, was passed on William Wallace, have been preserved, and the first part runs thus [1]: " William Wallace, a Scot and of Scottish descent, having been taken prisoner for sedition, homicides, depredations, fires, and felonies, and after our lord the king had conquered Scotland, forfeited Balliol, and subjugated all Scotsmen to his dominion as their king, and had received the oath of homage and fealty of prelates, earls, barons, and others, and proclaimed his peace, and appointed his officers to keep it through all Scotland : you, the said William Wallace, oblivious of your fealty and allegiance, did (1) *along with an immense number of felons, rise in arms and attack the king's officers and slay Sir William Hezelrig, Sheriff of Lanark,* when he was holding a court for the pleas of the king; (2) did with your armed adherents attack villages, towns, and castles, and issue brieves as if a superior through all Scotland, and hold parliaments and assemblies, and, not content with so great wickedness and sedition, did counsel all the prelates, earls, and barons of your party to submit to the dominion of the king of France, and to aid in the destruction of the realm of England."

No date is assigned either to the beginning of these deeds, or to the attack on Hezelrig, but contemporary

[1] *Chronicles*, i. 139-142.

English authorities place the latter in May 1297,[1] and mention also an attack on Ormsby, the English justiciar, as having taken place at Scone in the same month, Wallace and Sir William Douglas being the leaders on the latter occasion.[2]   Hemingburgh also relates that Ormsby " being forewarned escaped with difficulty, leaving much spoil to the enemy, which, when they had gathered, they proceeded, not now in secret as before, but openly, putting to the sword all the English they could find beyond the Scottish sea, turning themselves afterwards to the siege of the castles."   Thus both the sentence on Wallace and Hemingburgh's narrative prove that in May 1297 all the central part of Scotland north of the Forth was in open and successful insurrection against England.

At the very same time a rising on a large scale was in progress in the province of Moray,[3] which comprised, roughly speaking, the central and eastern parts of the modern county of Inverness, and all the modern counties of Elgin and Nairn.   At the head of the rising was Andrew de Moray,[4] and with him, as we know from the report of the English guardian of the province, were the burgesses of Inverness and many of the men of Moray.[5] We shall presently tell the tale of this little-known rising at length, but meanwhile it will suffice to say that the dates mentioned in the guardian of Moray's report leave no room for doubt that it had begun at latest by the middle of May.   About the same time there was trouble in the district of which Aberdeen was the centre,[6] for on 11th June Edward, then at Ospringe in Kent, addressed a writ to the Sheriff of Aberdeen strictly enjoining him to use every means in his power to arrest and bring to justice the armed bands of malefactors and disturbers of the peace who, the king has heard, are active in these parts.

Further south Macduff of Fife and his two sons had led out the men of that earldom,[7] with what result we

---

[1] Hemingburgh, Trivet, &c.   [2] *Ibid.*
[3] Bain, ii. 922.   [4] *Ibid.*   [5] *Ibid.*
[6] *Rotuli Scotiae*, i. 42.   [7] Stevenson, ii. 217.

shall see presently. So much, then, for Scotland north of the Forth and Clyde. By the middle of May at latest almost the whole of that vast and turbulent district was in open revolt, a condition in which a considerable part of it had certainly been for several months previously.

South of the Forth and Clyde, Lothian alone seems to have been undisturbed. In the west the Bishop of Glasgow and the Steward of Scotland were in the field before the end of May,[1] and were soon joined by the young Earl of Carrick,[2] Robert Bruce, the future king, while, as we saw, Wallace had descended on Lanark and slain Hezelrig, Edward's sheriff.

In the far south-west the country was up in arms as early as April, for on 13th June Edward, then in Kent, sent a letter of thanks to certain Gallovidian chieftains who had remained loyal to him.[3] As he thanks them "for repelling certain malefactors and disturbers of the peace, and recapturing castles taken by said malefactors in your parts," the rising clearly could not have begun later than April and probably was in full swing much earlier.

It is thus clear that by the month of May 1297 practically all Scotland outside Lothian was in revolt, and, looking to that fact, and to the condition of the times, the difficulties of communication and the like, and to the fact also that the risings occurred in widely separated districts, it is evident that long before May 1297 active hostility to England was rife in many different parts of the kingdom. The renewal of the War of Independence, accordingly, had its beginnings during these months and not in May 1297, as has hitherto been believed. That is to say, Edward was hardly over the border before the first mutterings of revolt made themselves heard. His campaign of 1296, therefore, had resulted in the defeat but not the conquest of Scotland : and it is significant that it was in the Celtic parts of the kingdom that these mutterings first became ominous, and

---

[1] Stevenson, ii. 192; Hemingburgh, &c.
[2] *Ibid.*   [3] Stevenson, ii. 177.

that the risings occurred which marked the spring and
early summer of 1297.

Two English chroniclers of the period describe the
leaders of the Scottish army in the summer of 1297 as
the Bishop of Glasgow, Andrew de Moray, the Steward
of Scotland, and William Wallace.[1] Hemingburgh
states that the Bishop of Glasgow and the Steward of
Scotland were "the fabricators" of the evil, while the
Lanercost chronicler is even more explicit, laying the
blame for the whole of the events of May and June 1297
at the door of the Bishop, who, "ever foremost in treason,
conspired with the Steward of the kingdom, named James,
for a new piece of insolence, yea, for a new chapter of
ruin. Not daring openly to break their pledge to the
king, they caused a certain bloody man, William Wallace,
who had formerly been a chief of brigands in Scotland, to
revolt against the king, and assemble the people in his
support." Compare this with Hemingburgh's narrative.
"In the month of May of the same year," he says, "the
perfidious race of the Scots began to rebel . . . William
de Ormsby, the king's justiciar, following steadily the
command of the king, was outlawing without distinction
of person all who were unwilling to take the oath of
fidelity to the king of England. But there was a certain
public robber, William Wallace by name, who had been
outlawed many times. He, when he was roaming and
fugitive, convoked all who were outlawed to himself, and
acted as if he were the chief of them, and they increased
to many people. With him also was associated the
aforesaid Sir William Douglas, who, at the surrender of
the castle of Berwick, had given himself up with his
men to our king on security of life and limb as aforesaid :
to whom the king had since restored everything, but he,
unmindful of these benefits, had become a robber allied
to a robber."

It is, of course, impossible to dogmatise from passages
like these, especially as, though written by contemporaries
of the men and events concerned, they were not set

[1] Trivet, Rishanger.

down on parchment till several years later. On the other hand, the fact that they were not set down till then means that they reflect the settled view in England regarding the causes and the course of those events, and the parts played by the various participators in them. Accordingly, though we cannot dogmatise from the passages quoted, we can draw certain general conclusions, concerning which it may be said that they are as near as it is possible now to get to the real truth of the events which preceded the appearance of several Scottish armies in the field in May 1297.

All the English chroniclers ascribe the beginning of trouble to the Bishop of Glasgow, but it must be clearly understood that what they have in view is not the series of disturbances and local risings which occurred in the winter of 1296–97, but the general uprising which became formidable in May 1297. The Bishop was certainly not the instigator of all and probably not of any, of the outbreaks which occurred during the winter months, but all the evidence goes to show that he was both the instigator and the organiser of the general revolt which came to a head a few months later. The outbreaks which occurred during the winter and the early spring, though they were due to the same general causes, had no direct connection with each other, and for that reason they did not become serious enough to attract the attention of the English chroniclers. But the Bishop of Glasgow viewed them otherwise. He was chafing against the interference of the English Church in the affairs of the Church of Scotland, and was only waiting for a favourable opportunity to embark on an attempt to throw off a yoke which bound the Church and the kingdom in one strong oppressive embrace. The outbreaks and disturbances during the winter of 1296–97 provided him to a limited extent with his opportunity. They disclosed a condition of things favourable to his schemes, and he straightway set to work to take advantage of them to organise a revolt on a large scale.

The remark of the Lanercost chronicler probably

indicates how he proceeded. Wallace, already an outlaw, had begun to attract to himself—doubtless by some of those exploits which Blind Harry revels in telling, and some of which, at least, must have a modicum of truth behind them—a large body of malcontents and outlaws in the Scottish midlands, and with them was performing various feats against the hated English. The Bishop, well-informed of all that was passing and eagerly plotting and planning for the overthrow of English domination, took prompt advantage of Wallace's doings to advance his own plans. " Not daring yet to break their pledged faith to the king," as the Lanercost chronicler has it, but, more accurately, not being yet in a position to throw off the mask, the Bishop and his allies encouraged Wallace and supported him to the best of their ability, which is the true meaning of the Lanercost chronicler's assertion that they caused him to revolt and assemble the people against the English king.

In all probability Sir William Douglas's association with Wallace at this stage was due to the Bishop. On general principles the Roman Catholic Church in Scotland was relentlessly opposed to the domination of England. During the months which had passed since Edward's march through Scotland in the summer and autumn of 1296 that opposition had been blown into a fierce flame of indignation by Edward's repeated presentation of English priests to Scottish benefices—a deliberate policy which had for its object the Anglicisation of the Scottish Church, and the consequent possible reconciling of the Scottish people to English rule by means of the great influence which the Church exerted in that age.[1] And in this connection it may here be noted that the English chroniclers record that Wallace's campaign in May and June 1297 was marked by fierce hostility to English priests and nuns, many of whom are alleged to have been slain and many others expelled from the country

[1] Any authoritative History of the Roman Catholic Church in Scotland. Professor MacEwen's *History of the Church in Scotland*, vol. i., is the most recent, and the most authoritative for our period.

with the greatest possible contumely.[1] Be that as it may, however, it was, beyond question, the Church of Scotland which, more than any class or community in the kingdom, inspired and kept alive the spirit of resistance to England throughout the long and bitter years of the War of Independence, and she it was who, in season and out of season, preached the sacred duty of war against the English yoke, and in the persons of her bishops and her priests often led the way on the field of battle itself. For while the people of Scotland as a whole were bitterly opposed to the yoke of England and were eager to throw it off, the Church of Scotland it was which possessed the means and the ability to give effective expression to that spirit, even to the extent of taking the lead in organising and supporting armed rebellion. And of all the leaders of the Church of Scotland during the period of the War of Independence the Bishop of Glasgow was the most able, as he was the most ardent and the most devoted in the cause of Scottish freedom.

Accordingly, the following facts are clear: (1) The Church of Scotland, with the Bishop of Glasgow as its militant leader, had been driven into fierce and implacable hostility to England, a hostility which would only be satisfied by the total overthrow of English rule in Scotland. (2) Throughout the winter and spring of 1296–97 Scotland was in an exceedingly disturbed state and local risings against the English occurred in widely separated districts. (3) The Bishop of Glasgow perceived in these the opportunity for which he had been waiting, and used the great power of the Church to foster the feeling of hostility to England, to foment rebellion, and generally to prepare the way for an insurrection on a large and organised scale. (4) Wallace, springing into fame as the leader of a large band of outlaws and malcontents, provided the Bishop with a magnificent instrument for furthering his plans. (5) Douglas, probably at the Bishop's instigation, joined Wallace, and thus brought to his standard both strength

[1] Hemingburgh.

and distinction, the latter a matter of much importance in that age. (6) In May Wallace attacked Lanark and slew Hezelrig ; raided Scone along with Douglas ; and thereafter, also with Douglas, swept through the district directly to the north of the Forth, slaying the English and besieging the castles. (7) In the same month the Bishop and the Steward of Scotland took the field in the west, and the young Earl of Carrick, Robert Bruce, hastened to join them in the hope of winning for his family the Crown of Scotland, to which he believed them to have an absolute right, and of which he believed them to have been unjustly deprived by Edward's award four and a half years before. (8) In the same month Andrew de Moray raised a formidable and successful insurrection in the province of Moray. (9) In the same month there were disturbances of some kind in the outlying parts of the sheriffdom of Aberdeen. (10) In the same month, or a little later, Fife was in rebellion under the leadership of Macduff of Fife and his two sons ; and (11) in the same month Galloway was in the throes of an insurrection which had probably been proceeding for some time.

Such are the facts. The following conclusions may fairly be drawn from them : The sudden outbreak of a revolt on a large and formidable scale in May 1297, which apparently took the English officials by surprise, was the direct outcome of the widespread disorder which had marked the winter months. That disorder owed its transformation into organised and formidable rebellion to the skill and the capacity of the Bishop of Glasgow and the successful operations of Wallace. Each of these was to a certain extent the complement of the other, and while it is, perhaps, going too far to say that neither would have had much chance of success without the other, it is, at least, probable that, had it not been for Wallace's exploits in the spring of 1297, the general rising planned by the Bishop might not have occurred so soon, which might or might not have been a good thing for Scotland. On the other hand there can be no doubt that the general rising planned by the Bishop was the initial cause of the success which attended the Scottish arms in 1297, as will be made clear in the next two chapters.

In the next place the outbreak of insurrection in Moray, Fife, the West of Scotland, and Aberdeenshire at almost the same moment as Wallace's and Douglas's attack on Scone, must have been the result of a common plan, for their practically simultaneous occurrence could not have been accidental, especially as the Bishop possessed, in the persons of prelates and priests in the Church who were as bitterly inimical to England as he was, and in the persons of certain knights and others, the means for laying his plans, and making preparations for a rising in all parts of the country at the same time. As events turned out, the rising in Moray, as we shall see presently, proved of vast importance, a fact which brings us to the last of our present conclusions.

Briefly put it is this. We have seen that two contemporary English chroniclers give the leaders of the rising as the Bishop of Glasgow, Andrew de Moray, the Steward of Scotland, and William Wallace. The Bishop, as we have seen, was the real inspirer and organiser of the rising, the Steward was his coadjutor, and William Wallace was the instrument he found and used. Why then do the English chroniclers place Andrew de Moray next in order to the Bishop among the leaders of the rising? They do so because, as we shall see in the following chapters, that is his right and proper place. The campaign which he conducted in Moray in the summer of 1297 has hitherto been either entirely neglected in the pages of Scottish historians or referred to only in a puzzled sort of way which has wrapped it in greater mystery than ever. But that campaign was of extreme importance both in its bearing on the battle of Stirling Bridge and in its bearing on the whole subsequent history of the War of Independence, and we shall, therefore, consider it at length in the chapters which follow. Meanwhile, however, the fact that the

place assigned to Andrew de Moray by the English
chroniclers is supported by the fact that he was the leader
of a successful and extremely important insurrection in
Moray, will suffice to support our conclusion regarding
the chroniclers' accuracy on this point.

But before we proceed to consider the campaign
in Moray, it will be well to have some idea of the
course which events took further south. At this stage,
however, we shall not examine these in any detail, as it
will be necessary to discuss them when we come to
consider the problems relating to the actions of Robert
the Bruce, the future king, during the early years of
the War of Independence. It will suffice to say meanwhile that acute dissensions broke out between the
leaders of the western campaign[1]; that Wallace, if he
had actually joined forces with the Bishop, the Steward,
and their followers, as his colleague Douglas certainly
had,[2] left them before the end of the first week in July,
and retired with a large following of common folk to
the secure fastnesses of Selkirk Forest[3]: and that the
other leaders of the western campaign capitulated to
a superior English force at Irvine on 7th July,[4] resistance, in view of their divided counsels, being useless.
The names of the chief men who thus capitulated have
survived. They were the Bishop, the Steward, Robert
Bruce, Earl of Carrick, the Steward's brother John, Sir
Alexander Lindsay, and Sir William Douglas.[5] It is
clear from the English official documents that Douglas
consented to the capitulation with a very bad grace,[6]
and some three weeks later he was cast into prison at
Berwick for failing to produce his hostages. There he
remained "very savage and very abusive" till after the
defeat of the English at Stirling Bridge, when he was
transferred to the Tower of London, where he died
two years later without having made his peace with
England. He had been stripped by Edward of all

[1] Hemingburgh.
[2] Stevenson, ii. 192.
[3] *Ibid.*, p. 202.
[4] *Ibid.*, p. 192.
[5] *Ibid.*, p. 192 ; Bain, ii. 907, 908, 909.
[6] Stevenson, ii. 205.

his lands and possessions, but he left behind him a young son who was to live to exact from England a great vengeance for the wrongs which he, his father, and his country had suffered, and to win in Scottish history undying fame and the honoured name of "The good Sir James."

Note.—It is a matter of common belief among Scottish historians that a letter issued by Edward on 31st January 1297 has reference to a condition of unrest in Scotland. As Professor Rait puts it: "In January 1297 the English governor, Warrenne, is ordered to prevent any correspondence between Scotland and the Continent; neither clerk nor layman is to leave the kingdom without special permission, and letters found on anyone are to be seized." A somewhat similar letter was also issued on 1st March, Kirkcudbright being specially mentioned, yet neither of these letters has the remotest connection with the condition of Scotland ! The letter of 31st January is one of no less than ninety-nine *in exactly similar terms* addressed to the mayors and bailiffs of all the principal towns of England, the Justice of Chester, the Justice of North Wales, the Warden of the Cinque Ports, and the Keeper of the realm and land of Scotland. They were issued in connection with the renewal of the war with France, and for no other reason. The Scottish letter of 1st March is in exactly similar case. It was one of several addressed to all the principal ports in both kingdoms whence " passage " to France was proposed to be made. See *Close Rolls*, Edward I, 1296–1302, pp. 81–83, for letters of 31st January, and p. 87 for those of 1st March.

CHAPTER IV

ANDREW DE MORAY'S CAMPAIGN IN MORAY

In the province of Moray, as elsewhere in Scotland, the outward and visible signs of English sovereignty were everywhere apparent. Inverness, the key of the Highlands, was garrisoned by a strong English force,[1] the castles of Urquhart, Nairn, Forres, Elgin, Lochindorb, and many another were held by Edward's men[2]; and from knight and noble, from churchman and layman, from burgess and landholder the oath of allegiance had been extorted. The burgess of Inverness woke daily to the knowledge that he was under English rule; from the great castle above him, overawing the town and the surrounding neighbourhood, the pennon of a knight of England flew; an English trumpet-call wakened time and again the echoes of the burgh; and in the narrow streets English knights and men-at-arms were too familiar figures. But in spite of all the ever-present display of English power, in spite of all the memories of Edward's recent visitation, and the fame of the warrior statesman king, to Inverness came throughout the winter and the spring rumours of discontents, of risings here and tumults there, and all the varied murmurings which presaged a coming storm. So we can picture to ourselves the little town lying huddled under the protecting castle, seemingly quiet, seemingly reconciled to the presence of its English masters, yet all the time full of smouldering wrath, a true reflection of the rest of the north, whose spirit required only a spark to set it aflame.

To Inverness on a day of May in the year of grace 1297[3] came the first faint rumour that the standard of

---

[1] Bain, ii. Various entries.   [2] *Ibid.*   [3] *Ibid.*, No. 922.

32

revolt had been raised again, that the English were to be driven from the land they cumbered with their presence. Then following hard upon the rumour came the news that young Andrew de Moray had escaped from his English prison, and had returned to his father's lands in Moray with the intention of raising the whole north against the English.[1] Sir Andrew de Moray himself was lying in the Tower of London [2] with many another good Scottish knight, but his tenants and vassals on his lands of Petty, Avoch, Croy, Alturlie, Boharm, and Botriphine were ready to follow his son in any attempt he should make to throw off the English yoke. The burgesses of Inverness, led by one of their number, Alexander Pilche,[3] listened eagerly to these tidings, and when they were followed by news that Andrew de Moray had actually hoisted the standard of revolt at his father's castle at Avoch, but seven miles away across the Inverness Firth, and that the men of Moray were hastening to him, the burgesses could no longer be restrained. With Alexander Pilche at their head, they flung off all semblance of allegiance to England, and betook themselves to Avoch and a bold bid for freedom.[4]

At Avoch they received warm welcome,[5] and there, perhaps, some of them, for the first time, began to realise the desperate nature of their undertaking. But there was no drawing back. It is true they were at the beginning but a part of a small body of men who had gathered round Andrew de Moray, but they were fired with the true heroic spirit, else they would not have been there. For though some of them may have entered on the adventure without pausing to count the cost, yet none of them but knew from the outset that English domination could not be overthrown without a stern struggle. And so let us picture that little army assembled at Avoch in the beginning of May 1297.

At their head is young Andrew de Moray, one of the chivalric figures of Scottish history. He is son and heir

---

[1] Bain, ii. 922.   [2] *Ibid.*, pp. 742, 960.   [3] *Ibid.*, p. 922.
[4] *Ibid.*   [5] *Ibid.*

of one of Scotland's greatest houses, bearer of an historic name, leader by virtue of his descent of the warlike men of Moray. His father and his uncle, great nobles both, lie in an English prison paying the penalty of patriotism, and he himself but a few months before was suffering a similar fate.[1] So he is under no illusion as to the strength of England or the character of the English king. He is only recently married;[2] he is young, gallant, and full of life and hope; he is heir to the great possessions of his family, the lands of Petty, Avoch, Boharm, Croy, and others, and the great estates of Bothwell; he is, in a word, one of the most favoured of the younger Scottish men of rank. If loyalty to Edward would pay anyone, it would pay him, yet here we find him prepared to put all to the touch on a venture of which no one knows better than he the tremendous danger.

With him, perhaps, is his uncle the priest, David, not yet Bishop of Moray, but already inspired by that patriotic spirit which was to lead him by-and-by to preach a holy war against the power of England, and play a great part in the winning of his country's freedom.[3] But next to Andrew de Moray in the present venture ranks not knight or churchman, but Alexander Pilche, burgess of Inverness.[4] He is de Moray's chief lieutenant and right-hand man, and it is upon the heads of these twain that the wrath of the English commanders in the north is presently to descend. And the men they lead, what of them? Burgesses of Inverness, as we have seen, and the men of Moray, landholders, tenants, and all the motley population of the countryside, with a sprinkling of churchmen, a priest or two perhaps, and one or more of the Dominican Friars of Inverness, that preaching brotherhood who were beloved of the common people, and had the gift of eloquence wherewith to stir men's blood.

Such was the army that assembled at Avoch to measure its strength against the might of England, an

---

[1] Bain, ii. 177.   [2] *Ibid.*, p. 1178.
[3] See Chapter XVIII.   [4] Bain, ii. 922.

army small at first in numbers, and but ill-equipped in arms, but an army moved by some strong compelling spirit, else assuredly it had never come together at all. We may wonder now, men have wondered for centuries, at the spirit which drove our fathers to such seemingly hopeless battle against such tremendous odds, but by that spirit it was that the freedom of Scotland was won. And as we gaze for a moment, through the mist of centuries, on the little army gathered at Avoch, an army embarked on what by all the rules of warfare was an impossible task, we get a glimpse of the composition of those other misty armies which, impelled by the same motives, made possible the impossible, and snatched victory out of the very jaws of death.

News of the gathering at Avoch soon spread far and wide, and eager men flocked to de Moray's standard. As soon as he was strong enough he embarked on an active campaign, and soon had the officers of England in the province in a state of serious alarm, for, wherever possible, they were attacked, and some were killed and others captured and cast into prison.[1] So serious did matters become that the guardian of Moray, Sir Reginald le Chen, despatched an appeal to Edward for help,[2] and a little later summoned his subordinates to take counsel with him at Inverness.[3] Thither, accordingly, Sir William Fitzwarine, the Constable of Urquhart Castle, betook himself on the morning of Sunday, 25th May.[4] But Andrew de Moray was well advised of the movements of his foes, and when the English knights were sitting in close conference in the Castle of Inverness, the object of their deliberations was hurrying with his men to prepare a surprise for Fitzwarine.[5]

The conference ended Fitzwarine got to horse. The times were troubled, so a strong escort rode with him, but he anticipated no danger, least of all from those rogues whose fate he had just been deciding. So by the old hill road which wound over the shoulder of Dunain,

---

[1] *Rotuli Scotiae*, i. 41.   [2] *Ibid.*
[3] Bain, ii. 922.   [4] *Ibid.*   [5] *Ibid.*

and thence by way of the Caiplich, where the burgesses
of Inverness were wont to cut their peats, he took his
way, a rough, uneven way no better than the hill tracks
which abound to this day. His escort was strong, well-
armed, and mounted, and a brave sight they made as they
rode along the parlous path, expecting no danger, and
discussing, perhaps, the chances of an onfall on the rebels
at Avoch before they fled in fear. For how could they
hope to stand against the knights and men-at-arms of
England? And so, armour clanking, accoutrements
jingling, they cantered on.

On a sudden came a slight sound, a faint whir-r-r, a
flight of arrows, a rush of armed men. The spot, be
sure, was well chosen, for well did Alexander Pilche and
the burgesses of Inverness know every turn, every evil
brae, every treacherous, boggy bit, every likely spot for
an ambush, on that weary road. Horses and men went
down before the wild onset, the air was full of shouts and
cries, the ringing of arms on armour, and the groans of
wounded men. In one brief moment the whole aspect
of the day was changed, and where before there had been
the quiet of a May evening, there was now the noise of
battle and a fierce confused melee. For a little it looked
as if not a man of all the English force would escape.
But they had two great advantages over their foes. They
were mounted, and they were clad in part at least in
armour of proof. And in right good stead did these
stand them now, for Fitzwarine and some of his men were
able presently to break clear of the melee, and, driving
their spurs deep into their horses' flanks, gained in safety
the shelter of Urquhart Castle. But they left behind
them two of Fitzwarine's principal followers, who fell
sore wounded into de Moray's hands,[1] and a number of
lesser men, whose fate is not recorded. They lost, too,
eighteen horses,[2] a grievous loss in a country where horses
accustomed to carry knights or men-at-arms were difficult
to obtain, and they had been compelled to flee before the
foe they despised. It was a great day for de Moray and

[1] Bain, ii. 922. [2] *Ibid.*

his little army. They had struck a strong blow for freedom, and they had won.

Once within the walls of Urquhart Castle, Fitzwarine
doubtless thought he was safe from further molestation.
Though he had lost some men and horses, that was but
the result of an unfortunate ambuscade, and the rogues
who had waylaid him would surely never dare to wage
open war on the forces of the English king. Besides,
was not the castle a place of great strength, constructed
and fortified with all the well-known skill of the English
military architect, and held by an ample garrison ? [1]

If such were his thoughts, he was doomed to speedy
disillusionment. Neither Andrew de Moray nor the
men who followed him were out on a mere foray. They
were engaged in a desperate effort to rid their country
of the English. And so while Fitzwarine slept, Andrew
de Moray and Alexander Pilche took counsel together.
They had met with considerable success, their men were
brave and eager, at the news of their victory recruits
would come pouring in. The iron was hot for striking.
They would strike, and that speedily. So in the first
grey dawn of the morning they roused their sleeping
men, and the little army of patriots set out blithely on
the next stage of their struggle for freedom. But
whereas the day before they had swooped down on
surprised and confused men, they were now marching
against a foe alert and ready and entrenched behind
strong walls.[2]

How far de Moray was influenced in his action by
the fact that another Scottish force was in the neighbourhood it is impossible to say, but doubtless it had something to do with his decision. For the times were
strange indeed, and boldness and promptitude might
have big results. He must have known that the
Countess of Ross was near at hand with a large following,[3] and he probably had no difficulty in guessing that
she was there in answer to a summons similar to that

---

[1] Mackay's *Urquhart and Glenmoriston*.
[2] Bain, p. 922.   [3] *Ibid.*

which had taken Fitzwarine to Inverness. For the Earl of Ross lay in an English prison,[1] and it behoved the Countess, if she would win his release and save his vast estates, to gain the favour of the English king. And so in the month of May, when Scotland was astir against her oppressor, the Countess of Ross was in the field on the side of England.[2]

Thus we have the stage set for an act that has both comedy and tragedy in it. So let us picture it for a moment as it appeared to Fitzwarine when he looked forth from the battlements of Urquhart on that Monday morning. Before him he sees a hostile array, whose intention to lay close siege to the castle is only too evident. Flushed with their success of the previous day, they have that in their demeanour which betokens trouble, and they are evidently led by men well skilled in the art of war. To his trained eye it is evident that this is no disorderly rabble, but a force to be reckoned with. It consists, as he can see, of two main elements, the followers of Andrew de Moray and the burgesses of Inverness,[3] and as he grasps that fact, he begins to realise that this rising is something more than a flash in the pan. For though the warlike men of Moray might follow a gallant young soldier like Andrew de Moray in a wild foray, it would require more than that to lead the burgesses of Inverness to dare the wrath of the English guardians of the king's peace.

As he ponders, he becomes aware of a stir in the besiegers' camp, and presently a mounted man appears riding towards the castle. He halts before the uplifted drawbridge, and with loud voice declares himself an esquire of that good friend of England and Fitzwarine, the Countess of Ross.[3] But Fitzwarine is suspicious. He sees a hostile army over against him. He knows he and his fellow-countrymen are held in detestation. What more likely then, than that the Countess of Ross is in league with the enemy. True, her husband is in Edward's hands, but so is the father of that troublesome young

<hr/>

[1] Bain, pp. 690, 742, 1395, &c.   [2] *Ibid.*, p. 922.   [3] *Ibid.*

knight, who is even now the leader of the rebel forces before him. And so he parleys, the drawbridge in all probability inexorably up, the Countess's esquire on the landward side of the moat.

What brings him here? What message bears he from the Countess? To which the esquire makes tactful reply. The Countess is near at hand, and sends her condolences. She is horrified at the news of the doings of the previous day, and Fitzwarine may be very sure she had no share in them. She is a staunch friend of England, and in proof thereof even now offers her assistance.[1] She will, if he desires, help him in the defence of the Castle; but none the less she counsels surrender as the better course, for the whole country is up, and his situation exceeding parlous. Fitzwarine likes not the look of things. He fears the Countess and her gifts, he distrusts her advice. And so, as he subsequently informs his royal master, he refuses her proffered aid "lest greater peril should befall him,"[2] and, dissembling his real motives, bids the esquire return the Countess his thanks, and inform her that he requires not her help, as he "trusts sufficiently to defend himself and the Castle."[2] So the esquire takes himself off, and Fitzwarine watches him make his way safely past the besiegers, a feat which does not tend to allay the English knight's suspicions.[2]

But the comedy is not yet over. Word is by-and-by brought to Fitzwarine that another army is approaching, and when he examines it he finds that it consists of the Countess of Ross's men. Her son is at their head, and sends word to Fitzwarine that he has come to his relief. But Fitzwarine, now more suspicious than ever, "believes that for evil he has come," and summarily rejects the offered aid. Whereupon the Countess's men retire to a little distance, there to wait upon events.[2]

That Fitzwarine had good grounds for his suspicions there can be no doubt. The Countess's position was peculiar. Her loyalty to Edward was quite plainly dictated by the hope of favours to come. But if this

---

[1] Bain, p. 922.　　　　[2] *Ibid.*

rising proved successful, what would her loyalty to
Edward avail her ?   Moreover, the sympathy of her own
men was probably with the men they were in arms against,
and it is likely that her son had more than a similar
feeling for, as well as a lively friendship with, Andrew
de Moray.   So she found herself very unpleasantly
placed.   If she attacked de Moray's men, she ranged
herself definitely on the side of England.   If she lent no
aid to Fitzwarine, Edward would exact full payment.
So she temporised.   Let Fitzwarine surrender the Castle
and depart in peace.[1]   He would not ; then let her men
aid him in its defence, but let them make no attack on
de Moray.   And so she endeavoured to sit uneasily on
two stools, the while de Moray and his men tried to
take the castle, and Fitzwarine did his best to keep
them out.

The Countess of Ross disposed of for the time being,
the issue lay between Fitzwarine and the besiegers.
While the negotiations between the would-be allies went
forward, Andrew de Moray and his men, cognisant no
doubt of the true inwardness of the proceedings, had lain
amused spectators of the parleyings.   But now the time
had come for them to take a hand in the game.   So in
true knightly fashion, for Andrew de Moray was nothing
if not a very perfect knight, Fitzwarine was summoned
by herald to surrender.[2]   The summons, of course, was
rejected, and Andrew de Moray and his men sat down
before the walls to a determined siege.

The element of comedy now enters again.   The English are within the castle ; closely besetting them without
are the burgesses of Inverness and the men of Moray ;
while within easy distance of both lies the army of the
hesitating Countess of Ross.   She dare not attack de
Moray ; she must do something to deserve Fitzwarine's
good graces.   At last she hits on a scheme.   Fitzwarine's
supplies are scanty.   She will order her son to send him
provisions for the castle.   How the son carried out his
mother's commands we do not know, but carry them out

he did, for Fitzwarine's own account of his action is on record.[1]

The provisioning of the castle deprived the besiegers of any chance they might have had of starving it into surrender. So they determined on the desperate expedient of a night assault,[2] and in the half-darkness of a June night made a bold attempt to carry the castle by storm. The besieged were on the alert, however, and a fierce struggle ensued. For a time the issue was in doubt. The English held the advantage of position, but they were doughty fighters those Scots, and would win in if men could. But the night was short, the half-darkness began to disperse, and every minute gained was worth an hour to the defenders. Still the Scots stuck grimly to their task, and the English were hard beset. Fitzwarine's son[2] and William Puer,[2] a knight or esquire, were slain. Another knight was sore wounded,[2] and of lesser men not a few were killed.[2] But the walls were strong and high, and the attack was held at bay till the day came, and Andrew de Moray realised that now only at great cost could the castle be taken. So he called off his men, and reluctantly determined to abandon the siege for the time.[2]

Though frustrated in their attempt on Urquhart Castle, neither Andrew de Moray nor his followers were unduly disheartened. They had suffered some losses, it is true, but they were still undefeated, and they had been suffered to march away from Urquhart without molestation. What their destination was the men of Moray did not know, but no doubt their young leader had some good object in view. Their expectations were soon realised. The Countess of Ross had spoiled their little campaign. What more fitting than that they should teach her a sharp lesson? So northwards to Ross they took their way, and the Countess by-and-by got tidings that her Castle of Balconie was in danger at their hands.[2] Thus Andrew de Moray achieved a four-fold purpose. He kept up the spirits of his men by waging

[1] Bain, p. 922.   [2] *Ibid.*

successful war in the very territory of the foe who had foiled them at Urquhart; he taught the Countess of Ross that he was a formidable enemy, and that armed adherence to England had its penalties; he got in the rear of her army, cut her communication with Ross, and rendered her situation in Inverness-shire precarious; and, lastly, he secured a place which provided at once a convenient centre whither recruits from the northern parts could gather, and a safe retreat for his men.

What size of army he now had we have no means of knowing, but that it was considerable is certain, for he was able to divide it into two parts, one of which lay round Avoch and the other round Balconie.[1] The strategic advantages of such a division a glance at the map will make clear. He was not only able to harass the English over a wide area, but he made it impossible for them or their allies to advance against either Avoch or Balconie without laying themselves open to attack on their flank or rear. And harass them he did. Throughout the long days and the short nights of June the English knew no respite, and the name and fame of Andrew de Moray and Alexander Pilche waxed great in the land.

How often during those days must Sir Reginald le Chen have looked eagerly from the Castle of Inverness for signs of a messenger from England. For, as we have seen, on the first sign that the rising was like to prove formidable, a courtier had been despatched to Edward with the tidings, and while Andrew de Moray and his men were setting the Highlands on fire, their oppressors' cry for help was being carried to distant England as fast as horses' hoofs could bear it. Edward's response was instant and emphatic.[2] The rising must be stamped out at once and completely. Nothing must be left to chance. The force for the chastisement of these insolent rebels must be in every way sufficient, and precautions must be taken which would render a rising in the future unlikely.

[1] Bain, p. 922.　　　　[2] *Rotuli Scotiae*, p. 41.

The messenger to whom these orders was entrusted was a near neighbour of Andrew de Moray—Sir Andrew de Rait,[1] of Rait Castle, near Nairn, who a few weeks later carried to Edward from his servants in the north several letters, including Fitzwarine's before-mentioned, giving particulars of the rising and the measures taken to deal with it.[2] Whether or not Sir Andrew had ridden southwards with Sir Reginald le Chen's appeal for help, I know not, but on 11th June he received at Ospringe, in Kent, or the day of the arrival of the news from the distant north—the orders for the suppression of the rising being issued on the same day—a grant of the lands in Scotland of his brother, Gervase de Rait,[3] so in all probability he it was who brought the tidings to Edward.

The orders were contained in letters addressed to Henry le Chen, Bishop of Aberdeen ; Sir Gartenet, son of the Earl of Mar ; John Comyn, Earl of Buchan and Constable of Scotland ; and Sir Alexander Comyn, his brother, ordering them to raise at once all their own forces and the forces of the whole Sheriffdom of Aberdeen, and to proceed forthwith to the relief of Urquhart Castle.[4] Now, as it happened, earlier on that same 11th of June, John Comyn, Earl of Buchan, had left Ospringe for Scotland in the company of John Comyn of Badenoch, Alexander de Balliol, Alexander, Earl of Menteith, Reginald de Crauford, Master Nigel Campbell, and William Bisset.[5] For Edward I was about to embark on a great campaign in Flanders, and in order to keep as many as possible of the Scottish knights and nobles under his own eye and away from temptation, he had ordered a large number of them to accompany him, and given to others who were still his prisoners in England the choice of going with him or continuing in confinement. So on this 11th day of June the Earl of Buchan and his companions had set out for Scotland under safe

---

[1] Stevenson, ii. 212   [2] *Ibid.*, ii. 213.   [3] Bain, ii. 893.
[4] *Rotuli Scotiae*, i. 41 ; Bain, ii. 961 ; Stevenson, ii. 211.
[5] Stevenson, ii. 175.

conduct from Edward to make themselves ready to fight
in his war on the Continent,[1] and on that same day
Edward received tidings of yet another rising against his
power in the kingdom whither they were bound. They
must thus have missed Sir Reginald le Chen's messenger
by the narrowest of margins, and though they may have
known that there was trouble in the west of Scotland
and Argyll, and that an English army was even then
assembling for the invasion of their native land, they rode
northwards without any suspicion that they themselves
were soon to be involved, and that the tumults of which
they had heard were part of a great national uprising.

We may imagine, then, the little cavalcade riding
towards Scotland on their own various affairs bent, talk-
ing much of the approaching campaign in Flanders, discussing desultorily, perhaps, the folly of those in Scotland
against whom the forces of England were even then
gathering, and grumbling one to another of the strong
hand and the exactions of the English king. For though
they perforce acknowledged Edward's overlordship, they
liked the new condition of things little, and were loyal to
their English master only because they deemed resistance
worse than useless.

To them riding in this mood through England comes
unexpectedly Sir Andrew de Rait.[2] He has ridden hard
to overtake them, and when he reaches them loses no
time in handing his letters to the Earl of Buchan, and
making known his tidings.[3] Great is the excitement that
thereupon ensues, and long and animated the discussions,
for Andrew de Moray is known to most of the company ;
he is, indeed, a near kinsman of the two Comyns,[4] and
his action may have consequences of which he never
dreamed.

The rest of that northward journey must have been
full of interest. As they drew near the Border they
would learn that the Bishop of Glasgow, young Robert
Bruce, Earl of Carrick, Sir William Douglas, and the

---

[1] Stevenson, ii. 175.
[2] *Ibid.*, ii. 212.
[3] *Ibid.*
[4] B. P., ii. 126.

Steward of Scotland, were at the head of a great force in arms against England ; that one William Wallace, whose doings had lately caused some stir, was in command of another force by no means small ; and that " beyond the Scottish sea " (*i.e.* the Forth), whither they were going, the whole country was said to be up. How they must have discussed the pros and cons of the situation. They were Scotsmen all of them ; but the Comyns liked not Bruce, and he was evidently at the head of the western rising. On the other hand, Andrew de Moray was their kinsman, and none knew better than the Earl of Buchan and John of Badenoch that the whole north hated the English yoke. As for themselves, they, too, would gladly cast it off if they dared ; but were the times yet ripe for such an undertaking ? Not a year ago the whole might of Scotland had been humbled at Dunbar, and they themselves were but come from the presence of the English king in order to make ready to accompany him to Flanders, and the consciousness of his power was still upon them. And so, in the first week of July, they came to Aberdeen.

In Aberdeen the four men entrusted by Edward with the task of pacifying the north, speedily met to consider what their course should be. Of the four the Bishop, Henry le Chen, was least troubled with doubts, for he had proved an active supporter of England, and his loyalty to Edward was less open to question than any of the others. As for Sir Gartenet, was he not the heir of an ancient Celtic house and brother-in-law of young Robert Bruce, Earl of Carrick, who was even then at the head of a rising in the south-west ? No need to inquire on which side his sympathies lay ; but, like the Comyns, he probably judged that the time for successful resistance was not yet. Moreover, his father, the earl, was an involuntary guest of Edward in England, albeit at that very moment, though Sir Gartenet knew it not, he was riding homewards[1] in order to equip himself for the expedition to Flanders, like many another Scottish knight who preferred war to restraint or imprisonment.

---

[1] Stevenson, ii. 185.

Let us try to picture to ourselves that meeting of King Edward's men. They had their royal master's letter before them with his peremptory orders "strongly enjoining them" to proceed to Urquhart Castle without any delay.[1] Its relief accomplished, and measures taken to strengthen it against future attack, they were to take vigorous steps for the suppression of the rising, the two Comyns especially being ordered to remain in the north until the disturbances had been completely quelled. And, ended the arrogant king,[2] "do ye comport yourselves with the vigour I expect of you, that I may rightly commend in this business your diligence and fidelity." The Bishop, we may be sure, was all for instant action, for obeying Edward's orders unhesitatingly and implicitly. The others were torn with doubts. They were on the horns of a dilemma if ever men were. How they must have cursed Andrew de Moray for putting them in the position in which they found themselves. But they knew that Edward's orders would have to be obeyed. For not only were they prisoners released on parole, but they were conscious that disobedience was worse than useless. Already they must have had tidings of the capitulation of one Scottish army at Irvine. There, on 7th July, the Bishop of Glasgow, Robert Bruce, Earl of Carrick, the Steward of Scotland, Sir William Douglas, and various other knights and nobles, had been compelled to make peace with the English force which had marched against them, and the rising in the west was over.[3] At the same time a second English force of 300 horse and 10,000 foot was advancing by way of Berwick in support of the first army,[4] and of it, too, the four in Aberdeen must have had cognisance. So with one English army, in victorious spirit, in Ayr, and another near Berwick; with the Scottish army in the west dispersed without a struggle; and with only a little known esquire, William Wallace, and some common men in arms against England in all the district to the south of

---

[1] *Rotuli Scotiae*, i. 41.

[2] *Ibid.*

[3] Stevenson, ii. 192.

[4] *Ibid.*, p. 202.

the Forth,[1] it behoved all who wished to stand well with Edward to make it plain that they had never faltered in their fealty. Accordingly, about the 12th July, Edward's "diligent and faithful friends," mindful of "the faith and love in which they were held by him," set out from Aberdeen "without any delay" to comport themselves in Moray with the vigour to which they had been so "strongly enjoined."

If they thought, however, that their task would prove easy, that the news of Irvine, which Andrew de Moray was certain to have received, would cause the rising to collapse, they were speedily disappointed. Andrew de Moray and the men he led were made of better stuff than that. Two months had now elapsed since de Moray had taken the field, and he had not been idle in the interval.

He had not permitted his force to lie long in the neighbourhood of Avoch and Balconie. If the Castles of Urquhart and Inverness were too strong for him, others were not, and from the Beauly to the Spey the adherents of England felt the weight of his hand. In his orders to the Bishop of Aberdeen Edward himself has placed on record that the patriots in Moray had in May killed some of his officers and cast others into prison,[2] and against the persons and property of those who still remained Andrew de Moray throughout the summer directed his attentions. The guardian of Moray, Sir Reginald le Chen, he singled out especially, and between the beginning of May and the end of August his lands were laid waste, his goods despoiled, his castles burned, and he himself eventually captured and imprisoned.[3]

Now, Sir Reginald le Chen was by marriage a connection of de Moray, he having married one of the heiresses of the Morays of Duffus, a house to which the Morays of Petty and Bothwell were closely related.[4] But the Chens were interlopers without any real sympathy for the land in which their lot was cast, and they had

---

[1] Stevenson, ii. 202.   [2] *Rotuli Scotiae*, i. 41.
[3] Bain, ii. 931, 1737.   [4] B. P., ii. 122.

proved strong and staunch supporters of the English king. Their Castle of Duffus, the ancient home of the family from which de Moray was sprung, was accordingly now become an English stronghold, a fact which must have galled young Andrew exceedingly, as at a later date a similar happening galled Bruce's friend, the gallant Sir James Douglas. So when at the head of a force so numerous that in their report to Edward the English leaders termed it "a very large body of rogues,"[1] he swept through the province of Moray towards the Spey, midway between Forres and Elgin he turned aside, and descending furiously on the lands of Duffus, laid them waste, captured the castle, and gave it to the flames.[2] Then having taught Sir Reginald le Chen that loyalty to Edward must cost him dear, and having removed the reproach from the ancient de Moray home, he led his men across the Spey[3] to the Banffshire lands of his family, to Boharm, where stood one of his father's principal castles. There amid his own people, and in a country of bog and wood with the swift-flowing Spey running through it, he was in an admirable situation for awaiting the coming of the force which he must by this time have known was advancing against him from Aberdeen. The Spey, moreover, was in these days the eastern boundary of the province of Moray, and Andrew de Moray knew full well that it was, as it had been for many centuries before, and was to be for many centuries afterwards, the natural protection, as its fords, where it flowed through the flat country, were the natural gateway of Morayland. By these same fords many a host had crossed to conflict with the men of Moray, and through them many a king in war array had ridden. Less than a year before Edward himself, with a mighty army, had passed them, and had Andrew de Moray been possessed of the gift of divination he might have seen far down the centuries another Highland host waiting on these same banks for another hostile army, marching to another and a final contest for the Crown of Britain.

[1] Stevenson, ii. 212.   [2] Bain, ii. 931, 1737.   [3] Stevenson, ii. 212.

CHAPTER V

"AND as we were in Launoy, upon the Spey," wrote Edward's liegemen to him from the security of Inverness on 25th July 1297,[1] "and as we were in Launoy, upon the Spey, on the Tuesday before the feast of St. Mary Magdalene, there met us Andrew de Moray with a very large body of rogues, the number of which Sir Andrew de Rait, your bachelor, can show you, according to what he learned from the people of their company. And there the aforesaid rogues betook themselves into a very great stronghold of bog and wood, where no horseman could be of service." Thus succinctly do " his loyal and faithful Henry, by the grace of God, Bishop of Aberdeen," and his fellow leaders report "to their liege lord, the very noble and very excellent prince, and their dear lord, Sir Edward, by the grace of God, the noble King of England," the tale of what befell them in the north. But there is a significant concluding paragraph to the letter. "And since it would be too long a business to write and send to you all the points and occurrences which have happened, and the condition of the country in all matters, we pray you to have the goodness to give credence to Sir Andrew de Rait, your bachelor, who can tell you these affairs in all points, for he was in person at all these doings." The ostensible reason that "it would be too long a business" to set forth in writing all the happenings of the campaign may be the true explanation of the omission of any information of the kind which Edward so ardently desired,

---

[1] Stevenson, ii. 212.

D

but that there is another and a much more probable explanation we shall presently see.

It was on or about 15th July[1] that the two forces came face to face "in Launoy, upon the Spey." Where precisely Launoy was has been much discussed, but it is now clear that it is the Norman-French rendering of "the Enzie." In a journal or diary of Edward I's invasion of Scotland in 1296, written in Norman-French, it is stated that on 24th July Edward left Cullen, advanced to the country of "Lannoi," and encamped "en Lennoy," on the river Spey. On the next day, 25th July, the diarist states that he crossed the Spey, and on the 26th that he reached Elgin.[2] "Lannoi," "Lennoy," and "Launoy" are, therefore, all clearly the same word, and there cannot be the least doubt that they are an attempt at the phonetic rendering of the Norman-French equivalent for "the Enzie," L' Annoi, L' Ennoy, and L' Aunoy being almost identical with the pronunciation of Enzie, with the French article prefixed. It was the fashion in the Norman-French of the period to run the article preceding a proper name beginning with a vowel and the name itself into one word, and in another document, written at Inverness on the same day as the report to Edward and in the same connection, the name of John of the Aird appears as "John de Laarde,"[3] instead of as John del Ard, which would have been the strictly correct rendering. The Enzie comprises, roughly, the large district on the east bank of the Spey, in which Gordon Castle is situated. In the thirteenth and fourteenth centuries it was covered with wood, and was one of the principal royal forests in the north of Scotland. Just inside its western boundary was a great bog, extending eastward from the Spey, and long famous as the Bog of Gight, immediately to the north of which Gordon Castle was afterwards built. The road from Aberdeen to Inverness had perforce to run through the Enzie and skirt the Bog of Gight in order to reach the ford across the Spey at Bellie, and the district was therefore an ideal

[1] Stevenson, ii. 212.   [2] Cottonian MSS.   [3] Bain, ii. 923.

one in which to lie in wait for the approach of an enemy.

To Andrew de Moray, therefore, there were two courses open. He could await Edward's men on the western bank of the Spey, and endeavour to dispute the passage of the river, or he might attempt an ambuscade on the opposite side at the Bog of Gight. He determined on the latter course, for several reasons probably. In the first place, the Bishop and the Comyns would be on the lookout for trouble at the river, and, as it was the height of summer, its crossing would present little difficulty to them. In the second place, on the eastern bank, Andrew de Moray was in a district well known to him, a district, moreover, full of natural advantages and in close proximity to his own strong castle of Boharm, to which he could retreat if the worst came to the worst. And in the third place, the Bog of Gight offered splendid opportunities for an ambuscade, and a secure refuge from the attacks of mounted men.

Be that as it may, Andrew de Moray, with a very large body of men, met the advancing foe hard by the Spey. If he had planned a surprise he was disappointed. In the Bishop, the Comyns, and the son of the Earl of Mar, to say nothing of Sir Andrew de Rait, he was dealing with men accustomed to Highland methods of warfare, and men, moreover, who must have known of the success which had attended the ambush laid by Andrew de Moray for the constable of Urquhart Castle. They had to reckon too on the possible hostility of the greater part of the country through which their route lay, so once they had left their own particular district behind they would advance with every precaution known to mediæval war. And so, striking through Aberdeenshire by the track which had known the tramp of countless armies, they would come to the castle of Cullen, the last royal stronghold on their side of the Spey. There, probably, awaited them tidings of Andrew de Moray's advance, and of his destruction of the castle of Duffus. He could not, therefore, be very far away, he must be possessed of a stronger force than they had imagined, and it was hardly likely that they would be allowed to cross the Spey unopposed, or make their next halting-place, Elgin, without molestation. So at daybreak on a July morning they would march out of Cullen, for Elgin was a long day's march away, and it behoved them, if they would reach it in safety, to perform their journey in the full light of day, and at the same time spare their men as much as possible, for they knew not what might lie before them.

Thus it was that Andrew de Moray, when his advancing foes came into view, would see that to attack them then was hopeless. They were marching in battle order, and as he looked from his own men to theirs he would see that, though the advantage of numbers was probably with him, the advantage of arms and armour and of horsemen was with them. We can imagine him sitting on his horse, with his followers clustering behind him, a motley throng of townsmen and countrymen, gazing anxiously at the approaching force. Himself a mailclad warrior, he would know full well the enormous value of armour and mounted men in those days of hand-to-hand fighting, and as he glanced from the well-appointed host before him, its armour glittering in the July sun, its spear-points gleaming brightly, its ranks arrayed for battle, to the eager, light-armed throng behind him, he would know that the chances were too desperate, and that he must not risk a battle. So reluctantly the order to retreat would be given, and the patriots would retire into the " great stronghold of bog and wood,"[1] beside which, largely because of the secure refuge it offered, their young leader had elected to await the coming of his enemy. For in it "no horseman could be of service,"[2] and into its recesses therefore the invaders dare not venture.

So far the advantage seemed to lie with Edward's men, but in truth they were in a difficult situation, for

---

[1] Stevenson, ii. 212.   [2] *Ibid.*

they had yet to make the passage of the Spey, and that in the presence of a hostile and undefeated army. So they appear to have had recourse to negotiation, as Sir Andrew de Rait seems to have been sent to see if Andrew de Moray could be brought to reason.[1] The situation was undoubtedly full of piquancy. The leaders of the opposing forces, as we have seen, were friends and near relatives, and apart from that neither the Comyns nor the son of the Earl of Mar could have had much stomach for the task on which they were engaged. But now that their kinsman, young Andrew, had seen their strength, he might consider it wise to come to Edward's peace, or at least to oppose them no further. But if such was their hope it was speedily disappointed, for Andrew de Moray remained in the field, and all the satisfaction Sir Andrew de Rait obtained was the knowledge that he and his friends were opposed by "a very large body" of men.[2]

Andrew de Moray, however, was unable to dispute the passage of the Spey, and that in itself is proof of the strength of Edward's force and the skill with which it was led. So presently the invaders came to Elgin,[3] which, almost exactly a year before, Edward himself had entered at the head of his victorious army.[4]

As soon as they crossed the Spey the invaders found plenty of evidence of the extent of the insurrection, and as they advanced through Moray they had to exercise the utmost vigilance, for "the rebels" were numerous, active, and skilfully led. From Elgin their route lay by way of Forres and Nairn to Inverness, and it was with Andrew de Moray ever threatening them that they accomplished the perilous passage of the Findhorn, and at last, a day or two later, came to Inverness.

Although the burgesses of Inverness formed a valuable part of Andrew de Moray's army, and although one of their number, Alexander Pilche, was his chief lieutenant, the castle of Inverness still remained in the hands

[1] Stevenson, ii. 212.   [2] *Ibid.*
[3] *Ibid.*   [4] Itinerary.

of Edward's men.[1]   Accordingly when Henry le Chen and his allies reached Inverness they found one strong place remaining in which the friends of England could take counsel together.   Thither accordingly they summoned the few remaining adherents of Edward to meet them, and very soon after Sir Reginald le Chen had given his cousin and his companions eager welcome, the constable of Urquhart Castle, the Countess of Ross, John of the Aird, and others came into the town.[2]   So now, on the high ground round the castle, a strong force pledged to the service of England lay, and while its leaders were engaged within the castle walls in laying plans for the suppression of the rising, below, in the narrow streets of the burgh, the wives and children of the patriotic burgesses whispered fearfully of the fate which was likely to befall their husbands and sons, their fathers and brothers, who had joined themselves so gallantly to Andrew de Moray.

In the castle, however, there was little of the elation of victory.   From Sir Reginald le Chen the newcomers heard a tale of disaster, of lands ravished, of strong places laid waste, of English officers captured, of Edward's men killed, of contumelies innumerable inflicted on all who adhered to England.   They heard, too, of the ever-increasing power of Andrew de Moray, and though they might hearten one another with the recollection of the recent capitulation at Irvine, they could not but recognise that they were face to face with no ordinary undertaking.   They found too that, like most of themselves, Edward's adherents in Morayland had no real enthusiasm for their task ; but the sons of Reginald le Chen and John of the Aird were in English prisons,[3] while the husband of the countess still lay with Andrew de Moray's father, a captive in the Tower of London. Of all the company gathered in the castle of Inverness on that July day, therefore, probably three only were

[1] Stevenson, ii. 209-213 ; Bain, 922.
[2] *Ibid.*, 209–214 ; Bain, 923.
[3] Bain, ii. 177 ; No. 985 ; *Ibid.*, 923.

whole-hearted in their loyalty to England—William Fitz-warine, the English constable of Urquhart Castle, Edward's faithful Bishop of Aberdeen, and Sir Andrew de Rait, who but a brief six weeks before, on the very day of his setting out with the king's despatches for Scotland, had received from Edward the gift of all his brother's, Gervaise de Rait's, lands in the northern kingdom.[1]

The immediate result of the conferences in the castle seems to have been a spate of letter-writing on the part of the English faction, and a determination to send Sir Andrew de Rait to Edward to report to him personally of the progress, or the want of progress, of events in the north.[2] So on 24th and 25th July the leaders of what we may call the expeditionary force, and the constable of Urquhart Castle, Sir Reginald le Chen, and the Countess of Ross, busied themselves with the composition of letters to Edward, in which a very great deal was said in commendation of the Countess of Ross and very little regarding the fortunes of the expedition. In one letter from the Bishop, the Earl of Buchan, and Sir Gartenet of Mar, the rising is described as "non modicus," by no means small,[3] and in another it is stated that, in accord-dance with Edward's orders, the Earl of Buchan and his brother are to remain in the north "for the great damage which is in the country."[4] In neither letter is there any mention of any success having attended their efforts hitherto, but "since it would be too long a busi-ness to write" concerning "all the points and occurrences which have happened, and the condition of the country in all matters," they pray Edward to give credence to Sir Andrew de Rait, "who can tell you these affairs in all points, for he was in person at all these doings."[5]

There is only one inference to be drawn from this. The writers of the letters had nothing very satisfactory to report, and it was therefore better in every way that the tidings of their non-success should be carried to

[1] Bain, ii. 893.   [2] Stevenson, ii. 209–214.
[3] *Ibid.*   [4] *Ibid.*   [5] *Ibid.*

Edward by word of mouth. In the event of their messenger falling into the hands of "the rebels" the letters would convey no encouragement or information of value to them, while Sir Andrew de Rait could be trusted to put matters in the best possible light for the Bishop and the Comyns when he came to explain their endeavours and the position of affairs to the king.

That this is the true interpretation to be placed upon the letters, a letter from Hugh de Cressingham, King Edward's most able and most hated official in Scotland, seems to show clearly. Sir Andrew de Rait was at Berwick on his way southward on August 5th, at which place Cressingham at that time lay. De Rait of course reported to Cressingham the condition of things in the north, and showed him the letters he was carrying to the king. Whereupon Cressingham, in a long letter to Edward on the affairs of Scotland generally, comments thus on the situation in the Highlands. "The peace on the other side of the Scottish Sea is still in obscurity, as it is said, as to the doings of the earls who are there. But at all events we hope that if our business succeeds well on the day of Saint Laurence as to the Bishop of Glasgow and the others, as far as the people on the other side of the Scottish Sea are concerned, we hope soon to have them at our pleasure by God's grace. Sir Andrew de Rait is going to you with a credence, which he has shown to me, and which is false in many points and obscure, as will be shown hereafter, as I fear; and therefore, sire, if it be your pleasure, you will give little weight to it." [1] From all of which it is plain that Cressingham not only regarded the situation in the north as serious, but that he had grave suspicions of the men who were supposed to be engaged in endeavouring to restore Edward's sovereignty in those parts.

When Sir Andrew de Rait left Inverness he was accompanied by a clerk of the Countess of Ross, Bernard de Monte Alto,[2] a member of the family whose head in

---

[1] Stevenson, ii. 226–227.   [2] *Ibid.*, p. 214.

the north was the hereditary Sheriff of Cromarty.[1] A small escort of armed men rode with them, and making all the haste they could they reached Mar before the end of July. There they found the earl newly returned from England, and on hearing whither they were bound he charged Sir Andrew with a message to Edward and handed him a credence as evidence of his authority to speak for him.[2] Pushing southward by way of Strathearn, Sir Andrew was made the bearer of yet another message and credence, this time from Malise, Earl of Strathearn, who, to quote the credence, prayed the king " to have the goodness to believe Sir Andrew de Rait, the bearer of this letter, in the matter which he will tell you verbally from me. Greeting. May God keep you, body and soul." [3] So armed with many credences and bearing many letters, Sir Andrew de Rait in due time left Berwick and the doubting Cressingham behind him, and hastened Londonwards. And as we leave him riding through England we can only regret that the tale which he by-and-by unfolded to Edward was not written down and stored away with the letters and credences which he carried so far, and which, nearly six hundred years afterwards, were taken from the dark recesses where they had lain so long to cast new light on the deeds by which and the men by whom the independence of Scotland was won.

[1] See various entries in Bain.
[2] *Ibid.*, p. 214. [3] *Ibid.*, p. 215.

CHAPTER VI

ABERDEENSHIRE IN REVOLT

WITH the riding away of Sir Andrew de Rait from Inverness our direct knowledge of the progress of events in the north ceases. But by a careful study of the materials which bear indirectly on the situation, it is, I think, possible to piece together a fairly accurate narrative of what happened.

We left the Bishop of Aberdeen, the Earl of Buchan, Sir Gartenet of Mar, and Sir Alexander Comyn with all their own forces and those of the whole Sheriffdom of Aberdeen at Inverness on 25th July. With them were the Countess of Ross and her men, Sir Reginald le Chen, John of the Aird, Sir William Fitzwarine, and various others who still gave allegiance of a kind to Edward. But formidable though this force seemed, it was altogether unequal to the task imposed upon it. It had reached Inverness, but it had not brought Andrew de Moray to book; it had not even succeeded in compelling him to fight; and it had certainly not dispersed his army, which was even then very probably hovering in the near vicinity and causing the invaders considerable anxiety. The latter, moreover, were in something of a quandary. They had now been a full fortnight absent from Aberdeen, and with that town and the surrounding country stripped of its defensive forces, save for a small garrison in the castle of Aberdeen, common sense demanded that they should not be away a day longer than necessary. But Edward's orders were explicit. The Bishop and Sir Gartenet were to proceed to Urquhart Castle without delay, see the condition of it, and thereafter, in consultation with Fitzwarine, " provide and direct that the castle might be so strengthened and garrisoned that no damage or danger might in any way occur to it," while the Comyns were to remain in the north until order had been restored.[1]

It is possible that the Bishop and Sir Gartenet actually visited Urquhart Castle prior to the date on which we find them in Inverness, for between their crossing of the Spey on 15th July, and the first letter dated from Inverness on 24th July, there was just time for them to have done so and returned to Inverness. The point, however, is immaterial. The fact of importance is that they and the Constable of Urquhart Castle, Fitzwarine, were all at Inverness on 24th and 25th July. It has been suggested that thereafter Edward's instructions as to the strengthening of the castle were carried out, and that in the late summer or autumn of 1297 the still existing massive entrance towers which guard the only landward approach were built. This, however, as we shall presently see, is impossible, and it is much more likely that the towers were built either soon after its capture by the English in August 1296, or during the four years' occupation which succeeded their successful siege in the closing months of 1303. Be that as it may, however, on 25th July 1297 the English faction were gathered in force in Inverness making arrangements for their future proceedings. As a result of their cogitations it was decided that the Earl of Buchan and Sir Alexander Comyn should, in accordance with Edward's instructions, remain for the meantime in the north, and that the Bishop should return forthwith to Aberdeen.[2] Thus the force at the disposal of Edward's servants was reduced very considerably, and the prospects of the patriots in consequence were materially improved.

Good cause was there for the Bishop to hurry to Aberdeen, though on 25th July he probably knew it not. His anxiety so far had been caused merely by his knowledge of the undefended condition of the Sheriffdom and his suspicion of the loyalty of the people. But, as it happened, the whole wide district of which Aberdeen is the centre, was even then in a turmoil, and the very

[1] *Rotuli Scotiae*, i. 41. [2] Stevenson, ii. 212.

sheriff who held the castle of Aberdeen for Edward had thrown off his allegiance. On 23rd July Cressingham reported to Edward that Wallace was then lying with a body of men in Selkirk Forest;[1] on 11th June Edward had addressed a writ to Sir Henry de Latham, Sheriff of Aberdeenshire, strictly enjoining him to use every means in his power to arrest and bring to justice the armed bands of malefactors and marauders who were perpetrating robberies and other enormities in his district;[2] and on 1st August the Earl of Warren wrote to Edward that " we have sent to take Sir Henry de Latham, who is in your Castle of Aberdeen, and there makes a great lord of himself. But whether he is yet taken or not we cannot as yet certainly inform you, for at the departure of this letter we have as yet had no answer from any of those who went to take him; but if he be caught he shall be honoured according to his deserts."[3] But Sir Henry de Latham was not caught, for on 2nd February following his lands in Lancaster were seized because he was "a rebel and adherent of the Scots."[4]

Now, Blind Harry tells us that towards the end of July Wallace led his men north, that he swept through Buchan, and that on 31st July he was at Aberdeen. Blind Harry's statements have usually to be received with great caution, and his chronology is often far astray, but on this occasion his narrative fits in to a certain extent with the facts revealed by the official documents just quoted. It is true that he makes Wallace first destroy the shipping in Aberdeen harbour, then harry Buchan, then sweep through the north as far as a place which he calls " Crummade," which is usually assumed to be Cromarty, but is probably Crimond, and finally return to Aberdeen on 31st July—an obviously impossible feat if Wallace was in Selkirk Forest on 23rd July.

Let us take a bird's-eye view of the situation as it was in the third week of July 1297. In the south-west a Scottish army had taken the field and capitulated. In

---

[1] Stevenson, ii. 202.
[2] *Rotuli Scotiae*, i. 42.
[3] Stevenson, ii. 217.
[4] Bain, ii. 972.

the east, Macduff of Fife had led out the men of the
earldom, and had suffered defeat, he himself and his
two sons being at the end of July captives in the hands of
Malise, Earl of Strathearn.[1] On the Borders a great
English army was assembling for the crushing of such
pertinacious Scots rebels as still kept the field.[2] In
Selkirk Forest Wallace was lying with a considerable
force.[3] In the north Andrew de Moray had shaken the
power of England severely, and his insurrection was
growing in magnitude daily. In the outlying districts of
Aberdeenshire there was considerable unrest, but not
sufficient to keep the English force which dominated the
north-east from advancing against de Moray. Thus, in
the third week of July, in the province of Moray alone
was resistance to England being actively and successfully
maintained. With the invasion of Moray by the troops
from Aberdeen the situation underwent a complete
change. As soon as the men who had held that district
for England were a safe distance away Aberdeenshire rose
in revolt, and Sir Henry de Latham, the sheriff of the
county, throwing in his lot with the "rebels," the castle
of Aberdeen itself fell into their hands. As the Earl of
Warren wrote from Berwick to inform Edward of this
fact on 1st August,[4] the outbreak and the seizure of
the castle must have occurred at least a week earlier,
and as Wallace was in Selkirk Forest on 23rd July he
could in consequence have had no share in it. But as
for some time before the battle of Stirling Bridge on 11th
September, Wallace was certainly north of the Tay, the
probability is that on learning of the successful rising in
Aberdeen he immediately hastened thither, and joined
forces with Sir Henry de Latham and his followers.
Thus to a certain extent Blind Harry is right. But in
ascribing to Wallace the harrying of Buchan and the
sweeping of the north to "Crummade," he is simply
crediting his hero with the deeds of other men. For if
"Crummade" is really Cromarty, it is clear that the

---

[1] Stevenson, ii. 217.   [2] *Ibid.*, ii. 200–203
[3] *Ibid.*   [4] *Ibid.*, 217.

minstrel has simply transferred Andrew de Moray's northern campaign to Wallace, while the harrying of Buchan, if it is not an echo of Bruce's famous "herschip of Buchan" ten years later, probably describes accurately enough the doings of the "rebels" in Aberdeenshire in the last week of July 1297. At all events it is clear that Andrew de Moray's campaign was the direct cause of the Aberdeenshire rising, and with that rising English power in the north-east collapsed like a house of cards.

When the news of the condition of things in their own districts first reached the invaders of Moray we do not know, but it was certainly after 25th July, else Sir Andrew de Rait had not departed as he did. So we may imagine the warrior-bishop setting out from Inverness in the assurance that the Comyns whom he was leaving behind would put a speedy end to the insurrection, and that he himself would ere long be lording it again in Aberdeen. But he could not have proceeded far on his way before tidings of the "tumults" in Aberdeenshire met him. At first, probably, he would not regard them as serious. They would seem to him merely outbreaks of a nature to be expected when the country was denuded of troops. As he proceeded eastwards, however, further messengers would meet him, and, realising at last that the situation was dangerous, he would send couriers hurrying to the Comyns urging them to return to their own districts without delay. The Comyns would require no urging. Already, possibly, they knew of Sir Henry de Latham's revolt and of the doings in Aberdeen and the surrounding districts, for that very courteous and very skilful warrior, Andrew de Moray, would almost certainly take care that tidings of such demoralising import would reach his cousinly opponents at the earliest possible moment. And so by and by there was mounting among the men of the Comyn force, and the last of the army which was to have brought Andrew de Moray and his men to reason was hurrying eastward at the top of its speed.

Then came the patriots' opportunity. Flushed with

the certainty of triumph which the sight of their foes in full retreat gave them, they descended on the castles still held for England, and in a very short time these were all in their hands. How they fell, unfortunately we know not, but it must have been at this time, for when the men of Moray gazed less than six weeks later from the slopes of the Abbey Craig at the great English army which lay over against them across the Bridge of Stirling, they were heartened to hear that in its ranks was that same Constable of Urquhart Castle,[1] whom, with others of Edward's men, they had driven headlong from the north so short a time before. Sir Reginald le Chen, Edward's guardian of Moray, did not, however, escape thus easily. He was captured by the patriots, probably on the fall of the castle of Inverness, and remained for a time a prisoner in their hands.[2]

With the fall of the castles of Urquhart and Inverness, such northern knights and nobles as had remained in half-hearted allegiance to Edward in all probability came to terms with Andrew de Moray, and he, with an army now swollen to large dimensions and eager for the fray, swept through Moray, marched in triumph through the country of those who had so lately thought to overwhelm him, and joined forces with the rest of the patriots. Those who had been so lately the friends of England offered no resistance. The principal men among them, the Bishop of Aberdeen, the Comyns, the Earl of Mar and his son, and the Earl of Strathearn, were content to wait upon events, while many of their followers betook themselves with eagerness to the army of the patriots. Perhaps the private messages which the Earl of Mar and the Earl of Strathearn confided to the ear of Sir Andrew de Rait at the end of July were assurances to Edward that they had no hand in the troubles which had by that time broken out in their own districts; but the Earl of Mar did not return to England to accompany his liege lord to Flanders, nor did the Earl of Strathearn send the captured Macduff of Fife and his two sons to the Earl

---

[1] Bain, iv. 1835. [2] Ibid., ii. 1737.

of Warenne, who was so anxious to give them their deserts. All of which shows how the wind was blowing, and how Edward's "friends" were trimming their sails to go with it if it blew fair for Scotland.

Unfortunately we know nothing of the details of the campaign in the north-east in August 1297, but the end of the first week of September found a large Scottish army, under the command of Andrew de Moray and William Wallace, waiting on the north bank of the Forth for the coming of the English. There we may leave them for a little, while we consider some other matters which call for attention.

Sir Andrew de Rait had meantime reached Edward, related to him his account of the happenings in the North of Scotland, and handed him the commendations he carried in favour of the Countess of Ross. Edward had also received Cressingham's despatch informing him of the progress being made towards the pacification of Scotland, and containing his assurance that he would soon have "the people on the other side of the Scottish Sea . . . at our pleasure, by God's grace." Sir Andrew de Rait, no doubt, put the best face on matters which he could, and the letters he brought, coupled with the complete collapse of Bruce's and Douglas's rising in the south-west, and Cressingham's confident assurance that he would soon have the people on the other side of the Scottish Sea at his mercy, caused Edward to believe that the complete success of his arms in Scotland was only a matter of a very short time—if, indeed, it had not already been secured. Moreover, he was in a mood for believing the best, for he was just about to start for Flanders, and it jumped with his desires to believe that he was leaving no difficult Scottish problem behind him.

This brings us to the question of the Letter of Safe-Conduct issued to Andrew de Moray on 28th August, a question which has caused a good deal of rather unnecessary difficulty to many people. Here, as in most historical matters, dates and details are of importance. Sir Andrew de Rait was at Berwick on 5th August.

Edward sailed for Flanders on 22nd August. Before sailing he himself ordered letters of safe-conduct to be issued in favour of Hugh, son of the Earl of Ross, and Andrew de Moray, as these letters themselves bear.[1] They were not actually issued until 28th August,[2] six days after the king had sailed. Now, in those days the journey from Berwick to London was not accomplished in a day. Six years later, in 1303, it took the Earl of Ross and a mounted retinue eighteen days to travel from London to Berwick,[2] and if we deduct four days, which were spent at York, we are left with fourteen days of actual travelling.[3] Sir Andrew de Rait would probably not take quite so long, but, as he left Inverness on 25th July and did not leave Berwick till 5th August, it cannot be said that he was travelling at any appreciably greater rate of speed than the Earl of Ross. It is, therefore, safe to say that at the very least he took eleven or twelve days between Berwick and London, and may easily have taken more. He would thus arrive in London only a few days before Edward sailed, and his tidings would be the last the king received from the north of Scotland before his departure for Flanders.

From Sir Andrew's story Edward would of course gather that Andrew de Moray was the head and forefront of the trouble in Moray, and it was quite natural, therefore, for him to conclude that the peace of the north could best be maintained by having that stormy petrel removed from the ways of temptation. The obvious method of securing that lay to his hand. It was a method he often used, and generally with success. Young Andrew's father was still a prisoner in the Tower, and would probably gladly exchange his prison for the continental field of war. Many of his brother nobles of Scotland had already agreed to do so on the terms which Edward demanded, namely, that they should find sufficient security and give hostages for their good behaviour while in Flanders with the English king. These hostages Edward insisted, in most cases, should be their

---

[1] Stevenson, ii. 227.　　[2] *Ibid.*　　[3] Bain, ii. 1403.

E

eldest sons, and already the Earl of Athol, John Comyn, the younger of Badenoch, and Richard Siward,[1] among others, had either delivered, or agreed to deliver, their eldest sons as such. Moreover, a week or two before he sailed, the king announced further that his pleasure was "that the Scots prisoners delivered to him, to go with him in his foreign war, shall find good security without delay, and send to their friends in Scotland to give mainprise before the king's lieutenant. And let them write accordingly."[2]

So the mystery of Andrew de Moray's safe-conduct vanishes. Edward simply offered to take the Earl of Ross and Sir Andrew de Moray to Flanders on condition that, like their friends, they gave their sons as hostages ; and the fathers, who of course knew nothing of the doings in the north, and were anxious after a year's captivity in the Tower to breathe the free air of heaven once more, agreed to his terms. So they wrote to their sons explaining, no doubt, the position of matters, and enclosing letters of safe-conduct from the king, which at that time were very necessary adjuncts if one wished to travel in any degree of safety. The interesting thing about these safe-conducts is that they were both issued on the same day and in identical terms, and that they state the reason of their issue to be that each of the two fathers, "detained in our prison within our Tower of London, is sending for his son to come to him immediately, in order that he may speak to him by our permission."[3] If the sons came there was no doubt that the fathers would go to Flanders, and thus Edward would in the simplest possible manner secure the removal of young Andrew de Moray from the north of Scotland.

It has to be observed that in taking this action Edward was not guilty of anything discreditable. It was not, as has often been suggested, a mere subterfuge to get Andrew de Moray into his hands by fair means or foul. He simply made to Sir Andrew de Moray an

[1] See various entries in Bain's *Calendar*.
[2] Bain, ii. 944.   [3] Stevenson, ii. 227.

offer similar to that which had already been made to, and accepted by, many of Sir Andrew's fellow-captives, an offer, too, which was quite in accordance with the chivalric ideas of the times. Had young Andrew de Moray given himself up as a hostage, there is not the slightest reason to suppose that he would have been treated differently from the other hostages in similar case to himself, or that he or his father would not have been released on Sir Andrew's return from Flanders.

CHAPTER VII

ANDREW DE MORAY AND WILLIAM WALLACE

It is unnecessary to retell here the well-known tale of the battle of Stirling Bridge. Every Scotsman knows how Warrene and Cressingham lay on the south side of the Forth gazing across the river at the Scottish army posted on the slopes of the Ochils; how Cressingham, against Warrene's better judgment, insisted on crossing the narrow bridge which spanned the Forth, in order to destroy the enemy whom he despised; how the Scots allowed part of the English army to cross unmolested; how, while these were still in disorder, the Scots, charging impetuously down upon them, put them to utter rout; and how the remainder of the English army fled in dismay before their triumphant foes. These things are part of the heritage of every Scot, and we need not dwell upon them now, but shall pass from them to consider such of the details of the battle as bear more particularly on our present narrative.

I do not think there can be any doubt in the mind of anyone who has read thus far, as to what was the composition of the Scottish army at Stirling Bridge. It was composed of "the common men" of Scotland, and was drawn for the most part from those districts in which Andrew de Moray and William Wallace had just been waging successful war; that is to say, from the province of Moray and the counties of Banff, Aberdeen, Kincardine, Forfar, Perth, Stirling, and Dumbarton. What the size of the Scottish army was it is, of course, impossible to say, but it is unlikely that it exceeded 10,000 men, and probably was considerably less. The English army has been placed by patriotic chroniclers at

50,000 and over, which, of course, is ridiculous. On 23rd July Cressingham reported to Edward that in the middle of the month he had a force at Roxburgh of 300 covered horses and 10,000 foot.[1] By the end of August this force had doubtless been augmented somewhat, but it is unlikely that at Stirling Bridge it numbered more than 10,000.

When the Scottish army rushed down on the disordered English at the bridge a fierce mêlée took place. Friend and foe were mixed up together, and the struggle resolved itself into a hand-to-hand fight of the most desperate description. Like the young and ardent warrior he was, Andrew de Moray fought in the thickest of the fray, and when the day was lost and won, he was found lying severely wounded in the midst of the slain.[2] Wallace was thus left sole leader of the triumphant Scottish army, and at their head he pursued the fleeing English to the border.

Among those slain at Stirling Bridge was Sir Richard de Waldegrave, the constable of the castle of Stirling The Earl of Warrene heard of his death before he turned his horse's head southwards, and stayed his flight long enough to entrust the custody of the castle to his own kinsman, Sir William Fitzwarine, the late constable of Urquhart Castle.[3] Fitzwarine, however, did not enjoy his new honour long, for Stirling Castle was soon starved into surrender.[4] Thus Fitzwarine, who had had more than his share in the events of the summer, fell at last into the hands of the Scots, and remained a captive in their midst until April 1299.[5]

The battle of Stirling Bridge was fought on 11th September, and on 11th October Wallace was at Haddington on his way to an invasion of England.[6] In the interval Dundee Castle and nearly all the castles of Scotland still held by England had surrendered, and so complete was the triumph of the patriots that on 11th

---

[1] Stevenson, ii. 202.   [2] Fordun.
[3] Stevenson, ii. 233 ; Bain, iv. 1835.   [4] Bain, iv. 1835.
[5] *Ibid.*, ii. 1062.   [6] Original Letter in Archives of Lubeck.

October "the leaders of the army of the realm of
Scotland" were able to declare to "the Mayors and
Commons of Lubeck and Hamburg" that the kingdom
of Scotland had been "recovered by war from the power
of the English." Into the space of one short month all
these events had been crowded, and Wallace, fully occupied as he thus was, could clearly have had no time
for the numerous other deeds attributed to him during
the same month by Blind Harry. These may, perhaps,
have occurred at some other time, but they could not
have occurred between 11th September and 11th October
1297.

It is usually said that, at the council held at Perth
soon after Stirling Bridge, Andrew de Moray and William
Wallace were elected "leaders of the army of the kingdom of Scotland." This may or may not be true, but it
is at all events clear that at the battle itself they were the
leaders; and after that victory a council may well have
been held in order to give their leadership the appearance
of legal sanction. However that may be, they appear
after Stirling Bridge with the official title, "leaders of the
army of the kingdom of Scotland." In three contemporary documents they are thus designated. The first of
these is the letter already referred to written at Haddington on 11th October. The two others are dated at
Hexham on 7th November.[1] In all of these the order
of the names is the same, namely, "Andrew de Moray
and William Wallace, leaders of the army of the realm
of Scotland." In each of these, moreover, the two leaders
are stated to be acting with the consent of "the community of the same realm." After 7th November
Andrew de Moray's name no longer appears. Round
these simple facts a great web of mystery has been woven,
but if they are examined in the light of all that has gone
before, it will, I think, be apparent that the mystery no
longer exists.

Prior to the battle of Stirling Bridge, Andrew de
Moray and William Wallace, in spite of the success which

[1] Hemingburgh.

had attended their arms, occupied a somewhat equivocal position in the eyes of Scotland. The events of July and August had taken those magnates of Scotland who were fully cognisant of them completely by surprise, but considerable though the successes of the two young esquires, and especially of Andrew de Moray, had been, they had not yet been of such a nature as to lead the knights and nobles of the north and east to regard Andrew de Moray or William Wallace as of the first importance in the affairs of Scotland. It was one thing by a combination of fortuitous circumstances to destroy for the moment English power in the north and east. There would be another story to tell when they met a real English army in the field. So most of the knights and nobles of the north and east stood aloof, hoping that victory would incline to the side of their countrymen, but certain in their own minds that the motley host led by Andrew de Moray and William Wallace would go down like chaff before the might of England.

Such was the situation on the eve of the battle of Stirling Bridge, and great, therefore, was the responsibility which rested upon the shoulders of the two young esquires who were about to pit their own inexperience and their undisciplined host against the proven leaders and the trained and well-armed army of England. But they hesitated not, and because in their youthful courage and ardour they dared what older and more experienced men would not have dared, the freedom of Scotland was won.

By the victory of Stirling Bridge the whole situation in Scotland was completely altered, and the two leaders of the victorious army became at a single bound the most powerful men in Scotland, and the directors, for the time, of their country's destinies. Had they both lived, the name of Andrew de Moray would probably be held to this day in as high veneration as that of Wallace. But Andrew de Moray was mortally wounded at Stirling Bridge, and it was left to William Wallace to reap the fruits and push home the advantages of the victory. By the ability with which he rose to the occasion he became, on Andrew de Moray's death, the sole leader and the recognised champion of the cause of Scottish freedom, and by his subsequent exploits and his heroic death attained to a place in the hearts of his countrymen to which no Scotsman before or since has ever approached. But the very greatness of the place which he occupied in the imagination of Scotsmen led to the growth of a mass of legend which distorted the true facts of his career, and gave rise to numerous difficulties, many of which have only in recent years been cleared up, and some of which still remain. Among those the relations of Andrew de Moray and William Wallace have hitherto occupied a foremost place, and much ink has been spilt in unsuccessful efforts to solve the seeming mystery of the bracketing of their names together as " leaders of the army of Scotland," a mystery which seemed to be intensified by the fact that Andrew de Moray's name was placed first. It is a mystery which, I venture to think, can be regarded as a mystery no longer.

It is curious how many investigators insisted on increasing the difficulty of their investigations, by assuming that Andrew de Moray was *killed* at Stirling Bridge. Of the details of that battle we have unfortunately little authentic information, but if one thing is certain it is that Andrew de Moray was not killed, but only wounded in the struggle. That he died afterwards from the effects of his wounds is true, but his death was not immediate, and he probably lived for several weeks after the battle. As to the wound, Fordun, whose authority on this point cannot be questioned, is quite explicit. " Hugh de Cressingham was killed," he says, " and all his army put to flight. Some of them were slain with the sword, others taken, others drowned in the waters. . . . Of the nobles on his (Wallace's) side, the noble Andrew de Moray alone, the father of Andrew, fell wounded." When we find that statement confirmed by the subsequent appearance of Andrew de Moray's name along with that of Wallace as one of the leaders

of the army of Scotland, it is a little difficult to understand why investigators should have insisted on increasing
their difficulties by assuming that he was killed at Stirling
Bridge, and therefore could not have been Wallace's
colleague a month or seven weeks after the battle.
In order to meet their new difficulty, they were compelled, quite unhistorically, to release Andrew's father,
Sir Andrew, from the Tower, and this in spite of the
fact that in none of the documents is Wallace's colleague
termed " Sir Andrew." He is always simply " Andrew
de Moray." Compelled at last to abandon that solution,
some investigators took refuge in vague suggestions that
Wallace either as an act of grace or as an act of policy
bracketed the young heir of Petty and Bothwell with
himself, thus showing that the true obstacle to the
solution of the problem was an inability to get away
from the overshadowing personality of Wallace. To
put it shortly, they were unable to realise that Wallace's
appearance as a potent force in Scottish history dated
from Stirling Bridge and not from a period anterior to
it. A brief consideration of all the facts, however, should
now place the relations of Andrew de Moray and William
Wallace in their true light.

After the battle of Stirling Bridge, Wallace, the
unwounded leader, led the Scottish army south. He
was at Haddington on 11th October, as we have seen,
and from there advanced into the north of England.
Andrew de Moray meantime had been removed wounded
from the battlefield, and it is possible that he may have
been carried north, for his castle of Bothwell was at that
time in the hands of the English, and in the north he
had left a young and newly-married wife. Whether
that be so or not, however, one thing is clear, and that
is that when the letter was sent to Lubeck on 11th
October Andrew de Moray was still supposed to be
alive. Immediately thereafter the Scottish army marched
into England, and during the three weeks of marching
and warfare which ensued the news of Andrew de Moray's
death, if it had occurred in the meantime, could hardly

have reached them. It must always be remembered that communication in those days was at the best of times exceedingly slow and precarious, and during a Scottish invasion of England must have been almost impossible.

Very little now remains of the mystery either of the bracketing of the names of Andrew de Moray and William Wallace together as the leaders of the army of Scotland, or of the placing of Andrew de Moray's name in the first place, for in the light of all the facts I have stated there is little mystery left to dissipate. To Andrew de Moray much more than to William Wallace were due the events which made Stirling Bridge possible, and the chief share in that victory itself was likewise his. That is why his name appears before Wallace's as one of the two leaders of the army of Scotland.

A brief recapitulation of the facts which we have elucidated will make this clear. The beginning of July had seen the apparent collapse of the great rising which had promised so well. The Bishop of Glasgow, the Earl of Carrick, Sir William Douglas, the Steward, and other magnates from whom so much had been expected had capitulated, and with their capitulation the backbone seemed to have gone out of the revolt. Wallace, the noted outlaw, had not, it is true, surrendered, but throughout almost the whole of July he had lain in Selkirk forest attempting nothing, and giving the English commanders no cause for anxiety, as Cressingham's despatches make clear.[1] Throughout all the rest of Scotland, save in the province of Moray, the same spirit of indecision prevailed, and Cressingham looked forward with arrogant confidence to a speedy re-establishment of English sovereignty.[2] Moray, however, upset all his calculations. The success of the revolt there led directly to a successful rising in Aberdeen and the neighbouring counties, and that in its turn caused Wallace to leave the recesses of Selkirk forest, and make common cause

---

[1] Professor Murison in his *William Wallace* comes to the same conclusion regarding Wallace's doings in July (p. 83).

[2] Stevenson, ii. 205, 207, &c.

with the north-eastern counties. With the whole country from the Beauly to the Tay up in arms the power of England in all that wide district collapsed, and Andrew de Moray with his victorious army swept south, carrying everything before him, and receiving as he went great accessions to his strength. When at last he effected a junction with the forces now commanded by Wallace, he it was who must have occupied the superior position, for he it was who had made possible the campaign on which they were now embarked; he it was who had displayed all the qualities of leadership and waged successful war against the English during the preceding four months; and he it was who had brought to the common cause an army tried and proven—an army numerous, confident, and elated with past victories.

It must be remembered, moreover, that Wallace, at the period with which we are at present dealing, was not yet the known and accepted champion of the cause of Scottish freedom. He was merely one of several leaders who had roused different parts of the country against England, and in his own special district, the Scottish Midlands, he had gained considerable successes, and was looked up to as a warrior of courage and repute. Andrew de Moray occupied a precisely similar position in the north, where the name of Wallace, if it was known at all, was known simply as that of a man who had performed doughty deeds of valour against the English in the south.

The name and fame of Andrew de Moray, however, were greater in the Midlands and the south in the summer of 1297 than were the name and fame of Wallace in the north. For while Wallace was as yet at best a name only in the north, de Moray's was a very real and important personality in the Midlands and the south, for he was heir to the great barony of Bothwell,[1] and, because of his father's and uncle's captivity in England, the actual head for the time of the great house of Bothwell. Now, the castle of Bothwell lay

[1] Bain, ii. 1178.

on the north bank of the Clyde in the lower ward of Lanarkshire, and the lordship of Bothwell comprised a large stretch of country in the same county. So great were his possessions that Sir William de Moray of Bothwell, young Andrew's uncle, was known as "le Riche," and his castle of Bothwell was regarded as a place of such strength and importance that it was strongly garrisoned by Edward in 1296,[1] and at a later date conferred by him, for his principal residence and stronghold, on the trusted soldier whom he made his commander-in-chief in Scotland and guardian of the northern kingdom, Aymer de Valence, Earl of Pembroke.[2]   Thus young Andrew de Moray was in 1297 the chief representative in Scotland of one of her greatest houses, and head of the most powerful family in the district with which the earliest authentic exploits of Wallace are associated.

For some reason or other Edward treated the Morays of Petty and Bothwell with unusual severity. We have already seen that many Scottish knights and nobles were released in order to accompany Edward to Flanders long before any suggestion of a like nature was made to Sir Andrew de Moray. Sir William de Moray ("le Riche") was, however, among those who went to Flanders.[3]   In spite of that he was not permitted to return to Scotland, but was kept in England under conditions of considerable severity, and eventually died there in poverty. It is when contrasted with his treatment of other Scottish nobles, many of whom rebelled and made their peace with Edward more than once, that this treatment of the de Morays appears in its most significant light, and it is difficult to resist the conclusion that the English king treated them as he did because he had good reason to fear that they would never be really reconciled to his rule in Scotland. Colour is lent to this view when we remember that Sir Andrew died in the Tower of London, that his son, young Andrew, received his death wound fighting against England, and that young Andrew's son, the third Andrew, in his turn fought gloriously against

---

[1] Bain, ii. 1867.   [2] Bain, ii. 1214.   [3] *Ibid.*, ii. 942.

the third Edward, and played a great part in defeating
that king's attempt to reduce Scotland to the position of
a vassal state.[1]

It is also a remarkable fact that after Stirling Bridge
the Scots under Wallace never won a victory in the open
against any English force which can fairly be described
as an army. The strategy of Falkirk, moreover, is as
different from the strategy of Stirling Bridge as it is
possible to conceive. Even the most ardent admirers of
Wallace are compelled to admit that Falkirk should
never have been fought at all, and all manner of
unconvincing reasons, ranging from dissensions among
the Scottish leaders to suggestions that the Scots were
taken by surprise, have been advanced to account for the
battle. Of the latter suggestion it is sufficient to say
that the disposition of the Scottish army shows that its
leaders were not taken by surprise, while on the other
hand it may be added, if they were, it would reflect
anything but credit on their generalship, as a glance at
the history of the campaign will make clear to anyone.
But if the strategy which lost Falkirk was the direct
antithesis of the strategy which won Stirling Bridge, it is
also the case that the strategy which won Stirling Bridge
was very similar to that which Andrew de Moray had
displayed in his northern campaign. Andrew de Moray,
it will be remembered, had, in the words of Edward's
own officers, waited the coming of the invaders of Moray
beside "a great stronghold of bog and wood," into which
he would be able to retire if the advancing force seemed
likely to prove too strong for him. And retire into it
he did, to the annoyance of Edward's officers, for its
condition was such that in it "no horseman could be of
service." He thus took up a position which gave him
excellent opportunity both for attack and defence. The
same is true of Stirling Bridge. Against an army posted
on the slopes of the Ochils "no horseman could be of
service," while the opportunity of attack which the position offered the story of the battle makes clear. At

[1] See various entries in Bain for treatment of the Morays.

the same time the wild country to the rear of the Scottish position, a country of hill, morass, and forest, offered a safe retreat in case of defeat, for there, too, " no horseman could be of service." [1]

At Falkirk these positions were reversed. The Scottish army stood purely on the defensive in a situation which had few natural advantages, and from which, in the event of misfortune, there was no easy means of escape. It must be confessed that it hardly looks as if the brain which conceived the plan of battle at Falkirk was the same as that which conceived the plan at Stirling Bridge.

It is also of some importance to observe that the strategy evinced by Andrew de Moray's son, Sir Andrew de Moray, the Regent of Scotland from 1332 to 1339, was of a nature very similar to that exhibited by his father in 1297, and was just as successful. So that in the de Morays military genius seems to have been hereditary, a fact which, while not of course conclusive in regard to Stirling Bridge, is at least suggestive. The conclusion on the whole matter, therefore, would seem to be that Andrew de Moray possessed military genius and military training, William Wallace those qualities which go to make a great guerilla leader. Without the former neither the campaign which made Stirling Bridge possible nor the battle of Stirling Bridge itself would have been fought or won, while without the latter there would have been possible neither the successful campaign which succeeded Stirling Bridge, nor the deeds which in the years from 1297 to 1305 gave William Wallace so tremendous a hold upon his countrymen and caused him to come to typify in English eyes that irreconcilable spirit of the Scots which could be neither conquered nor conciliated.

[1] Sir James Ramsay in his *Dawn of the Constitution* thus describes the Scottish position. " On the opposite side of the river Forth Wallace confronted them, at the foot of the Ochil range, at a distance of about a mile from Stirling Bridge. At his back he had the Ochils, his left rested on the river Forth ; in front he had a low swampy meadow, with a causeway leading up to the then Stirling Bridge : a horseshoe bend of the stream covered his right flank, and secured him from any attack except along the causeway. No spot could be better chosen."

It is, probably, hardly necessary now to endeavour to show that Andrew de Moray's insurrection in Moray formed part of the plan engineered by the Bishop of Glasgow. The facts we have elucidated speak for themselves on that point. There are, however, some other facts and arguments which go to support this view. In the first place it is impossible to believe that Andrew de Moray's rising was merely a local ebullition, that it had no connection with the doings of the patriots elsewhere. Andrew de Moray had had too much experience of the power of England to indulge in the dangerous game of raising impossible insurrections, and, moreover, his father was a prisoner in Edward's hands. So when he took the step he did, he must have taken it deliberately and with the knowledge that others were taking similar action elsewhere. In this connection we have already commented on the significance of the fact that his insurrection began at almost the same time as Wallace's and Douglas's attack on Edward's Justiciar, Ormsby, at Scone, and almost simultaneously with other risings elsewhere. In the next place Andrew de Moray had a close connection with the Church militant in the person of his uncle, David de Moravia, who was parson of Bothwell in 1296,[1] a canon of Elgin in 1297 or 1298,[2] and Bishop of Moray from 1299 to 1326.[3] This David was one of the most ardent and single-hearted patriots of his time, and won for himself the high honour of Edward's special hate. We shall meet him frequently in the course of our narrative, so meantime we need say no more. Our present point is that in David de Moravia the Bishop of Glasgow found a willing coadjutor, and that through him it would be a natural and simple matter to influence young Andrew de Moray. In the third place, Andrew de Moray had been a prisoner in Chester Castle,[4] and the little evidence we possess indicates that he owed his freedom to his own daring— in other words, that he escaped. For the five other

---

[1] Bain, ii. 212.   [2] Dowden's *Bishops of Scotland.*
[3] *Ibia.*   [4] Bain, ii. 177.

Scots who had been consigned to Chester with him were still in captivity there in September 1300.[1] Accordingly, as an escaped prisoner he would be eager to strike a blow at England, and as on his escape he would be certain to visit his uncle, David de Moravia, if for no other purpose than to discover how the interests of his family had been affected by the events of the previous year, that patriotic prelate would have full opportunity for enlisting his services in the schemes of the Church militant. In view of all these facts it seems impossible to doubt that Andrew de Moray's insurrection in Moray was part of a general plan, while both that fact, and all the facts we have been considering regarding his career in 1297, prove that the English chroniclers were not writing at random when they placed him next to the Bishop of Glasgow among the leaders of the general uprising of May 1297.

[1] Bain, ii. 1156.

CHAPTER VIII

THE PLACE OF WILLIAM WALLACE IN
SCOTTISH HISTORY

THE battle of Stirling Bridge raised Andrew de Moray and William Wallace to a unique position among their countrymen. From being the leaders of two successful local risings, the two young esquires became, as we have seen, at a single bound the most powerful men in Scotland, and the directors for the time of their country's destinies. But Andrew de Moray was wounded unto death, and so the whole fruits of the victory, the glory, the power, and the opportunity passed to William Wallace. And right nobly did he use them. He was now no longer in the eyes of his countrymen simply a bold outlaw. He was one of the two leaders of the victorious army of Scotland, and presently, on Andrew de Moray's death, became sole "guardian of the kingdom of Scotland and leader of the armies of that kingdom." [1] The battle of Stirling Bridge, the death of Andrew de Moray, his own exploits, and his own qualities had all combined to make him the most powerful man in Scotland.

I do not propose to deal in detail in these pages with the career of William Wallace after the battle of Stirling Bridge, for the double reason that it is well known to every reader of Scottish history, and that I have little new to place on record regarding it. Readers who desire to refresh their memory, however, may be recommended to Professor A. F. Murison's *Sir William Wallace* in the "Famous Scots Series," or to Sheriff Æneas Mackay's masterly sketch in the *Encyclopædia of National Biography*.

[1] He is thus described in the charter granted by him, on 29th March 1298, to Alexander Scrimgeour.

F

In either they will find all the authenticated facts of Wallace's career fully set forth, while in Professor Murison's book many of the problems regarding him are discussed learnedly and adequately. We shall, of course, frequently meet him again in the course of this study of the War of Independence, but meantime it is unnecessary to do more than glance, very briefly, at certain salient facts.

After Stirling Bridge Wallace led the Scottish army south, and early in November invaded the north of England. For two or three months the northern counties were made to pay in part for all that Scotland had suffered at the hands of England during the preceding year and a half, and eventually the Scots returned to their country in January 1298 laden with immense spoil. A quotation from Hemingburgh will bring out clearly the extent and the effect of the inroad. "During that time," he says, "the praise of God ceased in all the monasteries and churches of the whole province from Newcastle-upon-Tyne to Carlisle; for all the monks, canons regular, and other priests, the servants of the Lord, had fled, with, one may say, the whole of the common folk, from the face of the Scots."

After his return to Scotland in January 1298, until the battle of Falkirk on 22nd July of the same year, Wallace maintained his position as sole leader of the army of Scotland and guardian of the kingdom, and that although the chief result of the battle of Stirling Bridge and the subsequent expulsion of the English had been the rallying, for a time, of the whole country to the cause of freedom. The very knights and nobles, who in the summer of 1297 had been endeavouring to suppress the efforts of the patriots, threw off their allegiance to Edward; and when, in January 1298 and again in May of the same year, the Scottish nobles were summoned to a Parliament at York, they "neither came nor sent." No better evidence could be adduced of the completeness of the patriots' success, or of the readiness of all classes in Scotland to throw off the English yoke at the first

favourable opportunity. Dunbar had humbled the pride
of the Scottish magnates, and led them to believe resistance to England impossible—at least while Edward lived.
Stirling Bridge and an English army in headlong flight
encouraged them to think that independence, even in
Edward's lifetime, was not so impossible as they had
thought; and the events which followed Stirling Bridge,
especially the accomplished facts of the expulsion of the
English from Scotland and the return of the Scottish
army with great spoil from a successful invasion of the
north of England, convinced them that Edward's might
was not so invincible as it had seemed. So, to put it at
its lowest, they accepted the situation, and for a time at
least Scotland presented an almost solid front to her foe.

Among the rest the magnates of the north and north-
east lost no time in accepting the new condition of things.
The Countess of Ross abandoned her efforts to obtain
the release of her husband, and he remained a prisoner
in the Tower until September 1303; the Bishop of
Aberdeen continued to perform the duties of his diocese;
the Earl of Buchan became one of the most active of the
patriots, and as late as 1303 was one of the Scottish
ambassadors to France; Sir Gartenet of Mar, Sir
Alexander Comyn, and Sir Reginald le Chen likewise
abandoned the cause of England, the son of the last, who
since the battle of Dunbar had been a prisoner in Kenil-
worth Castle, being in August 1299 one of several
prisoners exchanged for Englishmen captured by the
Scots;[1] and John Comyn, Lord of Badenoch—the same
Red Comyn who was afterwards slain by Bruce—early
threw in his lot with the patriots, became in 1299 one of
the guardians of Scotland, and commanded the forces
of Scotland against England with varying success until
February 1304.

The very fact, however, that the magnates of Scotland
had thrown in their lot with Wallace rendered his position one of extreme difficulty. For Wallace was but the
younger son of a small Scottish knight, and the great

[1] Bain, ii. 1062, 1076–77, 1099.

magnates were not likely long to be content to play second fiddle to him. Moreover the most powerful family in Scotland, the Comyns, were near relations of Balliol and strong supporters of his claim to the Scottish Crown, to which, indeed, they were next in succession, if Edward's award had been right and if Balliol's direct line failed. Accordingly, it was not in the nature of things that they should be content to submit to the leadership of Wallace for any length of time. So long, however, as Wallace was at the head of a victorious and devoted army his position, though difficult, was almost unassailable. But Falkirk changed all that, and with his overthrow on that disastrous day his resignation of both leadership and guardianship was inevitable. This brings us to the only other point relative to Wallace with which we shall deal meantime.

We have already noted that the armies which Andrew de Moray and William Wallace led to victory in 1287 were composed of " the common folk " of Scotland, as was also, for the most part, the army which Wallace commanded at Falkirk. This is strikingly brought out by Hemingburgh, who tells us that Wallace " was joined by an immense number of the Scots, for the community of the land followed him as their leader and chief. Moreover all the followers of the magnates adhered to him ; and as for the magnates themselves, they were with our king in body, but their heart was far from him." Of the accuracy of this statement there can be no question. Wallace was followed by and relied on " the common folk " of Scotland, a fact which was at once his strength and his weakness. To that fact he owed whatever measure of success and all the enormous influence which were his, and it was Edward's realisation of that and all it meant which won for Wallace the fierce malignant hate of the English king. The feudal aristocracy of Scotland Edward could understand and believed he could conciliate. Wallace represented the mass of the people whom Edward could neither understand nor conciliate. Yet if they remained in open hostility to England his sub-

jugation of Scotland would never be complete. Hence
his determination to capture at all costs the man who
was in himself the embodiment of that popular hostility,
and who was in addition a warrior of skill and daring
and a leader who had won the heart and the imagination
of the people. Hence, also, the undoubted fact that
Edward himself, and all Englishmen great and small,
came to regard Wallace not only as their most formidable foe but as the one serious obstacle to the establishment of English dominion in Scotland. And hence,
accordingly, Edward's cruel and unchivalrous treatment
of Wallace, his judicial murder of his most gallant enemy.
If the people whom Wallace represented could not be
conciliated they might be cowed. If Wallace steadfastly
refused to own Edward as his sovereign he might be
barbarously done to death as a traitor. Thus not only
would he be put out of the way, but his fate would
prove a terrible warning to the Scots. So ran the argument, an argument too common in that age, but an
argument in the case of Scotland foredoomed to failure.
For far from cowing Scotland, far even from destroying
Wallace's influence, the execution of Edward's most
honourable foe and Scotland's most consistent patriot
filled " the common folk " of Scotland with an undying
hatred of England, and but increased their determination
to throw off her yoke at the first opportunity.

But if Wallace were executed because he was the
embodiment of the national resistance of Scotland to
English domination, in that very fact lies the true secret
of the influence he exerted and the part he played during
the seven years which elapsed between the battle of
Falkirk in July 1298 and his execution in August 1305.
After Falkirk he never again commanded a Scottish army
in the field, but the influence he exerted was none the
less very great, and to him more than to any other man
was due the growth of that spirit of determined hostility
to English domination which became at last almost a
second nature to the common folk of Scotland, and which
had such far-reaching results in the history of the two

nations.   And so though his name does not occur very often in the history of the five years immediately succeeding Falkirk, yet when we read during these years of such things as Edward's officers reporting [1] that in some districts " all the country was rising," and that elsewhere [2] a castle was attacked by a force of " four knight-bannerets, 240 men-at-arms, *and seven thousand footmen*," we see his influence at work, the influence of his deeds, his example, and his ardent genius, on the spirit of " the common folk " of Scotland, on the men who, to " an immense number, had followed him as their leader and chief."

[1] Stevenson, ii. 431–35.   [2] *Ibid.*

CHAPTER IX

THE CAUSES OF THE WAR OF INDEPENDENCE

So far nothing has been said in this study of the War of Independence in regard to the controversies and the actions which were the direct cause of the war, but we have now reached a stage when it is necessary to examine these. We shall, accordingly, proceed to consider (1) the English claims to the overlordship of Scotland; (2) the character of Edward I, especially as disclosed in his dealings with Scotland; and (3) the attitude of the Bruces, and especially of the future king, in the early years of the controversy and the war.

Unfortunately, in regard to the first of these questions, even writers of repute have, until recently, been unable to approach this matter of the English claims without a strong bias in favour of their own country; and though now there is a general tendency to admit that the English claims had no real foundation, were in fact unreasonable and tyrannical, there still lingers a feeling among many writers, that Edward I had some justification for his action—(1) Because there was some question of homage due by Scotland to England; (2) because Edward believed sincerely that he was the feudal overlord of Scotland; and (3) because he was invited by the Scots themselves to intervene and act as arbiter during the confusion which followed the death of the Maid of Norway.

These arguments may be dismissed very briefly. In regard to the first, various Scottish kings owed homage to the English king for lands which they possessed in England. On one or two occasions the English king endeavoured to make this the excuse for extorting homage for the kingdom of Scotland as well, but it was always indignantly and emphatically repudiated. In the next place the whole history of the two kingdoms and of their relations to each other during the centuries preceding the death of the Maid of Norway, is in itself an emphatic contradiction of any such theory—is, indeed, entirely inconsistent with any such relationship. In the third place, on the one solitary well-authenticated occasion on which Scotland was compelled to yield temporary submission to England, owing to the capture of William the Lion at Alnwick in 1174, the Treaty of Falaise, which embodied that submission, was completely abrogated, and the independence of Scotland restored in the most unequivocal manner, by the Treaty of Canterbury in 1189. And in the fourth place, no English writer of repute is able to point to a single well-authenticated act, or a single well-authenticated document which supports the English contention. While these things are so, however, I am content to rest the whole Scottish case on the broad fact, above stated, that the whole history of the two kingdoms for centuries prior to the death of the Maid of Norway is absolutely inconsistent with any such relationship. How any thinking person can read that history and retain any belief in the English claims is beyond comprehension.[1]

But what of Edward's sincere belief that he was the feudal overlord of Scotland? Well, the people who, in their endeavours to find excuses for the English king, advance that theory have a very heavy onus upon them. It is for them to prove it, and that no recent writer has succeeded in doing. Three incontrovertible facts stand in the way. In the first place, after the death of Alexander the Third, Edward did not take the steps which, had he been, or believed himself to be, the feudal superior of Scotland, he would, in accordance with the principles

[1] For full statements of the case for and against the English claims see Sir James Ramsay's *Dawn of the Constitution*, Professor Tout's *Edward I* in the "English Statesmen" series, and his volume on the period in the *Political History of England*, Appendix to Robertson's *Scotland under her Early Kings*, &c., &c.

and daily practice of feudal law, have been entitled to take. In the second place, when he eventually put forward his claim to the overlordship of Scotland, he carefully suppressed all the evidence which told against that claim, the most notable example of this being his citation of the Treaty of Falaise as a proof that William the Lion had surrendered the independence of Scotland, and his suppression of the Treaty of Canterbury, which abrogated the Treaty of Falaise in the fullest possible way. In the third place, when on 2nd June 1291 Edward met the competitors to the Crown of Scotland for the second time, not only was a protest from the *communitas* of Scotland against the claim to overlordship deliberately suppressed, but the official record of the meeting was itself deliberately falsified in order to make it appear that the competitors conceded to Edward not only the overlordship but also the direct dominion of Scotland. As Sir James Ramsay remarks : " The grant of the direct dominion would have involved the entire incorporation of Scotland. The words to that effect must have been interpolated later when Edward found that the rights of an overlord would not serve his purpose." At all events, there can be no question that they were interpolated without the knowledge or consent of the Scots, as the documents put in at the time by the Scots themselves prove. Finally, Sir James Ramsay draws attention to the fact that even before Edward had made his first demand for the admission of his overlordship, at Norham on 10th May 1291, he had confidentially informed his barons in council [1] that he contemplated conquering Scotland as he had conquered Wales. [2] And yet we are

[1] Annals of Waverley ; Annals of Worcester.
[2] Compare Mr. K. H. Vickers in his *England in the Middle Ages*, which forms Vol. III. of Professor Oman's *History of England*. Published only a month or two ago, it was not available when these pages were written, and I have only seen it on the eve of going to press. It is written from the English standpoint, and the fact that he describes Wallace as " having murdered the Sheriff of Lanark in a particularly brutal way,"—which is utter rubbish—will sufficiently indicate the unlikelihood of his straining anything in favour of the Scots. Yet he says of this period : " It was no secret in England that he (Edward) had the definite intention of subduing Scotland to his will when he summoned

asked to believe that Edward was sincere and honest in his attitude towards Scotland. He may have been, but in the face of facts like these a little more than mere assertion is necessary to carry conviction. The Scots who lived through these strenuous years, at all events, had no doubts on the matter. Said the nobles and community of the kingdom in their letter to the Pope in 1320: "We continued to enjoy peace and liberty . . . until Edward, the late king of England, *in the guise of a friend and ally*, invaded and oppressed our nation, at that time without a head, unpractised in war, and suspecting no evil."[1]

This brings us to the next argument, which is that Edward was invited by the Scots themselves to intervene, and act as arbiter during the confusion which followed the death of the Maid of Norway. Which is quite true, but is no justification for his subsequent behaviour. On the contrary, it puts it in a worse light than ever, for it means that he abused the confidence reposed in him, and took advantage of the difficulties of the Scots and the divided state of the kingdom to demand from them, in return for his good offices, an acknowledgment of his overlordship, which, once obtained, he intended to use as a lever for the complete subjugation of Scotland to England.[2] He obtained this recognition of overlordship, moreover, in a manner which leaves no doubt of his deliberate bad faith. In response to the request of the contending parties in Scotland that he should act as arbiter, he requested the Scottish nobles and prelates to meet him at Norham, on the English side of the border, on 10th May 1291.[3] At the same time he summoned his northern barons to join him there with their followers

the claimants to appear before him at Norham, at the same time promising that the appearance of Scottish suitors on English soil should not be taken as a precedent."

[1] Acts of Parl., i. 114, &c.

[2] Again compare Mr. Vickers. "Ever an opportunist in the best sense of the word, Edward, when events played into his hands, seldom failed to make the most of his opportunity. *This is true of all his policy, but most of all his dealings with Scotland.*" (The italics are mine.)

[3] Foedera.

on 3rd June.[1] When on 10th May he met the Scottish
nobles and prelates he demanded that, as a preliminary
to any further proceedings, they should acknowledge
him as lord paramount of Scotland. Taken by surprise, the Scots asked for delay, and were given twenty-
four hours to think the matter over. On the expiry of
the twenty-four hours they asked for further delay, and
were granted three weeks.[2] Now, mark this. Edward
had summoned his military forces to meet him, as we
have seen, by 3rd June, that is to say, he would
have a strong force at his command on the Scottish
border at the very moment when the period of grace
granted to the Scots had expired. The Scots, on their
part, would be unable to offer any resistance. They had
gone to Norham in good faith, and were totally unprepared for war. Remember, too, that it was the thirteenth
century, and that the interval of three weeks granted
them would, accordingly, give them no opportunity of
assembling an army or of making known Edward's
demand to the country at large. The kingdom, too, was
divided and distracted, and the rival claimants to the
Crown were not likely to sink their differences at a
moment's notice in order to offer opposition to Edward,
even if such a course had been possible, which it was not,
or if they had all been united in a common determination
to resist Edward's claim to overlordship at all costs,
which they were not. Some of them, at least, were willing
to purchase a Crown at the price of homage to Edward,
and that Edward knew full well, and certainly acted
upon when he put forward his demand at Norham.[3]

Accordingly, effective opposition to Edward's demands
was out of the question, and when the adjourned con-

---

[1] Foedera. [2] Foedera. Rishanger.

[3] Compare Mr. Vickers: "The claimants, given a day to think the
matter over, asked for a longer time, but though Edward granted this
request he showed that he had decided to enforce his claims. He . . .
did not hesitate to take advantage of his opponents' weakness to press a
demand at a time when it could not well be rejected." But they were
not yet his opponents, merely men who had asked him to act as judge in
a dispute between them. And the judge took advantage of his position
to further his own ends !

ference met on 2nd June all the competitors agreed
to accept his conditions. Edward then demanded the
surrender of the Scottish castles, and the Scots perforce
had to obey. Sir Herbert Maxwell, who for some
obscure reason is always trying to make out Edward I
a model of chivalry, honesty, and sincerity, says of the
transaction : "It is clear that Edward did not at this
time entertain any sinister designs of annexation, because,
although it had been agreed that he was to hold the
kingdom and castles for a space of two months after
he had given his award, in fact he restored the kingdom
to the four guardians and the castles to their keepers on
the very day on which they were surrendered, namely,
11th June. The king did not pronounce his award till
17th November 1292, seventeen months later." But in
this, as in many other of his alleged facts, Sir Herbert
Maxwell is wrong. The castles were not restored to
their keepers, but remained in the custody of English
custodians, as many entries in the documents of the
time very clearly show.[1] Moreover, Edward insisted
that the whole community, priests, nobles, knights,
landholders, burgesses, and free tenants should take
the oath of allegiance to him, and for this purpose
commissioners were appointed throughout Scotland.
The administration of the oath was ordered to commence on 13th July 1291, and to continue for fourteen
days. Those who went to the place appointed for them
to take the oath but refused to take it, were to be
arrested and detained till they complied ; those who
did not appear but sent a reasonable excuse were to
be remanded till the next Parliament ; those who neither
appeared nor sent an excuse were to be dealt with
severely.[2] Which had the truer conception of Edward I,
the twentieth-century Scotsman, who, in endeavouring
to palliate his conduct, so misrepresents his actions, or
the fourteenth-century Scots who had been the victims of

[1] See various entries in Stevenson, Bain, &c. Also Ramsay's *Dawn
of the Constitution* for a full account of the various steps by which
Edward gained and kept possession of the castles.
[2] Bain, ii. 124. Foedera.

his oppression and his double-dealing, and who solemnly placed on record that "in the guise of a friend and an ally" he invaded and oppressed the nation, and treacherously endeavoured to place it under his heel?

On 17th November 1292, as we have seen, Edward declared John Balliol to be king of the Scots. On 19th November the kingdom and castles of Scotland were formally made over to the new king; and on the following day he did homage to Edward and swore fealty to him as his overlord. On 30th November he was crowned at Scone, but returned southwards immediately to spend Christmas with Edward at Newcastle. There he received the first unmistakable evidence of Edward's intentions. By the Treaty of Brigham, on 18th July 1290, it was solemnly agreed, among other things, that no native of Scotland should be required to plead to any suit, civil or criminal, out of the realm. Despite this, when Balliol had been only a fortnight a king, a burgess of Berwick appealed to Edward from a decision of the Scottish courts. Balliol at once protested, reminding Edward of his solemn promises in regard to this very matter, and requesting him to observe them. I commend Edward's reply to those who still believe in the honour or honesty of the English king. He had strictly kept all his promises, as the Scots well knew, he said. But it was clearly within his province to review the decisions of the judges whom he himself, as lord superior, had appointed in Scotland. He, however, wished to deal plainly with the Scots, and therefore he let them know at once *that, though he had submitted to be bound by certain promises, made for a time, and while the throne of Scotland was vacant, now that a king had been appointed, he did not intend to be hampered by those promises for the future. He would hear appeals, or any other questions properly brought before him from Scotland.* By this time Balliol had arrived at Newcastle, and in order that he might be under no delusions as to Edward's intentions the English king sent for the Scottish prelates and nobles who had accompanied their king, and told them plainly that *no promise, concession, or notification ever placed on parchment should keep him from hearing appeals from Scotland, or otherwise exercising his rights of overlordship.* He further warned them that he would cite the king of Scotland to appear in England as and when he might think fit.

Nor was this all. Not content with these plain intimations of his intention to break, as and when he pleased, his plighted word, Edward demanded the abrogation of the Treaty of Brigham, and on 2nd January 1293, two days after the English king had spoken so plainly to Balliol's advisers, Balliol, yielding to one wonders what threats or cajoleries, cancelled the treaty and released Edward and his heirs from every " article, concession, or promise " therein contained. In other words, as Professor Tout, English historian and admirer of Edward I as he is, puts it, " Edward sought to extract from the submission of the Scots consequences which had no warranty in custom, and made Scottish resistance inevitable." As a result, appeals were carried from the Scottish to the English courts, most extraordinary rules being laid down for the regulation of these. The king of Scotland, for example, was made a party to every suit brought under review ; his attendance was required at the hearing of an appeal in order to justify the proceedings of the inferior court, and he was made personally liable in damages, both to the appellant and to the lord superior, for any miscarriage of justice. So high-handed and so absolutely unheard of are these rules that, as Sir James Ramsay well says, " they can only be taken as proof of a settled purpose of driving Balliol to extremities." [1]

To that sober judgment we may add this. The appeal of the Berwick burgess, which provided Edward with so convenient a handle, was almost certainly engineered by Edward himself. Here are the facts.[2] In October 1291 Marjory Moigne of Berwick brought an

---

[1] See Ramsay's *Dawn of the Constitution*, and authorities there cited, for full narrative.
[2] Stevenson, i. 377, &c.

action against Roger Bartholomew, likewise of Berwick, and in May 1292 judgment went against Roger. On 7th December 1292 Roger lodged an appeal to Edward, thus taking a step which no Scotsman had ever taken before. Edward, with remarkable promptitude, took up the hearing of the appeal, *and in three weeks from the date of its lodging*, namely, on 22nd December 1292, judgment was given by the English court. In any circumstances, so rapid a disposal of an appeal would have been remarkable, but in the special circumstances of this appeal it can only be described as sinister. Now, Edward himself was at Berwick during the whole of June 1292, and from 14th October to the end of November in the same year, engaged in hearing the pleas of the competitors and in considering and giving his decision. Roger Bartholomew's appeal bears that, on 7th December 1292, he, " in the presence of the lord king himself at Berwick . . . had petitioned " against the judgment of the judges appointed by " the said lord king, lord superior of the kingdom of Scotland, while the said kingdom was in his hands, by reason of his overlordship of the said kingdom." [1] These facts admit of one conclusion only. Roger Bartholomew was instigated or encouraged by Edward or his servants to appeal to the English king, and thus provide Edward with a pretext for drawing still tighter the bonds which he had fastened on Scotland. How effectively he made use of the opportunity thus given we have just seen.

Some of the results of Edward's tortuous policy we have seen in the foregoing pages. Its immediate result was that Balliol was goaded by repeated acts of interference in the affairs of Scotland into renouncing, in October 1295, the homage which had been extorted from him, and into entering into an alliance with France against England. In March 1296 the War of Independence began, and Edward marched with a mighty army towards what, it is impossible to doubt, had been, ever since the death of the Maid of Norway, the goal of his ambitions, the conquest of Scotland and its annexa-

[1] Stevenson, i. 377, &c.

tion to England.[1] His path was strewn with broken vows. He had plotted the downfall of Scotland " in the guise of a friend and ally." And yet he is acclaimed by many Englishmen and one or two Scotsmen as the soul of chivalry, sincerity, and honour.

If it be thought that I am laying too much stress on the evil aspects of Edward's character, my reply is that in the interests of historical truth it is necessary, for these were the real causes which lay at the root of the policy which made Scotland and England bitter foes for three hundred years. Moreover in recent times certain Scottish writers, in a quite natural revolt from the distorted pictures of the older historians, have striven so hard to be fair to Edward that they have gone to extremes, and the limit has been reached by Sir Herbert Maxwell in the series of volumes on the War of Independence which stands to his name. To Sir Herbert, Edward I is very much of a hero, and the treatment he accords him is in marked contrast to that which he metes out to Bruce. Edward's broken vows are palliated. He is always " noble " and " chivalrous," always actuated by high motives in his treatment of Scotland. His conception of a united kingdom is " statesmanlike," his treatment of his conquered foes, save Wallace, is " generous," and much more to the same effect. On the other hand Bruce's oaths and his alleged numerous breakings thereof are set forth with the utmost care and without palliation. His behaviour during the years from 1296 to 1306, when he was but a young man—he was only twenty-two in 1296—is painted in dark colours, with the most extraordinary inaccuracy, and without any real effort to understand his motives. These, indeed, are said to have been of the basest. " It would be idle to refuse to see in Bruce's dutiful attitude to King Edward the anxiety of the heir to secure his rich inheritance. So hardly shall they that have riches——! " and much more

---

[1] Again compare Mr. Vickers : "The opening thus afforded was eagerly seized, and from the very first Edward showed that he meant to assert his authority over Scotland."

to the same effect, the inheritance in this case being the estates of Bruce's father in Scotland and England. For this sort of stuff it is difficult to have anything but contempt. As we shall presently see, Bruce's behaviour during these years is quite understandable, and, in many ways, quite consistent. But, for the moment, I am concerned with the state of mind which treats Edward from one standpoint and Bruce from another. If it were so disgraceful a thing in Bruce to break his oaths, it was very much more so in Edward; and if these things are to be reckoned in the count, it is, I think, easier to forgive the young knight than the old crusading king who, with the sanctity of oaths ever on his lips, tried by every device of treachery and guile to bring Scotland under his sway, and in the attempt brought upon her and her people woes innumerable. Even Professor Tout is fain to admit that in his dealings with Scotland "Edward never lost sight of his own interests, and it is clear that he took full advantage of the needs of the Scots to establish a close supremacy over the northern kingdom."

It was not, however, only in his dealings with Scotland that Edward showed little regard for his oath when these clashed with his interests. Professor Tout thus sums up his character on this point.[1] "Hot and impulsive in disposition," he describes him, "easily persuaded that his own cause was right, and with a full share in the pride of caste, Edward committed many deeds of violence in his youth, and never got over his deeply rooted habit of keeping the letter of his promise while violating its spirit." Compare this with the estimate of Sir James Ramsay,[2] whose fair and judicial treatment of the history of this period, and of other periods, has won the admiration of all historical writers. "Legal-minded to a fault," he says, "he could take a somewhat extended view of what was due to himself, and a somewhat contracted view of what was due to others. The motto inscribed on his tomb by a later age, 'Pactum serva' (Keep your word), was not one that could

[1] *Pol. Hist.*, iii. 137. [2] *Dawn of the Constitution*, p. 522.

G

honestly be claimed on his behalf. We cannot describe him as one 'who sweareth to his neighbour and disappointeth him not: yea though it were to his own hindrance.' Where his interests required it he could be content to keep his word 'in the spirit of a peddling attorney.' As we have seen, he could disown the most solemn engagements, and if that did not suffice, he could even stoop to falsification of documents. Equivocation and chicane were his worst faults, the faults of a man bent upon having his own way, yet anxious at the same time to find justification for all that he does." Thus between the judgment of the friendly historian and the impartial critic there is little difference. The former agrees with the latter that Edward did not hesitate to break his oaths in order to advance his own interests; and if anyone desires a proof of this, apart from Edward's dealings with Scotland, let him read, for example, the tale of the events which led to the Welsh War of 1282.[1]

Two estimates of Edward's character from the pens of contemporaries of his own may complete the picture. The first is from Nicholas Trivet, a contemporary admirer of Edward. "His disposition was magnanimous," he says, "but he was intolerant of injuries, and reckless of dangers when seeking revenge, though easily won over by a humble submission." The second is by an English friar, an adherent of Simon de Montfort. Edward, he says, was "a valiant lion, quick to attack the strongest and fearing the onslaught of none. But if a lion in pride and fierceness, he was a panther in consistency and mutability, changing his word and promise, cloaking himself by pleasant speech. When he is in a strait he promises whatever you wish, but as soon as he has escaped he forgets his promise. The treachery or falsehood whereby

[1] Mr. Vickers: "In the light of subsequent events it is almost impossible to believe that he had not already decided on his later course of conduct. . . . Edward's arbitration was just and legal, for once the terms were synonymous, but when equity and legal technicality came into conflict there was not a moment's doubt as to which course he would pursue."

he is advanced he calls prudence; the way whereby he arrives whither he will, crooked though it be, he regards as straight; whatever he likes he says is lawful, and he thinks he is released from the law as though he were greater than a king." These words were written long before Edward began to put his designs against Scotland in force, yet can anyone deny that they describe with appalling accuracy the man who " in the guise of a friend and ally" sought to make Scotland his own? So much for the honour, chivalry, and sincerity of the English king. Was it in ignorance or irony, I wonder, that a later generation engraved on his tomb in Westminster Abbey the words " Pactum serva " (Keep faith)?

There remains the question of the so-called "statesmanlike" conception of Edward's Scottish policy. We are told repeatedly that his dream of a united kingdom, which should embrace the whole island of Britain, was statesmanlike in the highest degree, was worthy of the master-mind of the greatest of the Plantagenets. Along with that belief is found often the equally erroneous belief that it would have been a good thing for Scotland and England had Edward been successful in his designs. Even Professor Tout shares those beliefs. Edward, he says, "has rightly been praised for his clear conception of the ideal of a united Britain, which brought him into collision with Welsh and Scots. His foreign policy lay as near to his heart as the conquest of Wales or Scotland, or the subjection of priests and nobles. He was eager to make Gascony obey him, anxious to keep in check the French king, and to establish a sort of European balance of power, of which England, as in Wolsey's later dreams, was to be the tongue of the balance. . . . Yet if his methods of attaining his objects were sometimes mean and often violent, there was a rare nobility about his general purpose." It is a pity Professor Tout does not define that "rare nobility." In the rest of the passage we have just quoted he, unconsciously perhaps, gives us the key to Edward's general purpose, but where is the rare nobility of it? He was merely consumed with a devouring ambition, a passion to make himself arbiter of Western Christendom and master of all Britain. It was an age of warfare, and Edward more than any of his contemporaries was possessed with the lust for dominion and conquest. But is there any nobility, rare or otherwise, in that? Elsewhere in these pages I characterise it as the unholy ambition of a masterful king, and that, when stripped bare of all its trappings, it undoubtedly was. Moreover, if Edward's conception of a united Britain was statesmanlike, then there were many great statesmen before him, for there was hardly a king, Scottish or English, who in the preceding centuries did not dream a similar dream, and not a few of them sought to bring it to fruition. But to Edward alone did there come a really promising opportunity of realising that dream, and he alone had the combination of qualities, good as well as evil, evil as well as good, which made it possible to seize the opportunity with some prospect of success.

As to the belief that it would have been a good thing for both Scotland and England had Edward succeeded in his designs, it is only necessary to say this. The whole subsequent history of the two countries proves the contrary to the fullest possible degree, and the history of Ireland and Wales under English dominion confirms this conclusion irrefutably. It is easy to theorise about what might have been, but the facts must be faced fairly. Had England after the death of Edward I been ruled by a series of strong and statesmanlike kings, had England known how to win the loyalty of a conquered country, had England been content to devote her energies to the affairs of Britain and to these alone, and had there been in Scotland no sense of nationality, no deep-seated hatred of English domination, it is conceivable that, in time, the conquest of Scotland might have had the best results for both nations. But as things were it cannot be denied that these essentials were altogether lacking, and in consequence only chaos, strife, and suffering could have been the result. And when we take a broader sweep, when we bear in mind all that we have noted in the foregoing pages, it is impossible to imagine, even had there been no Bruce, even had the succeeding kings of England been strong and statesmanlike, that the Scots would ever have submitted to the domination of England. And that, after all, is one of the two true tests of Edward's statesmanship, the other, as we shall presently see, being the results. Judged by the first of these tests Edward's statesmanship fails, and fails lamentably. For it exposes itself to us as a statesmanship that took no heed of difficulties, that paid no attention to essentials, that failed to take account of the future, that, in a word, had no real understanding of either the nature or the probable results of the policy on which it proposed to embark.

When tested by results the judgment on Edward's Scottish policy must be the same. It has, perhaps, never been more fairly or more accurately stated than by Professor Hume Brown, whose moderation and fair-mindedness are beyond question. Says he,[1] " In truth, national prejudice apart, in regard to the relations of the Scottish and English peoples Edward is not an inviting figure in British history. He found two kindred nations, which for a century had been involved in no serious quarrel; and by the time he had done his work he had evoked international antagonisms which bore immediate fruit in incessant wars that lasted for two centuries and a half, and which can never be wholly effaced from the memories of the two peoples." That seems to me to be the final judgment alike on Edward I and on his dealings with Scotland, and when one thinks of it an awful judgment it is.

[1] *History of Scotland*, i. 155.

CHAPTER X

THE TRUTH ABOUT THE BRUCES (1286-1292)

WE come now to the vexed question of the part played by the Bruces both in the controversies which preceded the War of Independence, and in the opening years of the war itself. In recent years, as I have already remarked, some Scottish writers have loved to parade the alleged vacillations and oath-breakings of the Bruces, and especially of the young Earl of Carrick, the future king, as if in these things they were unique, while there are not wanting suggestions that young Bruce in some way played a particularly treacherous part towards his country, and even towards Wallace. As a result it has become an accepted maxim of Scottish history that the behaviour of the Bruces from 1290 to 1306 was in every way reprehensible, and successive writers have exhausted their store of adjectives in heaping opprobrium upon them. Yet, as we shall presently see, for this view of the behaviour of the Bruces there is practically no historical warrant, and much of the indignation which has been wasted on their alleged iniquities has not the slightest foundation in fact.

Viewed from a nineteenth and twentieth century standpoint these oath-breakings, in which the War of Independence abounds, and which were not by any means confined to the Bruces, have an ugly look. But in the thirteenth and fourteenth centuries they were not regarded in the same way. Oaths of fealty were, as a matter of fact, very largely mere formalities, a fact which was quite well understood by both parties to the transaction. They were binding, as a rule, only so long as the party to whom the oath was taken was in a position to make it effective. Moreover, it was not the oath as such that was important, but the acknowledgment of feudal dependence which it signified. But neither the oath nor the acknowledgment was of such extraordinary sanctity or binding force as some people would appear to imagine. Legally, they put the inferior in the position of a rebel if he repudiated or acted contrary to his allegiance to his superior. Morally, the breaking of them was not regarded as in any way reprehensible. In short, the man who took and broke an oath of fealty was in almost exactly the same position as any subject of the British Empire, who for any cause becomes a rebel to-day. Legally, he is a rebel and a traitor, but from the ethical standpoint his conduct may be beyond reproach.

I have not seen it argued anywhere that the king, the nobles, the prelates, and barons, the burgesses and the free tenants of Scotland were guilty of any sin on account of their breaches of fealty. Yet, so far as oaths were concerned, they broke their oaths just as flagrantly as the young Earl of Carrick afterwards broke his. Accordingly, if oath-breaking as oath-breaking is to be reckoned a flagrant crime in Bruce, it must also be reckoned as such in every Scot who repudiated his fealty to Edward in 1295 and 1296.

It is, moreover, a matter of sober history that, with the single exception of William Wallace, every Scotsman of note in the War of Independence who had come to man's estate before 1305, took the oath of fealty to Edward time after time, and broke it over and over again. Nor were the Scots unique in this. On many occasions throughout his reign Edward I was at variance with different sections of his own people, and on most of these occasions these people broke their oaths of allegiance. We need look no further than the period of the War of Independence itself for abundant evidence of this. In January 1297 the entire clergy of England broke their oaths of fealty, and were promptly outlawed by the king, who told them, "If ye keep not your homages and oaths for your baronies, neither am I bound to you in anything." In the same year Roger Bigod, Earl Marshal of England, and Humphrey de Bohun, the Constable, refused to serve Edward overseas unless he himself were there; and when Edward threatened compulsion, they raised so strong an armed force that he had to give way. But the earls and their allies had none the less broken their oaths of fealty. Many more instances could be given, but these will suffice. I have said enough to show how these oaths were regarded in their own time, and by what standards they must be judged.

There are, however, one or two other points which must be kept in mind when the matter of the oaths of the Scots, and more particularly of the Bruces and their leading adherents such as the Bishops of St. Andrews and Glasgow, are under discussion. In the first place it is a rule of law even to the present day that an oath or obligation extorted by force or under compulsion is not only not binding, but is null and void and of no effect from the beginning. That was just as well understood in the thirteenth and fourteenth centuries as it is to-day. In the next place, many Scots who took those oaths of fealty took them because they really believed that all hope of resistance was at an end, which is almost equivalent to the " essential error " which in law is regarded as providing a good reason for the abrogation of a contract. And, in the third place, some who took them broke them, because they sincerely believed it was their duty so to do. When a mere oath conflicts with duty, he would be a bold man who would maintain that it is duty which must go. Moreover, I must repeat, there is the uncontestable fact that the breaking of these oaths of fealty was not regarded at the time as anything of a very heinous nature. Bishops, priests, nobles, knights, landholders, burgesses, and free tenants all took and broke them with equal facility, and that in England, when the occasion arose, just as freely as in Scotland. Finally, we must remember Edward's own record in the matter of oaths. Not only does it serve as an example of the spirit of the times, but is in itself sufficient to exonerate completely every Scot who ever broke an oath to the English king.

When, however, the oaths of fealty of the Bruces are pointed to merely as evidence that at certain times and on certain occasions they were on the side of England, we are on different ground, and it is to that aspect of the matter we shall devote our attention. To begin with, it is absolutely essential to remember that the Bruces regarded themselves as the rightful heirs to the throne of Scotland, and were so regarded by a large section of the Scottish people. In order to make this plain, I cannot do better than quote Bruce the Competitor's own statement of his claim as printed in Palgrave's *Scottish Documents*, and summarised by him.[1]

" This declaration or deduction of title," says Palgrave, " sets forth the following facts. It states that William, King of Scotland, had one brother, David, Earl of Huntingdon, who had issue four children, namely, one son and three daughters. The son died without leaving any heir of his body ; the eldest daughter, Margaret, was married to the Lord of Galloway, by whom she had one daughter, Devorguilla." John Balliol's descent from Devorguilla is then deduced. " The second daughter, Isabella, was married to the Lord Bruce, who begot upon her one son, to wit, Robert Bruce, ' who now is ' ; and the third daughter was married to the Lord Hastings, from whom those of the line of Hastings are descended."

The following table will make these descents clear :

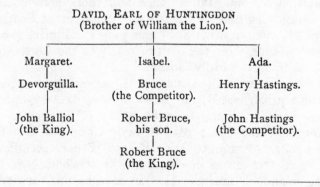

DAVID, EARL OF HUNTINGDON
(Brother of William the Lion).

Margaret.	Isabel.	Ada.
Devorguilla.	Bruce (the Competitor).	Henry Hastings.
John Balliol (the King).	Robert Bruce, his son.	John Hastings (the Competitor).
	Robert Bruce (the King).	

---

[1] Page xv, &c.

"Alexander II," continues the document, "having advanced almost to the verge of senile age, and there being no expectation of his having an heir of his body, assembled all the nobles and magnates of Scotland, the bishops and other clergy and laity, as many as could be brought together, at a certain day and place, in order to prevent the dissensions which would arise in the event of his death without issue. Unto this parliament or convention he declared the state of his age, and that he had no issue of his body; but that his uncle David had three daughters, the first of whom had a daughter and the second a son; and he enjoined them all, as they were bound to him by their allegiance, fealty, and homage, that they would decide and adjudicate between the parties —Which and whether of them should inherit the crown, the daughter of the eldest sister or the son of the second sister? And the great council being assembled together, they decreed and adjudged by all their own laws, and by the imperial and other laws, that the son born of the second sister should inherit in preference to the daughter born of the eldest sister. And all present, clergy as well as laity, unanimously declared the same as a true judgment to the king. Such judgment being given by the great council and accepted by the sovereign, he, King Alexander, took Robert Bruce, Lord of Annandale, who now is, by the hand, and presented him to all the nobles and magnates, clerks and laymen, then and there present, as his true and legitimate heir to the kingdom of Scotland; and all such magnates, by the king's command and in his presence, took the oath of fealty to the Lord Robert Bruce upon the Holy Gospels."

As it happened, Alexander II married again after the events just narrated, and a son, afterwards Alexander III, was born to him. On the death of Alexander III's daughter, the Maid of Norway, Alexander II's direct descendants came to an end, and Bruce, accordingly, claimed the throne in virtue of the settlement made in the reign of Alexander II. In fact, he put forward his claim before the death of the Maid of Norway, and both before and after her death he appeared in arms in support of it. There can be no question, moreover, that many of the magnates, the clergy, and the laity of the kingdom regarded him as the rightful king, while that ancient body, the seven earls, likewise declared in his favour.[1]

When at last the various competitors had agreed to submit their claims to Edward I as arbiter, Bruce based his claim on the double ground of his recognition as heir in the time of Alexander II and his descent. Balliol, his chief rival, was a great-grandson of David of Huntingdon, whereas Bruce himself was a grandson, and therefore nearer in degree to the last three sovereigns. We need not go into all the pleadings and counter-pleadings here. Suffice it to say that Edward eventually decided in favour of Balliol, basing his judgment, it is important to notice, on the English law of descent, and making no mention whatsoever of Bruce's claim as the recognised heir of Alexander II.

Of late years it has come to be accepted that throughout the proceedings Edward acted with scrupulous fairness, and that his decision was legally correct. Neither of these conclusions, however, is final, and in regard to the first readers would do well to consult Sir James Ramsay's *Dawn of the Constitution*, wherein all the facts are marshalled with great clearness. The material fact is there brought out that the judgment was the judgment of the twenty-four arbiters appointed by the English king, and that the eighty Scottish arbiters, forty appointed by Balliol and forty by Bruce, had, contrary to the accepted opinion, no voice in it.

Another fact, equally important, is also brought out, namely, that Edward so succeeded in manœuvring matters that the case was tried and decided by English law. This of course does not imply any deliberate unfairness on his part towards any individual competitor. His object was to forge another link in the chain of Scottish subjection to England, and from his point of view the application of English law in the competition

[1] Palgrave, 14–21.

for the Scottish Crown was therefore a very important matter. Taken along with his acknowledgment as Lord Superior, it afforded, from a legal standpoint, emphatic evidence of the subordination of Scotland to England. In point of fact, however, it was a purely tactical advantage, and was more worthy of a pettifogging lawyer than of a statesman. Moreover, though the competitors were manœuvred into acquiescence, it was a reluctant acquiescence, which must have left a sense of grievance behind it. When eventually the decision came to be given, this sense of grievance would naturally be greatly aggravated in the case of a competitor who felt that by the application of English law to what was a purely Scottish matter, his case had been prejudiced. Which was exactly the position in which Bruce found himself; and though at the time he was not in a position to make any effectual protest, there cannot be the slightest doubt that neither he nor his son nor his grandson ever regarded the decision as anything but grossly unjust to them, and as one which must be overturned on the first favourable opportunity.

As to the legal accuracy of the decision, that is still more or less of an open question. According to English law it was possibly sound, though the point at issue was novel and had never before been decided. But according to the law and custom of Scotland, as it then was, Bruce had the better claim. More than that it is unnecessary to say, save this. Bruce had been recognised in the time of Alexander II as heir to the Crown. His claim to it on the death of the Maid of Norway was therefore exceedingly strong, and in quite a different category from that of the other competitors; and in his own eyes, and in the eyes of a large and powerful party in Scotland, the Crown was therefore his beyond all question.

The names of the auditors appointed by Bruce and Balliol may be stated here,[1] as they give us some indication of the strength of the party which looked to Bruce as the lawful king. Bruce's auditors were :—The Bishops of Glasgow and Dunkeld ; the Abbots of Melrose and

---

[1] Foedera.

Jedburgh; Patrick, Earl of March; Donald, Earl of Mar; Walter, Earl of Menteith; John, Earl of Athol; Malcolm, Earl of Lennox; James, the Steward of Scotland; Sir William de Soulis (who in 1291 was Sheriff of Inverness); [1] Sir John de Soulis; Sir Nicholas de Graham (Linlithgow, Berwick, Roxburgh, Ayr, &c.) [2]; Sir John de Lindsay; Sir John Stewart; Sir Alexander de Bonkill; Sir William de la Haye (Sheriff of Inverness in 1296); [3] Sir David de Torthorald; Sir John de Kalantir; Sir William de Fenton; Master Adam de Crokedeak; Henry, Deacon of Aberdeen; Sir Walter de Lindsay; Sir Reginald de Crawford; Sir Colin Cambel; Sir William de Stirling; Sir John de Stirling of Moray; Sir John de Inchmartin; Master Robert de Merleye; Master William de Stirling; Master Thomas de Bonkill; Henry de Lematherton (probably the same who does homage as Henry de Lematone, parson of Douns in Perthshire); [4] Master William de Annandale; Master William de Gosford (parson of Castlemilke in Dumfriesshire); [5] Master Richard de Bouldon (parson of Edilstone, Peebleshire); [6] Brother Reginald de Rihal, monk of Melrose (who, in 1279, had twice been an envoy of Alexander III to Edward I); [7] Sir William de Conisburg (of Lanarkshire); Sir William de Preston; Sir Gilbert de Conisburg (of Ayrshire); and Sir Geoffrey de Caldecote.

Balliol's auditors were:—The Bishops of Saint Andrews, Aberdeen, Dunblane, Sodor, Candida Casa, (Whithorn), and Ross; the Abbots of Dunfermline, Holyrood, Cambuskenneth, Kelso, Tungland, Scone, and Cupar, and the Prior of St. Andrews; Walter, Archdeacon of Dunblane; John, Earl of Buchan; Gilbert, Earl of Angus; Malise, Earl of Stratherne; William, Earl of Ross; Sir Alexander of Argyll; Sir Andrew de Moray; Sir Geoffrey de Moubray; Sir Herbert de Maxwell; Sir Simon Fraser, the Father; Sir Patrick de Graham; Sir William de St. Clair (of Herdmanston in Haddington); Sir Reginald le Chen, senior; Sir Reginald

---

[1] Bain, ii. 560. [2] B. P., vi. 195. [3] Palgrave.
[4] Bain, ii. 212. [5] *Ibid.* [6] *Ibid.* [7] *Ibid.*, 162, 164.

le Chen, junior; Sir Nicholas de Haye (Sheriff of Perth); Sir Robert de Cambron de Balligarnach; Sir Richard Fraser; Sir John de Stirling of the Carse (in Stirlingshire); [1] Sir Andrew Fraser, Sir Michael de Wymes (Fife); Sir Michael Scot (Fife); Sir Richard de Stratton (Edinburgh); Sir William de Moray of Tullibardine; Sir William de Melgedrom (Sir William de Melkedrum or Meldrum, Sheriff of Aberdeen in 1292, and landholder in Aberdeenshire),[2] Sir Ralph de Lascelles (lands in Fife and, apparently, Edinburgh)[3]; and Sir David de Graham.

Many of the names in these lists will become familiar to us from their frequent appearance in the following pages. Leaving the fourteen churchmen among Bruce's auditors out of account, almost every one of his twenty-six lay auditors, who lived till 1306, fought for his grandson when he made his final bid for the Scottish Crown. Of Balliol's twenty-five lay auditors the most important were connected with him by blood, and in consequence, after the death of the Red Comyn—who was Balliol's nephew, and after Balliol's deposition was regarded as representing the claims of the Balliols to the Scottish Crown—many of them became the mortal foes of the future king. Several of them, however, threw in their lot with Bruce when he revolted finally, while almost every one of them fought on the Scottish side during the wars which preceded Edward I's final invasion in 1303.

The chief interest of the lists, however, lies in the evidence they afford of the strength of the following of the two principal claimants to the Crown. Apart from the clerical auditors a glance at the lists is sufficient to show that there is not much to choose between them, though Bruce's list perhaps contains more " names of fame " than does Balliol's. The Earls of March, Mar, Menteith, Athol, and Lennox, and the Steward of Scotland in themselves constitute a formidable party, and with them are found such powerful magnates as Sir William

---

[1] Bain, ii. p. 199. [2] *Ibid.*, pp. 587, 832.
[3] *Ibid.*, pp. 213, 1869, 1870

and Sir John de Soulis, Sir John and Sir Walter de Lindsay, Sir Alexander Stewart of Bonkhill, Sir William de la Haye, Sir Reginald Crawford, Sir Colin Campbell, Sir John Stirling of Moray, Sir William Stirling, Sir John de Inchmartin, and Sir William de Fenton. Another remarkable feature of these names is that while every part of the country is represented, the representatives from north of the Forth and Clyde are especially notable, among them being the Earls of Mar, Menteith, Athol, and Lennox, Sir Colin Campbell, Sir William de la Haye, Sir John Stirling, Sir John de Inchmartin, and Sir William de Fenton. Balliol's most prominent auditors were his own blood relations, the Earls of Buchan, Angus, Strathern, and Ross, Sir Alexander of Argyll, Sir Andrew de Moray, and the two Reginalds le Chen, while others of importance were Sir Simon Fraser, Sir Michael de Wymes, Sir Nicholas de Haye, Sheriff of Perth, Sir David and Sir Patrick de Graham, and Sir William de Meldrum, Sheriff of Aberdeen. But as in Bruce's case so in Balliol's. The representatives from north of the Forth and Clyde are here, too, especially notable, including as they do the Earls of Buchan, Angus, Strathern, and Ross, Sir Alexander of Argyll, Sir Andrew de Moray, Sir Reginald le Chen, senior, Sir Reginald le Chen, junior, the Sheriffs of Perth and Aberdeen, and several more. In fact if we take the lay auditors of Bruce and Balliol together, out of the fifty-one no less than thirty-two belong to Scotland north of Forth and Clyde, while so far as power and influence are concerned they are incomparably superior to the southern representatives.

In regard to the clerical auditors we need say little. Bruce had fourteen of these, Balliol fifteen, while so far as position went Balliol's were infinitely the greater, comprising, as they did, six bishops, seven abbots, one prior, and one archdeacon, as against Bruce's two bishops, two abbots, one dean, one monk, and eight priests. But the churchmen, with one or two exceptions, were not identified with either claimant to the extent that the lay auditors were; and when the War of Independence came they, as a rule, used their influence to the utmost on behalf of Balliol, Andrew de Moray, Wallace, Comyn, or Bruce, whenever any of these were in the field, irrespective of what claimant or party these might represent. The impelling purpose of the Church was the preservation of the freedom of Scotland and the Scottish Church, and to that the person of the king was a secondary consideration. It is well to remark, however, that the Bishop of St. Andrews, who was one of Balliol's auditors and a strenuous supporter of his claims, was not the bishop who afterwards played so great a part in the War of Independence. Balliol's bishop was William Fraser. His more famous successor was William Lamberton, who was elected to the see in 1297.

Enough has been said now to show that the party which in 1290 and 1291 looked to Bruce as the rightful king was influential and powerful. We need only add that as early as September 1286, that is barely six months after the death of Alexander III, Bruce put forward a deliberate claim to the Crown, and supported it by armed force. In his view, and in that of his supporters, a female could not succeed to the throne of Scotland, and he was therefore the rightful sovereign. In order to secure his rights, moreover, he and his supporters entered into a solemn agreement at Turnberry, 20th September 1286, those who thus bound themselves together in support of Bruce's claims being [1] Bruce himself and his two sons; Patrick, Earl of March and his three sons; Walter Stewart, Earl of Menteith and his two sons, Alexander and John; James, the Steward of Scotland, and his brother, Sir John Stewart of Bonkill; and Angus Macdonald of the Isles and his son Alexander. Thus, not only was Bruce's claim to the crown backed by an influential and powerful party, but it was a claim in which he had the fullest faith, a claim which he put forward at a very early stage, which he endeavoured to make good by force, which he left no stone unturned to

[1] Stevenson, i. 22.

insist upon, and which he never abandoned but believed in to the day of his death. Born in 1274, his grandson, Robert Bruce, the future king, lived through all the years of controversy which followed the death of Alexander III in 1286, and was old enough to appreciate to the full the claims of his family, and to resent the injustice which they believed had been done them. In his eyes his grandfather was the rightful King of Scots, and when, by the death of both father and grandfather, he, in his turn, became the head of his family, he believed that on his brow ought lawfully to rest the Crown of Scotland. That is the fact which it is absolutely essential to bear in mind if his behaviour during the years from 1296 to 1306 is ever to be understood—those years during which, in the full flush of early manhood, he sought by every means in his power to win back for his family the inheritance which he believed to be theirs of right, and of which he believed them to have been unjustly deprived.

CHAPTER XI

THE TRUTH ABOUT THE BRUCES (1292–1298)

IF all the foregoing facts are kept steadily in view, it should not be difficult to understand the attitude and the actions of the Bruces in the years which followed the award of the Scottish Crown to John Balliol in November 1292. In what light they themselves regarded that award they made clear from the very beginning. Bruce, the Competitor, was then an old man of eighty-two, and therefore too advanced in years to endeavour to make good his claims to the Crown against the award of Edward I. But, far from abandoning these claims, on the very day on which Edward informed him that he had failed to prove his case, namely, on 5th November 1292, he formally resigned to his son Robert, Earl of Carrick, the father of the future king, all his claims to the kingdom of Scotland.[1] Henceforward, so long as John Balliol sat on the Scottish throne, the names of Bruce, the Competitor, and his son are absent from the Scottish documents of the period, and they may be looked for in vain among those who attached their seals to the deed by which, on 2nd January 1293, Balliol released Edward from all his promises and obligations of the previous two years.

Bruce the Competitor's son, that Robert Bruce who was Earl of Carrick in right of his wife, the Celtic Countess of Carrick, showed in what spirit he regarded the new King of Scots by refusing, on the death of his wife in 1292, to do homage to Balliol for the Earldom.[2] Instead he made it over to her and his son, the future king, then a youth of eighteen, and retired himself to Norway with his daughter Isabella, who in the following

---

[1] B. P., ii. 431. [2] *Ibid.*, p. 432.

year married King Eric of Norway.[1] Either shortly
before or soon after his father's, the Competitor's, death
in 1295 [2] he returned to England and got delivery of his
father's English estates,[3] and in October 1295 was appointed by Edward Governor of Carlisle.[4] Still steadfastly refusing to do homage to Balliol, he continued to
live in England, acting as Governor of Carlisle till October
1297, when, being deprived of his governorship [5] on account of the suspicion with which his son was regarded,
he retired altogether from the political scene, living in
retirement till his death in 1304.[6]

It is impossible to say whether or not the young Earl
of Carrick, the future king, did homage to Balliol for
the Earldom of Carrick and the lands of Annandale.
The most that can be said is that while it is probable
that he did, it is possible that he did not. But whether
he did or did not, there can be no question that Balliol's
repudiation of his allegiance to Edward in October 1295
absolved of their fealty all those who had done homage
to him after Edward's award. This is especially true of
those who were liegemen of Edward as well as of Balliol,
and of those who had taken the oath of allegiance to
Balliol because of Edward's award. If the young Earl
of Carrick had sworn fealty to Balliol, he came within
both these categories, and therefore had a double reason, so
far as oaths were concerned, for standing by his oath to
Edward rather than by his oath to Balliol. So there can
be no question of " perfidy " on his part here. In any
case it would be a hard doctrine to maintain that the
young Earl was guilty of " perfidy " because he did not
break his oath to Edward when Balliol and his adherents
broke theirs ! "

The two Bruces, and the Earls of March and Angus,
renewed their homage to Edward in his camp at Wark
on Easter-day, 25th March 1296.[7] For this the hostility

---

[1] B. P., ii. 432.   [2] Bain, ii. 706.   [3] B. P., ii. 432.
[4] Stevenson, ii 6.   [5] Bain, ii. 950.   [6] B. P., ii. 433.
[7] Hemingburgh. Mr. Bain assigns to 14th March 1296 a document in
which is recorded the homage to Edward of ninety Scotsmen of position.
(Bain, ii. pp. xxiii and 730.) Among them are the Earl of Lennox,

of the Bruces to the Balliols was not alone responsible, the Earl of Angus, indeed, having been one of Balliol's auditors in the competition for the Crown. But when, in October 1295, Balliol repudiated his allegiance to Edward, all "Englishmen" were expelled from the Court and their lands forfeited, a measure which was aimed principally at the Bruces, who were thus designated because of their refusal to recognise Balliol as king, and because of their lands and residence in England. The decree also struck, however, at other nobles and landholders who held lands in both countries, and were not prepared to throw over their allegiance to Edward, and therefore, of course, their lands in England, in order to adhere to Balliol. The Earls of March and Angus were among these. Hence their renewed homage to Edward at Easter 1296. As the forfeited lands of the Bruces were forthwith conferred by Balliol on his kinsman John Comyn, Earl of Buchan, the intensity of the feud between the Bruces on the one hand and the Balliols and the Comyns on the other is clearly evident.

It is hardly necessary now for me to endeavour to defend the Bruces for either their attitude or their actions in the years from 1292 to 1295, or for their appearance in the campaign of 1296 on the side of Edward. Their conduct from the very day of the

---

Sir Edmond de Ramsay, Sir Michael Scot, Sir John de la Haye, Sir Wm. de Mayor of Sandford, Sir John de Berkeley, Sir Wm. de Fenton, Sir David de Berkeley, Sir John de Cambron of Balligarnach, Sir John de Stirling of Moray, Sir Wm. de Mohaut (Monte Alto), Sir Adam de Valoignes, Alexander Fraser, John de la Haye, William Wiseman, Nigel de Carrick, Patrick de Graham, Alexander de Straton, John de Logy, and many more who played a great part in the wars of Bruce, and many of whom were supporters of his grandfather, the Competitor, in 1292 and earlier years. It is noteworthy that of the seventy-five or thereabouts who can be identified, about three-fourths (56) belong to Scotland north of the Forth and Clyde. Of the others a large proportion belong to Dumfriesshire and the Celtic West, Bruce's own country. Accordingly, if Mr. Bain's date were correct, these homages would prove that John Balliol was repudiated as king by many of Bruce's supporters at the first favourable opportunity and before the war actually began. Unfortunately, however, 1296 cannot be accepted as the correct year. Ample internal evidence shows that it must be 1304.

award of the Crown to Balliol had been quite consistent. They had refused to recognise him as king, and they had never ceased to hope and to work for their own succession to the Scottish throne. Their conduct down to the end of 1296, therefore, was not in any way perfidious or treacherous to Scotland. In 1296 they were in arms not against Scotland but against Balliol, and in view both of their own previous attitude and of the policy adopted towards them by Balliol and his friends, it is difficult to see what other course they could have taken.

It was, of course, in the interests of the Bruces to assist Edward against the Balliols. When the revolt was crushed he would in all probability be deposed, and the Crown might then be given to them as heads of the line next in succession according to Edward's own award. Fordun, indeed, has a story to the effect that Edward kept the Bruces faithful to him in 1296 by promising the Crown to the elder Bruce once Balliol had been disposed of. On Bruce's claiming the fulfilment of this promise Edward is said to have replied, "Have we nothing else to do but win kingdoms for you?" The story may or may not be true, but, as the events above narrated show, it was not necessary for Edward to purchase the Bruces' loyalty by any such promise. They could not, and would not, have fought against Edward in 1296, when victory would only have meant the establishment of their rivals on the Scottish throne more firmly than ever. They were animated in 1296, as they had been ever since the death of Alexander III, by the single purpose of gaining the throne which they fully believed to be theirs of right, and that purpose it was which inspired and directed the young Earl of Carrick in all the years which followed. That is the key to his actions, and that alone. He has been accused of all manner of mean and paltry motives in order to account for his indecision on some occasions, and for his adherence to Edward from 1302 to 1306, while many shady actions have been attributed to him which never in fact occurred. But in all his actions he was guided by that one single motive, was pursuing that settled, consistent purpose. This it is which explains even his apparent desertion of the national cause in 1302. For we shall see, in spite of the accepted belief to the contrary, that from 1297 to 1302 the young Earl of Carrick was actively engaged on the side of Scotland, and only made his peace with Edward when it became apparent to him that victory would mean only the victory of his rivals, or, to put it otherwise, when he realised that he was fighting in a cause which had become, for the time, the cause of the Balliols and the Comyns. Blame him from our twentieth century standpoint if you will, but remember that from the thirteenth century point of view his action was entirely justifiable.

Another fact must also be kept in view when judging the young Earl of Carrick's conduct between 1297 and 1306. In 1297 he was only twenty-three years of age, and, accordingly, the ardour, the optimism, and the inexperience of youth must be taken into account. We must avoid the common mistake of treating his doings during these years as if they were always the calculated and restrained acts of a man of mature age. The importance of this will be speedily apparent.

Early in 1297, as we have seen, occurred the first Scottish rising on a large scale. Hemingburgh tells us that on tidings of it reaching the North of England the young Earl of Carrick was summoned to Carlisle, of which his father was governor, and compelled to take a new oath of fealty to Edward. Evidently, therefore, if the story is true, his ambitions were at least suspected in English official circles. Hemingburgh then relates that he was despatched to lay waste the lands of the rebels, and in pursuance of his orders raided the lands of Sir William Douglas, one of the Scottish leaders, and made captive his wife and children, but that shortly afterwards he threw in his lot with the patriots, declaring that his oath of fealty had been extorted from him by force, and that he could not fight against his own flesh and blood. Whether or not the story is true in all its details, it is certain that the young Earl did join the Scots in May or June 1297, and if it is the case that he did first devastate the lands of Douglas, it is quite possible that this was an act of private revenge, for Douglas was certainly fighting on the side of Balliol in 1296, whichever party he may have belonged to before or after that date.

The reason of the young Earl of Carrick's sudden change of sides in 1297 should now be evident. He was young and ardent, and when several strong Scottish forces, animated only by the desire to throw off the yoke of England, appeared in the field, he judged the moment for making good his family's claims had come. Everything seemed in his favour. Balliol had abdicated and was in exile; nearly all the leaders of the Balliol party were captives in England, Balliol's two most powerful partisans, his kinsmen, Sir John Comyn of Badenoch, and the Comyn Earl of Buchan among them; Edward, if he had not definitely refused to place the Bruces on the Scottish throne as Fordun relates, had at all events annexed the kingdom, and was administering it as his own; two at least of the leaders of one of the Scottish armies in the field belonged to the Bruce faction, viz., the Bishop of Glasgow and James the Steward; and the rising as a whole was more or less the work of the Bishop. And so the young Earl of Carrick took the decisive step of throwing off his allegiance to Edward, thus declaring plainly that he was determined to make a bid for the Scottish Crown.

Young Andrew de Moray and William Wallace had no part in the fiasco which ensued a few weeks later. Bruce and his companions were in the West, and on the approach of an English force, which was weaker in foot-soldiers but stronger in mounted men-at-arms than the Scots,[1] they capitulated on terms. Their action, however, was not dictated by fear, as is sometimes suggested, but by dissensions in the ranks of the Scots

[1] Hemingburgh.

themselves, as Hemingburgh impartially records. The
cause of these dissensions is obvious. It was the old
question of the claims of the Balliols and the Bruces.
Young Andrew de Moray was of course a partisan of
his kinsman Balliol, while, so far as can be judged from
Wallace's actions both then and subsequently, he, too,
was in favour of Balliol. Sir William Douglas, moreover, had defended Berwick for Balliol against Edward
in the previous year, and is not likely to have been won
over to Bruce's side by the recent devastation of his
lands and the capture of his wife and children. As
against these, the Bishop of Glasgow, James the Steward
and his brother, and Alexander de Lindsay backed the
claims of the Bruces, whom the young Earl of Carrick
was present in person to represent. At the date of
the capitulation, it is true, Andrew de Moray was conducting a successful campaign in the North—concerning
the fortunes of which the Western army was of course
ignorant—but that does not alter the fact that the Bruce
and Balliol parties were at variance, while it must also
be remembered that Douglas was still with the Western
army, and that Wallace was either with it or not very
far away. With such acute divisions existing, effective
resistance to the strong English army was out of the
question, and accordingly its leaders, or certain of them,
agreed to surrender on terms, those who thus capitulated
being the Bishop of Glasgow, the Earl of Carrick, the
Steward of Scotland and his brother John, Alexander de
Lindsay, and William Douglas.[1] Neither Andrew de
Moray nor William Wallace had any part in this transaction, as we have already seen, and it is important to
observe that those who agreed to it were all members
of the Bruce party with the single, and perhaps doubtful,
exception of Sir William Douglas. It is also significant
of the light in which the rising, or at least the Western
rising, was regarded in England that in addition to
agreeing to give up his infant daughter Marjorie as a
hostage [2]—a condition which does not seem to have been

---

[1] Stevenson, ii. 192–200.   [2] Bain, ii. 910.

implemented—the Bishop of Glasgow, James the Steward, and Alexander Lindsay had to become guarantees for the Earl of Carrick's loyalty till that condition was fulfilled.[1] Plainly, therefore, the young Earl of Carrick was regarded by his contemporaries in both Scotland and England in 1297 as bidding for the Crown of Scotland, and his action both in joining the rising and in capitulating when all hope of success seemed gone, was clearly dictated by that motive.

The capitulation at Irvine on 9th July 1297 did not, however, as is usually stated, put an end to the young Earl of Carrick's breach with England in that year. He probably agreed to the capitulation with a bad grace—he was only twenty-three, remember, and the other leaders being his father's contemporaries doubtless regarded him as an enthusiastic but inexperienced young man who should be advised by them. At all events the young Earl delayed to give his hostages and otherwise fulfil the conditions of the capitulation at Irvine;[2] and though a document dated at Westminster on 14th November 1297, by which the Bishop of Carlisle and Sir Robert Clifford were empowered " to receive to the King's peace Robert de Brus, Earl of Carrick, and his friends as seems best to their discretion,"[3] is sometimes cited as evidence that Bruce did come to Edward's peace in 1297, it is obviously no evidence at all. On the contrary it supports all the evidence we possess in pointing to the opposite conclusion.

Between the date of the capitulation at Irvine, 9th July, and the above writ of 14th November, the battle of Stirling Bridge had been fought and won, and the November writ makes clear that up to the beginning of that month the Earl of Carrick had not been received to Edward's peace. We know also that by 5th August the Earl had certainly not implemented the conditions of the Irvine capitulation;[4] while on the 13th of October Carrick's father, the elder Bruce, was deprived

[1] Bain, ii. 910.   [2] Stevenson, ii. 226.
[3] Bain, ii. 961.   [4] Stevenson, ii. 226.

of the governorship of Carlisle, the Bishop of the diocese being appointed keeper of the castle and the demesne in his place [1]—a fact which admits of but one interpretation. In November and December 1297 the Scots, under Wallace, were in the North of England, and Hemingburgh tells us that about the same time Sir Robert de Clifford, the English Warden of the Western Marches, crossed the Solway and ravaged Annandale, returning to Carlisle on Christmas Eve. Towards the end of February 1298 he repeated his raid and burned the town of Annan. There is no reason to question Hemingburgh's accuracy in regard to these expeditions, and as the Earl of Carrick was Lord of Annandale (he appears as such in documents of March and October 1296) [2] he could hardly have been in Edward's peace when his lands were being thus devastated. Then we find, on 4th June 1298,[3] an order being issued for the distraint of the goods and chattels in Essex of Robert de Brus, in order to pay his debts to the Exchequer, debts which, as we shall see presently, had been expressly postponed by Edward in October 1296.[4] Such an order would hardly have been issued had he been in Edward's peace.

On 3rd July 1298 [5] Edward crossed the border on the expedition which resulted in the defeat of Wallace at Falkirk on 22nd July; and Hemingburgh, who gives us a full and graphic account both of the campaign and of the battle, tells us that the Earl of Carrick held Ayr and the West for the Scots, while Wallace with the main Scottish army lay in the interior of the country. He also narrates that after the battle Edward seized Stirling, and after lying there for some time marched to the West. At his approach, he says, Bruce burned the castle of Ayr and retired into Carrick, whither Edward would have pursued him had not the want of provisions stopped his progress. So he turned into Annandale, took Bruce's castle of Lochmaben, and

---

[1] *Bain*, ii. 950.   [2] *Ibid.*, pp. 732, 850.
[3] Stevenson, ii. 285.   [4] *Ibid.*, p. 114.   [5] Itinerary.

then departed out of Scotland by the western borders. Doubts have been cast on Hemingburgh's story for reasons which we shall consider presently, but it is confirmed in a most striking way by the known itinerary of Edward on his return from Stirling, which was by way of Abercorn, Edinburgh, and Linton to Ayr, which he reached on the 26th August, and thence, after a stay of seven days, by way of Tibbers and Dalgarnock to Lochmaben, where he stayed for two days, recrossing the border into Cumberland on Saturday, 6th September 1298.[1] That is to say, from Ayr he did strike across country in a south-easterly direction, taking the shortest route to the English border and Carlisle, and passing through part of Bruce's lands of Annandale, and resting at his castle of Lochmaben by the way, which is exactly what Hemingburgh says he did do. He left Ayr on the 1st or 2nd September, and was at Carlisle by the 8th of the month at latest,[2] a fact which bears out Hemingburgh's narrative still further, for it proves that he wasted little time on the march from Ayr to Carlisle.

[1] Itinerary.   [2] *Ibid.*

CHAPTER XII

THE TRUTH ABOUT THE BRUCES. SOME ELEMENTARY CONSIDERATIONS

THE doubts which have been cast on Hemingburgh's narrative are based on two documents, one of which bears the date 3rd July but no year,[1] and the other no date at all![2] Mr. Bain, however, assigns them both tentatively to 1298, while Stevenson, in whose collection the latter first appeared, puts it at some indefinite period in 1297. Obviously, therefore, neither of these documents can be founded on as proving that Bruce was on Edward's side in 1298, unless those who advance them as evidence are prepared to prove that they belong to that year. This, however, they make no attempt to do. They simply accept Mr. Bain's tentative dates unhesitatingly or with slight doubt, and proceed to erect an elaborate structure upon them. Thus Mr. Andrew Lang observes[3] that in June 1298 "we find Robert Bruce, the future king, busy in Edward's service in Galloway," and, later, that, after Falkirk, "manifestly the conscience of that ever-shifting politician (Bruce) condemned him."

There can, however, be no question that neither of these documents belong to either 1297 or 1298. The first, dated 3rd July, year unmentioned, records that " Robert de Brus, Earl of Carrick and Lord of Annandale," being then at his castle at Turnberry-in-Carrick, " begs a renewal of protection on behalf of his bachelors Sir John de Wigton, Sir John de Seton, and Sir Walter Haket, who are with him in the king's service in

---

[1] Bain, ii. 995.   [2] Stevenson, ii. 178 ; Bain, ii. 1049.
[3] *History of Scotland*, i. 186, 188.

Galloway, and are going to the place where the King
is, and whose late protection expired at the Nativity
of St. John Baptist last," that is on 24th June.   Now
both Sir John de Wigton and a Sir John de Seton (first
the father, later the son) appear on record from the very
beginning of the troubles in 1296 down to Bruce's
coronation and after, and nearly always on the side of
England, save in the years from 1297 to 1301.[1]   Of
Sir Walter Haket there is no further record.   So obviously this document might refer to any of the years
during which the Earl of Carrick was undoubtedly
Edward's liegeman, namely 1296 and from 1302 to
1306.   There is no evidence, internal or otherwise,
which makes 1297 or 1298 preferable to these or even
so probable as these.

On the other hand, as we have seen, the Bruces, father
and son, were actively engaged on the side of Edward in
1296.   Moreover, on 14th May in that year they were
commissioned by the English king,[2] then at Roxburgh,
to proceed to their ancestral lands of Annandale and
Carrick—which, it is important to remember, had been
confiscated by Balliol in the previous year and conferred
on John Comyn, Earl of Buchan.[3]   Their orders were
to receive to King Edward's peace their own vassals and
the men of the adjacent parts.   These instructions were
carried out so well that on 15th October in the same
year the following tangible token of Edward's favour
was granted the Earl of Carrick.[4]   Beginning "Edward,
by the grace of God," &c., it goes on, "Whereas we
have great trust in our faithful and loyal Robert de
Bruce, Earl of Carrick, for the good service which he
has done, we command you to cause to be postponed all
debts in which he is bound to ourselves in our exchequer,
and cause him to have such terms therein that he can
easily pay them; provided always that postponement
continue during our pleasure."   There can be no doubt
that the sale of Bruce's goods in June 1298 was due

[1] Bain, ii.   Various entries.   [2] Foedera.
[3] Hemingburgh.   [4] Stevenson, ii. 114.

to the cancellation of this grant, the cancellation in its turn being due to the young Earl's continued rebellion.

It is thus evident that the Earl of Carrick was in Galloway, Annandale, and Carrick "on the king's service" throughout the summer of 1296. He would, accordingly, be at his castle of Turnberry-in-Carrick sometime during that period, and from the castle of "Turnberry-in-Carrick" the letter of 3rd July is written. In the next place, Sir John Wigton was in 1296 active on the side of Edward, for on 21st March of that year he attached and imprisoned "a Scottish traitor for absenting himself from his lands to avoid serving in the army against the Scots."[1] In the third place, the letter is a request for a protection for Sir John Wigton and two other knights "who are going to the place where the king is." On 3rd July 1296 the king was in the parish of Alyth[2] in the south-east of Forfar on his famous march to the North of Scotland, but Bruce, of course, could not know that. From 6th to 13th June Edward had been at Edinburgh, from 14th to 20th June at Stirling, and from 21st to 25th June at Perth.[3] The most the Earl of Carrick could know on 3rd July, therefore, was that Edward had left Edinburgh and reached Perth, whence he intended to advance further north. Hence the vagueness of the phrase "are going to the place where the king is." In view of all these facts, Bruce's presence in Galloway and at Turnberry-in-Carrick "on the king's service" in the summer of 1296, the mention of Sir John Wigton as being then active on the English side, and the fact that Edward was, on the date on which the letter was written, somewhere in Scotland, though precisely where Bruce was uncertain, all seem to prove that the letter of 3rd July on which so many assumptions have been founded was written on 3rd July 1296.

The other document, that which Stevenson assigns to 1297 and Bain to 1298, does not present much real difficulty. It is a draft memorandum regarding letters

---

[1] Bain, ii. 822.　　　　[2] Itinerary.　　　　[3] *Ibid.*

which are to be written to various magnates ordering
them to provide troops for a campaign in Scotland.   The
first entry runs, " A closed letter to the Earl of Carrick
to come with as many men-at-arms as he can.   [And
that he bring with him 1000 foot soldiers of the chosen
men of Kyle and Cunningham, Cumnock, and Carrick.]
Of Carrick and Galloway 1000 men according to the
discretion of the Earl of Carrick, and that he bring them
with him in his company."   A number of other names
and requisitions follow, the total number of foot summoned being given as 8100.

Now in view of all that we have elucidated regarding
the Earl of Carrick's actions in 1297, that year may at
once be discarded as the date of the draft memorandum.
There remains Mr. Bain's tentative 1298.   Hemingburgh's narrative and the other facts we have considered
make that year impossible, and even if we discard
Hemingburgh altogether the remaining facts seem irreconcilable with 1298.   There is the document itself to
consider, however, and its evidence is convincing that
1303 must be the date.

In 1303 Edward was preparing for a final invasion of
Scotland, and on 9th April of that year he ordered
various levies from the North of England to meet him at
Roxburgh five weeks after Easter, viz. on 12th May.[1]
With the exception of the Earl of Carrick and Sir
Richard Siward the names and the numbers are practically
the same as in the draft memorandum, while a later entry
shows that the Earl of Carrick and Sir Richard Siward
were summoned at the same time to supply the number
of men mentioned in that memorandum.   An extract or
two will suffice to show that the dated document of 9th
April 1303 is simply the draft memorandum in its final
and official form.   In the draft Sir Richard de Brun is
to be ordered to bring 1000 men from Cumberland.
The entry in the dated document is the same.   And so
with Sir Robert de Lengleys and Sir Walter de Stirland
who are to bring 1000 men from Westmoreland and

[1] Bain, ii. 1351.

Kendal; with Sir William de Dacre who is to bring 700 from Lancaster; with Sir John de Fitz Marmaduke who is to bring 500 from the Bishopric of Durham, and various others. Moreover, a note of the above levies, including the Earl of Carrick's and Sir Richard Siward's, which though undated Mr. Bain himself assigns to 1303 and which cannot possibly belong to any other year, concludes with almost the identical concluding words of the undated draft memorandum. The latter, as translated by Mr. Stevenson, runs, " And 40 masons to make . . . 40 . . . tiers. And 200 ditchers . . . from Northumberland and York, one half from the one county and the other from the other." The former, as translated by Mr. Bain, concludes, " Also 40 masons to hew stone, 40 carpenters, and 200 ditchers from Northumberland and York equally." In both, moreover, Sir Robert Clifford is charged to inform the inhabitants of the bishopric of Durham that the king will be at Durham three weeks after Easter, and will hear their complaints against the Bishop.

There can be no possible doubt, therefore, that both these undated documents, the draft memorandum translated by Mr. Stevenson and assigned by Mr. Bain to 1298, and the undated note of levies assigned by Mr. Bain to 1303, refer to one and the same thing. Now Easter in 1303 was on 7th April,[1] and three weeks later, the time at which Edward expected to be at Durham, would therefore be about the end of that month. We find that Edward actually was in the county of Durham on 30th April 1303,[2] and in the city itself from 3rd to 5th May.[3] In 1297, however, he was never further north than Cambridge,[4] while in 1298 he spent Easter (6th April) at Westminster,[5] and did not begin his northward journey till the last week of that month, reaching Cambridge only on 17th May,[6] and Durham not till 16th June.[7] So the evidence is conclusive not only that 1297 and 1298 are impossible dates for the draft memorandum, but that 1303 is the only possible year. Accordingly

---

[1] Itinerary. [2] *Ibid.* [3] *Ibid.* [4] *Ibid.*
[5] *Ibid.* [6] *Ibid.* [7] *Ibid.*

Hemingburgh's narrative, corroborated as it is by the other facts we have elucidated, must stand, and it must be accepted as an incontrovertible historical fact that the young Earl of Carrick never fulfilled the terms of the capitulation of Irvine, but bore an active share in the resistance of the Scots during the closing months of 1297 and all through 1298.

Soon after the battle of Falkirk Wallace is said to have resigned the Guardianship, and John Comyn of Badenoch and Sir John de Soulis are likewise said to have been appointed Joint-Guardians in his place. Whether this is probable or not we shall see presently. In August 1299, at all events, there was a meeting of the Scottish leaders in Selkirk Forest, but it was not by any means a peaceful gathering.[1] Fierce dissensions broke out among them, and so heated did the discussion become that Sir John Comyn took the Earl of Carrick, his future slayer, by the throat, while his kinsman, the Earl of Buchan, seized the Bishop of St. Andrews, that William Lamberton who afterwards served Bruce so well.[2] This is usually cited as evidence that the Bishop was a partisan of Bruce, and it is nearly always stated that the fracas was a fracas between the Comyn and Bruce factions. This, however, was not the case, as we shall afterwards see. Meanwhile it will be sufficient to observe that the Bishop was the friend and ally of Wallace, to whom, indeed, he had owed his election to the Bishopric two years previously. To that friendship, and not to any friendship with Bruce, was due his participation in the quarrel.

Among others present at the meeting were the Earl of Menteith, the Steward of Scotland, Sir David de Graham, and Wallace's brother, Sir Malcolm Wallace. Wallace himself was not present, and the fracas was caused by Sir David de Graham, a member of the Balliol party, demanding his lands and goods on the plea that he was going abroad without leave. Sir Malcolm Wallace indignantly objected to Graham's demand, and each thereupon giving the other the lie drew his dagger.

[1] Bain, ii. 1978.   [2] *Ibid.*

Into the ensuing scuffle the Comyns and Bruce and the Bishop were drawn as already described. Eventually peace was restored, and it was finally agreed that the Bishop, the Earl of Carrick, and Sir John Comyn should be Guardians of the realm, the Bishop having custody of the castles as principal.[1] It is clear from all this that the parties of the Balliols and the Bruces were at loggerheads, and that old rivalries were as active and irreconcilable as ever; and the election of the Bishop of St. Andrews, Wallace's friend, as principal Guardian *with the custody of the castles*, is a striking proof of the intensity of the jealousy existing between them. Neither the Earl of Carrick nor John Comyn could agree to the other having the custody of the castles lest his own interests should be prejudiced thereby.

In that same month of August 1299 the Earl of Carrick and Sir David de Brechin invaded Galloway and attacked Lochmaben Castle, then held by an English garrison;[2] and in November the three Guardians—the Bishop, the Earl of Carrick, and John Comyn—were besieging Stirling Castle, whence on 13th November they wrote to Edward offering to accept the mediation of the King of France.[3] Thereafter we hear no more of the Earl of Carrick till February 1302, that is to say, two and a half years later,[4] though Sir Herbert Maxwell, with his usual inexplicable anxiety to depreciate Bruce, says in one place, "All this time Robert Bruce, Earl of Carrick, was acting with a duplicity extraordinary even in those times of divided allegiance," and in another, "All this time the Earl of Carrick continued to act a double part." It is difficult to know how to characterise these statements, for, as we shall see presently, there is not a vestige of evidence of any kind to support them, nor does Sir Herbert cite any authority for them.

In 1300 and again in 1301 Edward I invaded Scotland in force. In the former year Caerlaverock Castle was captured,[5] in the latter Bothwell.[6] The winter of

---

[1] Bain, ii. 1978.   [2] *Ibid.*, 283.   [3] *Ibid.*, 1109.   [4] See *infra*.
[5] Rishanger; and the contemporary ballad, "The Siege of Caerlaverock."   [6] Bain, ii. 1235.

1301–02 was spent in Scotland,[1] and it is during this period that we hear of the young Earl of Carrick again, for the first time since the siege of Stirling in November 1299.   Yet we are asked to believe that during these two and a half years he was playing a double part, and behaving with a duplicity extraordinary even for those days !   From 1st November 1301 to 31st January 1302 Edward I was at Linlithgow,[2] and negotiations of some kind were entered upon between him and the Scottish Guardians, for on 26th January 1302 he ratified a truce with the Scots till St. Andrew's Day, 30th November 1302,[3] though he still refused to acknowledge Balliol as king or the Scots as allies of France, by whose mediation the truce was granted.   Early in February 1302 Edward left Linlithgow for England,[4] and on the 16th of the month, being then at Roxburgh, he pardoned Hector Askeloc for the slaughter of Cuthbert of Galloway, the pardon being granted at the request of the Earl of Carrick.[5] Ten weeks later, about 28th April 1302, the Earl and his tenants came to Edward's peace.[6]   It may well seem incredible, but it is nevertheless true, that it is on these two last-mentioned facts, occurring both of them in the spring of 1302, and on these alone, that the charges brought against Bruce by modern writers of having been guilty of duplicity, treachery, shiftiness, and the like during 1299, 1300, and 1301 are based !   Not a shred of evidence of any other kind is produced ; and no such evidence can be produced, for it does not and never did exist.   On the contrary, every one of the authentic facts regarding Bruce's conduct during these years proves him to have been consistent, honourable, and absolutely straightforward in both his actions and his attitude.   The truth of this statement we shall now proceed to see.

It is usually stated that Wallace resigned the Guardianship soon after the battle of Falkirk, and that Sir John Comyn and Sir John Soulis were appointed in his place. But Fordun, who is given as the authority for the state-

---

[1] Itinerary.   [2] *Ibid.*   [3] Foedera.
[4] Itinerary.   [5] Bain, ii. 1291.   [6] *Ibid.*, 1303.

ment, does not say so, though many writers hastily
assume that he does. What he says is that Sir John
Comyn was appointed Guardian on Wallace's resignation,
and that within the five years which succeeded that
event Soulis was also appointed. Which is not only
very different from saying that Comyn and Soulis were
appointed at the same time, but also happens to be
correct. Now there is in existence a letter written by
Philip, King of France, to " Robert de Brus, Earl of
Carrick, and John Comyn the younger, Guardians of
the Kingdom of Scotland," &c. It is dated 6th April,
but no year, and Mr. Bain assigns it tentatively to 1302.[1]
On this assumption, which is quite erroneous, certain of
Bruce's traducers have hastened to base further ridiculous
charges against the patriot king. Anything was good
enough to besmirch his memory with, so they did not
think it worth while to inquire whether Mr. Bain's
tentative date was correct. Yet their whole case, even
then a stupid one, depended on 1302 being the year when
the letter was written ! But the letter, as it happens, was
written in 1299 not in 1302.

The letter is addressed by Philip to Bruce and Comyn,
the Guardians of Scotland, the magnates, " and the whole
community his dear friends." It begins by wishing
them " health and hope and fortitude in adversity," and
urges them to persevere in their resistance. For he " is
moved to the very marrow by the evils brought on their
country through hostile malignity," and praises them
" for their constancy to their king and their shining
valour in defence of their native land against injustice."
Regarding the aid which they ask, " he is not unmindful
of the old league between their king, themselves, and
him, and is carefully pondering ways and means of help-
ing them. But bearing in mind the dangers of the road,
and dreading the risks which sometimes chance to letters,
he has given his views by word of mouth to William,
Bishop of St. Andrews, for whom he asks full credence."

Now we have seen that Edward, on 26th January

[1] Bain, ii. 1301.

1302, ratified a truce with the Scots till St. Andrew's Day, 30th November 1302. This he did by express agreement with the King of France, and the treaty embodying it, which was ratified by Edward on 26th January 1302, had been signed by Philip on Christmas Day 1301. Accordingly, Philip's letter to the Guardians urging them to continue their resistance and promising help is hardly likely to have been written three months after he had obtained nearly a year's truce for them. On the other hand, during the negotiations for peace between England and France in 1299, Philip had tried to get the Scots and their king included,[1] but after months of parleying agreed, in June 1299, not to insist on these conditions provided Edward gave Balliol up to the Pope.[2] To these terms Edward agreed, and on 14th July 1299 ratified the treaty.[3] The war with Scotland therefore continued, but ultimately on 30th October 1300 Edward, being then at Dumfries on his return from a very barren invasion of Scotland, consented, at the request of the King of France, to a truce with the Scots till 21st May 1301.[4] A few weeks after the expiry of the truce Edward again invaded Scotland,[5] and again, at the instance of the King of France, agreed ultimately to a long truce, the above-mentioned truce of January 1302.[6]

It is evident from these facts that the letter of the King of France to the Scottish Guardians is very much more likely to have been written in April 1299, when Philip was doing his best to have the Scots and their king included in his treaty of peace with England, or in April 1300, a truce being by his mediation obtained in October of that year, than in 1302. Moreover, we know, as a matter of fact, that Lamberton was in Flanders in the spring of 1299, as were also " the Abbots of Melrose and Jeddeworth, John de Soulis, knight, and other Scots enemies." [7] Now the Abbot of " Jeddeworth " is one of the Scots envoys expressly mentioned in King Philip's letter, and as the phrase

[1] Foedera. [2] *Ibid.* [3] *Ibid.* [4] *Ibid.*
[5] Itinerary. [6] Foedera. [7] Bain, ii. 1071.

"other Scots enemies" is wide enough to cover "John Wissard, knight," the other envoy mentioned in King Philip's letter, it must be admitted that the evidence in favour of 1299 as its date is exceedingly strong. The only possible objection to it, in fact, is its direction to "Robert de Brus, Earl of Carrick, and John Comyn, the son, Guardians of Scotland, in the name of King John," but that objection is based on the assumption that neither Carrick nor Comyn were Guardians prior to the meeting in Selkirk Forest in August 1299. That assumption, however, as we shall now see, is altogether unwarranted.

Wallace, as we have seen, is said to have resigned the Guardianship soon after the battle of Falkirk, which was fought on 22nd July 1298, but the spy's report of the meeting which was held in Selkirk Forest in August 1299 does not say either that the Bishop of St. Andrews, the Earl of Carrick, and John Comyn were *then* elected in his place, or that the two last-mentioned had not been Guardians before. In order to understand this fully it is of the greatest importance to realise the nature and closeness of the relations existing between the Bishop and Wallace, and in order to bring these out in all their bearings I cannot do better than cite Edward's own presentment of his case against the Bishop for his behaviour during the years from 1296 to 1304. It occurs in his complaint to the Pope in 1306.[1]

"The people of Scotland," he says, "by the abetment and procurement of the Prelates and Clerics of the land, having rebelled against the king, under the guidance of William Wallace, their chieftain and leader, Lamberton forthwith adhered to him. At this juncture the Chapter of St. Andrews had duly elected Master William Comyn, a good man and true, and who was always faithful to the king, but William Wallace and his party, by force and duresse, compelled the Chapter to elect Lamberton in his stead, who then entered upon the temporalities of the See.

[1] Palgrave, clxiv. 331-40.

"Being then made Bishop, Lamberton continued at the Court of France, together with other of the great men of Scotland, the King's enemies, labouring continually to do all the harm and injury in his power against his liege lord, until peace was finally concluded between France and England." (This refers to 1303 as well as to 1298 and 1299.) "And after the conclusion of said treaty, he, Lamberton, by letters patent under his seal, urged and excited the prelates, earls, barons, and all the commonalty of Scotland, they being the king's enemies, to carry on the war vigorously, until the Bishop and other Lords in France could return to Scotland. And this he did in open violation of his oath, as was notorious and well known." (That is the oath which, in common with the rest of Scotland, Lamberton, then Chancellor of Glasgow, had sworn in 1296. He took no other oath of allegiance to Edward between that date and 4th May 1304.)

"Moreover, the Bishop addressed his special letters sealed with his seal, to the traitor Wallace: and prayed that for the love of him, the Bishop, he, Wallace, would do all possible hurt and damage to the King of England. And Lamberton also wrote to his officers in Scotland to employ a portion of his own provision for the sustenance of Wallace."

In view of that plain statement can there be any possible doubt as to the position in which Wallace and the Bishop stood to each other, and the bearing of that relationship both on the Bishop's part in the fracas at the meeting in Selkirk Forest in August 1299, and his election as principal Guardian on the same day? Let it be noted, too, that Edward's charges above quoted refer to the whole period from 1297 to 1304, that during all these years, therefore, the Bishop was the staunch friend of Wallace, and that, during these same years, he was not in any sense a partisan of Bruce.

Now, Philip's letter of 6th April is addressed to "Robert de Brus, Earl of Carrick, and John Comyn the younger, Guardians of the Kingdom of Scotland in the name of the famous and illustrious King John, and the venerable fathers the bishops, abbots, and priors, and the earls, barons, and other magnates and the whole community of the Kingdom." It cannot be by accident that there is no mention there of William Lamberton as one of the Guardians, or that Carrick and Comyn are not addressed as two of the Guardians, but simply as " the Guardians." Then at the end of the letter Philip says that he has given his views by word of mouth to William, Bishop of St. Andrews, whom he commends to the Guardians, and for whom he asks full credence. Had the Bishop at that time been one of the Guardians, not only would such a commendation have been unnecessary, but all mention of the fact that he was a Guardian would not have been omitted. But he is commended to the Guardians not as a fellow-Guardian but as Bishop of St. Andrews.

Now, as we have seen, the Bishop of St. Andrews was in France in the spring of 1299. In June 1298 he had been consecrated at Rome,[1] and there cannot be any doubt that in 1299 his presence in France was due to the fact that he was then on his homeward journey from Rome. During his absence from Scotland the disaster of Falkirk had occurred, and in France the Bishop probably first heard the tidings, and then or later met the envoys from Scotland who had been sent to seek assistance from the French king. Like the good patriot and the friend and colleague of Wallace that he was, he remained at the French Court, lending his powerful aid to the pleadings of the Scottish envoys, and was eventually chosen by Philip as the bearer of his message to the Scots. That he was neither one of the Guardians, nor one of the original envoys, explains Philip's commendation of him to the Guardians on his return to Scotland after an absence of over a year, during which many things had occurred and many changes had taken place.

We have thus elucidated that in April 1299 Lamberton was not one of the Guardians, that he was in France, that

---

[1] Dowden's *Bishops of Scotland*.

envoys from Scotland were at the French Court, that negotiations were proceeding for a truce between France and England, which should include the Scots, and that the Earl of Carrick and John Comyn were in all probability Joint-Guardians of Scotland—all of which is in exact accordance with the terms of Philip's letter. The conclusion, therefore, is irresistible that the letter was written in April 1299, not in April 1302; that Bruce and Comyn were then Joint-Guardians of Scotland, as the letter says they were; that the Bishop of St. Andrews, on his return from Scotland in the summer of that year, was elected the third and the principal Guardian, in order to hold the balance between the conflicting claims and interests of Comyn and Bruce, and that he owed his appointment to the fact that he was a partisan of neither of these magnates, but was a faithful friend and colleague of the great patriot Wallace, was himself a man of powerful personality, and was a *persona grata* with the King of France.

[*Note.*—Since the foregoing was written a fact has come to my notice which places the accuracy of these conclusions beyond question. In Vol. II. of the *Scots Peerage*, p. 218, there is a foot-note which states that a writ has recently been discovered granted by Robert Bruce, Earl of Carrick, in his own name and that of his co-Guardian, John Comyn, and *dated 2nd December* 1298. It is suggested in the note that, in view of this, the meeting in Selkirk Forest may have been in August 1298 instead of 1299. Curiously enough I at one time entertained a similar idea, but on examining the evidence found it to be impossible. For one thing William Lamberton was consecrated Bishop of St. Andrews at Rome early in June 1298, a fact which makes it impossible for him to have been in Selkirk Forest on the 12th of August following. In the next place Edward I himself was throughout August 1298 in Scotland, his itinerary from the 1st to the 31st of that month being Stirling, Torphichen, Stirling, Abercorn, Braid (Edinburgh), Glenross (Peebles), Linton (Peebles), Ayr, and the letter reporting the meeting makes it perfectly clear that at the time when it was held, viz., 12th August, Edward was nowhere near Scotland. The same letter, moreover, which is dated 20th August, announces that at the end of the meeting, the Earl of Carrick left that same day, viz., 12th August, for

Annandale and Galloway, and we know as a fact from another document, above referred to, that in August 1299 the Earl of Carrick did raid that country, attacking his own castle of Lochmaben, then held by an English garrison, and threatening the town of Annan. There is other evidence, equally conclusive, to show that 12th August 1299 is the date of the meeting in Selkirk Forest and Lamberton's election to the Guardianship. But the foregoing will suffice. The writ of 2nd December 1298, therefore, is not only strictly in accordance with the facts as we have elucidated them, but confirms them in the fullest possible way. Accordingly there can no longer be any doubt that soon after Falkirk Wallace did resign the Guardianship, and that the young Earl of Carrick and Sir John Comyn of Badenoch, "the Red Comyn," became Joint-Guardians in his place, with the double object of uniting the rival houses of Bruce and Balliol in the war against England and of safeguarding their conflicting interests. It is also clear that one of the first acts of the new Guardians was to despatch envoys to the King of France in the autumn of 1298, or winter of 1298–99, with what result we have just seen.]

CHAPTER XIII

THE BRUCES AND THE COMYNS, 1298-1304

For nearly four years the young Earl of Carrick remained one of the Guardians of Scotland, and during all that time there is not the slightest suggestion of any kind in any contemporary record or authority that he was otherwise than loyal to his colleagues and to the cause which he and they represented. The infamous suggestion to the contrary has its sole basis in the imagination, the gross carelessness, and the prejudice of certain nineteenth and twentieth century writers. Early in 1302, however, *and after a truce of nearly a year's duration had been entered into*, he, for reasons which we shall consider presently, made his peace with Edward, and about the end of April took the oath of allegiance to the English king. For a considerable period before then, however, he had ceased to act as one of the Guardians, and, probably towards the close of 1301, Sir John Soulis was appointed in his stead. At all events Sir John Soulis appears on record as a Guardian on 23rd February 1302,[1] on which date, in that capacity, he wrote to the King of France in regard to the truce which had recently been concluded between Edward on the one part and the French and the Scots on the other; while in the autumn campaign of 1301 he likewise appears on record as one of the leaders of the Scottish forces in the field.[2] Now Sir John Soulis, it will be remembered, and his brother Sir William, had been two of Bruce the Competitor's auditors in the competition for the Crown; and when in 1306 the young Earl of Carrick again raised the standard of revolt, he

---

[1] Acts of Parl. of Scotland, I., Appendix, p. 98.
[2] Stevenson, ii. 431, 432.

was one of the first to join him. On the other hand, his mother was one of the five daughters of Alexander Comyn, Earl of Buchan,[1] and he himself was therefore a full cousin of the Earl of Carrick's contemporary, John Comyn, Earl of Buchan, and a kinsman of Carrick's great rival Sir John, the Red Comyn, of Badenoch. It is possible, therefore, to regard his appointment to the Guardianship as having been made in either the Bruce or the Comyn interest, but I prefer to suggest that he was appointed on Bruce's resignation because he was repugnant to neither the Bruce nor the Comyn faction, because he was known to be animated by intensely patriotic motives in his opposition to England, and because he was a knight of proved courage and worth. At all events, it is significant that he suffered the interests of no faction to affect his hostility to England, that he fought under the banner of the Comyns as readily and as gallantly as under the banner of the Bruces, and that he came to be regarded by Edward himself as one of his most dangerous and most implacable adversaries.[2]

On 16th February 1302, as we have seen, Edward I pardoned a murderer at the request of the Earl of Carrick, and shortly before 28th April the Earl was received to Edward's peace. In October following there is reason to suppose that he attended Edward's Parliament at Westminster,[3] and thenceforward, until the slaying of Comyn in February 1306, he was ostensibly loyal to the English king, and even assisted him during his invasion of Scotland in 1303 and 1304.[4] In considering this apparent desertion by the Earl of Carrick of the cause of Scottish freedom two preliminary facts must be kept clearly in view, (1) he went over to Edward openly and in no treacherous or underhand manner, and (2) he went over during a period of prolonged truce, that is to say, he did not desert his colleagues at a time when they were actually in the field.

[1] B. P., ii. 256.
[2] See various entries in Stevenson and Bain.
[3] Bain, ii. 1334.   [4] Bain. Various entries.

In going over to Edward in 1302 the Earl of Carrick was, perhaps, from some points of view, guilty of un-patriotic conduct, but there was nothing perfidious in his action. In view of the fierce criticism and the misrepresentation to which he has been subjected, this cannot be too strongly insisted upon. Moreover, in taking the step he did he was actuated by the same motives as had guided all his actions. Ever since 1297 he had fought on the side of Scotland, and had been for more than three years, 1298–1301, one of the Guardians of the kingdom. But while his colleagues in the Guardianship were fighting for the restoration of Balliol or one of his line, the Earl of Carrick was fighting for his own claim to the throne. At the same time there can be little doubt that with both John Comyn and the Earl of Carrick patriotic motives played a part, though with each the moving cause was unquestionably the claims of his family to the Scottish Crown. Their interests were, therefore, bound to clash in the end, and it says a good deal for them, and especially for the Earl of Carrick, that they fought together against Edward for so long.

Comparatively little is known of the happenings in Scotland from 1299 to 1302, but everything we do know shows that the Comyns were in the ascendant and were, moreover, steadily improving their position. They had several powerful factors in their favour. There was their own immense territorial and family influence. There were the facts that Balliol had been King of Scotland, that he had revolted against the aggression of England, and that he had only surrendered after the destruction of his army, and in face of immensely superior forces. There was the great influence of Wallace, who had always been careful to make clear that he was fighting for "King John." There was the influence of the Church, which as early as 1290 had been cast mainly on the side of Balliol, and which after 1295 was almost wholly exerted in his favour. And, finally, there was the fact that while Balliol had actually sat on the throne, the Bruces were as yet only claimants to it, and had, moreover, in 1296 fought on the side of England. Accordingly from the very outbreak of the war down to the surrender of the Comyns and their allies in 1304, there can be no question that the Comyns, as representing the Balliols, occupied the stronger position. At intervals, as after Falkirk in 1298, events may, perhaps, have seemed to turn in favour of the Bruces, but the Comyns always succeeded in reasserting themselves, and the later phases of the first part of the war show them to have acquired a complete ascendancy.

In both 1300 and 1301, as we have seen, Edward I invaded Scotland, and the little we know of these campaigns is sufficient to indicate the relative position of the Comyns and the Bruces. In the former year Galloway was the scene of the English operations, and a strong Scottish force which harassed the English considerably was under the command of John Comyn the Guardian, his kinsman the Earl of Buchan, and Sir Ingelram de Umfraville, who belonged to the Balliol party.[1] In the previous year, as we have seen, the three Guardians—the Bishop of St. Andrews, Carrick, and Comyn—had attempted to obtain a truce. In July or August 1300 the attempt was repeated, this time by Comyn the Guardian, the Earl of Buchan, and the Bishop of Whithorn,[2] but as Edward would make no concession, and as the Comyns demanded the restoration of King John, nothing came of it. Edward met with little success in his campaign, however, and by 30th October he was glad to agree to a truce till Whitsunday (21st May) 1301, on the intercession of the King of France. It is clear from these facts that in 1300 the Comyns were in the ascendant in Scotland, and the fact that they entered into negotiations for the restoration of King John, apparently on their own initiative, neither the Bishop of St. Andrews nor the Earl of Carrick being mentioned, is of peculiar significance.

Long before the expiry of the truce Edward was making preparations for another Scottish invasion, and

[1] Rishanger.   [2] *Ibid.*

in July 1301 he was over the border again.[1] The campaign, however, was as abortive as that of the preceding
year, and though Edward remained in Scotland from 5th
July 1301 to 18th February 1302 the capture of Bothwell
Castle was his only achievement of any note. The invasion was brought to a close, as we saw, by the ratifica-
tion at Linlithgow on 26th January 1302 of the truce
obtained by the good offices of the King of France, a
truce which was to extend till 30th November 1302.
But while Edward was engaged in the siege of Bothwell
Castle in September 1301, the Scots were very active in
Ayr and the West.[2] Lochmaben Castle was in dire
straits from their attentions, and on 7th September Sir
John Soulis and Sir Ingelram de Umfraville attacked it
with a force which its English constable estimated at
four knight-bannerets, 240 men-at-arms, and 7000 footmen.[3] They failed to capture the castle but burned the
town.[4] At the same time the Earl of Buchan, Sir
Simon Fraser, Sir Alexander de Abernethy, and Sir
Hubert de Morham were "with their power" not far
away, and "all the country was rising because the
English officers had no troops to ride upon them."[5]
Moreover, when Soulis and Umfraville, after suffering some losses at Lochmaben, turned towards Nithsdale and Galloway, there, too, the country rose with
them.[6]

About the same time the new castle of Ayr was in
danger, the constable informing the king that on 3rd
October "the Scots were in Carrick before the castle of
Turnberry with 400 men-at-arms and foot-soldiers enough
. . . and within these eight days wished to attack Ayr
Castle and injure the country at the king's peace.
Wherefore they beg the king to send succours quickly,
for the Scots are in such force that they cannot withstand them. They have heard nothing from Earl Patrick
(the Earl of March), to whom they understand the king
has given the keeping of the country: at which (that is at

---

[1] Itinerary.   [2] Stevenson, ii. 431–5.   [3] Ibid.
[4] Ibid.   [5] Ibid.   [6] Ibid.

hearing nothing from the Earl) they wonder much."[1]   The
presence of the Scots before Turnberry and Ayr was due
to the invasion of the West by the Prince of Wales, who,
while his father entered Scotland by Berwick and proceeded by way of Peebles, Lanark, and Glasgow to Bothwell, set out from Carlisle to subdue the west.   He got
as far as Turnberry and the new castle of Ayr, but
being threatened by a strong Scottish force which hung
on his flank he retreated to Carlisle, which he reached in
the first week of October.[2]

Now it will be noticed that in this western campaign
it is the Balliol party who are again prominent.   With
the single and doubtful exception of Sir John Soulis all
those mentioned as leaders are Balliol's men.   The Earl
of Buchan, Sir Ingelram de Umfraville, and Sir Alexander
Abernethy, were strong partisans of Balliol, and remained
opponents of Bruce to the very end, while the little we
know of Sir Hubert Morham indicates that he, too, was
of the Balliol party.   Sir Simon Fraser, who afterwards
won high fame as a knight and a patriot, and was executed under circumstances of great cruelty in 1306, was
likewise a partisan of Balliol, his father having been one
of Balliol's auditors in the competition for the Crown.
Sir Simon himself had fought for Balliol at Dunbar,[3]
was carried captive to England, and was released in order
to accompany Edward to Flanders in 1297, where he
rendered good service and won the high regard of the
English king, who both then and subsequently bestowed
on him many signal marks of his favour.   In 1298 he
accompanied Edward on his Scottish campaign, and received from the English king the gift of a horse "for
his own riding."   In the following year he had his lands
in Scotland restored to him and was appointed to the
responsible post of Warden of Selkirk Forest, in which
capacity we find him performing various feats of arms
against the Scots and being treated as a trusted and
valued servant by the English king.   Yet in 1301, while

[1] Bain, ii. 1236.   [2] Ibid., p. 1239.
[3] For this and following statements see entries in Bain.

at Wark Castle on the Tweed, he suddenly went over to the Scots, carrying away with him the horses and armour of a fellow-knight. That he should have deserted at such a time the English service in which he stood so high, again suggests that in 1301 the cause of the Scots looked like being triumphant and that Fraser's own friends, the Comyns, were in the ascendant.

From these facts it seems clear that in 1300 and 1301 the Comyns were at the head of the most powerful party in Scotland, and that the triumph of the Scots would mean the triumph of the house of Balliol. The cause of Bruce, therefore, was languishing, yet there is not the faintest indication of any kind that he was otherwise than loyal to his colleagues. On the contrary the fact that during the campaign of 1301 his castles of Lochmaben and Turnberry were still held by English garrisons, and that the Earl of March was in command of all that district for England, proves that he was still an open enemy of England. But the position had already become impossible for him. He found himself one of the leaders of a cause which, if successful, would mean the downfall of his own hopes, and it is to his honour that in such circumstances he remained loyal to his colleagues so long. The few facts which we know about the campaign of 1301 perhaps indicate the difficulty of his position, for while the fact that his name is not preserved in any of the scanty records of the campaign may mean nothing, it at least suggests that he had ceased to play a very active part in the opposition of the Scots, though he had not yet actually abandoned their cause. Such a course would have been perfectly legitimate and natural, for it is not in human nature, and especially it was not in fourteenth-century human nature, for a man to fight for a cause whose triumph would in his eyes be a disaster.

It will, of course, be argued that the cause for which Bruce fought from 1297 to 1301, and which he abandoned in 1302, was the cause of Scotland. But that is the twentieth-century point of view, regarding which we

K

shall have something to say later. Meanwhile it will be sufficient to remark that while Bruce and the Comyns were undoubtedly fighting for a free Scotland, they were each fighting for their own hands as well, and a free Scotland under a king of Balliol or Comyn blood was as unthinkable to Bruce as a free Scotland with the young Earl of Carrick or his father on the throne was to the Comyns. And so also with Edward I. He, too, was fighting for his own hand, and the war accordingly ultimately became in reality a contest between three men or groups of men for the prize of the Crown of Scotland. Once that fact is grasped much that to modern eyes seems strange becomes clear, and we hold the key not only to the actions of the Bruces, the Balliols, and the Comyns from 1286 to 1303, but to the actions of the Bruces and the Comyns from 1303 onwards, and to all the actions of Edward I from the beginning to the end of his dealings with Scotland.

When that is understood it will, I think, be admitted that, as I have already remarked, Bruce's behaviour throughout 1300 and 1301, when things were clearly shaping themselves in a way which was likely to prove fatal to his ambitions, was creditable to him. Doubtless, he still hoped against hope that events would take a turn in his favour, but even when it must have become apparent that this was unlikely he did not forthwith abandon his colleagues, but remained in hostility to England. This seems to me to indicate that so long as there seemed a chance of the Scots being successful against England he was prepared to sink his own claims for the good of the greater cause, leaving the question of the Crown to be decided at some future date. Indeed, when the course of events from 1297 to 1302 is looked at as a whole, and especially when the association of Bruce and John Comyn in the guardianship from 1298 to 1301 is considered, it seems to me impossible to resist the conclusion that some sort of agreement or understanding actually existed between Bruce and the Comyns, whereby, probably, the question of the Crown was postponed until such time as Scotland was freed from the domination of England. Such an understanding would explain not only the association of Bruce and the Comyns in these years, but also the events which culminated in the death of John Comyn in February 1306. In that age, however, and in the peculiar circumstances of the situation, such an understanding would have to stand an almost intolerable strain, and the moment it began to appear that victory would mean victory not so much for Scotland as for the Balliols the breaking-point would be reached. Be that as it may, however, it must, at all events, be reckoned in Bruce's favour that when the situation had finally become impossible he did not jeopardise the cause for which his colleagues were fighting by deserting it during a time of actual warfare, but waited until the campaign on which they were then engaged was over, and a truce of nearly a year's duration had been signed, and then, and only then, and during a period of peace, did he cut himself loose from a cause which it was no longer possible for him to support.

In stating the case for Bruce thus it must not be supposed that I am losing sight of the fact that there were many people of all classes in Scotland who were animated by purely patriotic motives, and did not care very much whether a Bruce, a Balliol, or a Comyn sat on the throne, so long as that throne was the throne of a free Scotland. The men who followed Andrew de Moray and William Wallace, the men who in fact made possible the resistance from 1297 to 1304 and the subsequent success of Bruce, were men of that type. It was, indeed, because of these men, and because of their courage, their patriotism, and their example, that Comyn and Bruce ever took the field at all. But for the present we are engaged on an attempt to unravel the tangled skein which has gathered round the actions and the motives of the future king, and to place these in their true perspective. And so our attention is necessarily concentrated for a time on the rivalries and ambitions of the Balliols, the Comyns, and the Bruces, for unless these are understood it is impossible to comprehend either the attitude and the actions of the Comyns and the young Earl of Carrick from 1297 to 1304, or the course of events which eventually placed the latter on the throne of a free Scotland.

CHAPTER XIV

BRUCE AND LAMBERTON

From the date of his surrender to Edward in April 1302 to the day of the slaying of the Red Comyn in February 1306, the Earl of Carrick, as we have seen, remained ostensibly loyal to Edward and even assisted him during his invasion of Scotland in 1303-4. It is probably unnecessary now to point out that this assistance was due not to any desire to stand well with Edward or to any treachery to Scotland, but entirely to his rupture with the Comyns in the previous year and his hostility to them, they being now in full command of the Scottish forces in the field, and against them Edward's operations being chiefly directed. From a sentimental or patriotic point of view we in the twentieth century may regret the fact, but we must admit that from the fourteenth-century standpoint his action is at least understandable and requires no imputation of mean motives to explain it.

I have said that from 1302 to 1306 the Earl of Carrick was "ostensibly loyal" to Edward. The phrase is used advisedly, for, on 11th June 1304, he and William Lamberton, Bishop of St. Andrews, entered into a solemn agreement at Cambuskenneth,[1] whereby, "in view of future dangers," and "in order to resist the attempts of rivals," they agreed that in all time coming they would assist each other against all persons whatsoever, that neither would undertake anything without consulting the other, and that each would warn the other of any danger. In the words of Mr. Andrew Lang, "this meant that Lamberton was still working

[1] Palgrave, p. 323.

for the independence of the Scottish Church, and that Bruce was still hankering after the Scottish Crown." As the Earl of Carrick was then high in Edward's favour, was indeed assisting him at the siege of Stirling, and only three days later was served heir to his father's English estates, doing homage for them on the 17th of June 1304 and having his debts to the Exchequer respited by Edward, Bruce's traducers naturally put the very worst construction on his behaviour. As before, however, they ignore the essential facts, and we shall, therefore, consider them briefly.

In March or April 1304 the Earl of Carrick's father, the elder Bruce, had died,[1] and the Earl was now, accordingly, in his own eyes, and in the eyes of many in Scotland, the rightful King of Scots. In the previous year Edward had invaded Scotland in great force, had advanced as far north as Kinloss in Moray, and had captured every Scottish stronghold of importance except Stirling. He had spent the winter in Scotland; and in February 1304 John Comyn of Badenoch and all the Scottish leaders in the field, save Wallace and Simon Fraser, had surrendered, on almost their own terms, to the English king. In June, Stirling Castle was being besieged, and its fall was only a question of time, for so broken were the Scots that only a few scattered bands remained in the field. During the invasion of 1303 Lamberton and other Scottish envoys had been in Paris, but on 20th May of that year a treaty of peace was signed between England and France, from the terms of which the Scots were excluded. Despite this the Scots envoys when writing to John Comyn, the guardian, to inform him of the fact, exhorted their countrymen to be of good courage, bidding them "now if ever quit yourselves like men."[2] Some months later the envoys had returned to Scotland, and in February 1304 they had surrendered along with John Comyn the guardian. Lamberton is mentioned among the others who thus surrendered, and by 4th May 1304 he had done homage

---

[1] Bain, ii. 1493.   [2] Foedera.

to Edward, his lands being restored to him on that date.[1]

Now, as we have seen, Lamberton was a partisan of neither the Balliols nor the Bruces. He was a churchman first and last, and from the beginning to the end of the struggle his conduct had been dictated by the dominating purpose of securing the independence of the Scottish Church. All through these years of varying hope he had worked and fought courageously, tenaciously, and unsparingly with that goal in view. From the beginning he had allied himself with Wallace, for in Wallace he recognised the force on which the cause he had at heart must ultimately depend, the force of the popular sentiment of Scotland, and through good and ill report he stuck by Wallace, as Edward's complaint to the Pope shows. But a free Scotland without a king was as unthinkable to him as it was to Wallace or to any other knight or prelate of that age, and accordingly at the outset he took the natural course of working and fighting for the restoration of the king who had already sat, and who, in the eyes of the Scots, still sat upon the Scottish throne. While that was so, however, he was not thirled to the party of the Balliols. He was no mere partisan. While the Comyns were in the main fighting for the restoration of the Balliols, Lamberton was fighting for the freedom of the Church and the kingdom of Scotland, and the personality of the king was to him a matter of minor importance. And so when, in the spring of 1304, the cause of Balliol had tumbled into ruin, Lamberton was both free and ready to look elsewhere for the saviour of his Church and his country.

His thoughts naturally turned at once towards the Earl of Carrick, now by the death of his father a claimant in his own right to the Scottish throne. Lamberton, of course, was not ignorant of the causes which had led the young Earl into the English camp, and he was familiar, too, with his character, his known skill as a warrior, and

[1] See Bain for all these facts.

his natural qualities and abilities. Bruce the king did
not obtain all those gifts of head and heart which won
for him a kingdom and the love and devotion of countless men only when he ascended the Scottish throne,
though far too many people write as if, by some strange
miracle, he did. Lamberton, too, was of course aware
that the downfall of the Comyns was Bruce's opportunity.
They had played their game and lost. The field was
now clear for Bruce to play his. And from what the
worthy Bishop knew of his one-time fellow-guardian,
play it at the first favourable opportunity he was sure
he would.

There is, moreover, one other point. Not only had
the Comyns played and lost, but they do not seem to
have played skilfully. Courage they had, but not, apparently, military skill. It was left to knights like Sir
Thomas Maule at Brechin, Sir Alexander Bosco at Glen-
urquhart, and the young Sir William Oliphant at Stirling
to redeem in Edward's last Scottish campaign the fighting fame of the Scots and show what might have been
done had the armies in the field been led with ability.
And so not only had the Comyns gone down before
Edward, but Lamberton must have realised that under
their leadership the cause he had so much at heart would
never be victorious.

In entering into their agreement of 11th June 1304
Bruce, as we shall henceforth call him, and Lamberton
were undoubtedly breaking their oaths to Edward, but,
nevertheless, they deserve very little of the censure which
has been lavished upon them on that account. Two
blacks, of course, do not make a white, but in judging
their conduct towards Edward, Edward's conduct towards
them and their country, which, it must never be forgotten, lay at the root of the whole matter, must not be
lost sight of. The man who " in the guise of a friend
and an ally" had filched away the freedom of Scotland, and
had now but twelve years after that first act of perfidy,
and because of it, completed to all seeming the conquest
of the country in blood and fire, had no reason to com-

plain if those whom he had wronged sought to fight him with the weapons which he had used against them. And if that be remembered it will be seen that it is not Bruce and Lamberton, but the much-lauded Edward, who suffers by the comparison. For while Bruce and Lamberton laboured under a sense of injury and injustice, Edward, merely to gratify his own selfish ambitions, stooped to perfidy of a description to which the simple fealty-breaking of Bruce and Lamberton is not in any way comparable.

It is often argued that Bruce was guilty of base ingratitude and worse to the king who had loaded him with gifts and favours. But was he? Edward had deprived Bruce of a kingdom, and thought to compensate him by the gift of a few acres of land, most of which by the way was in actual fact Bruce's own, and a few pounds in money. And Bruce is not only accused of base ingratitude, but is subjected to all manner of vilification because he did not humbly accept this as sufficient, and straightway cease to scheme for the recovery of the kingdom of which he had been robbed by his supposed benefactor! There is surely something seriously wrong somewhere in the reasoning which characterises that as base ingratitude.

The plain fact of the matter is, Edward sought by every means in his power to attach Bruce to himself, just as he sought to attach every other great magnate in Scotland. He is often praised for the " generosity " of his treatment of the Scottish knights and nobles who rebelled again and again. But in truth there was no real generosity in it. There was policy, which is a very different thing. Edward knew quite well that he could not hold Scotland by force. But he considered he might hold it if he succeeded in convincing her natural leaders that it was to their best interests to stand by him. Therein lies the real explanation of his treatment of "rebels" like the Comyns and of his treatment of Wallace. The latter is the true test of his alleged "generosity." He had nothing to gain by " generosity " to Wallace, and so had him put to death with every imaginable form of cruelty. He had something to gain by "generosity" to the Comyns, the Bruces, the Frasers, the Umfravilles, the Stewarts, and countless others, and so dealt diplomatically with them—and won in the nineteenth and twentieth centuries a spurious reputation for generosity to a land which he had drenched in blood and upon which he had inflicted untold miseries in an unholy attempt to gratify his own selfish ambition.

We have already had occasion to observe that much confusion exists in the minds of many people as to the motives which impelled the Comyns, the Bruces, Lamberton, and various others during the long struggle with England. At one time these motives are described as purely selfish. At another, the very men who are said to have been actuated entirely by these motives are said to have betrayed or deserted the cause of Scotland, a cause which, if their motives were purely selfish, never, of course, had any existence for them. As a matter of fact all these men were very human products of their age, and were animated, like men before and since, by a mixture of motives. It may be that selfish motives predominated, but nevertheless it may safely be asserted that Balliols, Bruces, and Comyns alike, as well as bishops, priests, and other men, such as Andrew de Moray and William Wallace and many another, were not animated solely by selfish ambitions or selfish purposes. No Scotsman of the period, whatever his rank, class, or condition, was reconciled to the subordination of Scotland to England. All alike were anxious to be governed by their own king, their own countrymen, and their own laws. All alike hated the domination of England, and all alike resented the condition of vassalage which had been imposed upon them. The proof of these assertions is written large on the whole history of the War of Independence, and both the foregoing and the succeeding pages contain abundant demonstration of it. It is true that other factors often intervened to complicate those clear issues, but while the importance of those factors was frequently very great we must avoid the too common mistake of supposing either that they were the only factors or that they were the only ones which mattered. And so when we see that Lamberton throughout his career was working for the freedom of the Church of Scotland, and Bruce for his own accession to the Scottish throne, we must not let our realisation of these facts lead us to suppose that no real desire for the freedom of Scotland, no real desire for the welfare of their fellow-countrymen, found any place in the hearts or the schemes of the patriotic Bishop or the future king.

With that word of warning we may proceed to sum up the facts which confronted Bruce and Lamberton in 1304. Those which Bruce had to face were as follows :

(1) Edward I had annexed the kingdom which Bruce regarded as his of right. (2) Bruce believed that if Edward I had dealt fairly by his grandfather in the competition for the Crown, he himself would now be sitting on the Scottish throne. (3) Therefore he, Bruce, owed nothing to Edward, who in showing him favour was manifestly endeavouring to persuade him to accept the situation. (4) The rival line, who had owed the Crown to Edward, had just been crushed, and apparently finally crushed. (5) But Scotland was as far as ever from being reconciled to English domination, though for the moment she was compelled to accept it. (6) With the downfall of the Comyns he himself, as head of the House of Bruce, would probably be able to rally the greater part of Scotland to his side, if he took the field and claimed the Crown. (7) But experience had taught him that so long as Edward was alive, and vigorous and active, success, if it could be gained at all, could only be gained after a long and bloody struggle. (8) Edward, however, was an old man, and in the natural order of things could not be expected to live much longer. (9) Edward's son and heir was a wastrel, was weak, foolish, incompetent, pleasure-loving, and devoid of nearly every kingly quality. (10) Edward's death, accordingly, would be Scotland's

and, therefore, Bruce's opportunity. (11) For Edward's death, therefore, he must wait, but meantime he must have his plans in shape in order to be prepared for eventualities, and in order also to be in a position to forestall any move on the part of the Comyns. (12) And, at the same time, he must take care to give Edward no reason to suspect his intentions.

Those who love to parade Bruce's alleged attitude to Edward and Edward's attitude to Bruce from 1303 to 1306 would do well to examine their position with the foregoing facts kept steadily in view. I would only ask them this question. When they talk so indignantly of Bruce's posing as a loyal subject of Edward during these years, the agreement between Lamberton and himself being all the time in existence, do they mean to suggest either that he should have rebelled at once, or that he should have proclaimed upon the housetops his intention to endeavour to enforce his lawful rights at the first favourable opportunity, or that he should have complacently acquiesced in Edward's usurpation of his rights, or that he should have taken no steps to make possible his claiming them when the opportunity offered, or that by declining Edward's gifts, by refusing to do homage, and by absenting himself from Parliament, he should have excited the suspicion of the English king and so enabled him to foil his cherished purpose?

The facts which Lamberton had to face in 1304 were very similar to those which Bruce had to face, with the exception, perhaps, that Lamberton was not so ardent a believer in Bruce's indefeasible right to the throne as Bruce himself was, though, as he had been Chancellor of Glasgow before he became Bishop of St. Andrews, he had in all probability been in favour of the Bruce claim to the Crown in 1291 and 1292, Glasgow being in the sphere of influence of the Bruces and their friends, and the Bishop of Glasgow having been one of Bruce the Competitor's auditors. In addition to the facts which weighed with Bruce, however, Lamberton had a number of others ever before him. (1) He was as determined as ever to secure, if possible, the freedom of the Scottish Church from English interference. (2) That could only be secured if the kingdom of Scotland were free. (3) The war conducted for so long, with so many hopes, first of all by Andrew de Moray and William Wallace, then by Wallace, then by Bruce and Comyn, then by Bruce, Comyn, and himself, and finally by the Comyns aided by Wallace, had ended in total failure. (4) He himself had been compelled to surrender and to take the oath of fealty to Edward. (5) But the oath had been given under compulsion and accordingly was not binding. (6) Even if it were legally binding his duty to the Church came first, and as his duty to the Church demanded that he should lose no opportunity of freeing it from the domination of England, no oath could stand in the way. (7) In any case he could, if necessary, obtain absolution for breaking any oath the observance of which would be contrary to the higher interests of the Church. (8) In view of the complete failure of the Comyns he could no longer place any hope or reliance on them. (9) With the downfall of the Comyns went the possibility of Balliol's ever returning to Scotland as king. (10) Wallace, too, was no longer the power he had been, but even if he were, in whose name were they to fight now that Balliol was out of the question? (11) A leader was necessary who with courage and military skill would combine power, position, and influence. (12) There was one man, and one man only, who possessed the necessary qualities and essentials, and who in consequence could solve the difficulty created by the improbability of a successful rising ever taking place in favour of Balliol. (13) That man was Robert Bruce, Earl of Carrick, who believed himself to be the rightful King of Scots, and was so regarded by a powerful party among the nobility and by many of the people of Scotland. (14) Lamberton himself either knew, or was convinced in his own mind, that Bruce would attempt to gain the Crown on the first favourable opportunity. (15) He knew, also, that the attempt once made would not be lightly abandoned. (16) Accordingly, if the Church of Scotland were ever to regain her freedom Robert Bruce was the man on whom she must henceforth depend.

Thus in 1304 Bruce and Lamberton were drawn irresistibly together by the devotion of each to the purpose which had guided all their actions during the previous twelve years. On the one hand if Bruce achieved his purpose Lamberton achieved his, while on the other hand, without the powerful aid of the Church Bruce could hardly hope to be successful. And so on 11th June 1304 they entered into a solemn and binding agreement which had for its ultimate object the winning of the freedom of Scotland—the freedom of the Crown, the Church, and the Community—and they did so even though at that very moment the consciousness of the power of Edward I was heavy upon them, even though they had recently taken oaths of fealty to him and might have to take them again, and even though the road on which they purposed to set out seemed long and dark and difficult. They did so because they believed to the uttermost in the justice of their cause, because they believed that they owed neither loyalty nor allegiance to the king who had extorted their oaths by compulsion and who had deprived them by fraud and force of their lawful rights and heritage, and because they believed that they were justified in using any means to compass the downfall of the tyranny which had erected itself on a foundation of falsehood, cunning, hypocrisy, and blood. By the irony of circumstances it is the apologists of Edward I, the king who never kept an oath when it was to his advantage to break it, the king who waded through a sea of lies and blood to the conquest of a free and friendly kingdom, it is his apologists who throw at the wronged and suffering Scots charges of perjury and perfidy, though they followed but a long distance away, and with far greater cause and with far less sin, the example set them by their much be-praised English oppressor.

CHAPTER XV

WILLIAM WALLACE AND ROBERT BRUCE

WE have now cleared Bruce of most of the charges which have been brought against him, but one still remains, and that perhaps the most monstrous of all, for not only is it vile in itself, but is based on nothing but a series of unwarranted assumptions, and is made to appear worse by assumptions of another kind. Moreover, it is a charge so vile that it should never have been brought unless it were capable of the fullest proof, and that, on the admission of those who bring the charge, it certainly is not. As a matter of fact, as we shall see presently, all the evidence we possess points to the exactly contrary conclusion, but before we examine that evidence we shall consider the charge itself and the manner in which it has been built up, as an excellent example of the method by which Bruce has been made to figure in the pages of modern historians as a shifty schemer, a base conspirator, a false friend, and a traitor to comrade, king, and country.

The charge is that Bruce was probably a witness of the trial and execution of Wallace, and that " we cannot doubt, alas, that he was consenting to the doom of Wallace, for he and Bishop Lamberton attended Parliament at Westminster three weeks later, when a fresh arrangement was made for the governance of Scotland." [1] And again, " What can be said in defence of Bruce's repeated presence in Edward's Parliament and Council about the time when Wallace was hurried to death? He was an English subject, it is true, and as such bound to regard Wallace, his former comrade, as a rebel, and to serve

[1] Sir Herbert Maxwell.

King Edward loyally in all things. But if that is held to justify his indifference to Wallace's fate he was involved in the greater dishonour by the secret treaty then existing between him and William de Lamberton. Of treachery to king, to comrade, or to both, Robert de Brus can scarcely be acquitted." [1] Which as a judgment is as wrongheaded as the supposed facts on which it is based are inaccurate and misleading. None the less the charge against Bruce of having behaved basely and treacherously to Wallace, and of having been a willing or at least an unprotesting witness of his trial and execution, has passed, largely as a result of the passages just quoted, into the domain of history.

I remarked above that the charge was based on a series of unwarranted assumptions, which it will be well to expose briefly before we go further. To begin with, there is neither evidence nor warrant for the assumption that Bruce was probably a witness of the trial and execution of Wallace. In the second place, the assumption that Bruce attended Parliament three weeks after Wallace's death is, as we shall see, demonstrably false. In the third place, the statement as to Bruce's " repeated presence in Edward's Parliament and Council about the time when Wallace was hurried to his death " is, as we shall also see, entirely devoid of foundation. And, in the fourth place, the assumption that, supposing these things were true, they prove that Bruce was "guilty of treachery to king, to comrade, or to both," is utterly fallacious and illogical. They might all be true and yet reflect not the slightest discredit or dishonour upon Bruce.

I have also remarked that the charge, based as it is on a series of unwarranted assumptions, is made to appear worse by assumptions of another kind. These are, briefly, (1) That Bruce in 1305 was, for some reason or other, under a greater obligation to support and defend Wallace than was any other Scot of the time—and that though Bruce had been actively opposed ever since 1302 to the

---

[1] Sir Herbert Maxwell

cause for which Wallace had been fighting; (2) That the relations between Bruce and Wallace ever since 1297 had been very much closer than those between Wallace and other Scottish leaders; and (3) That, accordingly, Bruce's "treachery" to Wallace was of the blackest description. For these assumptions, needless to say, not a particle of evidence is produced, but nevertheless they form, unconsciously perhaps, the gravamen of the charge brought against Bruce in relation to Wallace's trial and execution.

This last point demands a little further attention, for it really goes to the root of the apparent animus to Bruce which has caused so much misconception of his actions and motives. With Bruce's traducers the enormity of his supposed crime lies in the idea that Bruce the later patriot behaved basely and treacherously to Wallace the earlier patriot, that is to say that the one patriot betrayed the other, and that other his one-time comrade who had fought for the same cause as himself. For that monstrous conclusion there is not one iota of evidence. It all hangs on the simple fact that Wallace, the great patriot, was cruelly done to death by Edward I at a time when Bruce, the future patriot, is alleged to have been high in the favour of the English king. Between these two circumstances, however, there is not necessarily the remotest connection, but so obsessed are Bruce's traducers with the great personality and the sad fate of Wallace that they are unable to see that neither of these things has anything to do with the question of whether Bruce "was consenting to the doom of Wallace" or not. That question must be judged on its own merits, and not on the merits of Wallace or the supposed demerits of Bruce. Yet it is on these two latter that it has been judged, which is sufficient to condemn the judgment utterly. An examination of the charges and the alleged proofs will make this clear.

In the first place, no proof whatsoever is advanced for the assertions that Bruce was consenting "to the doom of Wallace," and that he was indifferent to his fate, save the unfounded statement that Bruce was present at an

L

English Parliament three weeks after Wallace's execution, a fact which, even if true, which it is not, cannot be regarded by any unprejudiced person as supplying the slightest warrant for so monstrous a charge.   Beyond this no evidence that is even plausible is produced, for none such exists.   In the second place, we are asked : "What can be said of Bruce's repeated presence in Edward's Parliament and Council about the time when Wallace was hurried to his death?"   The statement contained in that question, as we shall see later, is simply not true, but we may estimate its value meantime by a reference to the accuser's own catalogue of Bruce's deal-ings with Edward.   He there cites Bruce's doings in 1305 as follows[1] :—

" 20th March : Is with King Edward at Westminster : petitions the king to give him de Umfraville's lands in Carrick, which is granted.

"Attends Edward's Parliament in Lent.

"August : Is probably a witness of the trial and execu-tion of Wallace.

" 15th September : Is ordered by the king to appoint a keeper of Kildrummy Castle."

It may at once be said that this " catalogue of vices " for 1305, if I may call it so, is misleading, but, taking it at its face value, where is the evidence in it of Bruce's "repeated presence in Edward's Parliament and Council about the time when Wallace was hurried to his death ? " It is simply not there, and it is not there because it does not exist.

Wallace was tried at Westminster, and executed on 23rd August 1305.   Bruce attended Parliament at Westminster in Lent, a Parliament which sat from 28th February to 21st March.[2]   Thereafter he returned to Scotland, and *in spite of all assertions to the contrary, did not attend the Parliament which met at Westminster in September, three weeks after Wallace's death.*[3]   Lamberton

---

[1] Maxwell's *Bruce*, p. 122.
[2] *Memoranda de Parliamento*, 1305 (Rolls series).
[3] *Ibid.*, p. xlix. ; Bain, ii. 1691.

was one of the ten Scottish commissioners elected to that Parliament, but Bruce was not, and as we shall see, not only did he not attend that Parliament, but almost certainly was not even in London either then or later.

I have said, however, that the "catalogue of vices" above quoted is misleading. It is misleading in the sense that it states, under date 20th March, that Bruce was with King Edward at Westminster, and then gives a separate line to the entry, "Attends Edward's Parliament in Lent." The casual reader would naturally interpret this to mean that two separate and distinct attendances are meant, whereas as a matter of fact they are one and the same, Bruce's presence with the king at Westminster on 20th March arising out of, being in fact an actual part of, his attendance at the Lent Parliament, which, as above noted, sat from 28th February to 21st March. The reference to Bruce's probable presence at the trial and execution of Wallace is also misleading. It is founded on the veriest guess-work, and should, therefore, find no place in such a catalogue.

Assuming, however, for the sake of argument and in order to demonstrate in all its weakness the case against Bruce, that Bruce was present at some Parliament or Council about the time when Wallace was hurried to his death, how is anyone to know whether at such Parliament or Council he stood up in any way for Wallace or not? In the next place, how by any stretch of the imagination can the presence of Bruce or Lamberton or any other Scot at Edward's Parliament held three weeks after Wallace's execution be interpreted as evidence that they were "consenting to his doom"? Is it suggested that Bruce and those other Scots should have deliberately absented themselves from that Parliament as a protest against Wallace's death, and if that is what is meant can it be explained what possible good purpose could have been served by their doing so? Again, in what sense was Wallace a comrade of Bruce? Certainly not to any great extent in 1297 if the story of that campaign is read aright, and hardly from 1299 to 1301 when Bruce,

Comyn, and the Bishop of St. Andrews were the guardians of Scotland and Wallace is practically unheard of. After 1302 Bruce was not only not in any sense a comrade of Wallace, but was actively opposed to him, and however regrettable from a sentimental point of view this may be, it makes the high-falutin' accusation of treachery to comrade very childish stuff indeed.

The hollowness of the foundations on which rests the case against Bruce for his alleged consent to Wallace's doom having been thus exposed, we are now in a position to examine the true facts regarding his behaviour in the year of Wallace's death. We saw that in September 1305 a Parliament met at Westminster, the first, it may be noted in passing, which had been held since that which Bruce attended in March 1305.[1] This Parliament consisted of ten Scottish commissioners and twenty or twenty-two English commissioners, and it was held for the one specific purpose of framing an Ordinance and appointing officials for the government of Scotland.[2] Bruce was neither a Scottish nor an English commissioner,[3] yet Bruce's unkindest critic will have it that[4] "once again at this Parliament Bruce and Lamberton had sworn a new and more elaborate oath of allegiance on the Lord's Body, the Holy Relics, and the four Evangels. Having done so they set out for the north to take the part assigned to them in the new constitution of Scotland." The authority which he gives for this statement[5] is Bain's abstract of the "Ordinance by the king for the settlement of Scotland," but strange to say there is absolutely nothing which can bear such an interpretation either in that abstract or in the Ordinance itself, which is printed in full in Palgrave's *Parliamentary Writs*.

The Earl of Carrick's name is twice mentioned in the record which contains the Ordinance. It occurs first in the narrative which sets forth that "the King at his Parliament last Lent (March 1305) signified by the

---

[1] Palgrave's *Parliamentary Writs*.   [2] *Ibid*.   [3] *Ibia*.
[4] Maxwell's *Making of Scotland*, p. 109.   [5] Bain, ii. 457.

Bishop of Glasgow, the Earl of Carrick," and certain others that the Scots should elect a certain number of Commissioners to his Parliament to be held at Westminster, and so on. It occurs secondly in the Ordinance itself, where it is ordered that "the Earl of Carrick shall place Kildrummy Castle in the keeping of one for whom he shall answer," an entry of course which not only does not imply that Bruce was then in London, but suggests that either Edward or the Parliament were not too certain of his loyalty. At all events, the assertion that Bruce attended that September Parliament is seen, *on the authority on which it is made*, to be altogether devoid of foundation, as is likewise the assertion that by the Ordinance some part was assigned to him in the new constitution of Scotland. Accordingly the conclusion that Bruce's presence at that Parliament means that "he was consenting to the doom of Wallace" stands exposed in all its nakedness.

The absence of Bruce's name from the list of those appointed to administer the affairs of Scotland is so remarkable as to demand particular notice. If Edward at this time, that is in the closing months of 1305, had such implicit faith in him as has been so frequently asserted, the omission is indeed extraordinary. The truth, however, seems to be that Bruce's detractors have confused two very different things. They regard the favours which they say were heaped upon Bruce by Edward as evidence of Edward's faith in and affection for Bruce. The first by no means implies the second, and, as we have already seen, these favours are much more likely to have been dictated by a desire to conciliate Bruce than because of any particular faith in him or special affection for him. The omission of his name from the Ordinance suggests, at all events, that at the time there was some particular reason for not entrusting him with any share in the administration of Scotland.

A brief examination of the Ordinance will show how striking the omission is, and also how suggestive is the only reference to Bruce in the Ordinance itself. Four

pairs of justices are appointed for the whole of Scotland—
justices of this nature being, it may be remarked, in that
age extremely important officials—but Bruce is not one
of them, and that though Galloway is one of the four
districts into which Scotland is divided for the purpose.
As Galloway included the whole of the modern district
of that name, and all the West of Scotland south of the
Firth of Clyde—the other three districts being Lothian,
the country "between Forth and the mountains," and
the country "beyond the mountains" [1]—the fact that
Bruce was not appointed one of the justiciars in the
district in which he was the leading magnate possesses
considerable significance.   Moreover, twenty-one sheriffs
were also appointed, and though Bruce had recently been
Sheriff of Lanark [2] and Constable of Ayr Castle,[3] he
was not appointed either to that sheriffdom or to any
other.   The sole reference to him is that already mentioned, and in the circumstances its exact terms are
important.   It runs: "Also it is resolved and let it
be commanded to the Earl of Carrick that he place
Kildrummy Castle in the keeping of a man for whom
he shall answer," words which not only suggest a lack
of confidence, but imply that the Earl was not then
in London.

Now let us glance at the known facts regarding
Bruce in the first half of 1305, and contrast these with
the terms of the Ordinance.   In March 1305 Bruce
was one of three Scots—the others being the Bishop of
Glasgow and Sir John Moubray—consulted by Edward
during the sitting of the Lent Parliament as to how
Scotland should be represented at another Parliament
to be held later in the year.[4]   This is of so much importance to a true understanding of Bruce's position
in 1305, that we shall quote the terms of the document wherein Edward's demand of Bruce and his two
colleagues is set forth, and their answer given.   It

---

[1] Bain, ii. 1691.   [2] *Ibid.*, p. 1420.   [3] *Ibid.*, p. 1437.
[4] *Parliamentary Writs*, and *Memoranda de Parliamento*, 1305,
p. xlix.

is headed " Memorandum concerning the state of the kingdom of Scotland," and runs as follows : [1]

" Opinions given by the Bishop of Glasgow, the Earl of Carrick, and John de Moubray, in answer to the questions upon which the king had commanded them to advise. (1) Concerning the place and time of holding a Parliament on the affairs of Scotland. Answer—The place at the will of the king, but let it please him to consider the situation of his people of Scotland. The time also at his will ; but it seems to them that such Parliament cannot be conveniently held before the feast of St. John the Baptist then next (24th June). (2) Concerning the persons who are to come to Parliament. Answer—Two bishops, two abbots, two earls, two barons, and two for the *communitas*, one from this side of the Forth and one from beyond the Forth, to be elected by the *communitas* of Scotland at their assembly. (3) Concerning the persons who are to remain in Scotland for the defence of the same. Answer—The ' custodes ' and officers of the king, together with the *communitas*, will be sufficient to defend the said land.

" The premises being read before the king and Council, the king replies to the following effect : (1) The king agrees that the Parliament of Scotland shall be held in three weeks from St. John the Baptist, viz. 15th July. (2) That it shall be held in London. (3) And that the ten, to be elected by the whole *communitas* as before mentioned, shall come to the Parliament for the whole *communitas* of the land of Scotland. (4) And as to the defence of Scotland, let the same be entrusted to the ' custodes ' [2] and ministers of the king, and to the *com-munitas* of Scotland, *in such manner as the Bishop of Glasgow, the Earl of Carrick, and John de Moubray shall consent and ordain.*" (The italics are mine.) The memorandum is dated 26th March 1305, and a further memorandum records that the assembly at Perth was to

---

[1] *Parliamentary Writs*, and *Memoranda de Parliamento*, 1305, p. xlix.
[2] The "custodes" were John de Segrave "on this side Forth"; John Earl of Athol "beyond the Forth"; and William Earl of Ross "beyond the Spey."—Bain, ii. 1669.

be held on 28th May,[1] and the Parliament at London on 15th July. The Parliament was afterwards prorogued to 15th August, and finally to 15th September.[2]

The memorandum speaks for itself. It shows Bruce one of Edward's right-hand men in regard to the affairs of Scotland, it shows him being consulted on important and delicate matters regarding that kingdom, it shows him charged with the delicate task of assembling the whole *communitas* of Scotland and conducting an election of Scottish representatives to a Parliament in London for the settlement of the government of Scotland, and, finally, it shows him entrusted with the supremely important matter of providing for the defence of Scotland. Nor is that all. In that same month of March Bruce petitioned Edward to give him the lands forfeited by Sir Ingelram de Umfraville in Carrick, and the request was granted.[3] Shortly thereafter he set out for Scotland, and in due course the *communitas* of the kingdom met at Perth on or about 28th May.[4] Soon after the assembly at Perth Wallace was captured, was hurried to London, and was there executed on 23rd August. A few weeks later the Ordinance for the government of Scotland was framed, and the name of Bruce, of the man that is who only a few short months before had been one of Edward's right-hand men in regard to the affairs of Scotland, is conspicuous by its absence from the list of those to whom the affairs of that country are now entrusted. More than that, his name, on the one occasion on which it is mentioned in the Ordinance, is mentioned in a way which suggests very strongly that he no longer enjoyed the confidence of the English king, or was at least regarded with suspicion by him or his principal advisers.

So much for the Ordinance, but what may perhaps be regarded as the indirect evidence of the Ordinance does not stand by itself. It is confirmed by three other facts which admit of no dispute. In March 1305 Bruce,

---

[1] *Parliamentary Writs*, 1, Chron. Abstract, p. 66.
[2] *Ibid.*, p. 67.   [3] Bain, ii. 1657, 1658.   [4] *Ibid.*, p. 1619.

as we saw, asked for and obtained Sir Ingelram de Umfraville's lands in Carrick. On 10th October of the same year Edward ordered all de Umfraville's lands to be restored to him with the exception only of certain in the possession of Henry de Percy,[1] "to which Ingelram de Umfraville asserts hereditary right," and which "are not to be disturbed, but Ingelram may sue at law if he pleases." But there is no exception in favour of Bruce for the lands of de Umfraville conferred on him only six months before.

The second fact is of much more serious import; and it is significant of the extraordinary confusion of mind which exists among the traducers of Bruce that it is actually cited as the final proof alike of his iniquities and of the confidence and affection with which he was regarded by Edward down to the very eve of the slaughter of the Red Comyn. As one of them puts it,[2] "there exists one piece of evidence to show that de Brus stood high in Edward's favour up to the very eve of his crime, namely that on 8th February 1306 the king directed that the scutage due by de Brus, on succeeding to his father's English estates, should be remitted." This means that the writer, and others following him, have misread the document in question, and have completely misunderstood a very simple matter.

One would imagine from the passage quoted that scutage was a fine or casualty due by an heir on succession to his estates. It was, however, nothing of the sort. Far back in Anglo-Saxon times the warrior who failed to follow his king to the field had to pay a fine. In the twelfth century the custom was revived, but, as Bishop Stubbs says,[3] "instead of being a punishment it was now regarded as a privilege; those tenants of the Crown who did not choose to go to war, paid a tax of two marks for the knight's fee." It was in fact a commutation of the feudal duty of military service, and its original purpose was on the one hand to enable

---

[1] Bain, ii. 1696.　　　[2] Maxwell's *Bruce*, p. 128.
[3] *Constitutional History*, ii. 516.

a knight to avoid going on military service against his will, and on the other to provide the king with the means of obtaining a warrior in his place. In time scutage became a favourite device of the king for raising money, but by the beginning of Edward I's reign it had, as a tax, ceased to be remunerative, and was in consequence seldom resorted to. "The few taxes of the kind raised by Edward I," says Stubbs, " seem to have been collected almost as an afterthought, or by a recurrence to the old idea of scutage as commutation for military service. The scutage for the Welsh war of 1282, for instance, appears in the accounts of 1288, and the scutage of the twenty-eighth, thirty-first, and thirty-fourth years of the reign appear so late in the reign of Edward II as seem nothing better than a lame expedient for pecuniary exaction."

With that authoritative statement before us let us examine the alleged "remission" to Bruce which is regarded as so signal a sign of Edward's favour. "The king to the Treasurer and Barons of Exchequer," it runs. "As the late Robert de Brus, formerly Earl of Carrick, had his service with the king's army in Wales in the fifth and tenth years for one knight, as appears by inspection of the rolls of the marshalcy, he commands them to discharge Robert de Brus, his son and heir, of the scutage." [1] That is to say, Edward, in 1305, attempted to extort from Bruce a sum of money alleged to have become due by his late father for non-appearance in the Welsh wars of 1277 and 1282, and that though on 17th June 1304 Edward himself had commanded that "diligent search" should be made "for all debts due by Robert de Brus, Earl of Carrick, or his ancestors, and meanwhile that all these be respited!" [2] It was proved, by inspection of the rolls, that Bruce's father had fulfilled his service in these wars, and that accordingly no scutage was due. Edward in consequence was compelled to abandon this "lame expedient for pecuniary exaction" from Bruce, an expedient which, looking to

[1] Bain, ii. 1743.   [2] *Ibid.*, 1548.

the time which had elapsed since the date of the incurring of the alleged debts, namely twenty-nine years in the one case and twenty-four in the other, was in any event peculiarly mean and oppressive. Will anyone now venture to suggest that the abandonment of the claim was either a " remission " to Bruce, or a mark of Edward's regard for him ?

The third fact, when read in the light of all that has gone before, is the most significant of all. By the Ordinance Edward had appointed his nephew, John of Brittany the younger, to be guardian of Scotland, but as he was not able to proceed immediately to take up his duties, Edward, on 26th October 1305, wrote to the Bishop of St. Andrews, John de Sandale, Chamberlain of Scotland, Robert de Keith, and John de Kingston, informing them of the fact and committing the custody of the kingdom to them until the first Sunday in Lent 1306,[1] at which time John de Brittany would arrive. At the same time he commanded " the bishops, abbots, priors, earls, barons, and all the bailies and faithful men of the king in Scotland, and the whole community of the said land," to obey " the said Bishop, John, Robert, and John, or any two of them, in all things." [2] Six months before, as we have seen, Bruce had been one of the three men to whom the custody and defence of the kingdom had been committed. Now he is passed over for Sir Robert Keith and Sir John Kingston, just as a few weeks earlier he had been passed over in the Ordinance for the settlement of Scotland.

We are now in a position to sum up the facts regarding Bruce during the year which witnessed the capture and execution of Wallace. In the first half of that year we see him high in the councils of Edward, enjoying, apparently, the confidence of the English king, being consulted on the affairs of Scotland and entrusted with matters of delicacy and importance in regard to that kingdom, and asking for and receiving the lands in Carrick of Sir Ingelram de Umfraville. This condition

---

[1] Foedera. [2] *Ibid.*

of things lasted down until at least the end of June 1305. Less than three months thereafter we find him fallen from favour, his name omitted from the names of those appointed to manage the affairs of Scotland, and his loyalty evidently regarded with suspicion. A week or two later we find Edward restoring to Sir Ingelram de Umfraville his lands in Scotland, including apparently those which had been conferred on Bruce six months previously; and about the same time, or very soon thereafter, we find proceedings being instituted by Edward against Bruce for doubtful debts alleged to have become due by his father twenty-four and twenty-nine years before. Finally, on 26th October we find four men being appointed temporary guardians of Scotland, a position which Bruce had lately held, and he not numbered among the four. Accordingly between the first six or seven months of 1305 and the last few months there is in Bruce's career a great gulf fixed. Can any reasonable doubt remain that that gulf was caused by the capture, the mock trial, and the cruel death of William Wallace —the man who had fought manfully and with singleness of purpose for his country's freedom, the man who had never bowed his knee to Edward or owned him as king, the man who had been, on occasion, to some extent at least, an associate of Bruce, and the man on whose powerful assistance Bruce was doubtless counting when the time should come for him to strike that blow for the independence of Scotland to which he had long been committed, and of which intention Wallace was almost certainly cognisant?

This last point is, of course, to a considerable extent conjectural. But it is based on the following facts. When Wallace was captured a number of documents was found upon him. These have not survived, but an inventory of them is in existence, from which we learn that they included "confederations and ordinances made between Wallace and the magnates of Scotland." It is possible that one of these confederations may have incriminated Bruce, or at least cast suspicion upon him, may indeed have been an agreement somewhat similar to that between Lamberton and Bruce. The latter, it will be remembered, was entered into on 11th June 1304, and Lamberton, as we have seen, was the tried and proven friend of Wallace. There is no evidence of any friendship or close association between Wallace and Bruce, but they must have met in 1297 in the early days of the rising, when Wallace's colleague, Sir William Douglas, was certainly with Bruce. In 1298 they may have been acting together, though Bruce, as we saw, was not with Wallace during the campaign which ended at Falkirk, he being then in Ayrshire and the west at the head of a separate force. Thereafter, as one of the guardians of Scotland from 1298 to 1301, Bruce must certainly have had dealings of some kind with Wallace and been associated with him to some extent. But these associations were never close, as all the facts we have elucidated show; and as long as Wallace was acting in the name or on behalf of Balliol they never could be close.

With the collapse of the Comyns early in 1304, however, the whole situation changed. Before then Wallace had probably realised, as Sir James Ramsay suggests, that to fight longer in the name of Balliol was hopeless, for Balliol " had proved a failure, and in fact had become a stumbling-block." [1] At all events that is certainly true of the situation as it must have presented itself to those who were still fighting or plotting in 1304 for the freedom of Scotland, as the agreement between Lamberton and Bruce indicates. Accordingly, it is difficult to avoid the conclusion that when that agreement was signed Bruce had in contemplation not only the obtaining of the support of the Church, but also the rallying to his side of Wallace and the great force of popular opinion which he represented. I go further and suggest that, in entering into his bond with Lamberton, Wallace's friend and ally, Bruce was in fact also entering into an alliance with Wallace; and that, whether any

[1] *Dawn of Constitution*, p. 497.

sort of agreement in writing ever existed between Bruce and Wallace or not, it was quite well understood that when the time came Wallace's influence would be cast into the scale on the side of Bruce. That conclusion is not, of course, absolutely proved, but many an historical conclusion has been arrived at and accepted on worse evidence. But be that as it may, there cannot be any doubt that the marked contrast in the relations of Bruce and Edward I in the first half of 1305 and the later months of that year was connected with the capture and execution of Wallace, to neither of which was Bruce in any sense a party, to the latter of which indeed he may have been actively opposed, and either of which was undoubtedly a severe blow to the cause which he had at heart and to which he was so deeply committed.

CHAPTER XVI

THE SLAYING OF THE RED COMYN

THERE remains now only one point to consider before we come to the slaying of the Red Comyn. We saw that in March 1305 Bruce was present at Edward's Parliament at Westminster, and that very soon thereafter he set out for Scotland in order to make arrangements for the holding of the assembly at Perth on 28th May. In view of the repeated assertions that later in the year Bruce was again in London, it will be well to inquire if there is any evidence to support this view. The only authority I have seen cited for such a belief is by Sir James Ramsay in his erudite and painstaking *Dawn of the Constitution*. He there states (p. 499) that, after the Ordinance for the government of Scotland had been framed and approved by the king, "the affair closed with performance of homage on acceptance of office by the Scottish councillors, including the Bishops of St. Andrews, Dunkeld, Aberdeen, and Ross, and the earls, John of Strathbogie, Earl of Athol, and Robert Bruce, Earl of Carrick."

The authorities he cites in support of this statement are Foedera, I. 974, and Matthew of Westminster, III. 125. In neither of these authorities, however, is the name of either the Earl of Athol or the Earl of Carrick to be found! Matthew of Westminster, who describes the homage, says that the Scottish councillors, whom he describes as two bishops, two abbots, two earls, and other barons took the oath, but mentions no names, while there is no document of any kind in Foedera in which the name of either Athol or Bruce appears at this time. The two earls elected to the September Parliament were Buchan and March, but March not appearing owing to illness, Edward himself appointed Sir John Menteith, Wallace's betrayer, to act in his place. In Matthew of Westminster's narrative it is the ten elected commissioners who take the oath, and the two earls he has in mind are the two whom he supposed to be among the commissioners.

The Foedera reference is clearly a slip, and is due probably to the short document already quoted, in which the Scots are commanded to render obedience "to the aforesaid Bishop, John, Robert, and John," this referring back to the other document of the same date, in which their names are fully set forth, viz. the Bishop of St. Andrews, John de Sandale, Robert de Keith, and John de Kingston. But only a few months earlier John, Earl of Athol, and Robert, Earl of Carrick, were among the guardians of Scotland, which probably explains how Sir James Ramsay fell into this error when he glanced at the document of 26th October, in which only the Christian names of the four temporary guardians are mentioned.

This brings us to the final piece of evidence in regard to Bruce's whereabouts in the latter half of 1305. In the memorandum of 26th March 1305, the Bishop of Glasgow, Bruce, and de Moubray replied to Edward's question as to "who should remain in Scotland for the defence of the same," that is to say during the summer and autumn of 1305, that "the 'custodes' and officers of the king, together with the *communitas*, will be sufficient to defend the said land," the "custodes" being John de Segrave "on this side the Forth"; John Earl of Athol "beyond the Forth"; and William Earl of Ross "beyond the Spey." Edward's reply to the suggestion was, "As to the defence of Scotland, let the same be entrusted to the 'custodes' and the ministers of the king, and to the *communitas* of Scotland, *in such way as the Bishop of Glasgow, the Earl of Carrick, and John de Moubray, shall consent and ordain.*" (The italics are mine.)

This at once disposes of the probability of the Earl

of Athol having been in London in the autumn of 1305.
As one of the " custodes " he would, of course, remain in
Scotland " for the defence of the same." As to Bruce,
John de Moubray was the only one of Edward's three
Scottish lieutenants elected to the September Parliament,
and it is therefore in the highest degree unlikely that
either Bruce or the Bishop of Glasgow left Scotland in
the summer or autumn of 1305. In pursuance of their
instructions, they would remain to provide for the defence of the kingdom according to the very full powers
conferred upon them ; and it seems to me not very wide
of the mark to suggest that they would be the more
eager to do so as these powers gave them an unexpected
and an unrivalled opportunity for laying their plans
against that day of reckoning with England which was
never far from their minds. It may even be that therein
lies the true explanation of the absence of their names
from those of the representatives elected to Edward's
Parliament by the *communitas* of Scotland at Perth, and
also of the choice of Sir John de Moubray as one of
these representatives, he being a relation and strong
partisan of the Comyns. It would be a simple matter
for Bruce and the Bishop to declare their inability to go
to Edward's Parliament, and so to arrange matters that
de Moubray should be chosen. These, however, are
matters of speculation, but the fact nevertheless remains
that when, little more than six months later, Bruce's
sudden act of violent passion led to a premature attempt
to carry out his deep-laid schemes, his whole subsequent
course of action showed that he and the Bishops of
Glasgow and St. Andrews and others of his friends were
acting in accordance with plans which had been considered long and carefully. But whether these plans
were matured in the summer and autumn of 1305 or
not, it is at all events clear that not a particle of
evidence of any kind exists to support the suggestion
that Bruce was in London in the latter half of 1305,
while on the other hand every fact we possess indicates
that after his departure from London in April 1305

he never again set foot on English soil save as an open foe.

The tale of the slaying of the Red Comyn is so well known that we need not repeat it here, though we shall have to glance at an English version of it presently. Meanwhile it is enough to say that in the fourteenth century many versions of the story were current, as Barbour himself tells us, but in general details they all agree. The differences, as we should expect, depend on the sympathies of the writers, the English versions having it that the murder was premeditated, while the Scottish versions agree in attributing Comyn's death to a violent outburst of sudden passion on Bruce's part, when it became clear to him that Comyn had betrayed or intended to betray him.

In view of all we have elucidated regarding the relations of the Comyns and the Bruces during the preceding twenty years, it is clear that the Scottish versions are right in so far as they say that the slaying of the Red Comyn was not premeditated, but was due to a sudden and violent quarrel. But whether Comyn had actually betrayed Bruce, or even threatened to betray him, is quite another question. In all probability, however, the tale of treachery owed its origin to a later generation, anxious to find what they thought a fitting excuse for the quarrel and its fatal result. But to us, with all the story of the preceding twenty years before us, it is evident that the long and bitter rivalry of the Houses of Bruce and Comyn is sufficient in itself to account for the quarrel ; and when we remember that in 1299 the relations of Bruce and the Red Comyn were such that Comyn took Bruce by the throat at a Council of the Scottish leaders, it is hardly surprising that in 1306, when that rivalry had become greatly intensified, they should have come to blows at a meeting which was held for the express purpose of trying to come to some arrangement regarding the thorny problem of the future of the Scottish Crown.

In order that we may see on what flimsy grounds the idea of premeditation rests, however, it may be well to glance at Sir Thomas Gray's version of the story—the most circumstantial version on the English side. He tells it thus :

" At this same time Robert de Brus, Earl of Carrick, who retained a strong following through kinsmanship and alliance, always hoping for the establishment of his claim of succession to the realm of Scotland, on the 4th of the kalends of February in the year of grace 1306 sent his two brothers, Thomas and Neil, from Lochmaben to Dalswinton to John Comyn, begging that he would meet him (Robert) at Dumfries at the Minorite Friars, so that they might have a conversation. Now he had plotted with his two brothers aforesaid that they should kill the said John Comyn on the way. But they were received in such a friendly manner by the said John Comyn that they could not bring themselves to do him any harm, but agreed between themselves that their brother himself might do his best. The said John Comyn, suspecting no ill, set out with the two brothers of the said Robert de Brus in order to speak with him (Robert) at Dumfries, went to the Friars (Church) where he found the said Robert, who came to meet him and led him to the high altar. The two brothers of the said Robert told him secretly : ' Sir,' they said, ' he gave us such a fair reception, and with such generous gifts, and won upon us so much by his frankness, that we could by no means do him an injury.' ' See,' quoth he, ' you are right lazy ; let me settle with him.'

" He took the said John Comyn, and they approached the altar.

" ' Sir,' then spoke the said Robert de Brus to the said John Comyn, ' this land of Scotland is entirely laid in bondage to the English, through the indolence of that chieftain who suffered his right and the franchise of the realm to be lost. Choose one of two ways, either take my estates and help me to be king, or give me yours and I will help you to be the same, because you are of his blood who lost it, for I have the hope of succession through my ancestors who claimed the right and were supplanted by yours; for now is the old age of this English king.'

"'Certes,' then quoth the said John Comyn, 'I shall never be false to my English seigneur, forasmuch as I am bound to him by oath and homage, in a matter which might be charged against me as treason.'

"'No?' exclaimed the said Robert de Brus; 'I had different hopes of you, by the promise of yourself and your friends. You have betrayed me to the king in your letters, wherefore living thou canst not escape my will—thou shalt have thy guerdon!'

"So saying, he struck him with his dagger, and the others cut him down in the middle of the church before the altar. A knight, his (Comyn's) uncle, who was present, struck the said Robert de Brus with a sword in the breast, but he (Bruce) being in armour, was not wounded, which uncle was slain straightway."

The manifold absurdities in this story hardly require to be pointed out. It contains an account of a plot for the murder of Comyn, to which only Bruce and his brothers were privy; it reports a conversation of the most secret kind between Bruce and his brothers; and it represents John Comyn as too high-minded to dream of breaking his oath of allegiance to Edward. It is sufficient to say that Bruce and his brothers must have been very extraordinary people if they babbled of plots and conversations of such a nature—for the benefit of the English chroniclers apparently! As for the rest, it is plain that the English version, like the Scottish, simply sought to put the best gloss it could upon the story from its own point of view.

We may therefore sum up the whole matter by observing that the quarrel, with its fatal termination, was simply the climax to all that had passed between the Bruces and the Comyns during the previous twenty years, and that the mere fact that it occurred when it did is sufficient to prove that it was unpremeditated. The last thing Bruce could have desired was to precipitate the crisis at that moment. For Edward yet lived,

and the time was, therefore, not yet ripe for the revolt
which Bruce and his friends were planning.

Now that we have brought Bruce to the parting of
the ways it may be well to re-state briefly the main facts
which we have elucidated regarding himself, his father,
and his grandfather.   These are as follows:

1239.   Bruce the Competitor recognised as heir to
Alexander II.

1274.   Birth of Robert Bruce the future king.

1286.   *March* 19.   Death of Alexander III.

September.   Bruce the Competitor takes up
arms in support of his claim to the Crown,
and enters into a bond at Turnberry with
his principal supporters.

1290.   *September.*   Death of the Maid of Norway.

October 1.   Bruce the Competitor again takes up
arms in support of his claim to the Crown.

October 7.   Fraser, Bishop of St. Andrews,
appeals to Edward, and recommends John
Balliol as one whom Edward can trust.

November or *December.*   Bruce and the Seven
Earls also appeal to Edward.

1291.   *May* 10.   The Scottish magnates meet Edward
at Norham.

June 2.   The competitors acknowledge Edward
as overlord.

1292.   *November* 5.   Edward informs Bruce the Competitor that his claim has failed.   Bruce the
Competitor resigns to his son Robert Bruce,
the elder, all his claims to the kingdom of
Scotland.

November 17.   Edward awards Balliol the Crown.

November or *December.*   Bruce, the elder, refuses
to do homage to Balliol, makes over his
earldom of Carrick to his son, the future
king, and retires to England.

1293.   Bruce the elder's daughter marries the king of
Norway.

1295. *March.* Death of Bruce the Competitor.

October. Bruce, the elder, appointed Governor of Carlisle.

October. Balliol repudiates his allegiance to Edward.

October. Lands of the Bruces forfeited by Balliol and conferred on John Comyn, Earl of Buchan.

December. Edward prepares for invasion of Scotland.

1296. *March.* Bruce, the elder, and Bruce, the future king, accompany Edward towards Scotland, and renew their homage to him.

March 26. The Scots invade England.

March 28. Edward I invades Scotland.

March 30. Sack of Berwick.

May 14. The Bruces commissioned by Edward proceed to Annandale and Carrick and receive their own vassals and the men of the adjacent parts to Edward's peace.

October 15. Bruce thanked for his services by Edward, and his debts to the Exchequer postponed.

1297. *April* and *May.* General uprising in Scotland.

May. Bruce, the future king, joins the rising.

July 7. Bruce, the Bishop of Glasgow, Sir William Douglas, and others capitulate at Irvine.

August 5. Conditions of Irvine capitulation not yet fulfilled by Bruce.

September 11. Battle of Stirling Bridge.

October 13. The elder Bruce deprived of the governorship of Carlisle.

November 14. Bruce, the future king, not yet come to Edward's peace.

November and *December.* The Scots invade the North of England.

November and *December.* Sir Robert de Clifford ravages Bruce's lands of Annandale.

1298. *February*. De Clifford again ravages Bruce's lands of Annandale and burns the town of Annan.

June 4. Bruce's goods in Essex distrained, the postponement of his debts granted in October 1296 being thus revoked.

July 3. Edward invades Scotland.

July 21. Bruce in command of Scottish army in Ayr and the west.

July 22. Battle of Falkirk.

August. Edward marches against Bruce. Bruce retires to Carrick.

August 26. Edward reaches Ayr.

September 4. Edward captures Bruce's castle of Lochmaben.

September 6. Edward re-enters England.

December 2. Bruce on record as joint Guardian of Scotland with John Comyn the younger of Badenoch.

About *December*. Ambassadors sent to the king of France.

1299. *April 6.* King of France sends letter to Bruce and Comyn the guardians by the hand of Bishop Lamberton.

August 12. Meeting in Selkirk Forest, at which Lamberton added to Bruce and Comyn in the guardianship. Quarrel regarding Wallace's lands, and John Comyn seizes Bruce by the throat.

About *August 20.* Bruce invades Galloway and attacks Lochmaben Castle, which is held by an English garrison.

November. Bruce, Comyn, and Lamberton engage in the siege of Stirling Castle.

November 13. Bruce, Comyn, and Lamberton write Edward offering to accept the mediation of the king of France.

1300. *July.* Edward invades Scotland, captures Caerlaverock, and eventually agrees to a truce till May 21, 1301.

1301. *July.* Edward again invades Scotland, and remains there during the winter of 1301-2.

November. Negotiations between France and
England for truce which shall include Scots.

December 25. French king signs truce, which
includes Scots, till November 30, 1302.

1302. *January* 26. Edward ratifies truce with French
and Scots till November 30, 1302.

February 16. Edward pardons a murderer at
the request of Bruce.

April 28. Bruce comes to Edward's peace.

1303 and 1304. Bruce assists Edward during his invasion of Scotland and the siege of Stirling
Castle.

1304. *February.* The Comyns surrender to Edward.

June 11. Bruce and Lamberton enter into a
secret bond against all men.

June 17. Debts due by Bruce's ancestors to
English Exchequer respited.

1305. *March.* Bruce attends Parliament at Westminster and asks for and receives de Umfraville's lands in Carrick.

Bruce consulted by Edward as to how Scotland should be represented at a Parliament
to be held later in the year.

April. Bruce, charged along with the Bishop
of Glasgow and John de Moubray to carry
through the election of Scottish representatives to a Parliament in Westminster, and
entrusted, along with them, with the defence
of Scotland, departs for Scotland.

May 28. Meeting at Perth, at which representatives elected.

July. Wallace captured.

August 23. Wallace executed.

September 15. Parliament to settle affairs of
Scotland meets in Westminster. Bruce not
a member.

October. Ordinance promulgated for govern-

ment of Scotland. Bruce given no share in
the government, but ordered to place Kildrummy Castle in charge of a man for whom
he shall answer.

October 10. De Umfraville's lands restored to
him, including those bestowed on Bruce six
months before.

October 26. The custody of Scotland committed
to the Bishop of St. Andrews, John de
Sandale, Robert Keith, and John Kingston.
Bruce omitted, though six months before he
had been one of three to whom the custody
of Scotland was committed.

1305–6. *December–January.* Edward tries to extort
from Bruce debts alleged to have become
due by his father more than twenty years
before; he fails in the attempt, the debts
never having been in existence.

1306. *February* 10. Bruce slays the Red Comyn.

Any intelligent reading of that record must make
clear that after the award of the Crown to Balliol there
was a deep and bitter feud between the Bruces on the one
hand and the Balliols and the Comyns on the other;
that on the very first opportunity after the deposition of
Balliol, Bruce, the future king, threw in his lot with the
Scots; that from that date—May 1297—until the
beginning of 1302 he took a leading part in the resistance
of the Scots to England; that in February 1302, a long
truce between Scotland and England having been just
entered into, he made his peace with Edward, the old
feud between himself and the Comyns having come to a
head once more; that on the renewal of the war he fought
on the side of England until the downfall of the Comyns
was complete; that immediately thereafter he began to
plot with Lamberton to gain the Crown of Scotland for
himself; that nevertheless he remained high in the
confidence of Edward till shortly before the capture of
Wallace; and that from and after the capture of Wallace

he was regarded by Edward with ever-growing distrust and treated by him with signal and repeated marks of suspicion and disfavour. The picture thus disclosed may not be a picture of the ideal patriot hero of legend and romance, but it is a picture of a very human man who possessed more than his share of the virtues of his day and generation, and is a picture very far removed from the mendacious caricatures which represent Robert the Bruce as a shifty, sordid, selfish schemer, a traitor to his comrade and his country.

CHAPTER XVII

THE NORTH FROM 1297–1304.

It is now necessary for us to retrace our steps a little in order to examine the position in Scotland north of the Forth and Clyde [1] during the eight years which followed the battle of Stirling Bridge, namely the years from 1297 to 1305. On the death of Alexander III in 1286 six guardians [2] were appointed to govern the kingdom during the minority of the Maid of Norway, three being chosen to represent the country north of Forth and three the country south of Forth, a fact which is sufficient in itself to demonstrate that the north was regarded as every whit as important in the polity of the kingdom as the south. A glance at the names of the guardians suggests, however, that the north was the more important district, the guardians from beyond the Forth being William Fraser, Bishop of St. Andrews, Duncan, Earl of Fife, and Alexander Comyn, Earl of Buchan, [3] while the guardians from the south were Robert Wishart, Bishop of Glasgow, John Comyn of Badenoch, and James the Steward. [4] That is to say one of the southern guardians belonged to Scotland north of the Forth, where the bulk of his possessions lay and whence he took his territorial title. The Comyns, of course, had lands in Galloway, but there is no getting away from the fact that John

---

[1] In order to avoid confusion it may be well to state again that the expression " Scotland north of the Forth and Clyde " is used throughout to mean roughly Scotland north of a line drawn from a little north of Renfrew on the Clyde to Bo'ness on the Forth, including the portions of Argyll and Kintyre which geographically are south of the Firth of Clyde, that is to say all Scotland to the north of Antonine's Wall. See Introduction.

[2] Fordun.   [3] *Ibid.*   [4] *Ibid.*

Comyn of Badenoch was essentially a Highland magnate. It is also a significant fact that not one of the guardians had any connection with Lothian. They were all representative of Celtic Scotland.

The John Comyn who was one of the guardians in 1286 is not the same as the John Comyn who was Bruce's colleague in the guardianship from 1298 to 1301, who thereafter was the principal guardian till 1304, and who was slain by Bruce in February 1306. The latter was "the Red Comyn," or John Comyn the younger as he is termed in the documents of the period. The former was the Red Comyn's father, and was known to his contemporaries as "the Black Comyn." He it was who married John Balliol's sister Alianora, and their son, the Red Comyn, thus came to represent the claims of the House of Balliol after the deposition and exile of John Balliol.[1] We have seen how ardently the Red Comyn upheld these claims, and how from 1298 to 1304 he led the Scottish armies in the field against Edward.

Now I invite attention to the following facts: (1) From and after August 1299 two out of three guardians, the Red Comyn and the Bishop of St. Andrews, represented Scotland north of the Forth. (2) During the campaigns of 1300, 1301, 1302–3, and 1303–4, the Scottish armies in the field were commanded chiefly by the Red Comyn himself, or by his kinsman the Earl of Buchan, or by both. (3) The strength of the Comyn following lay in Scotland north of the Forth, where between them the Earl of Buchan and John Comyn of Badenoch ruled the whole vast and warlike district from Buchan to Lochaber. (4) From 1301 to 1304 the resistance of Scotland was almost entirely due to the two Comyns and the Bishop of St. Andrews. (5) During Edward's great invasion of 1303–4 all the resistance with which he met was in Scotland beyond the Forth,[2] with

---

[1] B. P., vols. i. and ii., under "Badenoch" and "Buchan," and various entries in Bain, &c.

[2] Bain, ii.   Various entries.

the single exception of Stirling Castle. (6) In Scotland beyond the Forth the Comyns made their last stand, and in Scotland beyond the Forth resistance to England continued long after it had ceased elsewhere, as we shall see presently.

When these facts are read in the light of all that has gone before, and especially in the light of Andrew de Moray's campaign and all that followed thereon, their significance is apparent. In the old Celtic kingdom of Scotland, Scotland beyond the Forth and Clyde, lay the real hostility to English domination and the real strength of the resistance to England. The same hostility was present, though to a lesser degree, in Celtic Scotland to the south of the Clyde, that Celtic west which included roughly the whole west country from Clyde to Solway ; and thence, too, the resistance to England derived a considerable part of its strength. But what of Saxon Lothian ? During all the years from 1297 to 1304 once, and once only, does it appear on the page which tells the tale of the Scots' struggle for freedom, and that is in 1303 when a Scottish army, under the command of John Comyn of Badenoch and Simon Fraser of Oliver Castle in Peebles, made a forced march by night from Biggar—which is not in Lothian—and surprised and routed an English army at Roslin. Lothian, in fact, played no part whatsoever in the resistance to England from 1297 to 1304, an attitude which, as we shall afterwards see, she maintained during the struggle from 1306 to 1314.

From September 1297 until June 1303 Scotland north of the Forth was almost entirely free of the English, the only mention of the presence of any of them in all that district during these years being in 1300, when, in a draft of the truce concluded in October of that year, it is stated : [1] " As to the towns of St. John (Perth), Dundee, Ayr, Banff, they must keep themselves by truce, and as best they can, till Pentecost next." As these names occur in a part of the document headed " The Order for the Scots' War," and as all the places held by England are

[1] Bain, ii. 1164.

mentioned specifically, it is clear that in all Scotland north
of the Forth, only Perth, Dundee, and Banff were in
English hands, and that they were very precariously held.
It is strange, indeed, to find them occupied by the English
at all, and the explanation probably is that they had been
captured during successful English raids.   The terms in
which they are referred to, moreover, seems to indicate
that their captors had little hope of holding them for
any length of time just then.   The year 1300 had witnessed an invasion of Scotland by Edward himself, and
though he did not penetrate as far as Perth, the castles
of Edinburgh, Linlithgow, Stirling, Kirkintilloch, Selkirk,
and Bothwell were, among others further south, at that
time in his hands, and Perth probably fell as the result of
a raid from one of these places, or was taken by a force
landed from the English fleet.   During "the Scottish
war" the English fleet was always in evidence, especially
on the east coast, and there can be little doubt that
Dundee and Banff owed their temporary capture in 1300
to this cause.   But neither Perth nor Dundee remained
long in English hands, and it is not likely that Banff was
any exception.   It is worth noting, however, that Banff
Castle seems at that period to have been peculiarly accessible by sea, for, as we shall see, in 1309 at a time when
the whole northern district—including the sheriffdom of
Banff itself and the very sheriff who had been appointed by
Edward in 1305—was enthusiastically on the side of
Bruce, the castle was still held by an English garrison,
and was receiving supplies from English ships.

In 1303 Edward determined on a supreme effort to
bring the resistance of Scotland to an end, and early in
May crossed the border[1] at the head of a strong and
well-equipped army, with the intention of marching
through the kingdom and reducing it everywhere to his
obedience.   That intention he succeeded in carrying out
to a very large extent, the Scots being able to offer little
effective resistance, though Sir Thomas Maule boldly
held the castle of Brechin against the invaders until he

[1] Itinerary.

was killed on the castle wall, and Stirling Castle defied all the might of England during a siege of three months. Edward's route was by way of Edinburgh, Perth, Aberdeen, Banff, and Elgin to Kinloss and Lochindorb,[1] his forces penetrating still further north, and on his return south Comyn, the guardian of Scotland, came in and made peace with him at Strathord on 9th February 1304. Only the castle of Stirling seems then to have remained as a visible sign that his conquest of Scotland was not complete. Before its walls, accordingly, Edward sat down on 22nd April, expecting doubtless a speedy surrender. But for three months the heroic garrison, under their gallant constable, Sir William Oliphant, defied him, and it was not until 20th July that he succeeded in reducing the last strong place remaining in the hands of the Scots.[2] Well might he now think that the subjection of Scotland was complete.

Scotland, however, was by no means yet finally subdued. There were still unconquerable spirits who refused to bow the knee to England, and these maintained for many months a species of guerilla warfare. Chief among them was Sir William Wallace, with whom for a time was the gallant Sir Simon Fraser of Oliver Castle, while in the north the Bishop of Moray still refused to come to Edward's peace. Their resistance was gradually worn down, however, and with the capture of Wallace in July 1305, followed by his execution on 23rd August in the same year, the last hope of the independence of Scotland seemed at an end. But as the darkest hour is that before the dawn, so the darkest hour in Scotland's history was the forerunner of the dawn of Scotland's freedom. But before we pass to consider the great struggle which placed on Bruce's brow the Crown of a free Scotland, we must examine the part played by the north in the dark years of 1303, 1304, and 1305.

[1] Itinerary.
[2] See Bain for various entries relating to siege and capture of Stirling Castle.

Edward's stay in the province of Moray in the autumn of 1303 extended to exactly six weeks.[1] He reached Elgin on 10th September, and the period between then and 21st October he spent for the most part between Kinloss and Lochindorb. His armies he meanwhile sent far and wide, and either then or within a few months thereafter most of the northern castles fell into the hands of his men. Round the events of these months a considerable mass of legend and tradition has gathered, and, as it is well-nigh impossible to disentangle the true from the false, I shall do no more than mention very briefly one or two of the better-known episodes.

Chief among these is the heroic tale of the siege and capture of Urquhart Castle, and it is pleasing to be able to record that of all the northern stories relating to this period, it is the least open to objection. We may, indeed, go further and accept it as on the whole an accurate account of a real event, for though the authorities on which it rests—Holinshed and Boece—are not beyond reproach, yet the internal evidence goes far to prove that in this instance they have got hold of a genuine narrative. It is sufficient to say here that in making the gallant defender of the castle one Alexander de Bosco, they name a member of a family who at that time were prominent in the district, but who long before either Boece or Holinshed wrote had ceased to have any connection with Inverness-shire.[2]

I need hardly retell the story—how the brave garrison and their commander refused to surrender, how, when all their provisions were exhausted, they sent the wife of de Bosco in the guise of a poor woman through the English lines, and how, when she was in safety, the remnant of the defenders, scorning surrender, made a great effort to cut their way through the besiegers, and fell to a man.[3] On the face of it, there is nothing improbable in the story. The War of Independence witnessed many actions

---

[1] See numerous entries in Bain and in Itinerary.
[2] Bain, ii. 163. B. P., iv. 44, &c.
[3] Mackay's *Urquhart* and *Glenmoriston*.

just as heroic, and the very force which sat down before Urquhart had probably but a few months before formed part of the English army under Edward himself, to which Sir Thomas de Maule had offered such bold defiance at the castle of Brechin.

Other notable tales of this period are the alleged defence of a "stark strength" on the Beauly and the long siege of the castle of Cromarty. The former rests only on the authority of Blind Harry, and is therefore open to grave suspicion, though it may be said that the Stockford on the Beauly was a very likely place for the passage of an invading army to be disputed, and that on the north bank of the river there still exist the remains of a fortification which commanded the ford.

Sir Thomas Urquhart is the authority for the siege of the castle of Cromarty, and though he, too, is not over-trustworthy, Hugh Miller tells of traditions current in his boyhood which tend to confirm the story. More important than that, however, is the fact that Sir Thomas Urquhart attributes the defence of the castle quite correctly to Sir William de Monte Alto or Mohaut, who, we know, was at the time heritable Sheriff of Cromarty and Constable of the Castle.[1] The story goes that Sir William held the castle against the English for seven years, that Sir William Wallace himself attempted its relief, that the English suffered on one occasion severe defeat, and that eventually it fell into their hands. The seven years correspond to the period from the middle of 1297 to some time in 1304, during which period Sir William de Monte Alto undoubtedly held the castle for Scotland, but no siege took place till after Edward's arrival in the north in the autumn of 1303— how long after we do not know. For the rest the story of a sturdy defence and Wallace's attempt at rescue may be true, but there is no historic corroboration of it, and we must be content to leave it at that.

However much of truth is to be found in all these tales, one thing at least is clear, the north did not make

[1] Bain, ii. 1691 (3).

N

a speedy or a tame surrender to Edward. Moreover, as we shall presently see, it never was, even after Wallace's death, reduced to the condition of peacefulness, which a too casual reading of authorities has led some people to imagine. It is true that several of the northern knights and nobles came very quickly to Edward's peace. The Countess of Ross, the Chens, the Raits, and their like hastened to his feet, but others, with the Church and the "middling men," stood aloof, and it was only after resistance was gradually crushed that many of them accepted the inevitable. There remained even then, however, some who refused to bow the knee, and among the hills and the mountains they found refuge and support. The truth of this statement I shall now proceed to demonstrate.

In 1304 Edward flattered himself that he had brought Scotland completely under his sway. Only Sir William Wallace and Sir Simon Fraser and a few broken men remained defiant, and of these his officers would soon make an end. In truth, he had good reason for his confidence. Seven years of warfare had left Scotland exhausted and seemingly crushed. Her armies had vanished, her leaders had been compelled one by one to surrender, her castles and strong places were in Edward's hands. Far different was her situation now from that in which she had found herself in 1297. Then she was recovering from the disaster of Dunbar, but the spirit of her people had not been humbled. Now she was spent and broken with seven years of warfare, years marked by few successes and many miseries, and years which had ended in seemingly irretrievable ruin. When one reads the history of these years as a whole, the wonder is not that Scotland was reduced to submission in 1304 and 1305, but that she should ever have ventured to dare the wrath of Edward again.

So certain was Edward himself that Scotland was now finally crushed, that he determined to treat the country with more generosity than on previous occasions, and to endeavour to secure her allegiance by reposing confidence in her people. So it came about that the last echoes of the war had hardly died away before many of the men who had borne arms against England were holding high office for England in the very districts in which their greatest exploits against England had been wrought. Thus, Sir William de Monte Alto, the gallant defender of the castle of Cromarty, was in September 1305 Sheriff of Cromarty for England,[1] while early in 1304 Alexander Pilche, burgess of Inverness, companion and chief lieutenant of Andrew de Moray, was keeper of the castle of Inverness for Edward.[2] Nothing could demonstrate more clearly the supreme confidence of Edward, and the belief of patriotic Scotsmen that so long at least as he lived further resistance was impossible. So, like certain of the Boer leaders after the Boer War, they entered the service of their conqueror, and by so doing secured at least that in their districts their fellow-countrymen were under the local administration of men of their own race. So in the north in 1304 we have England nominally triumphant. The Earl of Ross, at liberty once more, was Edward's devoted liegeman and his guardian of all the territory beyond the banks of Spey;[3] the Earl of Sutherland had come to Edward's peace, and died a year or two later still faithful to his new lord;[4] Sir Reginald le Chen and Sir Andrew de Rait were again, as they had been before Stirling Bridge, Edward's trusted officers in the north[5]; to Sir Alexander Comyn were committed "two of the strongest castles in the country," viz. those of Urquhart and Tarradale[6]; and Alexander Pilche was keeper of the castle of Inverness. The north might, therefore, well seem to be entirely at Edward's will. But in spite of appearances this was far from being the case, as we shall now see.

[1] Bain, ii. 1691 (3).   [2] *Ibid.*, p. 438.   [3] *Ibid.*, p. 1669.
[4] *Ibid.*, p. 1494, and *The Sutherland Book.*
[5] See numerous entries in Bain.
[6] Bain, ii. 1633. Tarradale is probably Red Castle in Ross-shire.

CHAPTER XVIII

HOW THE ENGLISH FARED IN MORAY IN 1304

THE first inkling we get of the unrest beneath the surface in the north is contained in a petition by John, Earl of Athol, to the king, sometime in 1304.[1] In it he prays Edward to supersede his order to deliver the castle of Aboyne to Sir Alexander Comyn till he is better advised, "for the land around it is savage and full of evil-doers, and the king has no other fortress where the country or his servants may be in safety to keep the peace." As Aboyne Castle was on the borders of Mar, and was not far removed from the country of the Comyns and the earldom of Athol, this extract throws a vivid light on the condition of the Highlands even in the very neighbourhood of Edward's most powerful liegemen. Our information regarding the state of the north, however, happily does not rest on this reference alone. There is in existence a document which gives a striking account of the dangers which Edward's servants had to encounter in the execution of their duties, and from it an extremely suggestive idea of the real condition of things in the north can be gathered.

Between 25th April 1304 and 28th February 1305 two of Edward's "clerks," James de Dalileye and John Weston, were engaged in "making an extent of all the king's lands in Scotland, both beyond the Scottish Sea towards Orkneye and on this side in Galloway and elsewhere." The account of the ingatherings and the expenses of the undertaking has happily been preserved, and from it the following particulars are taken. The curious may read the document for themselves in

[1] Bain, ii. 1633.

196

Bain's *Calendar of Documents relating to Scotland*, vol. ii. pp. 438–44.

From the discharge side of the account we learn that the clerks entered on the really serious part of their journey on 1st May 1304, for on that day sixteen men-at-arms, that is mounted, armour-clad men, were told off to accompany them as an escort, "inasmuch as during the war and the impending siege of Stirling Castle, *while the men of the parts beyond the mountains, and in Galloway and Carrick, had not yet fully come to the king's peace*, without such safe escort they could noways have done the work."[1] (The italics are mine.) From 1st May till 25th December did these sixteen men-at-arms escort the clerks, and their expenses at twelvepence each per day are duly noted down as amounting to £191, 4s.

Accompanying them, moreover, and apparently in command of the escort, was Sir Andrew de Rait, who, for the period from 1st May to 31st December, received for himself and his esquire the sum of £27, 12s., his payment being at the rate of 3s. a day. Thus the clerks were guarded by eighteen well-armed and well-mounted men when, in May 1304, they set out on their northward journey.

That escort, however, was soon found to be insufficient. Early in May they came to Aberdeen, but though their route thence to Banff lay through the territories of powerful magnates who had come to Edward's peace, the country was so far from being peaceful that the escort was doubled, and, in addition to the eighteen mounted men, twenty foot soldiers accompanied the king's clerks to Banff and thence to Elgin.[2] At Elgin they were in the province of Moray, and the ensuing entries make it clear that the district which had supported Andrew de Moray so loyally was still hostile to England.

From Elgin to Inverness the route of the king's clerks lay through the very heart of the long-famous fighting province, where so little was the rule of England regarded that Edward's officers were only able to enter on

[1] Bain, ii. 443.   [2] *Ibid.*

the last stage of their northward journey under the protection of a strong force, composed both of men-at-arms and foot soldiers provided by Sir Reginald le Chen, in addition to the original escort of eighteen mounted men. The entry relating to them is singularly expressive, especially when it is remembered that it is the sober entry of the king's clerks themselves. "And expense of divers men," it runs, "both men-at-arms and foot, of Sir Reginald le Chen escorting them from Elgin to Inverness, and there staying with them *on account of the imminent peril of enemies;* and escorting them back to Elgin." [1]

At Inverness they found Alexander Pilche in charge of the castle, and from him they received, on 24th June, the sum of 45*s.* for the rents of the burgh, which sum they duly credit themselves with in their accounts. [2] But further than Inverness they did not go, though their account expressly bears that they were charged with "making an extent of all the king's lands in Scotland both beyond the Scottish Sea towards Orkneye, &c." [3] It is a fair conclusion, therefore, that the reports they received of the state of the country further north, coupled with their own experiences since they had crossed the Spey, caused them to decide that to pursue their journey further would be exceedingly inadvisable. They record, however, [4] that they paid the expenses of two burgesses "sent from Inverness to a town called Wick in Caithness to arrest a vessel freighted with wools and hides, which refused to pay the king's customs. But when they arrived," the entry proceeds, "the merchants escaped by force with the ship, leaving one on shore, who was captured and put under good bail by the custom of the country to answer to the king." It does not appear whether the two burgesses were sent to Wick before or after the arrival of the king's clerks in Inverness, but it must almost certainly have been before, as the clerks do not seem to have stayed in Inverness long enough for two

---

[1] Bain, ii. 443.
[2] *Ibid.*, p. 438.
[3] *Ibid.*
[4] *Ibid.*, p. 441.

men to have made the journey to Wick and back. But the entry is valuable, apart from its own innate interest, as showing that the safety of the inhabitants of the north was not in serious jeopardy in the spring and summer of 1304, a striking contrast to the dangers which lay in wait for the servants of the English king in the same district at the same time.

Towards the end of June the king's clerks, still strongly escorted, returned to Elgin, and there they remained for fourteen days. But even in Elgin they were not safe, for they record that for these fourteen days they had to pay "the expense of twenty foot watching nightly while said James and John were in the town of Elgin, *through fear of some enemies who had not yet come to the king's peace.*[1] When at last they set out for Banff, they were in such fear that, in addition to their original escort, they were accompanied by twenty foot and Sir Reginald le Chen's men,[2] and it was not until they had left the province of Moray far behind them that they began to breathe freely once more.

In order to complete the picture, I may say that from Banff to Aberdeen there is no mention of an extra escort, but that from Aberdeen to Kincardine they were accompanied by "twenty foot and five men-at-arms,[3] besides the Thane of Cowie and his men," which indicates the presence of danger in that district. From Kincardine to Glasgow their ordinary escort is sufficient, but when they leave Glasgow the additional escort makes its appearance again. From Glasgow to Dumbarton the extra escort consists of ten foot, from Dumbarton to Renfrew of ten foot and ten men-at-arms, from Renfrew to Ayr of five men-at-arms and twenty foot, from "the town of Ayr to the town of Wigtown in Galloway" of "ten men-at-arms, twenty foot, and other men of the country"; from Wigtown to Kirkcudbright of twenty foot, and "from Kirkcudbright to the town of Dumfries, and staying there for seven days in the month of December 1304 watching nightly," of twenty foot.[4]

---

[1] Bain, ii. 443.　　　[2] *Ibid.*　　　[3] *Ibid.*　　　[4] *Ibid.*

Thus, after the province of Moray is left behind, the escort is not only much smaller, but there are no references to the "imminent peril of enemies," or any of those other graphic touches which light up the bald account of the expenses of the king's clerks in the north. It is interesting also to notice the districts other than Moray in which, on the return journey, the escort is strengthened. They are two in number, the district from Aberdeen to Kincardine, and that from Glasgow through the Celtic counties of the south-west to Dumfries. In the former the Braes of Angus were sufficiently near to give harbourage to desperate men; in the latter the inhabitants had ever shown a hatred of English domination, and from the more northern of them Wallace had drawn many of his men. And Wallace was, as a contemporary official document shows, still at large and causing anxiety to the English king.[1]

The extracts I have quoted show that in the north in the summer of 1304, that is to say seven or eight months after Edward's apparently conquering progress of Scotland in the previous autumn, there was not only considerable unrest and hostility to England, but that there were actually men in arms in the field against her. The north, contrary to the hitherto accepted opinion, had, in fact, not been pacified, and seemed in no immediate prospect of being pacified. It is natural to inquire who or what was responsible for this state of things? The latter part of the question requires no answer if we can supply an answer to the first part, for the detestation of the English was everywhere such that it required only a man of sufficient reputation, and an opportunity that seemed to give some promise of success, to bring numbers of eager men into the field. In the north in 1304 both of these conditions were to be found.

Let us take the latter first. Edward's invasion in 1303, as we saw, had not been immediately successful. He himself penetrated no further north than Kinloss, and there was much fighting and besieging in the Highlands

---

[1] Bain, ii. 1563.

after his departure. We do not know how or when the last fortress fell, but it may not have been until well on in 1304. However that may be, it is unquestionable that there was serious resistance long after Edward's departure, and it is reasonable to assume that the very fact of his departure gave new hope and vigour to those who were still holding out against him. It must also be remembered that Comyn, the guardian, did not surrender till February 1304, and that Stirling did not fall until July of the same year. The northern patriots had, therefore, in the summer of 1304 some reason for believing that their cause was not so desperate as, in the light of after events, it appears to us to have been; while the character of the country, and especially the proximity of the hills and forests, made the district an extremely favourable one in which to harass the enemy and maintain a guerilla war. All that was required was a leader, and a leader the province of Moray had.

In considering the career of young Andrew de Moray, we met once or twice his near relation, David de Moravia, who was parson of Bothwell in 1296, a Canon of Moray in 1297 or 1298, and Bishop of Moray in 1299. There has always been some doubt as to who precisely this David de Moravia was, but all the circumstances point to his having been a brother of Sir William de Moray of Bothwell and Sir Andrew de Moray of Petty, and thus an uncle of young Andrew, the hero of Stirling Bridge.

It has recently been stated that David de Moravia was a scion of the Tullibardyn branch of the House of de Moray, the statement being based on the facts that in the Scots College at Paris, of which, as we shall afterwards see, he was the founder, certain arms appear which are said to be his, and that these arms are those of the Morays of Tullibardyn, the progenitors of the present Murrays of Athole.[1] This evidence might be regarded as conclusive if the monument on which the arms are engraved had been erected in the fourteenth

[1] *Northern Chronicle*, November 1912.

century, and if, following on that, they could be assigned only to the Morays of Tullibardyn. But both these very necessary elements are wanting, and the alleged evidence, therefore, is of no value whatsoever.

David de Moravia founded the Scots College in Paris in 1325, but then, and for nearly 300 years thereafter, the foundation consisted simply of a fund the revenues of which were devoted to the support and education, at the University of Paris, of four poor scholars from the Diocese of Moray.[1] But habitation of their own, of any sort, the Scots scholars, as they were called, had none. In 1559 James Bethune, Archbishop of Glasgow and ambassador for Scotland at the Court of France, combined with a certain Thomas Winterhope in extending the foundation of the Bishop of Moray by setting aside a further sum of money for " poor scholars born in the country and kingdom of Scotland that they might study at the University of Paris." In 1603 James Bethune, dying, bequeathed the residue of his property and a house in Paris " to the poor scholars of Scottish nationality studying at the University of Paris." This house seems to have been occupied by the Scots scholars some little time prior to James Bethune's death, and it was the first habitation which they could call their own during all the 275 years which had passed since the Bishop of Moray's foundation in 1325. Under its roof the Moray and Bethune scholars resided until the year 1665. In that year the building, which is still known as the Scots College, was opened, and in it a memorial was erected to the Bishop of Moray and the Archbishop of Glasgow. This memorial takes the form of a black marble slab, and is surmounted by armorial bearings which are supposed to be those of David de Moravia and James Bethune. It is these armorial bearings which are now cited as conclusive proof that David de Moravia belonged to the family of Tullibardyn.

As this memorial was not erected until, at earliest,

---

[1] See *Scottish Historical Review*, iv. 399, for very full and interesting account of the College by Miss V. M. Montagu.

1665, it is, of course, clear that the armorial bearings assigned to David de Moravia are of no historic value unless it can be proved that they were a replica of arms known to have been borne by him in the fourteenth century. Not only is this impossible to prove, but it is, on the face of it, exceedingly unlikely that the seventeenth-century engraver had any authentic data to work on. On the other hand, the branch of the Morays who were prominent in the seventeenth century were the Morays of Tullibardyn. In 1606 Sir John Moray of Tullibardyn was created Earl of Tullibardyn, and in 1665 one of his descendants was Earl of Tullibardyn, and another was Earl of Athol.[1] It was, therefore, natural that, when engraving in 1665 arms for a bishop who bore the name of David de Moray, the artist should ascribe to him the arms of the House of Tullibardyn.

There is, however, another aspect of the matter. The very arms engraved in 1665 are not distinguishable from those borne by the Morays of Bothwell at the close of the thirteenth century. It is stated, by one upholder of the Tullibardyn theory,[2] that in 1296 the Bothwell arms were three mullets within a bordure charged with eleven roundels. These arms, however, were not the arms of Sir William de Moray of Bothwell, but those of Sir Andrew de Moray of Petty and Avoch, a brother of Sir William de Moray of Bothwell.[3] The arms of Sir William de Moray in 1292 are described as three mullets argent much defaced, and these seem identical with those ascribed to the Bishop of Moray in 1665.[4] In order to prove, therefore, that David de Moravia, Bishop of Moray, was a scion of the unimportant thirteenth or early fourteenth-century family of Tullibardyn, it is necessary to show, in the first place, that the arms in the Scots College are really his arms, and, in the second place, that these arms could only have been borne at the close of the thirteenth century by the

[1] B. P., i., under Atholl.   [2] Northern Chronicle, *supra.*
[3] B. P., ii. 125.   [4] *Ibid.*

Morays of Tullibardyn. As neither of these seem capable of proof, it is necessary to look elsewhere for the genealogy of the patriotic Bishop.

We saw that in 1296 David de Moravia was parson of Bothwell, that in 1297 or 1298 he was a Canon of Moray, and that in 1299 he was Bishop of Moray. His promotion, therefore, was exceedingly rapid, and must have been due to powerful influences. At that time the family of Tullibardyn were of very little importance, and with the heads of the families of Bothwell and Petty in captivity in England, it is not in the least likely that an obscure priest from Lanarkshire would have reached episcopal rank so speedily unless he had very special claims. Now if, as I believe, the parson of Bothwell was the youngest brother of Sir William and Sir Andrew, then during their imprisonment in England and after the death of his nephew, young Andrew, he would be for the time the head in Scotland of the Houses of Petty and Bothwell. Between them Sir William and Sir Andrew owned, as we have seen, the wide estates of Bothwell in Lanarkshire, and the lands and castles of Avoch, Petty, Croy, Boharm, Brachlie, Arturlies, Arndilly, &c., in the counties of Ross, Inverness, Moray, and Banff. If, after young Andrew de Moray's death in September or October 1297, the parson of Bothwell was the nearest representative in Scotland of the lords of these vast estates, it is easy to understand how he sprang in two short years from the humble position of parson of Bothwell to the proud position of Bishop of Moray, for though he was not formally appointed to the bishopric until 1299, he was actually elected in 1298. It was, moreover, not unusual for the de Morays to give one of their sons to the Church. Only fifty years had elapsed since another member of the family to which Sir William and Sir Andrew belonged, had died as Bishop of Moray, after having begun his ecclesiastical career as parson of the then family church of Duffus.[1] It must be admitted, therefore, that all the circumstances

[1] B. P., ii. 122. Dowden's *Bishops of Scotland.*

clearly point to David de Moravia having been a brother of the lords of Petty and Bothwell.

I regard this as of some importance, as it helps to explain many things otherwise obscure. As we shall presently see, David de Moravia played a very great part in the struggle for independence, and it is difficult to believe that he would have had the influence, which he undoubtedly did have in the north of Scotland, had he not been very closely connected with the great House of de Moray. Sir William de Moray and Sir Andrew de Moray were both dead before November 1300,[1] while young Andrew, as we know, died in 1297. Young Andrew, however, was succeeded by a son born in May 1298, eight months after his father's death.[2] Unfortunately, we do not know who the boy's mother was, but as his early years were spent in the province of Moray, it is probably safe to assume that she belonged to a northern family. At all events, the boy was brought up in Moray until 1303, when he was seized by Edward during his northern invasion and carried off to England. There he remained a prisoner until the battle of Bannockburn,[3] and it says much for the breed to which he belonged that on his return to Scotland he speedily became noted as one of the purest and bravest patriots of his day, and that in spite of his having spent the impressionable years from five to sixteen at the Court of England. Like his father and grandfather he bore the name of Andrew, and he it was who, in the wars of Edward Balliol, led the armies of Scotland, dying eventually regent of the kingdom in the year 1338, at the age of forty. It is certainly a fact of much significance that the family of Petty and Bothwell throughout the whole of the Wars of Independence displayed a spirit and showed a record which cannot be equalled by any other family of the time.

David de Moravia was among those who, in 1296,[4] did homage to Edward at Berwick, but after that date

[1] Bain, ii. 1178.
[2] *Ibid.*
[3] Bain, iii. 402.
[4] Bain, ii. 212.

he never appears as in any way friendly to England. Unlike the Bishops of Glasgow and St. Andrews, who many times came to Edward's peace and many times broke faith, David de Moravia, once he had thrown in his lot with the patriots, never wavered in his devotion to the cause of freedom. Like all Scottish Catholic churchmen of the day he was bitterly opposed to the claims of England, but in addition to that he seems to have been imbued with a spirit of loyalty and patriotism which would not permit him, even when all seemed lost, to bow the knee to England. He it was who kept alive the spirit of resistance in Moray, and he it was who in 1304 was the real leader of those who caused so much anxiety in the north to the servants of England.

We saw that Edward's clerks, engaged in "making an extent of all the king's lands in Scotland," were at Elgin in June and July 1304. While there they seized certain goods in the priory of Pluscardine, which had been stored there by the Bishop of Moray. They seized them because, as they said, the Bishop was the king's enemy.[1] These goods were carried to Berwick, where they were stored for nine months, and there an inquiry concerning them was held on 1st January 1305,[2] and there they were sold in February or March of the same year for £195.[3] It is clear from the entry not only that the Bishop of Moray was an open enemy of Edward in June or July 1304, when the seizure was made, but that he was such at the date when the entry was made, which was certainly not before March 1305. In all these official documents the language used is extraordinarily exact, and in this case the entry records that the goods were seized *and sold* for £195 "as the Bishop *is* the king's enemy." So, whatever the date of the entry, at the date of the actual selling of the goods the Bishop was recognised as an enemy of England, and that sale did not take place earlier than February 1305. There is no further mention of the Bishop in any contemporary record until 1306, when we learn from letters of Edward

---

[1] Bain, ii. 440.   [2] *Ibid.*, p. 1639.   [3] *Ibid.*, p. 440.

himself that he was one of the first to join Bruce, and was particularly active in obtaining recruits for his standard.[1]

In following the adventures of Edward's clerks, we saw that when in Elgin, in June 1304, twenty foot were engaged to watch nightly "for fear of some enemies who had not yet come to the king's peace." The remarkable thing about this entry is that it relates to a town which was in the very centre of Sir Reginald le Chen's district, and he, as we know, was a strong supporter of England. It is, therefore, not difficult to infer that the enemies whom Edward's servants had to fear were the Bishop of Moray and his men, and the force which the latter had at his command must have been very considerable, when such a lively dread of attack could exist in the minds of Edward's servants in Elgin itself.

We also saw that when Edward's clerks left Elgin, they were escorted as far as Banff by twenty foot and Sir Reginald le Chen's men, in addition to their own ordinary escort of eighteen mounted men. Clearly there was some very special danger to be apprehended in that district. It will be remembered that it was in Launoy, on the eastern bank of the Spey, that young Andrew de Moray in 1297 awaited the coming of the English force from Aberdeen. Launoy, or the Enzie, lies only six miles north of Boharm, and Boharm, with the neighbouring lands of Brachlie and Arndilly, belonged, as we have seen, to the Morays of Petty and Bothwell. The Bishop of Moray, therefore, had not only the men of his bishopric to draw upon, but the men of the lands of his family; and as these very lands had some time before been conferred on Aymer de Valence,[2] Edward's trusted Commander-in-Chief in Scotland, it was not likely that the men of Boharm would be consumed with loyalty towards England. The route to Banff thus lay along the verge of a district hostile to England, and that the danger to be apprehended was by no means inconsiderable, the strength of the force which accompanied the

---

[1] Palgrave, p. 330.   [2] Bain, ii. 1682.

king's clerks to Banff clearly shows. We thus see that in 1304, and in at least the early months of 1305, there was in the province of Moray and the neighbouring districts a considerable amount of active hostility to England, and that the men of Moray had an ardent and capable leader in the person of the Bishop of Moray.[1] How important a bearing these two facts had on the subsequent history of the War of Independence we shall see when we come to consider the campaigns of Bruce, the first of which, it is well to remember, began in February 1306, that is less than a year after the period at which we have now arrived.

[1] Full information regarding the family of De Moravia will be found in *Transactions of Inverness Gaelic Society*, vol. xxv. pp. 1–18. Balfour Paul's *Scots Peerage*, vol. ii. pp. 120–31 ; *Transactions of Society of Antiquaries*, vol. xxiv. pp. 462–9. Also numerous entries in Bain, Palgrave, Stevenson, &c.

CHAPTER XIX

BRUCE'S BID FOR A KINGDOM

WALLACE was executed in August 1305, and in October of that year Edward issued his Ordinance for the final settlement of Scotland. Though we have hints here and there that the country, especially in the north, was not yet entirely peaceful, Edward now thought, and it must be admitted he had good reason for thinking, that Scotland was finally subdued, and might henceforth be considered and treated as a part of England. He therefore proceeded, with the advice and consent of certain Scottish and English commissioners, to frame those regulations for the government of the country, to which we have already given so much consideration. In order to complete our view of the state of the north in the period between 1303 and Bruce's rising in February 1306, we shall, however, glance at them here in so far as they relate to Scotland "beyond the mountains." [1]

Edward's nephew, Sir John de Brittany, was appointed the King's Lieutenant and Warden of Scotland. For the administration of justice the kingdom was divided into four divisions, and over each division two justices, one a Scotsman and one an Englishman, were placed. Scotland "beyond the mountains" formed one division, and the justices for England were Sir Reginald le Chen and Sir John de Vaux. It was also decreed that there should be sheriffs, "natives either of Scotland or England, to be appointed or removed by the lieutenant or chamberlain at discretion . . . and that none should be appointed but the most efficient men and most profitable for the king and people and the maintenance of peace." For the north of Scotland five sheriffs were appointed,

[1] Palgrave's *Parliamentary Writs*, i. 160-3.

O

namely Sir Walter de Berkeley, Sheriff of Banff; William
Wyseman, Sheriff of Elgin; Alexander Wyseman, Sheriff
of Forres and Nairn; Sir John de Stirling, Sheriff of
Inverness; and Sir William de Mohaut (Monte Alto),
heritable Sheriff of Cromarty. Thus, in September 1305,
Edward believed, and behaved as if, Scotland had at last
been finally reduced to his sway. In little more than
four months he was to receive a rude awakening.

One provision of the Ordinance has for us a peculiar
significance. Among other things it was ordained "that
the customs of the Scots and the Brets be henceforth
prohibited and disused." This, of course, means that
the ancient laws and customs of the Scots and Picts were
still very much alive, and their prohibition is an indication of the position which the old Celtic traditions and
usages still occupied in the life of Scotland.

It was on 15th September 1305 that the Parliament which framed the regulations for the government of Scotland met at Westminster, and on 15th
October that the Ordinance embodying the result of
their labours was promulgated. On 10th February 1306
Bruce slew the Red Comyn at Dumfries, and on 27th
March he was crowned at Scone king of the Scots.
These dates show at once the futility of Edward's
dreams, and the spirit in which, in spite of all that had
happened, his pretensions were regarded in Scotland.

We have already discussed the slaying of Comyn and
the events which preceded it. After that desperate deed
Bruce seized and burned the castle of Dumfries, rode to
his own castle of Lochmaben, and summoned his friends
to him. At Lochmaben, however, he was in dangerous
proximity to a country friendly to the Comyns, and
knowing that there he could not long be safe, he rode
north to Glasgow, where the Bishop was his friend, and
thence to Scone. At Scone he was in the capital of the
ancient kingdom of Scotland; and it was in the ancient
kingdom itself, in Scotland north of the Forth, that he
made his first real bid for the Crown and the freedom of
Scotland. The slaying of Comyn had been an accident,

but whatever the causes that led to it, and whatever the motives which inspired the actions which preceded it, the deed itself was hasty and unpremeditated, and though by putting Bruce once and for all outside the pale of Edward's pardon, it compelled him to win Scotland or perish, it was not in itself that real call to arms for which eager spirits in Scotland had been waiting. Bruce rode from Lochmaben an outlaw surrounded, like many an outlaw before and since, by a band of faithful friends. To those whom he knew to be loyal still to the dream of a free Scotland, he sent tidings of his situation and of his determination to lead her as her king in a new struggle for freedom. Those who were willing to put all to the test of desperate fortune he summoned to his standard, and it he raised not at Dumfries or Lochmaben or Glasgow, but at Scone on the day when, by virtue of his descent and because of his reckless deed, he was crowned king of the Scots.

What was it that gave Scone its unique place in Scotland? Why was it that there her kings were crowned, and that from there Edward himself had thought it well to carry the palladium of the kingdom, the famous Stone of Destiny? The answer is simple to anyone who knows the history of Scotland, but it is an answer which contains a significance which has long been overlooked. Scone was the ancient capital of Scotland, the sacred place of her people and her kings, because it was the capital of that older kingdom which had conquered and welded into one the kingdom over which her kings reigned in the thirteenth century. That is a fact which is too often forgotten, but it is a fact which explains much that is otherwise inexplicable in the War of Independence.

Of old, Scotland was, like England, a conglomeration of small independent states or kingdoms. About the year 850 the Picts and Scots who dwelt to the north of the Firths of Forth and Clyde were united under Kenneth MacAlpin, and in the following centuries that united kingdom gradually conquered its southern neighbours. Immediately to the south of the Forth, comprising the modern counties of Clackmannan, Stirling, and Linlithgow, were two small kingdoms of mixed Celtic and Pictish blood, with a dash of English, which were for a time a sort of debatable land between the Celtic kingdom of Strathclyde and the English kingdom of Northumbria on the south, and the Picts and Scots on the north. The latter, however, now known as the kingdom of Alban, soon made good their claim to the debatable land, with whose people they had close ties of language and blood.

At the battle of Carham in 1018 Malcolm II, king of Alban, completely overthrew the forces of the English kingdom of Northumbria, whose territory extended along the east coast from the Humber to the Forth, and so completely shattered was the Northumbrian power that the whole of the territory to the north of the Tweed—that is Lothian—was ceded to Scotland, and has remained part of Scotland ever since. In the same year, 1018, Malcolm II became virtual master of Strathclyde, and his successor Duncan was ruler of all the modern kingdom of Scotland, with the exception of Caithness and Galloway. These two were by-and-bye added to the Scottish dominions, and at last Scotland, or Scotia, was ruled, at least nominally, by one king from the Tweed and the Solway to the Pentland Firth.

It is therefore clear that it was the Celtic kingdom of Alban, Scotland north of the Forth and Clyde, which was the creator of the mediæval and modern kingdom, and that she created it by annexing her neighbours. This fact it is which gives the key to much that is otherwise obscure in the history of Scotland from about the year 1200 onwards. The dwellers in Scotland north of the Forth and Clyde never forgot that it was they who had conquered the south; and for centuries, down even to our own day, the tradition of the conquest of the south by the north survived. In the beginning of the fourteenth century the memory of these things was real and living. Gaelic was still the language of the great bulk of the people outside the English Lothians. North of the Forth English was hardly heard save in a few of the burghs; and in most of these, with perhaps the exception of the Flemish town of Aberdeen, Gaelic was familiar to even the English-speaking burgesses. South of the Forth the earldom of Lennox was still a Celtic earldom, as was Bruce's own earldom of Carrick, which he inherited from his Celtic mother; and throughout all the wide district from the Forth and the Clyde to the English border, only in the conquered English Lothians was Gaelic a foreign tongue to the people. It has always been a tradition in the Highlands that both Wallace and Bruce spoke Gaelic. The wonder, indeed, would be if they had not, for they were both born and brought up in Gaelic-speaking districts, and Bruce, at least, had a Gaelic-speaking mother.

There is, moreover, another thing. The kings who, until the death of Alexander III, had sat on the throne of Scotland were Celtic kings. They might have been Normanised, though possibly the extent of their Normanisation has been exaggerated, but they sat on the Scottish throne because they were Celtic kings, the legitimate male descendants of the Celtic House which had made all Scotland its own. They were no English or Norman interlopers, and how much that fact counted for, the history of Scotland in the twelfth and thirteenth centuries makes abundantly manifest. Now, Bruce claimed the throne as a member of that Celtic House. He was no mere desperate outlaw gambling for a Crown or a gallows. He was an outlaw fighting for a Crown to which he had, at the very least, a very strong claim, and a claim, moreover, which not fifteen years before had found, and still found, many ardent supporters in Scotland. So claiming a Celtic throne, by virtue of his Celtic descent, he betook himself to the Celtic capital of the Celtic kingdom which had conquered all Scotland, and which during the preceding nine years had been the inspiration and the mainstay of the resistance to England, and there had placed on his brow the symbol which signified that Scotland once more had a king of her ancient blood.

Bruce was crowned at Scone on 27th March 1306 in the presence of a company small in numbers but great in gallantry, and a company which in itself showed very plainly whence the new-crowned king was to obtain the support without which he could never hope to sit on anything but a shadowy throne; a company, too, which was an admirable reflex of the real attitude of Scotland at the time. Yet, curiously enough, this plain key to the mystery of Bruce's success, a success which for centuries successive historians have found it beyond them satisfactorily to account for, has lain neglected or has been taken up only to be cast aside because its users lacked the knowledge or the imagination to apply it aright.

First on the list of the little gathering at Scone come four churchmen, the Bishop of St. Andrews, the Bishop of Glasgow, the Bishop of Moray, and the Abbot of Scone. The first three were the most powerful churchmen in Scotland, and their presence at Scone showed once again that the hostility of ecclesiastical Scotland to the pretensions of England was as deep-seated and determined as it had ever been. But the personality of the churchmen was as striking in some ways as the fact that they were the leaders of the Catholic Church in Scotland. Three of them at least had given strong and repeated proof of their hostility to England's claims, and three of them, the Bishops of St. Andrews and Moray and the Abbot of Scone, were "princes of the Church" in Scotland north of the Forth.

Come we now to the new king's lay friends. There was, first of all, his own near relatives, his four gallant brothers Edward, Nigel, Thomas, and Alexander; his nephew Thomas Randolph, afterwards Earl of Moray, and one of the paladins of the War of Independence; and his brother-in-law, Christopher de Seton, an English knight.

Next came Malcolm, Earl of Lennox; John, Earl of Athol; Gilbert de la Haye of Errol and his brother

Hugh; David Barclay of Cairns; Alexander Fraser; Walter de Somerville of Carnwath; David de Inchmartin; Robert Boyd; Robert Fleming; and last but, as the event was to prove, by no means least, the young James de Douglas. Others at that defiant coronation there were, but these are all the names that have come down to us. We shall presently consider, however, the names of many others who may or may not have been at Scone on that fateful 27th March, but who certainly were of Bruce's party in the early days of his kingship, and fought manfully for him at Methven. But for the moment we shall consider only the names mentioned, in order that we may see what clue to the history of the War of Independence they give.

Apart from Bruce's close family connections, and the churchmen already dealt with, eleven names are mentioned. Of these, two are great earls, the Earls of Lennox and Athol. The district of Lennox, as we have already seen, early came to form part of the kingdom of Alban. That kingdom was divided into a number of earldoms, which played an important part in early Scottish history, and the heads of which formed a body known as the Seven Earls. These earldoms were all Celtic earldoms, the earls were all Celts, and the earldoms themselves were situated in the purely Celtic part of Scotland. To them was sometimes joined in later times the earldom of Dunbar, whose head figures occasionally as one of the Seven Earls, but though the earldom itself was situate in the Lothians, the Earl was sprung from a Celtic House.[1] As a matter of fact there were, excluding Dunbar, nine Celtic earls proper in the Scotland of the twelfth and thirteenth centuries, not seven; and the body known to history as the Seven Earls included sometimes one and sometimes another of these. These earldoms were in reality the feudal equivalent for the old semi-independent provinces into which Alban had been divided, and they bore the old names. They were in the thirteenth century and at the

[1] B. P., iii. 239.

beginning of the fourteenth Angus, Athol, Buchan, Fife, Lennox, Mar, Menteith, Ross, and Stratherne. It will be noticed that Moray is not mentioned. The last Mormaer or Celtic Earl of Moray was slain during a rebellion in 1130, and between that date and Randolph's elevation to the earldom in 1312 there was no Earl of Moray. There are, however, good grounds for believing that the family of de Moravia were the representatives of the ancient Celtic House of Moray.

The province of Moray was for centuries one of the most turbulent districts in the kingdom of Alban. Its rebellions were frequent and formidable, and the men of Moray were known throughout the whole land as stark fighters and determined foes. Its rulers aspired repeatedly to the Scottish throne, and one of them, Macbeth, not only ascended that throne, but proved one of the strongest kings in the early history of Scotland. Other claimants to the throne—and in those early days there were many such—found always in Moray men eager and ready to fight for them. It was, indeed, the home of lost or desperate causes, and its turbulence was such that it proved to a long succession of Scottish kings a very difficult and thorny problem. That was why it ceased to exist as an earldom, and why in 1290 the Earl of Mar and the freemen of Moray described it, in an existing document to be afterwards referred to,[1] as a province which was under the immediate government of the king.

Moray was thus on a very different footing from the other earldoms, a difference which is emphasized by the existence of a large number of men who were known as the freemen of Moray. These were men who held their lands on condition of rendering military service to the king. They were virtually a garrison of king's men holding their lands from the Crown, and thus owning no feudal superior save the king. In the neighbourhood of the royal castles the lands thus held were held on the tenure known as castle-guard, their holders being

---

[1] Palgrave, p. 16.

charged with the special duty of garrisoning the royal castles. Their lands were called castle lands, and were distinct from the other Crown lands, the holders of which were obliged to render military or feudal services to the king other than the providing of men for a castle garrison. In the province of Moray these castle and Crown lands were very numerous, so numerous, indeed, that the province had a banner of its own—*Vexillum Moraviæ*—which all who held their lands of the king, whether barons, thanes, or freemen, were bound to follow.

Thus the province of Moray occupied an almost unique place in the Scotland of the twelfth and thirteenth and early fourteenth centuries. Throughout the rest of the kingdom the bulk of the population, outside the burghs, owned feudal superiors other than the king. Their banners it was they followed, and according as a great feudal lord declared for or against Bruce, so the vast majority of his vassals went into the field for or against the patriotic cause. In Moray there was no great feudal lord standing between the king and the people, and this it was which enabled the province to play the part it did in the War of Independence.

At the close of the reign of Alexander III, the earldoms of Scotland numbered thirteen. These were the nine Celtic earldoms already mentioned, and the earldoms of Dunbar, Carrick, Sutherland, and Caithness. Of these four, Carrick and Sutherland were Celtic earldoms in the fullest sense of the term, though their heads were not numbered among the "Seven Earls"; Dunbar was sprung from a Celtic House; and the territories of the Norwegian House of Caithness were, of course, situate in Scotland north of the Forth.[1]

By the time of Bruce several of the Celtic earldoms were in the hands of Norman or English knights, and it has in consequence sometimes been argued, by people who ought to know better, that they, therefore, ceased to be Celtic earldoms. What precisely they mean by

[1] See Balfour Paul for all these earldoms.

that it is hard to say. In Celtic Scotland the Norman
knights were not present as conquerors. Most of them
had acquired their lands by marriage into Celtic families
—they had a penchant for great Celtic heiresses, these
descendants of northern robber knights — and the
children of such unions proved no exception to the
well-known law that the children usually follow the
nationality of the mother, especially when, as happened
in these cases, they are brought up in the country and
among the people of the mother. It is nevertheless a
very common error to write of a Celtic earldom or a
Celtic family as having come to an end the moment
it devolved on a Celtic heiress who married a Norman
knight. An example or two will suffice to expose the
absurdity of this loose view. Many of the great Highland families of the present day are descended from
such unions, and yet no one would venture to assert
that the Frasers, the Stewarts, the Grants, or the
Campbells, for example, were not purely Celtic families.
It is worth remembering, moreover, that the Normans
who came to Scotland were already half-Celtic and that
they, therefore, very readily assimilated with the Scottish
Celts, many of whom, moreover, had like the Normans a
considerable quantity of Scandinavian blood in their veins.

How much this Normanisation theory has been over-
done, a glance at the facts will show. In Bruce's time
the Earl of Ross, the Earl of Sutherland, the Earl of
Athol, the Earl of Mar, the Earl of Stratherne, the Earl
of Lennox, and the Earl of Fife were all Celts.[1] The
Earls of Angus and Menteith, and Robert Bruce himself
as Earl of Carrick, had succeeded to these Celtic earldoms, through their respective mothers,[2] and the population of these earldoms was almost entirely Celtic.
Even the earldom of Buchan had only come to the
Comyns in the year 1214, when William Comyn married
the heiress of the last Celtic earl,[3] and it was not until
after the Herschip of Buchan, indeed because of it, that
the population began to cease to be predominantly Celtic.

---

[1] B. P., under these headings.   [2] *Ibid.*   [3] *Ibid.*

There remain only the earldoms of Caithness and Dunbar, the former of which had long ceased to be a Celtic earldom, and the latter of which lay in the English Lothians under the sway of a family of ancient Celtic descent. The last recorded appearance of the Seven Earls in their corporate capacity, in a document to which the term official may be applied, occurs in the year 1290, and the notable thing about it is that it is an appeal by these earls on behalf of Robert Bruce, Lord of Annandale, "the Competitor," grandfather of King Robert.[1] I cannot do better than quote the excellent summary of this remarkable document given by Sir Francis Palgrave.[2]

After explaining that it is a minute of proceedings instituted by the Seven Earls, and conducted for them by procurators appearing before the Bishop of St. Andrews and John Comyn, acting as guardians of Scotland, he proceeds to give its tenor as follows: "According to the ancient laws and usages of the kingdom of Scotland, and from the time whereof the memory of man was not to the contrary, it appertained to the rights and liberties of the Seven Earls and the *communitas* of the realm, whensoever the royal throne should become vacant, to constitute the king," and invest him with all the functions of government.   "And now, the throne being vacant by the death of Alexander III, and lest the Bishop of St. Andrews" (not Lamberton, King Robert Bruce's friend, but his predecessor, Fraser), "and John Comyn, acting as regents of Scotland, together with the small portion of the *communitas* adhering to them, should of their own authority appoint any king for the government of the kingdom, to the prejudice of the rights of the Seven Earls, and lest also John de Balliol should intermeddle in the kingdom or government of Scotland," appeal was hereby made to Edward, king of England, on account of the injury thus threatened, "in the name of the before-mentioned Seven Earls, and also of the bishops, abbots, priors, earls, barons, and freeholders of Scotland, and of the *communitas* to them adhering." [3]

[1] Palgrave, p. 14.   [2] *Ibid.*, p. ix., &c.   [3] *Ibid.*

Another appeal from the acts and jurisdiction of the guardians is made on behalf of the Earl of Mar, "and also of all the freemen of Moray, their kith, kin, and friends." It charges the regents with "entering the land of Moray, a land immediately subject to the dominion of the king of Scotland," and committing various ravages and depredations, "harrying and burning the lands and dwellings and barns of the freemen of the king of Scots therein." A third and last appeal is then made in the name and on behalf of Robert de Bruce, Lord of Annandale, claiming the Crown as the lawful and appointed heir of King Alexander. He complains that the guardians, "uniting with others of the kingdom, as well in prejudice of the rights of Bruce as in violation of the privileges of the Seven Earls," had intended to appoint John de Balliol to the vacant throne. Therefore "he, Robert de Bruce, so appearing by his procurator, appeals to the presence of Edward, king of England," and places himself, the Seven Earls, and all his kith, kin, and friends under the protection of the English king.[1]

In these appeals the antagonism of the Bruces and the Comyns may be noted, as well as Bruce's early and definite claim to the throne, and the support accorded him by the Seven Earls. The reference to the Earl of Mar and the district of Moray may also be noted. Meanwhile, the important point to bear in mind is that the Seven Earls, next to the king the most powerful force in thirteenth-century Scotland, in 1290 declared in favour of the claim to the Scottish throne put forward by the family of Bruce.

Although the foregoing appeal of the Seven Earls is the last official record of their appearance on the stage of Scottish history, there is one other mention of them which is of some importance to our narrative. In 1296, after John Balliol had defied Edward, a Scottish army invaded England, the same army which was a little later routed at Dunbar. The invasion is thus recorded by Rishanger: "At that time the Seven Earls of Scotland,

---

[1] Palgrave, p. ix., &c.

viz. of Buchan, of Menteith, of Stratherne, of Lennox, of Ross, of Athol, of Mar, and John, son of John Comyn of Badenoch, having assembled a strong army in the vale of Annandale," invaded England, and laid siege to Carlisle. Thus we see that at the end of the thirteenth century the Seven Earls were a real power in Scotland, that they certainly led her armies in war and attempted to settle her affairs in peace, that they all belonged to the old Celtic kingdom of Alban, and that they committed themselves at an early stage to the cause of Bruce in the competition for the Crown.

With all the facts we have just been considering before us, let us turn again to the gathering at Scone on 27th March 1306. We have just seen that two earls only were present, the Earl of Athol and the Earl of Lennox. But they were two of the Seven Earls, and between them they brought to Bruce's cause the whole of the wild and warlike district from Dumbarton up through the centre of Scotland to the borders of Moray. The Earl of Menteith and the Earl of Stratherne also joined Bruce,[1] though they are not mentioned as being present at his coronation, and as Bruce himself was guardian of the earldom of Mar for his youthful nephew, a boy of tender years, at that time under Edward's care in England, five of the ancient Celtic earldoms had ranged themselves on his side before the middle of June 1306. Of the others, the Earl of Buchan was a Comyn, and his mortal foe ; the Earl of Ross did not declare himself until the battle of Methven had seemingly decided Bruce's fate ; the Earl of Angus was hostile ; and the attitude of the Earl of Fife, then a young man of nineteen, and apparently still in ward in England, is unknown. But the Earl of Fife's sister made no secret of her sympathies. Though the wife of the Earl of Buchan, she hurried to Scone to claim the ancient privilege of her family of placing the Crown on the new king's head, and arriving after the coronation of 27th March, the ceremony was repeated on the 29th, in

[1] Palgrave, pp. 301-18.

order that nothing might be left undone which might enable anyone to say that Bruce had not been crowned with all due rites and observances.

Thus, so far as the Celtic earldoms were concerned, Bruce was in a strong position; and as by virtue of his kingship he had now a special claim on the men of Moray, a claim which, thanks to the Bishop of Moray, they were, with few exceptions, ready and eager to recognise, it must be plain to even the most incredulous that it was upon Scotland north of the Forth and Clyde that Bruce relied when he made his desperate bid for a throne, and that it was there he found the men and the support which enabled him to take the field in the early summer of 1306. For the moment, however, we are concerned more particularly with the evidence which the coronation affords of this. We have seen that apart from Bruce's own close family connections and four churchmen, eleven persons are on record as having been present at his coronation. Of these, two were the Celtic Earls of Athol and Lennox; and of the other nine, Gilbert de la Haye of Errol and his brother Hugh, David Barclay of Cairns, Alexander Fraser, and David de Inchmartin, belonged to Scotland north of the Forth and Clyde. The four others, William de Somerville of Carnwath, Robert Boyd, Robert Fleming, and James Douglas, belonged to Scotland south of the Firth of Clyde. Thus, excluding Bruce's four brothers, his brother-in-law, and his nephew, we find that among the fifteen companions of his coronation whose names have come down to us, no fewer than ten belonged to the old Celtic kingdom, to Scotland north of the Forth and Clyde, and that these ten were men of infinitely more consequence in Scotland than were the five from the south.

It is thus evident that a careful examination of the names of Bruce's companions at Scone should have afforded some clue to the mystery which has too long surrounded his movements in the critical years from 1306 to 1308, and if that had been done we should have been spared much false history and many misconceptions. Unfortunately, however, writer after writer started from the fundamental misconception that the independence of Scotland was won by the southern Lowlands. Yet at Bruce's coronation the Borders and the southern Lowlands were represented only by Robert Fleming, at that time a man of neither standing nor importance; by Robert Boyd, an obscure Ayrshire landholder; by Sir William Somerville of Carnwath, who owned a small estate in Lanarkshire; by the youthful James Douglas, who had neither lands nor following, the estates of his family having been confiscated seven or eight years before, and he himself being as yet young and untried; and by the Bishop of Glasgow. Thus from the very outset of Bruce's venture the representatives of the old Celtic kingdom were immensely superior, not only in numbers, but in power and influence, to Bruce's southern friends and allies; and it must be plain that without their aid his career as king would have been brief indeed.

CHAPTER XX

So far, we have been considering only the normal deductions which could hardly have failed to be drawn from all that was known of Bruce's coronation and the months which preceded Methven, if the subject had been approached with minds free of prejudice and with the true historical background kept firmly in view. We shall now proceed to see how accurate such deductions would have been, and how the only trustworthy evidence we possess bears them out in every particular.

Although the names of only fifteen of Bruce's companions at Scone are generally known, there exist numerous contemporary documents from which it is possible to compile a list of no less than 135 of those who had joined his standard before the battle of Methven on 26th June 1306. Although the majority of these documents have been accessible in printed form for many years, it seems never to have occurred to anyone either to compile such a list or to analyse and classify the names contained in them. Yet it was clearly the simplest method of arriving at a sound knowledge of the events of 1306, and of coming to a reasonable conclusion upon them. The two principal sources from which such a list may be compiled are Palgrave's *Documents* and Bain's *Calendar of Documents relating to Scotland*, while a few additional names may be gleaned from Balfour Paul's *Scots Peerage*. Of these Palgrave is, for our present purpose, by far the most important, for in it are printed two documents of unique value.

The first of these is headed [1] " The demands which

---

[1] Palgrave, pp. 301–18.

were made to the king for lands in Scotland in the year of his reign the 33rd," that is to say, in 1306. The first entry occurs in May 1306, and the entries continue throughout the year. The "demands" are petitions by English and Scottish adherents of Edward for the lands of men who had joined Bruce, and had thus forfeited their property. The great value of this list is, accordingly, at once apparent. The names of the "rebels" and their lands are set forth, the locality of the latter is often mentioned, and an illuminating phrase, such as "Who is with the Earl of Carrick?" or "Who is against the king?" is frequently added. When it is mentioned that over one hundred names occur on this list some idea of its value may be gathered. It is important to remember, however, that the names occurring are the names only of people who had lands or property worth coveting, and that with few exceptions the names are those of landowners. Accordingly, if over one hundred men of property were known in England to have joined Bruce before midsummer 1306, it is a reasonable inference that others whose names were not then known had also "rebelled," and that where so many landed men led, a large number of "the middling men" and "the common folk" of Scotland must have followed.

The second document, or series of documents, in Palgrave [1] to which I have referred is a list of "the king's enemies" sent to prisons in England. They are dated in the end of 1306, and in addition to the names of Bruce's queen and other ladies contain about a dozen names. Several of these occur also in the list of demands already mentioned.

From a careful examination of Bain's *Calendar*, a number of additional names, including the very interesting list of sixteen prisoners summarily executed at Newcastle by Edward's orders on 4th August 1306,[2] can be obtained, and from contemporary authorities cited in Balfour Paul's *Scots Peerage*, I have been able to obtain two or three more. The list thus compiled is accord-

---

[1] Palgrave, pp. 353–9.   [2] Bain, ii. 1811.

ingly extracted entirely from contemporary official sources, and is not therefore open to challenge on the ground of want of authenticity.

The list of Bruce's supporters in the spring and summer of 1306 numbers, as we have seen, 135 names. Of these, I have been unable to arrive at any conclusion regarding the locality with which six of them are connected. Three of these occur in one petition, and their lands are therefore probably contiguous. They are Walter Alich de la Brag, John Cokyn, and Sir Malcolm Everphme. The other three were among those executed at Newcastle in August 1306, William de Baa, Roger le Tailleur, and Ughtred le Marischal.

One hundred and twenty-nine names, therefore, remain. Of these, seventy-eight can be assigned to Scotland north of the Forth and Clyde, and fifty-one to Scotland south of the Forth and Clyde. But of Scotland south of the Forth and Clyde the whole west part was Celtic, and to that part thirty-five names out of the fifty-one for the whole south can, at a moderate computation, be assigned. Of the remaining sixteen, seven come from Roxburgh; six from Peebles and Selkirk, where the heroic Sir Simon Fraser was the moving spirit; two from Berwick; and one from an unknown locality.

These figures call for a closer examination. Twenty-six names are from Ayr, Renfrew, Dumfries, and Galloway. Now, Bruce's own Celtic earldom of Carrick lay in Ayr, and of these twenty-six names sixteen are from Carrick or its neighbourhood. Included in these are Sir Robert Boyd, Sir Reginald de Crawford, Sir Alexander de Lindsay, Simon Lockhart, Robert Cunningham, Sir Brice de Blair, and Sir Berin de Keith, all near neighbours of Bruce. The others are small men, and some, if not all of them, were vassals of Bruce. If to the sixteen Ayrshire names are added the five Dumfries names, the bearers of which were Bruce's own vassals or his close personal friends, and the three Galloway men, we find that twenty-four at least out of the whole fifty-one followed Bruce for what we may describe as reasons purely personal to himself. The remaining twenty-seven included such tried and proven patriots as Sir Simon Fraser of Oliver Castle, and his brother Thomas, who brought to Bruce's standard many of the men of Peebles and Selkirk, including the two specifically mentioned; Sir John Soulis, one of the late guardians of Scotland, who, like Sir Simon Fraser, had earned Edward's special rancour a year or two earlier, and the Bishop of Glasgow. That leaves us with twenty-one names for the rest of the south, the chief of which are James de Douglas, Sir William de Somerville, Sir Thomas de Somerville, John de Somerville, Sir Hugh Lovel, Robert de Nesbit, John Moray of Drumsagard, Sir James de Lindsay, and perhaps, though there is some doubt on the point, the Steward of Scotland.

Now, it must be admitted by anyone who knows the history of Scotland in the closing years of the thirteenth and the opening years of the fourteenth centuries, that the foregoing names do not of themselves make up a very formidable list, however imposing they may at a first glance appear. In mere numbers they form but a small fraction of the men of similar position in the southern counties whose names appear in the records of the period, while from the point of view of power or influence, few of them are of much account. The Bishop of Glasgow, Sir Simon Fraser, Sir John Soulis, Sir Alexander Lindsay, and Sir Reginald Crawford are the only names among them which carried much weight, or whose bearers were of much consequence in Scotland at the beginning of 1306. It is therefore a reasonable inference that outside his own immediate circle, and a small circle who were eager to seize any chance of resisting Edward's pretensions, Bruce did not receive much support or encouragement in the southern counties of Scotland when in 1306 he made his first bid for the Crown. It is noteworthy, too, that such support as he did receive came almost entirely from the west. English-speaking Lothian sent few volunteers to the standard of the new king.

It was far otherwise in Scotland north of the Forth and Clyde. Bruce came to Scone a fugitive, an outlaw, and a murderer, with no claim to the service of his vassals, as in Carrick and Annandale, with few ties of blood between him and the men whose aid he sought, and with no imposing force to lead them to believe that his cause was other than desperate. Yet sixteen of the leading men of Perthshire, the Earls of Athol, Menteith, and Strathearne among them; twelve from Angus and the Mearns; twelve from Aberdeen and Banff; one from the province of Moray; eleven from Fife; six from Lennox; four from Stirling; four from Argyll; and one each from Dumbarton and Clackmannan; seventy-eight in all, are on record as having taken the tremendous risk of joining Bruce in the early spring and summer of 1306.

Fifteen of Bruce's seventy-eight northern adherents belonged to Perthshire. First of all we find the three earls already mentioned, who between them were the feudal superiors of the whole modern county of Perth, and the two gallant brothers de la Haye. We find also Sir David de Inchmartin who, with William Rusky from the same county, paid for his patriotism with his life on the scaffold at Newcastle,[1] and Sir Malcolm de Innerpeffrey, who, though Edward's Sheriff of Clackmannan and Auchterarder, was, in the indignant words of an English official document of the time, " one of the first to join Sir Robert de Bruce, and wickedly abetted the Earls of Menteith and Stratherne in aiding said Robert." [2] Other prominent Perthshire names mentioned as among the king's enemies are those of Robert de Inchestour, Sir Alexander Menzies, and William Wychard of Aberdalgy.[3]

From Angus and the Mearns there came to Bruce a doughty companion of Wallace, Alexander le Scrimgeour, the Bearer of the Royal Standard of Scotland and Constable of Dundee. He and another patriot from the

---

[1] Bain, ii. 1811. [2] *Ibid.*, p. 1858.
[3] Except where otherwise indicated all the names contained in this chapter are taken from the sources already mentioned.

same county, Robert Wycher or Wishart, were soon to lay down their lives on the blood-stained scaffold of Newcastle, victims to Edward's lust for conquest and Edward's wrath.[1] From Angus and the Mearns came also Sir William de Mohaut, Sir John Siward, and John de Cambron of Balnely, all well-known knights in their day, and Lawrence de Angus, Master Ralph of Dundee, and several others.

Twelve names from Aberdeen and Banff appear on this Scottish roll of honour. Among them are those of Sir Walter de Berkeleye (Barclay), who, as we have seen, had been appointed Sheriff of Banff by Edward as recently as October 1305; Berkeleye's neighbour, Hamelyn de Troup; Sir Alan Durward of Fichele, a former Sheriff of Inverness; Thomas de Monimusk in Forglen; Sir Lawrence de Strathbogie, the owner of extensive lands in Caithness and Sutherland, as well as in Aberdeen and Banff; and one of the gallant family of Moray, Sir William de Moray of Sandford. With them, too, must be reckoned the young Earl of Mar, and three burgesses of Aberdeen.

At the head of those who hastened to join Bruce from the province of Moray was the patriotic bishop, David de Moray. With him went two others of the same name, Sir Alan de Moray of Culbin and Sir Walter de Moray, and the gallant young Andrew de Moray's friend and lieutenant, Alexander Pilche, burgess of Inverness, who had been, since 1304, keeper of the castle of Inverness for England. From Inverness, too, went Sir William de Fenton of Beaufort and his nephew, Patrick de Graham of Lovat, and Thomas de Dolays, of Dallas in Morayshire and Cantray in Inverness. There also declared for Bruce, a son of a former Sheriff of Inverness, in the person of John de la Haye, who held lands in the county, and Edward's Sheriff of Elgin, William Wiseman, who lived to do Bruce good service, but whose wife was carried away captive and clapped into prison by the chivalrous English king. Nor must

[1] Bain, ii. 1811.

we omit a gallant son of Moray, William de Botharm, who suffered in August 1306 a patriot's death at the hand of the executioner in Newcastle.[1]

Duncan, the Celtic Earl of Fife, was in 1306 only nineteen years of age, and at the time of Bruce's coronation was apparently under ward in England.[2] It was Edward's policy, wherever possible, to have the sons and heirs of Scottish magnates brought up in England, and as Duncan's father, the ninth Celtic earl, had died when his son and successor was only a year or two old, the English king had experienced no difficulty in assigning the infant earl to the care of an English guardian. In 1294 Sir Walter de Cambhou of Fife was appointed keeper of all the young earl's lands in Fife, Perth, Stirling, and Moray, a position which, of course, gave him great power.[3] By 1306 he was dead, and his son, Sir John de Cambhou, had succeeded him in his lands, and probably, though this is not clear, in his post as keeper of the earldom.[4] At all events Sir John must plainly have occupied a position of great power in the earldom. He was, moreover, lieutenant for the Sheriff of Fife in 1303,[5] and, when he declared for Bruce in 1306, his influence probably helped to bring many of the leading men of the county to Bruce's side. His career as a patriot, unfortunately, was brief. He was captured at Methven, and formed one of the victims of Edward's bloody assize at Newcastle in August 1306.[6]

Besides Sir John de Cambhou ten other of the leading men of Fife joined Bruce. First and foremost there was the Bishop of St Andrews, whose rebellion filled Edward with savage anger. Then there was Sir Michael de Wemyss and Sir David his son, whose defection Edward regarded with such wrath that he issued special orders to his Commander-in-Chief, Aymer de Valence, "to burn, destroy, and strip the lands and gardens of Sir Michael de Wemyss's manor, where we lay, and all his other manors, as the king has found neither good speech nor

---

[1] Bain, ii. 1811.   [2] B. P., under *Fife*.   [3] Bain, ii. 684, 701, &c.
[4] *Ibid.*, p. 1263.   [5] *Ibid.*, p. 1350.   [6] *Ibid.*, p. 1811.

good service in him; and this for an example to others; likewise to do the same, or worse if possible, to the lands and possessions of Sir Gilbert de la Haye, to whom the king did great courtesy when he was last in London, but now finds he is a traitor." [1]

Other Fife "rebels" included Sir John de Cambron of Balligarnach; Malise de Logy, who had served with Edward in Flanders; Thomas de Balkasky; Sir Adam de Valoines; Walter de Bickerton, seigneur of Kilconquhar; and Sir Andrew Gray.[2]

In the Earl of Lennox Bruce secured one of his bravest and most devoted adherents, and through him many men of the modern counties of Dumbarton and Stirling, a great part of which the earldom covered, followed the new king's standard. Among those who seem to have been the Earl's more immediate followers were John de Luss of Lennox, Alexander Folkard and Duncan his son, Anelf de Lenox, and Thomas de Cromenan in the county of Lennox. From Dumbarton there came also Sir Donald Campbell, and from the neighbouring county of Argyll his elder brother, Sir Neil Campbell. The brothers were the sons of Sir Colin Campbell of Lochow, the first MacCallein Mor, and their friendship with Bruce was hereditary, for Sir Colin was one of those named by Robert Bruce, the Competitor, in 1291, as supporters of his claim to the Crown.[3] Sir Neil and Sir Donald gave to Bruce the most devoted service, and of the former it is proudly said, and with truth, that "he adhered to King Robert Bruce in prosperity and adversity, and fought by his side in almost every encounter from the battle of Methven to that of Bannockburn."[4]

From the neighbourhood of Lennox also there came to Bruce's standard several other members of the patriotic family of Fraser, among them Sir Richard Fraser of Touch Fraser, in the county of Stirling, and Alexander Fraser, hereditary Sheriff of Stirling, lord of Ugtreth-

[1] Bain, ii. 1787.   [2] B. P., iv. 270.
[3] B. P., under *Argyll*.   [4] *Ibid.*

restrother in Fife and Cowie in Aberdeen, and successor to Sir Richard Fraser in Touch Castle. In 1306 Alexander Fraser was a young man, but by 1316 he was a knight, and in 1319 was Lord Chamberlain of Scotland. His mother owned lands in Caithness, and of his brothers one, Sir Simon, distinguished himself at Bannockburn, and is probably the ancestor of the Frasers of Lovat. This Alexander must be distinguished from another Alexander Fraser, who was lord of Cornton in Stirlingshire. He was a brother of the above-mentioned Sir Richard Fraser of Touch Castle, and, like him, joined Bruce in 1306. He is probably the Sir Alexander Fraser who is said by Barbour to have been captured at Methven, and certainly after that date he disappears from history.

The Alexander who became Lord Chamberlain and Sir Simon, his brother, are the two Frasers who joined Bruce in the north on his return to Scotland in 1307. We shall meet them again when we come to consider the events of that year. Meanwhile, however, it is necessary to warn the reader against confusing this Sir Simon with his more famous relations, the three Sir Simons of Oliver Castle in Peebles. The first of these was the brother of Sir Alexander's and Sir Simon's great-grandfather, John Fraser. The second, who died in 1291, was one of Balliol's auditors in the competition for the Crown; and the third was the famous Sir Simon Fraser, the hero of the battle of Roslin, the companion of Wallace, and the adherent of Bruce. He was captured in Kildrummy, and done to death in London with all the refinements of English cruelty, his head being placed on London Bridge, as a sign in Edward's eye of disgrace, but in reality as a token of highest honour, beside that of his friend and leader, Wallace.[1]

There is one other name belonging to Stirling appearing on the roll of honour, and it is worth recording for its own sake. Coweyn Mackassen, in the county of Stirling, early joined Bruce, but beyond that nothing is

[1] For full particulars of all these Frasers and their relationships, see B. P., vii. 420-8.

known of him. His lands were coveted by no less a person than Alexander, the queen's " chandeller," and with the appearance of Alexander's request on the roll of demands for the property of Scotsmen, Coweyn Mackassen, follower of Bruce, makes his first and last appearance on the page of history.

A few names yet remain to be considered. First among them is Angus of the Isles, whose exploits on behalf of Bruce are well known. With him there probably went to Bruce's standard Malcolm M'Culian, in the Isle of Kintyre, on whose lands Sir John de Ferrers cast covetous eyes. The name of John Biset, brother of Sir William Biset, Sheriff of Clackmannan, also appears. Sir William remained loyal to Edward, and from an entry in 1308 John appears to have abandoned the cause of Bruce.[1]   Finally, we find among those executed in August at the bloody assize at Newcastle, the name of Bernard de Mohaut.[2]   It has been assumed, on somewhat flimsy grounds, that he belonged to Peebles, but the burden of evidence seems rather to point to his having been one of the northern Mohauts. Now, it will be remembered that when, in 1297, the Countess of Ross sent letters to Edward from Inverness, she mentioned that " Bernard de Monte Alto, my clerk," was to accompany the bearer, Sir Andrew de Rait. Monte Alto was the Latin way of writing Mohaut, and we have seen what part the Monte Altos or Mohauts of Cromarty played in the wars of Andrew de Moray and Wallace. The Countess of Ross's " clerk " was almost certainly one of the Cromarty family, and when we learn that at the inquisition held at Newcastle after the execution of Bernard de Mohaut, the jury found that he owned " no lands or chattels," [3] there is every ground for believing that he must in that event have been either a " clerk " or a landless man, a young esquire for example. When we learn, further, that there was actually a Bernard de Mohaut a " clerk " and a member of a patriotic family, the conclusion is irresistible that

[1] Bain, iii. 49.   [2] Bain, ii. 1811.   [3] *Ibid.*

the man of that name executed at Newcastle was one
and the same with the one-time "clerk" of the Countess
of Ross.

Two names in the foregoing list require a little
further consideration. I have assigned Sir William de
Moray of Sandford to the county of Aberdeen.   There
is a small parish of that name in Lanark, and a Sandford
Bay and Sandford Lodge in Aberdeen.   There is no
clue to tell us which of these gave Sir William de Moray
his local designation, but, as in the demand for his lands
he is described as cousin of Sir Alan de Moray, who was
lord of Culbin (he is stated to have held lands in the
counties of Forres and Fife), I have preferred the northern
locality.   In any case, as his relationship to Sir Alan de
Moray shows, he was a member of the northern family
of that name.

There arises also the question of the Earl of Stratherne.
He certainly was of Bruce's party before Methven, but
in August 1306 he was a prisoner, and protested that he
had only joined Bruce under compulsion and in fear of
his life.   What degree of credence ought to be attached
to that statement it is impossible to say, but the story,
which is narrated at length by the Earl himself, does not
seem to have carried much weight at the time, and is,
on the face of it, almost incredible.[1]   At all events, it
is undoubted that the Earl of Stratherne was with Bruce
before the battle of Methven,[2] and that many men of
the earldom followed the new-crowned king to that
tragic field.

Let us now sum up the facts and the arguments
which the names of Bruce's supporters in 1306 disclose.
Fifty-one of these belonged to the southern counties,
the most prominent among them being the Bishop of
Glasgow; Sir Simon Fraser and his brother Thomas,
Sir Simon having been ordered, for his "rebellion" with
Wallace, to go into exile for four years at Christmas
1305; Sir Alexander Lindsay, who, in September 1305,
had been ordered, for the same reason as Sir Simon

---

[1] Palgrave, p. 319.   [2] *Ibid.*, p. 305.

Fraser, to remain out of Scotland for six months; Sir
John Soulis, who had been ordered to remain "south of
Trent" for two years; Sir Reginald Crawford, Sir
William and Sir Thomas de Somerville, John de Somer-
ville, Sir James de Lindsay, Sir Hugh Lovel, Sir Robert
Boyd, Sir Berin de Keith, Sir Brice de Blair, Simon Lock-
hart, Robert Cunningham, John Moray of Drumsagard,
Robert de Nesbit, and the young James de Douglas.
Among these there are but few really well-known names,
and not more than half a dozen are those of men who in
1306 were great territorial magnates.   Contrast this
with the northern list.   It contains five great earls, the
Earls of Athol, Menteith, Lennox, Stratherne, and Mar,
and the following "names of fame," Sir Gilbert de la
Haye and his brother Hugh; David, Bishop of Moray,
and his three relations, Sir William de Moray of Sand-
ford, Sir Alan de Moray of Culbin, and Sir Walter de
Moray; Alexander le Scrimgeour, Standard-bearer of
Scotland and Constable of Dundee; Sir Walter de
Berkeley, Sheriff of Banff; William Wiseman, Sheriff of
Elgin; Sir Malcolm de Innerpeffrey, Sheriff of Clack-
mannan and Auchterarder; Angus of the Isles; Sir Neil
and Sir Donald Campbell; Sir Alexander Fraser, here-
ditary Sheriff of Stirling; Sir Richard Fraser of Touch
Fraser; Sir Alexander Fraser of Cornton; Alexander
Pilche, constable of the castle of Inverness; Sir David de
Inchmartin; Sir Michael and Sir David de Wemyss; Sir
Lawrence de Strathbogie; Sir William de Fenton; Patrick
de Graham of Lovat; Sir John de Cambhou of Fife;
Sir John de Cambron of Balligarnach; Sir Adam de
Valoines; Sir Alan Durward; Hamelyn de Troup; Sir
William de Mohaut; John de Luss; and the whole
northern clergy led by the Bishops of St. Andrews and
Moray and the Abbot of Scone.   Merely to read the two
lists is to demonstrate the truth of the argument that it
is to Scotland north of the Forth and Clyde we must
look if we would solve the mystery of Bruce's doings in
the spring and summer of 1306, and read the secret of
the success which was ultimately his.

CHAPTER XXI

BEFORE AND AFTER METHVEN

For the period on which we have now entered the contemporary records can be supplemented by Barbour's heroic poem, "The Bruce," as well as by various English chronicles. "The Bruce" was completed in 1376, and as an historical document its value is far above that of Blind Harry's "Wallace." We know that John Barbour was Archdeacon of Aberdeen in 1357, and an auditor of Exchequer in 1384, and there is excellent ground for placing the date of his death in March 1395.[1] He must, therefore, have been born not later than 1330, and probably not earlier than 1320. He started, therefore, with a general knowledge of the events of the first quarter of the century; and when he made up his mind to write his poem, he exhausted every means at his disposal in order to obtain the fullest and most accurate information possible at the time when he wrote. In the result he succeeded in producing a poem, which in its details is astonishingly accurate, though in its general outline it is often vague. This has been proved repeatedly in recent years by the discovery of many contemporary English official documents. Its accuracy in detail may be judged from his list of Scottish prisoners taken at Methven; of these one only, Sir Alexander Fraser, does not appear in existing official records as having been captured on that fatal field. Of his vagueness in general outline, his account of the events which preceded Methven is a good example, and is in striking contrast to his detailed story of Bruce's adventures in Lorn and Lennox. The reason is that he probably drew

---

[1] See Mackenzie's *Barbour's Bruce*.

his information for the latter from the mouth of one of the participators in these events, while for the former no such authority was available. We shall see later that his account of Bruce's doings in the closing months of 1306 and the opening months of 1307, the period covered by Bruce's alleged concealment in Rathlin, is open to a similar criticism. But when all allowance is made, the fact remains that the poem is undoubtedly an historical document of the highest value.

Of the English chronicles there is one of special value for the military events of the period, Sir Thomas Gray's *Scalacronica*. It was written in 1356, when the author was a prisoner in Edinburgh Castle; and, as Sir Herbert Maxwell says, it is "of incomparable value to the student of Scottish and English history during the reigns of the first three Edwards. Incomparable because, alone among the chronicles of the time, it was written by a soldier who naturally viewed affairs from a different standpoint to that of the usual clerical annalist." As Sir Thomas Gray's father fought in almost every English campaign in Scotland from 1297 onwards, and as Sir Thomas Gray himself won his spurs in the Scottish wars of the third Edward, his knowledge, especially of the military events of the period, is unique; while the fact that he wrote his chronicle while a prisoner in Edinburgh Castle, enabled him to supplement his own knowledge from the books and documents, which, he tells us, he read in the castle, and from the mouths of the many Scottish knights and others with whom he talked during his two years' captivity.

It is curious that neither Barbour nor any other fourteenth-century writer gives any detailed or lucid account of Bruce's doings in the north, either in 1306 or in 1307 and 1308. Another curious thing is that no writer throws much light on the events of the months which elapsed between the murder of Comyn in February and the battle of Methven in June. Certain outstanding facts, such as the coronation, are mentioned, and interesting details concerning some of Bruce's companions,

James Douglas, for example, are given ; but of information of real value concerning the happenings of these months there is little or none. These omissions have doubtless coloured all that has since been written on the War of Independence, but that events of very great importance, both in themselves and in their subsequent results, did occur during these months we shall now proceed to see.

The first event of importance was the rallying to Bruce's side of the numerous northern knights and others whose names and consequence we have already considered. This it was which enabled Bruce to march against Aymer de Valence in Perth in the end of June with so strong a force that de Valence did not venture to accept its challenge to meet it on equal terms. Sir Thomas Gray's remark on this force is of interest, as it throws some light both on the composition and on the strength of Bruce's following. " Robert de Bruce," he says, " had gathered all the force of Scotland which was on his side, and some fierce young fellows easily roused against the English, and came before the town of Perth in two great columns, offering battle to the said earl and to the English." The phrase " Some fierce young fellows easily roused against the English " is suggestive of much, of which it is unnecessary, after all we have been considering, to point the explanation.

Barbour dismisses the events of the period between the coronation and Methven in a few lines. But three of these lines are of interest to us. After relating how Bruce received the homage of such barons as came to him, he goes on (I have modernised the words)—

> " And syne went over all the land,
> Friends and friendship purchasing
> To maintain that he had begun."

This is an excellent example of both that accuracy and vagueness in Barbour to which I have referred. The truth of the general statement which he makes is not open to doubt. It was a fact within his knowledge that

Bruce did so spend the interval between his coronation and Methven. But the expression " over all the land " is disappointingly vague, and the question remains, what parts did Bruce visit on this tour " friends and friendship " to obtain. The answer, I think, is clear. The list of names already given supplies it in one form, the knowledge of Bruce's own holdings and influence in the north supplies it in another, and the condition of the country itself in a third.

We saw that Bruce was guardian of the earldom of Mar for his youthful nephew, and it is on record that the castle of Kildrummy was in his keeping, probably as guardian of his nephew, as late as September 1305. Moreover, Bruce owned lands in the neighbourhood of Forres, and was keeper of the two great royal forests of Darnaway and Longmorn.[1] The condition of the northern districts we have already seen—their successful fight for freedom in 1297 under Andrew de Moray, their ensuing independence until 1303, and their prolonged resistance and disturbed condition in 1304 and 1305. There, accordingly, if anywhere, might Bruce expect to find the people " all ready at his will," and there, we may be sure, the patriotic Bishop of Moray was urging him to hasten. To Mar and Kildrummy, at all events, he must have gone, for the latter was in a position to offer a desperate resistance to a strong English army only a few months later, while the names of those who joined his standard from Inverness and Moray make it tolerably certain that he visited these parts also. As Alexander Pilche was constable of Inverness Castle for England, and as he is on record as having joined Bruce at this time, it may also be assumed that Inverness Castle was in the summer of 1306 in the hands of Bruce's party.

Elsewhere, meanwhile, Bruce's friends had not been idle. Everywhere north of the Forth and Clyde the Church was preaching a holy war, and though the Bishop of Glasgow had the misfortune to fall into English hands,

[1] Bain, ii. 1736.

the good work went on undaunted. David de Moravia, Bishop of Moray, was foremost among the patriot preachers, and the report of his doings drew on him Edward's especial wrath. With the Bishops of Glasgow and St. Andrews he formed the subject of indignant letters to the Pope, and repeated orders were issued to Aymer de Valence to effect his capture at all costs.[1] Happily, de Valence's efforts were unavailing, and, unlike his episcopal brethren of St. Andrews and Glasgow, David de Moravia escaped to fight for Bruce again ere long. Edward's complaint to the Pope concerning him is worth quoting, both for the light it throws on the state of affairs in the north and for the corroboration it affords of the accuracy of our narrative and our deductions thus far. It will be noted that the English king is unable to bring against the Bishop of Moray the charges of repeated oath-breaking, which form the burden of his plaint against the Bishops of St. Andrews and Glasgow. The document runs somewhat as follows :[2]

" The Bishop of Moray, by preaching so much against him, and by exhorting the flock of his bishopric to rebel with Sir Robert de Bruce, had incited them, nor does he yet cease to incite them daily as much as he is able, so that the flock of the bishopric of Moray who assembled to the help of the said Robert, and still hold themselves with him, have done this owing to the incitement, preaching, and exhorting of the said Bishop, because he told them that they were not less deserving of merit who rebelled with Sir Robert to help him against the king of England and his men, and took the part of the said Robert, than if they should fight in the Holy Land against pagans and Saracens." This last evidently rankled in Edward's mind, for he goes on : " He deceived Christians very much, aye by his false preaching and exhortation, and so has excited the people to join together to the effusion of Christian blood " ; and so, he concludes, the Bishop should be counted a murderer, and as Edward " has the ill-will of the said

---

[1] Bain. Various entries.   [2] Palgrave, p. 330.

Bishop very much at heart, let every representation and petition be made to the Pope against the said Bishop."

Several observations fall to be made on the foregoing complaint. To begin with, it was drafted after the capture of the Bishops of Glasgow and St. Andrews,[1] the former of whom was taken in Cupar Castle before the 8th June by Aymer de Valence,[2] and the latter of whom was certainly a prisoner by the end of July.[3] Mr. Bain, in his Calendar of Documents, assigns the date of the complaint to August, and this is probably correct. If that is so, then it has to be observed that at a date well after Methven we have Edward's own authority for saying that the men of Moray were still with Bruce. This is of considerable importance, but of even more importance is Edward's further statement that "the flock of the bishopric of Moray" had assembled to the help of Bruce, and that the Bishop was daily engaged in inciting the province of Moray to still further rebellion.

Among Edward's most consistent supporters in Scotland was Alexander de Abernethy. As early as March 1303 he is on record as a trusted servant of England, and from then onwards he rendered conspicuous service to Edward. In 1303 and 1304 he led expeditions against the patriots in Stratherne and Menteith, guarded the fords of the Forth to prevent the passage of Wallace or his friends, and did his best to capture the great patriot. From 1303 to 1305 he was custodier for England "of all the land from the Forth to the Scottish mountains," for which he retained sixty men-at-arms, besides foot. He also held the Sheriffdoms of Kincardine, Forfar, and Perth during the same period, and after the new Ordinance for the Government of Scotland, issued in October 1305, remained one of the most trusted and most influential of Edward's Scottish liegemen. In 1306 he took a prominent part against Bruce, and acted as one of Edward's chief lieutenants in Scotland north of the Forth. Till his death, which occurred some time after 1312, he fought on the side of

---

[1] Palgrave, clxii. 328-30. [2] Bain, ii. 1780. [3] *Ibid.*, p. 1812.

England, and at different periods between 1306 and 1312, filled the high offices of Joint Warden between Forth and Orkney, Warden between Forth and the Mountains, and Constable of Dundee.[1]

Soon after Bruce had left the neighbourhood of Scone, Alexander de Abernethy took the field openly against the new king, and from a despatch which he sent to Edward about the beginning of June 1306 [2] we learn something further of what befell during the period between Bruce's coronation and Methven. Bruce plainly had not been inactive. Forfar Castle had been captured, on his journey northward probably, and Abernethy reports that he found it burned and destroyed. He repaired it sufficiently to enable him, he thought, to hold out till relief came; from all of which it is clear that Bruce was not at that time anywhere in the neighbourhood—another indication that he visited the districts further north soon after his coronation. Even in Bruce's absence, however, Abernethy was not in an enviable position, and a further remark in his despatch shows very clearly to how great an extent Perthshire, Forfar, and Kincardine were on Bruce's side. He begs the king to command his son (the Prince of Wales) to be ready to assist him when needful, " and to cause him to chastise and prevent the Irish destroying the lands of his men of Fife and Gowrie with him in the king's service." The Irish, of course, are the Highlanders of Athol and Angus and the Mearns, and the fact that Abernethy was unable to protect the lands of his men in Fife and Gowrie from their depredations is a plain indication of the small extent of the support on which England could rely in these districts. The reference to the Prince of Wales is explained by the fact that as early as April 1306 Edward had made known that he and the prince were going to Scotland,[3] and that shortly afterwards to the prince was entrusted the task of leading an expedition to Scotland north of the Forth. The prince entered Scotland about the end of June, captured Lochmaben on 13th July,[4] was in the neighbour-

---

[1] See various entries in Bain.
[2] Bain, ii. 1793.
[3] *Ibid.*, p. 1763.
[4] *Ibid.*, p. 1803.

hood of Perth by 1st August,[1] and had taken Kildrummy by 13th September.[2] Abernethy's letter must of course have been written before the prince entered Scotland —otherwise he would naturally have appealed direct to the prince himself—and may with considerable certainty be assigned to May or early June, when intimation of the prince's impending advance must have been sent to Edward's lieutenants in Scotland, and when, as we know from the capture of Cupar, the English forces had begun to be active in the south-eastern part of Scotland north of the Forth.

By the beginning of June Aymer de Valence with a strong force had reached Fife, and succeeded in capturing Cupar, and in Cupar the Bishop of Glasgow.[3] Thence, probably on the news of the return of Bruce southwards, he retired to Perth, and there, on 26th June, he was challenged to battle by Bruce. He declined the challenge, and Bruce, lulled into a false security, was a few hours later taken by surprise, when many of his men were engaged in foraging, and the rest had laid aside their arms to prepare for the night's rest. A fierce hand-to-hand conflict ensued, but, outnumbered and taken unaawares, the Scottish army had no chance, and after a desperate confused mêlée they were totally routed.

Aymer de Valence's force at Methven consisted for the most part of the Scottish nobles who were opposed to Bruce, and their following. In the words of Gray, de Valence was accompanied by several " barons of England and several Scottish ones, descended from the blood of John Comyn, who all set themselves against the said Robert de Bruce." And later he tells us that after Bruce had retired from before Perth to prepare his camp at Methven, Aymer de Valence, " by advice of the Scottish lords who were with him in the town, friends of John Comyn and adherents of the English—the lords de Moubray, de Abernethy, de Brechin, and de Gordon, with several others—marched out in two columns." According to Barbour the English force outnumbered Bruce by

---

[1] Bain, ii. p. 1809.   [2] Ibid., p. 1829.   [3] Ibid., pp. 1780, 1809.

1500, and if this estimate is correct, it gives us a very good idea of the extent of the hostility which Bruce had to face in Scotland itself. For it must always be remembered that he had not only the whole might of England against him. He had the fierce enmity of the numerous blood relations and friends of the murdered Comyn to reckon with, and the hostility of those other Scotsmen who, for one cause or another, remained loyal to England. This it was which rendered his cause, desperate as it was before Methven, to all seeming hopeless after that fatal day ; and this it is which explains the savage relentlessness of the efforts of his foes to hunt him down.

The battle of Methven was more than a rout, it was a disaster. Sir David de Inchmartin, Sir Alexander Fraser, Sir David Berkeley, Hugh de la Haye, Thomas Randolph, and John de Somerville [1] were taken on the field, and the rest of the Scottish army was dispersed in all directions. Of the " two great columns " described by Sir Thomas Gray, Barbour tells us barely five hundred men remained with Bruce, and so complete was the overthrow that Bruce was compelled to take to the hills, for, in Barbour's graphic words :

> " He durst not to the plains go,
> For all the commons went him fro ;
> That for their lives were full fain
> To pass to the English peace again."

That the hills to which Bruce and his companions betook themselves were the mountains of Athol and Badenoch, Barbour makes quite clear. They " dreand (endured) in the Month their pain," he tells us explicitly, and :

> " Thus in the hills lived he
> Till the most part of his company
> Was riven and rent ; no shoes they had,
> But as they them of hides made,
> Therefore they went to Aberdeen,
> Where Neil the Bruce came and the queen,
> And other ladies fair and farand (handsome),
> Each one for love of her husband."

In Aberdeen, according to Barbour, the fugitives re-

[1] Barbour ; and Bain, ii. 1811.

mained for some time, until the English, learning of their whereabouts, advanced in force against them.[1] Whereupon they took to flight, and by way of the hills and Loch Tay came to Lorn. Their adventures thereafter are known to every reader of Scottish history.

Now, during his wanderings in the Grampians, Bruce was accompanied, Barbour tells us, by his brother Edward; the Earl of Athol; Sir William de Borqundoun, who seems to have been the knight who, in 1305-6, was Constable of Carstairs Castle; James Douglas; Sir Gilbert de la Haye; Sir Neil Campbell; and many others "that I their names can not say." These many others, it is safe to assume, included the Bishop of Moray and the other men of Moray, who, according to Edward's complaint above mentioned, were at that very time with Bruce. They included also, almost certainly, some of the men of Aberdeen and Banff who had joined Bruce's standard. When the presence of these northern adherents of Bruce is realised it is not difficult to see why in his desperate plight Bruce ventured to trust himself to Aberdeen. Moreover, the foes he might have expected to meet in that quarter, the Comyn Earl of Buchan and his friends, were still with Aymer de Valence, of whose army at Methven they had formed a considerable part. No advance had yet been made towards Aberdeen, and until that occurred Bruce could, accordingly, remain in comparative safety with his friends and supporters in Aberdeen and its neighbourhood. At all events, Barbour's statement on the point is explicit; and, as I have already remarked, Barbour's accuracy has been proved so repeatedly that in this matter it cannot be questioned, the more especially as it concerns the town with which, of all the towns in Scotland, he was best acquainted.

It is unnecessary to set forth in detail the further events of the year 1306, as these may be found in any Scottish history. A brief summary will serve for our purpose. On 11th August Bruce was defeated at Dalry, in Argyll, by the Lord of Lorn, and thereafter sent his

---

[1] De Valence was in Aberdeen by 3rd August. Bain, ii. 1810.

wife and daughter and the other ladies of the party to
Kildrummy Castle in charge of his brother Nigel and the
Earl of Athol. As we have already seen, a strong English
army, under the Prince of Wales, had meantime entered
Scotland, capturing Lochmaben Castle on 13th July,
and reaching Perth about 1st August. From there
they advanced north, and came to Kildrummy before the
end of August. On the news of their approach the
ladies were sent further north, and Nigel and his companions prepared to make a desperate defence of the
castle. By 13th September, however, the castle had
fallen, owing to treachery it is said, and Nigel Bruce,
Alexander Lindsay, Robert Boyd, and others of note
were captured. Nigel was executed shortly afterwards
at Berwick;[1] and the Earl of Athol, who escaped from
Kildrummy only to fall into the hands of the English a
little later, suffered the same fate at London on 29th
October.[2] Sir Simon Fraser, who had been taken before
the siege of Kildrummy, was put to death, with every
enormity known to English law, on 6th September.[3]

It had meanwhile fared badly with the queen and
the ladies. They had sought sanctuary at St. Duthus,
but the Earl of Ross violated the sanctuary and sent
them prisoners to England. The Earl of Ross, it will
be remembered, had suffered an imprisonment of six
years in England; and after his release in 1303 was entrusted by Edward with considerable power in the
North. There is nothing to show what his attitude
was during the critical spring and summer of 1306,
but probably, as I have already suggested, he held his
hand till he saw how events were likely to shape themselves. The presence of Aymer de Valence in the
North, in August 1306, very probably stimulated his
loyalty to Edward and caused him to give signal proof
of it by seizing the queen and her ladies. At all events,
Aymer de Valence was in Inverness some time during
the summer,[4] and in Aberdeen on the 3rd of August,[5]

[1] B. P., ii. 433.   [2] Ibid., i. 427.   [3] Annales Londoniensis, p. 148.
[4] Bain, ii. 1932.   [5] Ibid., p. 1810.

while on 11th August Edward himself thanked him[1]
for having "well settled affairs beyond the mountains and appointed wardens there." Be that as it may,
however, it is, on the face of it, unlikely that the queen
would have been found within such easy reach of the
Earl of Ross if he had been reckoned among King
Robert's foes. With the queen was probably captured
the wife of William Wiseman, Sheriff of Elgin, who
was consigned to prison at Roxburgh at the same time
as Bruce's daughter, Marjorie, was committed to the
custody of Sir Henry de Percy.[2]

Bruce meanwhile had succeeded in reaching Lennox,
where he was received joyfully by Earl Malcolm, who
till then had believed him killed at Methven. Thence,
closely pursued by the galleys of Lorn, he reached
Kintyre, where he received eager welcome from Angus
of the Isles, and was lodged in Angus's castle of Dunaverty. But even there he was not safe, for his foes were
hot on his track, and by 15th September Dunaverty
was closely invested.[3] They had come too late, however. Bruce again eluded them, and for the next four
and a half months Scotland knew him not.

---

[1] Bain, ii. 1820.   [2] Palgrave, p. 355.   [3] Bain, ii. 1833, 1834.

CHAPTER XXII

THE MYSTERY OF THE ISLAND OF RATHLIN

WE saw that about the middle of September 1306 Bruce left Dunaverty for the Island of Rathlin, and that there, according to Barbour, he remained hidden for four and a half months. Now, Rathlin lies only thirteen or fourteen miles south-west of Kintyre, and but four miles from the north coast of Ireland. In 1306 it formed part of the territories of the Bisets of the Glens of Antrim, who were warm adherents of Edward I, and as the island had a considerable population, it is hardly possible that, if Bruce and his friends did stay there for four and a half months, no news of their presence would have reached either Scotland or Ireland. On the face of it, therefore, Rathlin seems a strange place for the fugitives to have spent so long a period in, and the question, accordingly, at once arises, Is it certain that they did spend the winter of 1306-7 there? To that question a negative can be the only possible answer; and to the further question, Is there any evidence of their having spent that period elsewhere? we are bound to reply with an emphatic affirmative.

The authority for the Rathlin story is Barbour. Sir Thomas Gray, writing ten or twenty years before Barbour, makes no mention of it. He merely says that Robert de Bruce, on his return in 1307, landed from the Isles. Fordun, whose materials were collected prior to 1386, though those dealing with our period were not put into the form in which we now possess them until a number of years later, also makes no mention of Rathlin. He tells us of Bruce's wanderings, how he suffered all manner of hardships, " now left alone in the islands ; now alone, fleeing before his enemies ; now slighted by his servants, he abode in utter loneliness." But "God at length took pity on him ; and aided by the help and power of a certain noble lady, Christiana of the Isles . . . he, after endless toils, smart, and distress, got back by a round-about way to the Earldom of Carrick." It is thus clear that even among the learned men of Scotland in the fourteenth century, who had access to the books and documents of the period, and who must have talked often with many who had fought in the Wars of Bruce, there was apparently no knowledge, or tradition even, that Bruce had lain hidden for several months either in the Island of Rathlin or in any specific island. It is important, therefore, to consider exactly what Barbour does say concerning Bruce's sojourn in that island.

He tells us that Bruce stayed three days in Dunaverty, and then told his men to make ready :

"Toward Rachrin by sea to fare,
   That is an isle into the sea;
And may well in midways be
   Betwixt Kintyre and Ireland."

Then follow forty lines of description of the perils of the sea, the fury of the currents about the island, the making ready of the ships, and the perilous voyage—of 13 or 14 miles—all in the true Homeric style. And so he brings them safely to Rathlin, where, he tells us, the people did homage to Bruce, and during all the time he dwelt on the island brought him every day " victuals for three hundred men." As the island is only 6½ miles long and 1½ miles broad, and had a considerable popula-tion of its own, one wonders whence the victuals for 300 extra mouths for four and a half months could possibly have come ! Barbour wisely attempts no explanation. He leaves Bruce and his 300 on the island, while he takes up again the tale of the doings on the mainland.

But whence came the 300 ? If Barbour is to be believed, they fled with Bruce from Dunaverty, which, on the face of it, is most unlikely. To begin with,

Bruce could have had nothing like 300 companions with him when he reached Dunaverty, and in the next place, if we suppose he had, it is incredible that a fleet large enough to contain them all could have sailed thence without any tidings of its departure reaching his pursuers. For, as Barbour himself tells us, so closely were Bruce's foes pressing upon him when he sailed from the neighbourhood of Dumbarton for Kintyre that the Earl of Lennox, who was in the last galley, had to throw all his baggage overboard in order to escape capture. Moreover, Dunaverty itself was invested by the middle of September, that is to say within a day or two of Bruce's reaching it. Barbour tells us that Bruce stayed three days in Dunaverty. As his pursuers appeared before the castle by, at latest, 15th September,[1] their coming must have been immediately after, if not before, Bruce's flight thence. In all probability it was the appearance of the hostile force which caused Bruce's flight, but of that flight the English were unaware, for they sat down to a determined siege in the confident expectation that the fall of the castle would mean the capture of Bruce. It is, therefore, clear that no large fleet of galleys, such as that imagined by Barbour, could have borne the fugitives away from Dunaverty, for if it had neither Bruce's pursuers nor the besieging force could have remained in ignorance of it.

There is, however, a simple explanation of Barbour's statements. When Bruce returned four and a half months later, he was accompanied, Barbour says, by thirty-three galleys. As Barbour supposed that Bruce spent these four and a half months in Rathlin, he of course imagined that the galleys in which Bruce and his companions returned to Scotland were those in which they had sailed from Dunaverty. This is not only a perfectly reasonable explanation, but, as we shall presently see, may, with almost absolute certainty, be accepted as the true explanation. For I hope to show presently where Bruce actually did spend the winter of 1306-7,

[1] Bain, ii. 1833, 1834.

and where he obtained the men and galleys for his descent on the south-west in February 1307. Meanwhile, however, we may take it as tolerably certain that Bruce did not sail away openly from Dunaverty at the head of a lordly fleet, but that he fled in secret, accompanied only by a few faithful friends.

Barbour, as we saw, leaves Bruce and his 300 on Rathlin, while he takes up again the tale of the doings on the mainland. Then, the siege and capture of Kildrummy graphically described, and Edward disposed of at Burgh-on-Sands some months before his time, he returns to Bruce and Rathlin as follows :

> "To King Robert again go we,
> That in Rachrin with his men
> Lay till the winter near was gane,
> And of that isle his meat has tane.
> James of Douglas was angry
> That they so long should idle lie,
> And to Sir Robert Boyd said he :
> 'The poor folk of this country
> Are charged upon great manner
> Of us that idle lie here.'"

And so on in the true heroic style, the result of the dialogue being that Douglas and Boyd cross to Arran, capture valuable spoil at Brodick, and ten days afterwards are joined in that island by Bruce and his company, who arrive in thirty-three small galleys. A few days later comes the "fire of fate" and the attack on Turnberry, and Bruce once more has set the heather ablaze in Scotland.

It is, perhaps, unnecessary to point out how unhistorical the greater part of the foregoing tale is. Most of the Rathlin episode, with its disproportionate description of the ships, the perilous voyage, the homage of the people, and the feeding of the 300, is padding pure and simple. Barbour knew that Bruce had fled from Dunaverty to the Isles, and it is very possibly the case that at some period of his wanderings he visited Rathlin. Round these two facts Barbour's imagination wove the rest of the tale. For the purposes of his poem he had to account for the winter of 1306-7, and having heard that Bruce had been at Rathlin, he jumped to the conclusion that the whole four and a half months were spent there. The very vagueness of his tale shows that he was without first-hand information as to Bruce's doings during these months, and the very padding which, with poetic licence, he uses to cover up the gaps in his narrative serves to bring its essential bareness into relief.

Thus we see that the evidence for Bruce's sojourn of four and a half months in Rathlin is, on the face of it, open to grave suspicion. But have we any evidence, beyond negative criticism of Barbour himself, to set against his story? In the first place, we have the strange silence regarding Rathlin of the two Scottish authorities already mentioned (Fordun and Gray)—Gray may be termed a Scottish authority, as he drew his information from Scottish sources, and wrote his history in Scotland —and the only conclusion is either that they had never heard of Rathlin, or that they knew it to be but one of a series of places visited by Bruce in his wanderings and included by them under the general name of Isles. In the next place the *Chronicle of Lanercost*, the nearest chronicle in point of time to the events described and probably contemporary with them, a chronicle moreover compiled just over the Border, and therefore in close proximity to the events of which it speaks, states that Bruce "was lurking in a remote island," while Hemingburgh has it that he had gone "to the farthest isles of that region." Manifestly, Rathlin answers to neither of these descriptions. So far, then, the burden of what we may call the indirect evidence is distinctly against Rathlin.

We come now to evidence of a more direct kind. A chronicle of St. Albans [1] begins one of its sections with the heading, "How Robert the Brus fled from Scotland to Norway." It then goes on, "And at that same time was Robert the Brus much hated among the people of

---

[1] Quoted by Dr. Jamieson in Note at the end of his edition of Barbour's *Bruce*.

Scotland, so that he wist not what he was best to do; and for to hide him he went to Norway to the king that had spoused his sister; and there held him succour for to have; and Robert the Brus might not be found in Scotland." Later the chronicle tells "How Roberte Brus came again into Scotland, and gathered a great power of men for war upon King Edward," adding that he "before was fled into Norway for dread of death from the good King Edward." These statements are explicit enough; while the reason given for Bruce's choosing Norway, is, as we shall see, quite well founded, the chronicler's only error being that the king, who had spoused Bruce's sister, was by that time dead. As, however, he had been succeeded by his brother, who was thus Bruce's sister's brother-in-law, the error is not of much consequence.

Another chronicler, Rastell (1529), tells the same story; while Fabyan, who was Sheriff of London in 1493, after relating Bruce's defeat "in a plain near unto Saint John's Town" (*i.e.* Perth) adds: "And Robert the Bruce after his discomfiture and loss of his chief friends fearing lest the Scots, with such Englishmen as King Edward left there, would arise against him, all comfortless fled unto the King of Norway, and there abode during while King Edward lived."

The cumulative effect of these three statements is irresistible. Dr. Jamieson, in his well-known edition of Barbour's *Bruce*, poured scorn upon them, but his scorn was founded upon an error, for at that time the marriage of Bruce's sister to the King of Norway was unknown, and Dr. Jamieson could only explain the chronicler's assertion of it as "a misrepresentation of the affinity between Bruce and Richard de Burgh, Earl of Ulster, whose daughter he had married." But, now that the chroniclers' statements concerning Bruce's Norwegian connection have been proved to be correct, not only does Dr. Jamieson's objection vanish, but the very fact of their accuracy on such a point gives added weight to their statement that Bruce did go to Norway.

It will also be observed that the statements of the chroniclers as to the events before and after Methven, though concise, are astonishingly accurate, and accordingly, when they have been proved trustworthy in so many particulars, their statement that Bruce fled to Norway deserves credence, even if unsupported by other evidence. But that there is other evidence to support them, we have already seen in part, and shall presently see still further. Before proceeding to consider it, however, it will be advisable to explain precisely Bruce's connection with the royal family of Norway.

By the discovery of documents in recent years it has been proved beyond question than Bruce's sister, Isabella, was married in 1293, as his second wife, to Eric, King of Norway, the father of the Maid of Norway.[1] Though Eric died in 1299, he was succeeded by his brother Haco, who reigned until 1319. Thus the connection between Bruce and the reigning family of Norway was exceedingly close, as was also the connection between the two kingdoms. Eric's first wife was the daughter of Alexander III, and their daughter was the Maid of Norway; while Eric's second wife, the sister of Robert Bruce, was in 1307 the widow of one Norwegian king, the sister-in-law of another, and the sister of the new crowned King of Scots. So what more likely than that Robert Bruce, hard pressed by foes, his cause for the time to all seeming lost, should seek safety and a breathing-space in the Norwegian dominions?

One writer, in discussing the question of the alleged flight to Norway, commits himself to a very absurd remark. "Neither is it likely," he says, "that Bruce, had he gone to Norway, would have chosen for his return to Scotland a moment when his cause seemed utterly broken; when his friends, the Earl of Menteith, Sir Patrick Graham, and others had surrendered to Edward, and the coast was swarming with English and Highland galleys, in search of him." The inference apparently is that at Rathlin he, of course, knew of all

[1] B. P., ii. 432.

these things, and therefore chose that precise moment for his return to Scotland ! It should surely be obvious that the fact that he did return at that moment is a clear proof of the truth of Barbour's statement that Bruce was entirely ignorant of the severe losses which had befallen him after his separation from his queen in August. He was ignorant of the capture of his queen and his daughter, of the execution of his brother Nigel, the Earl of Athol, Sir Simon Fraser, and others, and of the surrender of many of his chief supporters. That being so, it surely follows—anyway for the credit of Bruce himself I hope it follows—that Bruce was much further away than Rathlin. If he was not it does not say much for him that he lay for four and a half months within fourteen miles of the Scottish coast, and did not venture to send any of his 300 companions to see what had befallen the friends who had risked so much for him. On the other hand, if he were in the Norwegian dominions the chances were all against any news reaching him after his flight from Scotland. Winter was setting in, the seas were wild and stormy, the means of communication were few and frail, and so far as he himself personally was concerned, his precise whereabouts was unknown. Accordingly the very reason so triumphantly advanced as a proof that Bruce did not go further afield than Rathlin is seen to be in reality an extremely convincing argument in favour of the Norwegian theory. Bruce returned when he did because he did not know either of the serious losses which had befallen him, or of the gathering of the English fleet off the western coasts. He did not know of these things because he was far removed from that quarter during the winter of 1306–7.

It will be observed that I have used the phrase " Norwegian dominions." At the period with which we are dealing the Orkneys still belonged to Norway, and, accordingly, when the English chroniclers spoke of Bruce as having gone to Norway, the authority on which they based their statement may quite well have meant Orkney. In any case, if Bruce actually went as far as Norway he certainly touched at Orkney on the way; but what I want to emphasize meanwhile is that the Norway of the English chronicles does not necessarily mean that he went beyond Orkney to the country which we know as Norway to-day. Orkney, it will be seen, thus fits in both with the statements that he went to Norway, and with the "remote island" of Lanercost and "the farthest isles of that region" of Hemingburgh.

Our evidence in favour of the Orkney or Norwegian theory is, however, not yet exhausted. There is a Mackenzie tradition of considerable antiquity that Bruce was received and entertained at Ellandonan Castle by Mackenzie of Kintail during his flight in the closing month of 1306. The tradition is mentioned in the Applecross Manuscript of 1669, and in Dr. George Mackenzie's MS., and it is undoubtedly founded both on traditions then existing and on manuscripts of an earlier date at that time in existence. Moreover, according to these manuscript histories, and to old tradition, the Mackenzies were then, as they had been for many years before, and were for many years after, at feud with Bruce's enemy, the Earl of Ross; while one manuscript states that the Mackenzie of Ellandonan of the day afterwards met Bruce at Inverness in 1307. Now, as we shall presently see, Bruce was at Inverness in 1307 and 1308, and he held an important Parliament there in 1312. So, all things considered, the Mackenzie tradition has a good deal to support it.

Then there is an Orkney tradition that Bruce in 1306 found sanctuary with the Laird of Halcro in Orkney, and a tradition in the family of Halcro that the laird of the day fought with Bruce at Bannockburn. Compare these with Boece's legend of the appearance of St. Magnus to the citizens of Aberdeen after the battle of Bannockburn, and the undoubted fact that Bruce made a grant of £5 from the fermes of Aberdeen to St. Magnus' Cathedral, Kirkwall.[1] Bruce, as we know, had the kingly gift of

[1] *Registrum Magni Sigilli* (1912 edition), App., i. 10; App., ii. 68. Also *Exchequer Rolls*, many entries.

never forgetting in prosperity the friends who had helped
him in adversity, as the long list of grants of land and
money to his supporters abundantly shows.   Nor was he
in the habit of making grants without good cause, and
we may therefore be certain that his grant to the cathedral
of St. Magnus was in recognition of some signal service
rendered to him.   Thus Boece's legend, and the grant to
St. Magnus, both go far to confirm the Orkney tradition,
and that tradition so confirmed coming on the top of all
we have just been considering seems to me to put the
finishing touch to the chain of evidence which makes it
as certain as an historical fact of such a nature can be,
that Bruce did find refuge in Orkney in the winter of
1306–7.

Once we admit the probability, at least, of this
theory, it is astonishing how other known facts, hitherto
in some ways rather baffling, fit into it.   It has probably
already occurred to the reader as strange that Bruce's
queen and daughter were sent to seek sanctuary at
Tain.   The king, who had not hesitated to commit
murder on the very steps of the high altar, must have
known that no sanctuary, however sacred, would have
availed him or his.   As a matter of sober fact I do not
believe that the ladies were sent from Kildrummy to
Tain with any such object.   They were sent from Kildrummy because it was realised that their safety there
was at best precarious, and it seems to me that the true
explanation of their presence at Tain is that they were
making for Orkney.   We have already seen that Bruce
and his company spent some time at Aberdeen after
Methven.   Thence, in all probability, they hoped to
escape by sea, as the Earl of Athol attempted to do a
few weeks later.   In all probability they abandoned the
idea as too dangerous, for that the danger was very real
the capture of Athol when he made his attempt proves.
We have seen already that in all his Scottish campaigns
Edward had a very considerable fleet operating off the
east coast, and there is no reason to suppose that he
departed from his usual custom on this occasion.   Hence

R

escape from Aberdeen was impracticable, hence also Bruce's dash for the west on the approach of an English force, and hence also the sending of the ladies north from Kildrummy by land. Again, I repeat, Tain could not have been their objective. They were only driven to the sanctuary of St. Duthus as a last resort, when, the Earl of Ross proving unexpectedly hostile, it seemed to afford them a last slender chance of safety. Their objective almost certainly was Orkney, where, under the banner of Norway, they would be safe, whither Bruce himself was to make if all else failed, and whither the Bishop of Moray had in all probability urged them and him to hasten.

We have already seen that the Bishop of Moray had drawn upon himself Edward's special wrath. By the beginning of August his brethren of St. Andrews and Glasgow, together with the Abbot of Scone, were prisoners in England. But he himself was still at large, in spite of all Edward's desperate eagerness for his capture. On 11th August we find the irate king writing angrily to Aymer de Valence on the subject.[1] After thanking his Commander-in-Chief for having "well settled affairs beyond the mountains," he goes on: "He is much surprised at not hearing from him whether the Bishop of Moray is taken or not, as he lately charged him and the Earl of Ross to see to this. Commands him to signify the fact for certain by the present bearer, as he much desires to have this Bishop's person in England, like those of the Bishops of St. Andrews and Glasgow."

Do we see in this reference to the Earl of Ross the key to the latter's seizure of the queen and her daughter? Be that as it may, Edward was disappointed of the Bishop's person, and the important point for us meanwhile is that the Bishop succeeded in escaping to Orkney. This we know from another letter of the angry king. On 6th March 1307 he wrote to Haco, King of Norway,[2] begging him "to arrest and send to him the rebel Bishop

<hr>

[1] Bain, ii. 1820.   [2] Close Rolls, 35 Ed. I, m., 12, *dorso*.

of Moray, who has been excommunicated by the Pope, and is resetted by some of Haco's subjects in the Isle of Orkney." By this time, of course, Edward knew of Bruce's return to Carrick, but he did not know that the Bishop had also in all probability returned to Scotland. News travelled slowly in those days, and the fact that Edward only learned of the Bishop's place of retreat after that patriotic prelate had left it in order to embark on a final and successful conflict with his old enemy of England, throws a vivid sidelight on the conditions of the period.

We have thus ascertained beyond the possibility of dispute that one at least of Bruce's chief supporters in 1306 was in Orkney during the winter of 1306–7. The important bearing that fact had on the subsequent history of the war we shall presently see, but meanwhile it will suffice to say that it is in itself a striking commentary on all we have just been considering regarding Bruce's doings in the winter of 1306–7, and the capture of his queen and daughter in the sanctuary of Tain.

CHAPTER XXIII

SOME PROBLEMS OF 1307

WE have not yet exhausted all the facts bearing on the question of Bruce's whereabouts in the winter of 1306–7, but in order to be in a position to place those which yet remain in their true perspective, it is now necessary to examine his doings in 1307.

In January 1307 Bruce was known to be in some island, probably Rathlin, between Scotland and Ireland, and, on the 29th of that month,[1] peremptory orders were issued to Sir Hugh Biset to join Sir John de Botetourte and Sir Simon de Montacute with a fleet in order to effect his capture. Bruce, however, eluded the English vessels, and landed in Arran about the beginning of February. Thence he crossed to his own earldom of Carrick, and there obtained a slight success over the English in the neighbourhood of his castle of Turnberry. Meanwhile, on 9th February his two brothers, Thomas and Alexander, along with Sir Reginald Crawford, had landed in Lochryan with 700 Irishmen. They were met on landing by the men of Galloway, under their chief Dugald Macdowall, and after a sharp conflict were totally routed. The two Bruces and Crawford were taken prisoners, and a day or two later were executed at Carlisle.

The news of Bruce's return very quickly reached Edward's ears, and troops were poured into Ayrshire and Galloway under the leadership of England's most skilful officers. It was during this period that most of the well-known romantic adventures of the fugitive king occurred. One slight success only attended Bruce's arms, Sir James Douglas capturing on 19th March his own castle of Douglas, and perpetrating the "Douglas

---

[1] Bain, ii. 1888, 1941.

larder." Famous in Scottish history though this episode is, from the historical point of view it is of little or no importance.

Sir Herbert Maxwell well sums up Bruce's position in these early months of 1307, when he says that "he had not an acre of land he could call his own; three of his four brothers and most of his trusty friends had perished on the gibbet; of his other supporters nearly all had given up his service as hopeless, and re-entered that of King Edward; his wife, his daughter, and his sisters were in English prisons."

Bruce, meanwhile, had taken refuge in the recesses of Galloway, but his hiding-place had been discovered, and his foes were closing in upon him from all sides. Aymer de Valence, Edward's most able general, was in supreme command of the forces, and with him probably were the 4000 foot, who mustered at Carlisle in February and March.[1] On the west Sir Henry de Percy guarded the approach to the sea[2]; on the south, in Wigtownshire, the men of Galloway were out in force under their chief Sir Dugald Macdowall[3]; on the east was Sir John de Botetourte with 70 horses and 200 archers[4]; while Sir Robert de Clifford and Sir John Wigton watched the fords on the river Cree.[5] From the north Bruce's implacable foe, John of Lorn, was hastening through Ayrshire with 22 men-at-arms and 800 Highlanders,[6] while another body of 300 English archers under Sir Geoffrey de Moubray was endeavouring to penetrate to Glentrool itself.[7] To meet all these converging forces Bruce had at most a few hundred ill-armed and ill-fed men, and only his own skill and the wildness of the country saved his little company from destruction and himself from capture and death.

Some time in March or in April—the date is uncertain—Aymer de Valence obtained information of Bruce's precise whereabouts, and a force of 1500 men was

---

[1] Bain, ii. 1902, 1913.   [2] Ibid. Various entries.   [3] Ibid.
[4] Ibid., pp. 1921, 1923.   [5] Ibid., p. 512.
[6] Ibid., p. 1957.   [7] Ibid., pp. 512, 1913

despatched up the Cree to endeavour to destroy him. Bruce, however, was on the alert, and catching his foes unawares on the hillside, in almost exactly the same manner as Dundee at Killiecrankie nearly four centuries later, he utterly routed them and drove them off the field with heavy loss.

We next hear of Bruce at Loudon Hill, in Ayr, nearly thirty-five miles to the north of Glentrool. There, on 10th May 1307,[1] he, with 600 men, met de Valence with a force said to number 3000. Bruce, however, with his usual skill, had chosen his ground well, and the end of the day found the English defeated and in full retreat.[2] The authority for the strength of Aymer de Valence's force is Barbour; but accurate though he usually is in his numbers, it must be admitted that there is some difficulty in accepting his Loudon Hill figures as correct, as the subsequent movements of the opposing forces show. After the battle de Valence retreated to Ayr. Three days later Bruce inflicted a defeat on another English force under Sir Ralph de Monthermer, and on de Monthermer also taking refuge in Ayr Castle, Bruce immediately invested it.

Now, obviously, if Bruce had only 600 men at the battle of Loudon Hill, it is incredible that he should have been in a position to besiege both de Valence and Monthermer in Ayr Castle three or four days after the battle, if the force of the former had amounted to anything like 3000 men. We are told, moreover, that the siege only lasted a short time, and that on the approach of further English troops Bruce was compelled to seek refuge again in the Galloway hills. The probability, therefore, is that Sir Aymer de Valence, whose castle of Bothwell was not very far away, had made an attempt with a small force to capture Bruce when he heard of his presence in Cunningham. Only thus can Bruce's ability to besiege him and Monthermer in Ayr Castle be explained, unless we are to believe that Bruce's army numbered more than 600 men. That it did so is unlikely. So far as Bruce's men were concerned Barbour was probably accurately informed, and, moreover, all the known facts bear him out in this particular instance. We are therefore driven to the conclusion that at Loudon Hill the English force was not large, and it is at least significant that throughout the rest of May and June the English held the west in strong force, and were unsparing in their efforts to hunt down the fugitive.

On 7th June 1307 Edward I died at Burgh-on-Sands, and from that moment the tide may be said to have turned in Bruce's favour. At first, however, it was hardly apparent. Throughout June, July, and August Aymer de Valence was exceedingly active,[1] but his efforts were fruitless, and towards the end of August he for some reason gave up his command and returned to England. Edward II had meanwhile proceeded south with his father's body, but he did not accompany it beyond Richmond, where he handed it over to the care of the Archbishop of York on 29th July.[2] Then, turning northwards again, he marched into Scotland by way of Carlisle, and advanced through Upper Nithsdale to Cumnock, which he reached about the second week of August.[3] There he remained to the 25th,[4] and then, without attempting anything further, he led the great army which had followed him back to England again. This inglorious retreat naturally afforded immense encouragement to Bruce, and the moment the English were over the border he swept down on Galloway and laid waste the lands of Sir Dugald Macdowall, who had sent his brothers to an ignominious death six months before. Then, according to the generally accepted story, he moved northwards in September or October 1307, leaving James Douglas to carry on the war in the south-west.

Such in brief outline is the tale of the events of 1307, as it has hitherto been told in Scottish history. It must,

[1] See many entries in Bain.
[2] Bain, iii. 2.
[3] *Ibid.*, 5.
[4] *Ibid.*, 7.

however, be obvious that there is nothing in that tale to account in any way either for Bruce's subsequent successes or for his sudden departure to the north in the closing months of 1307. It is merely a tale of a prolonged raid on the south-west which achieved no great success, and which apparently had no connection with any other movement elsewhere. We shall now, however, proceed to see that it was in reality part of a well thought out scheme, and that Bruce's advance to the north of Scotland was due to the success which had attended the efforts of those to whom had been entrusted the carrying out of the scheme in that quarter. We shall also see that in 1307, as in the ten preceding years, the events which took place in the north were much more important than those which occurred in the south, and that both in their immediate and their ultimate results.

As we have seen, Bruce landed in Carrick, his own earldom, in the early spring of 1307, and until September carried on a guerilla war in the south-west. ¿ In September he suddenly advanced to the north with a small force, and by the end of the year had defeated the Comyns at the battle of Inverurie, and begun the famous Herschip of Buchan. In explanation of this northern movement Mr. Lang simply says: "Bruce moved to the north, where, as the Forfar letter shows, he had hopes of finding partisans." He had hopes of finding partisans, that was all. Sir Herbert Maxwell is equally perplexed. "He moved northwards in order to raise the people in the national cause." No explanation is attempted. But why should he have moved northwards, without any adequate reason, on such an errand? To us, with all the facts we have elucidated before us, the answer presents little difficulty. The north held out no indefinite hopes. The north had already proved itself, and in the campaign of 1306 it had provided the bulk of Bruce's supporters. But none the less something more than that is necessary to explain the northward movement of 1307, and the astonishing success which attended it. After all, the campaign of 1306 had ended in a complete debacle, and though Bruce might have believed in 1307 that the north was still in sympathy with his cause, that in itself could hardly have been sufficient to entice him northwards at well-nigh the crisis of his fortunes, especially when it is remembered that in the north lay the country of the Comyns, his mortal foes.

At this stage the Bishop of Moray again appears on the scene. There is in existence a letter from the Earl of Ross to Edward II, written in the closing months of 1307,[1] wherein he asks pardon for having made a truce with Bruce, and explains that he was compelled to do so owing to Bruce having advanced into his territory with 3000 men. In the same letter he complains of the demands made upon him by the Bishop of Moray for the damage done to the Bishop's land by the Earl during the period when the Bishop was an outlaw. In October 1308 the Earl made complete submission to Bruce, and from that time onwards became one of his most powerful supporters, his son and heir, Hugh, marrying in the same year Bruce's sister, Matilda. The first witness to the deed of submission is the Bishop of Moray.[2]

Now, on 15th May 1307, the officer commanding for England at Forfar—almost certainly Sir Alexander Abernethy, though the name is missing from the document—reported[3] that he heard "that Sir Robert de Brus never had the goodwill of his own followers or the people at large, or even half of them, so much with him as now; and it now first appears that he has right, and God is openly for him, as he has destroyed all the king's (Edward's) power both among the English and the Scots, and the English force is in retreat to its own country, never to return. And they firmly believe, by the *encouragement of the false preachers who come from the host*, that Sir Robert de Brus will now have his will" (the italics are mine); and the writer himself believes, on the authority of Edward's officers, "both beyond and on this side of the mountains," whom he names, viz. Sir Reginald le Chen (Inverness, Nairn, and Moray), Sir

[1] Bain, iv. 399.   [2] Acts of Parl., i. 477.   [3] Bain, ii. 1926.

Duncan de Ferendrauth (Sheriff of Banff), and Sir Gilbert de Glenkernie (of the county of Elgin), "that if Sir Robert de Bruce can escape any way thither or towards the parts of Ross, he will find them all ready at his will more entirely than ever unless the king will be pleased to send more men-at-arms to these parts."

The importance of this letter can hardly be exaggerated. It is written on 15th May 1307; it speaks of the north as having been for some considerable time before that date roused on Bruce's behalf; it confesses that he possesses the goodwill of the people at large to an extraordinary degree; it reports that Edward's officers in the Highlands and the north-east are compelled to admit that the people in their districts are ready to rise *en masse* the moment Bruce appears, and that they are more devoted to him and his cause than ever; it declares that from Forth to the parts of Ross the whole country is openly for Bruce, and full of confidence that the day of the English is over; and, finally, it categorically ascribes this perilous condition of things largely to "the encouragement of the false preachers who come from the host."

Now, what do all these things mean? They mean, in the first place, that, during these fateful months in the spring of 1307, when Bruce was conducting his desperate forlorn hope in Galloway and Carrick, the north was rallying to his aid once again. They mean, in the second place, that at a date contemporaneous with Bruce's own descent on Carrick, in February 1307, his friends in the north were engaged in stirring up the people on his behalf. They must mean, in the third place, therefore, that his northern supporters knew both of his return and his plans; and they must accordingly mean, in the fourth place, that Bruce in the south-west and his friends in the north were acting in pursuance of an agreed upon plan of campaign. In no other way can the practically simultaneous renewal of the war in the north and the distant south-west be explained.

The question next arises, Who were these northern

patriots whose faith in their cause and their leader was so high as to inspire them to take yet another hand in the desperate game against England? Before we endeavour to answer let us consider for a moment the situation. Mr. Joseph Bain, in his admirable volume, *The Edwards in Scotland*, speaking of Bruce's return in February 1307, says he then for the first time learned "the tale of disasters and executions of his friends, and the desertion of his adherents, the Earl of Menteith, Sir Patrick Graham, and other chief men who had surrendered to Edward in November previous." The word "desertion" in such a context conveys an entirely erroneous impression. If there were any desertion it was on the part of Bruce, who in September had fled the country, abandoning to all seeming both his cause and his friends. So the surrender of some of the latter to Edward two months afterwards cannot fairly be described as "desertion." But the fact of their surrender throws a vivid light on the general situation. Methven had come and gone; Bruce himself had fled; many of his chief supporters were dead—his brother Nigel and his trusty friends, the Earl of Athol, Sir Simon Fraser, Sir David de Inchmartin, Sir John de Cambhou, Alexander le Scrimgeour, Ralph de Heriz, and Cuthbert de Carrick among them; many others were in English prisons, among them the Bishops of St. Andrews and Glasgow, the Abbot of Scone, Sir Hugh de la Haye, Sir Robert Boyd, Sir Alexander Fraser, Sir Thomas Randolph, and Sir Alexander Lindsay; some, like the Earl of Lennox and James Douglas, had fled with him; and those who remained were broken and scattered, leading the lives of hunted outlaws. Of these last some made good their escape—to the Orkneys and elsewhere; some succeeded in eluding capture, and lay hidden in the fastnesses of the Highlands till brighter days dawned; some, like the Earl of Menteith, Sir Patrick Graham, and Sir Walter Moray, were at length compelled, in the last extremity, to surrender. Thus at the end of 1306 Bruce's cause was seemingly broken beyond hope of recovery. Yet a month later, in the Highlands and in Galloway, eager men were following his flag in the field once more.

At the head of the patriots in the north we find the Bishop of Moray. From the letter and deed above mentioned we saw that he was with Bruce when he humbled the Earl of Ross in 1308; from the same letter and from Edward's letter to Haco on 6th March 1307 we know that he never, even in the darkest hour, abandoned Bruce's cause; while the Forfar letter of 15th May 1307, with its reference to "false preachers," makes it as certain as anything short of a definite mention of his name can be that he was at that date, and had been for some considerable time previously, at his old work of preaching a Holy War against England. For the rest, Edward's one time Sheriffs of Inverness, Elgin, and Banff, namely, Sir John de Stirling, Sir William Wiseman, and Sir Walter Berkeley, with Sir John de Fenton and Sir William de la Haye, both of the county of Inverness, and Sir David de Berkeley, are on record as having been with Bruce in his successful campaign against the Earl of Ross in 1308,[1] while Alexander Pilche appears at a later date as Bruce's Sheriff of Inverness. Of these Sir William Wiseman, Edward's Sheriff of Elgin; Sir Walter Berkeley, Edward's Sheriff of Banff; and Alexander Pilche, Edward's Constable of the castle of Inverness, are on record as having been "out" with Bruce in 1306; Sir John de Fenton is probably the son of the Sir William de Fenton of Beaufort who was also with Bruce in 1306, unless the name William in the 1306 list of "rebels" is an error for John; a Sir William de la Haye was Sheriff of Inverness in 1295–96; and a John de la Haye, "in the county of Inverness," is on record as having been with Bruce in 1306, which probably means that both father and son joined Bruce, unless, as is possible, some confusion existed in the mind of the copyist between the names of the two Inverness-shire knights, Sir John de Fenton and Sir William de la Haye; while Sir David de Berkeley has, of course, always been

---

[1] Acts of Parl., i. 477.   [2] Stevenson, ii. 17.

reckoned one of Bruce's earliest supporters. Of Sir John de Stirling there is no mention in 1306. He was a knight of Moray,[1] and was appointed Sheriff of Inverness[2] by Edward in September 1305, but does not appear in connection with Bruce until 1308.

It is therefore a fair inference that the men who aided the Bishop of Moray in rousing the north in the spring of 1307 were Alexander Pilche, Sir William Wiseman, Sir Walter de Berkeley, Sir William de la Haye, Sir John de Fenton, and Sir David de Berkeley, with perhaps Sir John de Stirling. Among the clergy who preached the Holy War were probably Master Walter Heroc, Dean of the Bishopric of Moray, and Master William de Crewsel,[3] precentor of the same diocese, who both witnessed the Earl of Ross's submission to Bruce in 1308; while the people to whom they preached, the people who filled the breasts of Edward's officers with such alarm in the spring of 1307, may best be described in the words of the same deed of submission as the " nobles, clergy, and laity " of Moray and the surrounding districts.

With all these facts, and the other facts which we have already elucidated, before us, we may now proceed, with some confidence, to reconstruct the history of the War of Independence after Bruce's flight from Dunaverty in September 1306.

---

[1] Bain, ii. 495. [2] *Ibid.*, p. 1691 (3). [3] Acts of Parl., i. 477.

CHAPTER XXIV

RECONSTRUCTION OF EVENTS FROM SEPTEMBER 1306 TO SEPTEMBER 1307

FROM Dunaverty Bruce fled northwards by sea. His companions were few—his brothers Edward, Thomas, and Alexander, the Earl of Lennox, Sir Gilbert de la Haye, Sir Neil Campbell, James Douglas, and perhaps Angus of the Isles are all we can venture to name with any certainty. In due time they reached Orkney, then part of the Norwegian dominions, enjoying perhaps on the way the hospitality of Mackenzie of Kintail at Ellandonan Castle. From Orkney Bruce himself and some of his companions may have gone to Norway, but, if so, their visit could not have been of long duration, for by the end of December 1306, at latest, they must have been back in Orkney. There they met other fugitives from the wrath of Edward, and there plans were laid for an immediate renewal of the war. If, in view of all we know concerning the disasters which had overtaken Bruce's cause on the mainland immediately after his flight, this seems improbable, a little further consideration will remove the difficulty.

Barbour tells us in the most explicit way that Bruce, on his return to Carrick, then first learnt of the disasters which had followed his flight. He says:

> " When that the King and his folk were
> Arrived, as I told you ere,
> A while in Carrick waited he
> To see who friend or foe would be,
> But he found little tenderness.

For the people were in such fear of the English,

> That they no friendship durst him show.
> But a lady of that countree,

270

That was to him in near degree
Of cousinage, was wondrous blithe
At his arrival, and speedily
Sped her to him, in full great haste
With forty men in company,
And handed them all to the King,
To help him in his warring.
And he received them in daynte
                (with joy, or in honour).
And her full greatly thanked he;
And asked for tidings of the Queen
And of his friends all eagerly,
That he had left in that countree
When that he put him to the sea.
And she him told, sighing full sore,
How that his brother taken was
In the Castle of Kildrummy.
And then destroyed so villainously;
And of the Earl Atholl also;
And how the Queen and others more
That to his party were holding
Were ta'en and led in-to England
And put in felon prison.
And how that Cristol of Setoun
Was slain, greeting she told the King,
That sorrowful was of that tiding."

Then follows a description of the king's grief, which it is unnecessary to quote. There has never been any question of the truth of this story. Not only is Barbour's authority on the point unchallengeable, but the story itself is quite in keeping with all the known facts.

Thus when the fugitives foregathered in Orkney under the shelter of the Norwegian flag, they believed that some of their friends at least were still holding out in Scotland; and it may not be altogether wide of the mark to suggest that the flight to the Norwegian dominions may have been undertaken partly in the hope of there securing such assistance as would make possible an immediate renewal of the war. However that may be, the essential fact is clear that in the winter months of 1306 Bruce was not aware that Kildrummy had fallen or that so many of his adherents elsewhere had been captured or destroyed. Accordingly, by all the laws of chivalry, to say nothing of policy, his return to Scotland at the earliest possible moment was necessary; and to him who was soon to be hailed by his contemporaries as the first knight in Europe the laws of chivalry always made irresistible appeal. Nor was this all. He would know that the fact of his flight was certain to be known to his foes, and would argue accordingly that they would not look for his return during the winter months. But if he were to defer his return till the spring or early summer not only would his enemies be on the alert, but his adherents would have abandoned hope, and his chances of success would be remote indeed. A campaign in winter or early spring, therefore, was not only necessary owing to the exigencies of the situation, but it promised more chances of success because his foes would probably be unprepared, and the conditions of the weather and the season—storm, snow, tempest, short days and long dark nights—would all be to the advantage of attacking forces operating in their own country.

Looked at from these points of view the events we are now approaching take on a new significance. They are seen to be the deliberate and necessary outcome of the position in which Bruce found himself towards the close of 1306, and they are seen to be closely related the one to the other instead of being, as they have hitherto been regarded, a series of more or less haphazard and fortuitous accidents, which owed nothing to, and in consequence reflected no credit on, the military genius of the first knight in Europe. The fact is, it has far too long been overlooked that Barbour was a priest, not a soldier, and that, consequently, while he was able to describe with fire and accuracy actual events, he was not able to appreciate the careful planning or the far-seeing military skill which lay behind them.

Now, what do we find early in 1307? Three separate and entirely unrelated raids occurring at almost identically the same moment—Bruce's own descent on Arran and Carrick, his brother's inroad on Galloway, and the northern patriots' onfall on the Highlands? To state it thus is to betray at once the absurdity of such a contention. The three raids occurred at almost the same moment, because, and only because, they had been planned to occur at almost the same moment. And so let us piece our narrative together.

The Bishop of Moray was in Orkney. Bruce and his companions were in Orkney. The situation in all its bearings was discussed and a definite plan agreed on. Bruce himself would rouse his own earldom of Carrick; his brothers would endeavour to get help from Ireland, and, with Sir Reginald Crawford, descend on Galloway; the Bishop of Moray would at the same moment once again raise the standard of revolt in the north. So from Orkney Bruce proceeded southwards, gathering recruits as he went. Mackenzie of Kintail probably contributed his quota in galleys and in men. Fordun tells us that " a certain noble lady, Christiana of the Isles," aided him with her " help and power." His friend and ally, Angus of the Isles, likewise did his share, and so " by a roundabout way," as Fordun puts it, thus bearing out our narrative, he " got back to the earldom of Carrick." It was on this roundabout way that he visited Rathlin. Bruce was far too skilled a soldier to descend on the mainland after a four months' absence without first spying out the land. So to Rathlin he took his way, a secluded island lying sufficiently near the Irish coast, to enable him to endeavour to obtain from Ireland the men he so sorely needed, and near enough to Scotland to enable him to send out some of his trusted comrades on a scouting expedition. Rathlin, too, was off the beaten track, and there he might lie in comparative safety for a week or two until his final preparations were made.

In reading the mass of contemporary documents published by Mr. Bain in his *Calendar*, and by other savants in other collections, no intelligent reader can fail to be impressed by the extraordinary efficiency of English organisation and English administration under the first Edward. This is especially true of the English administration in Scotland. The documents disclose an organi-

s

sation which can only be described as wonderful, and a knowledge of Scotland and Scottish affairs which is truly marvellous. Nothing is too small to escape the notice of Edward's officials. They seem to have had their spies everywhere, and the information which they transmitted in frequent reports to their royal master is, as a rule, extraordinarily full and accurate. All throughout the War of Independence this is abundantly evident, and the wonder is that the patriots ever should have made headway against an organisation so effective and a foe so well informed and so well served as Edward I. With the passing of the sceptre to the feeble hands of Edward II there came a vast change, and with it Scotland's opportunity. But in the early months of 1307 the greatest of the Plantagenets was still alive, and, though in feeble health, was consumed with a fiery eagerness to make an end of Bruce, which permeated to every corner of the vast organisation which he had created and still masterfully controlled. From the beginning of October 1306 to the beginning of March 1307, moreover, he made his headquarters at Lanercost,[1] where he was in close proximity to the Scottish border and in close touch with Ireland and the western coasts of Scotland and England. So he had early and full intelligence of Bruce's appearance in the western sea and of his arrival at Rathlin, for, as we have seen, on 29th January 1307 he ordered Hugh Biset to join Sir John de Menteith and Sir Simon Montacute with a fleet, in order " to put down Robert de Brus and destroy his retreat in the isles between Scotland and Ireland." [2]

This document disposes finally, to my mind, of the story that Bruce spent the four months from September to January in Rathlin; for it is incredible, looking to the many evidences we possess of the far-flung nature of Edward's sources of information, and the fiery zeal with which he urged on the hunt for the fugitive, that Bruce could have been in Rathlin for any length of time without information of his whereabouts reaching the

---

[1] Itinerary.   [2] Bain, ii. 1888.

English king. On the other hand, the fact that these orders were issued in January 1307 is a direct confirmation of the theory that Bruce visited Rathlin only on his return voyage from Orkney in December 1306 or January 1307. There he made final preparations for his descent on the mainland, and awaited news from the advance party, who had gone with Douglas to spy out the land, and from his brothers, who had crossed to Ireland in search of men for a descent on Galloway. Moreover, we should probably not be very far wrong in assuming that it was the efforts of the two brothers to raise a force in Ireland which gave away the secret both of Bruce's return and of his resting-place.

It will be remembered that Barbour made Bruce spend the winter in Rathlin with 300 companions—in itself an inherently improbable statement. As he puts Bruce's force at the same number when he returned to Carrick and attacked Turnberry, it is easy to see how he fell into his previous error. He was right in so far as he said that Bruce went to Rathlin with 300 men. His error lay in sending them there at the wrong time— namely, at the beginning instead of at the end of his wanderings in the western sea. So with the 33 galleys in which the 300 landed. They could not have sailed with Bruce from Dunaverty in September 1306, nor could they have lain all the winter at Rathlin. They both could and did come from the Island chiefs, who befriended the fugitive during his voyaging to and from Orkney.

The Lanercost chronicler tells us that with Bruce's brothers, when they landed in Galloway, was " the Lord of Kintyre and other large following." He also says that the Lord of Kintyre was among those captured, and that he was beheaded by Sir Dugal Macdowall and his head sent to Edward. In *Flores Historiarum*, however, we are told,[1] that the heads sent to Edward were "the head of Malcolm Makaillis, Lord of Kintyre, and the heads of the two leaders of the Irish " &c. This dis-

[1] Vol. iii. 327.

poses of many difficulties, among others of the statement often made that Angus Og himself took part in the Galloway raid, and the further statement, sometimes made, that he was captured and executed. For among those on record as having joined Bruce early in 1306 is one who figures in Palgrave's list as " Malcolm M'Culian in the Isle of Kentyr," who is obviously identical with the Malcolm Makaillis whom the English chroniclers took to be the Lord of Kintyre himself. We have, therefore, here unmistakable evidence that Angus Og sent men and ships to assist Bruce in the beginning of 1307.

Events now begin to shape themselves. Bruce raids Turnberry about the same time as his brothers Thomas and Alexander land in Galloway. But whereas Thomas and Alexander are totally routed, and pay the penalty for their failure with their lives, Bruce escapes from Turnberry with some spoil, and retires to the Galloway hills. Had his plans succeeded in their entirety, he would there have been in a strong position, but with his brothers dead and their force dispersed, he was little better than a desperate outlaw. Men do not, as a rule, flock to the standard of an outlaw, and especially not to that of such an outlaw as was Bruce, a man eagerly desired by the dreaded English king, a man on whose hands was the blood of sacrilegious murder, and on whose head was the curse of an outraged Church. So for a time Bruce's cause languished, his following dwindled, and he himself went in danger of betrayal and death. To this period belong these tales of his hair-breadth escapes, his courage, and his infinite resource, which are part of the heritage of every Scot.

Gradually, however, the tide began to show signs of turning. About 19th March Douglas perpetrated the " Douglas larder " ; a week or two later Bruce defeated the English at Glentrool ; and, moving thence to Cunningham and Kyle, gained recruits sufficient to enable him to beat de Valence at the Battle of Loudon Hill about the beginning of May, defeat Monthermer three days later, and lay siege to Ayr Castle. Meanwhile, in the distant north his Highland friends were doing their part manfully. Whether or not they actually came to blows with the English we know not, but their success at all events was such as to reduce Edward's officers in these parts to a state of terror.

So the spring passed and summer came. Edward I was sick unto death. The sceptre was slipping from his dying hands, and all men knew what manner of king his successor was like to prove. Bruce was waiting upon events amid the Galloway hills, whither he had been compelled to betake himself on the approach of a strong English force soon after he had laid siege to Ayr, and there he remained, hard beset, till the end of August. In the interval his great antagonist died at Burgh-on-Sands on 7th June, and his successor signalised the new order of things by marching into Scotland in August, and marching home again in September without accomplishing anything. Whereupon Bruce exacted fierce vengeance on the lands of the man who had sent his brothers to an ignominious death—Sir Dugal Macdowall —and then hastened north to place himself at the head of the movement which had assumed such promising dimensions in that quarter. The south, he saw, was still lukewarm or openly hostile. Six months of varying war had brought him few new adherents. No castle or strong place was in his hands. No man of note had declared for him. No large force was ready to follow him in the field. Not thus could a crown or the freedom of Scotland be won. So he turned to the north, which had followed him so gallantly little more than a year before, and which, in spite of all that had happened since, was still " all ready at his will more entirely than ever."

When I say this, I do not lose sight of the fact that in September Bruce's vengeance on Galloway was of so sweeping a nature that Edward II, then in Nottingham, issued orders that the Galloway men who had fled to Inglewood Forest to escape from Bruce, should there be received with their flocks and herds.[1]   But that fact does not alter the essential fact that the harrying of Galloway was in reality a successful raid on a hostile country, and that so far as the winning of the kingdom was concerned, it could not have, and did not have, any permanent result.   The ignominious retirement of the great English host across the border no doubt brought Bruce a number of recruits, and aided him vastly in his attack on the Macdowalls, but the plain fact none the less remains that, when he departed on his northward journey, he had neither land, village, nor castle in all the south that he could call his own, and was leader of but a small though gallant force.   The most that can be said is that the tide had taken a turn in his favour.   Glentrool and Loudon Hill had given it a slight start, the death of Edward I in June, and the inglorious advance and retreat of the English army in August and September, had together caused it to run a little more strongly ; and the harrying of Galloway gave it some further impetus ; but the flow was still weak and sluggish, and such record evidence as exists shows clearly that in the south-west Bruce's cause had not yet made any really substantial headway.

[1] Bain, ii. 14.

CHAPTER XXV

BRUCE AND THE EARL OF ROSS

It is unfortunate that we have no knowledge of the actual progress of events in the north in 1307, save such as can be gleaned from documents like the Forfar letter already quoted. But such documents are unhappily few and far between, and such as do exist are not supplemented to any great extent by the fourteenth century writers. It is this unfortunate want of perspective on the part of these writers which has led to the many misunderstandings of the War of Independence, and which has coloured all the so-called histories of the War, or of the period, in our own day. But in studying the history of the War of Independence, it should never be forgotten that Barbour and Fordun are both priestly writers; that by education and instinct the sympathies of both incline to the Teutonic part of the kingdom; that the calling and the careers of both brought them mainly into intimate connection with southern personages and southern influences; and that beyond the narrow radius of Aberdeen and the contiguous country the north was to both a closed book. In Barbour especially is this apparent. Within his limitations Barbour, it is true, is wonderfully accurate, but these limitations must always be borne in mind, as must also the fact already mentioned, that the priestly calling did not fit either Barbour or Fordun for understanding either the causes which lay behind the events they recorded or the motives which inspired the actions whose praises Barbour loved to sing. Nor must it be forgotten that "The Bruce" is a heroic poem, with Bruce and Douglas as its heroes, as the poet himself frankly declares in his opening canto. The poem, therefore, is not a history of the War of Independence, as it is often mistakenly regarded, but an epic poem whose motive is the singing of the heroic deeds of Bruce and Douglas. Bearing all these things in mind, let us proceed to consider the events in the north.

At the very outset we are met with a striking example of the limitations which we deplore in Barbour. He describes the battle of Loudon Hill — in May, remember — and then, having recorded de Valence's resignation or supersession — which event occurred in September 1307—he sings thus of Bruce :

> "Then wox his power mair and mair,
> And he thought well that he would fare
> Beyond the mounth with his men,
> To look who that his friend would be.
> Unto Sir Alexander the Fraser
> He trusted, for they cousins were,
> And his brother Simon, they two.
> He had need full well of more,
> For he had foes many ane ;
> Sir John Comyn, Earl of Bouchane,
> Add Sir John the Mowbray syne,
> And good Sir David of Brechyne,
> With all the folk in their leading,
> Were foes to the noble King.
> And, for he wist they were his foes,
> His journey northenwise he takes ;
> For he would see what kind of ending
> They would make of their menacing."

The many absurdities in the above passage hardly require to be pointed out. Bruce's power, as we have seen, can hardly be described as waxing more and more in August and September 1307 if the north is left out of consideration. Indeed Barbour himself only a dozen lines further on, after naming Bruce's companions on his northward journey, says he left behind him James Douglas "with all the folk that with him was," in order that he might endeavour to recover his own country, and adds, "He left him in to great peril." Hardly commensurate that with a power which was waxing more and more ! As for

the reasons of the northward journey they are of course
no reasons at all. Barbour had not the veriest idea why
Bruce went north when he did, and was reduced to in-
venting reasons which display at once his limitations as
an historian, and his lack of knowledge of events which
occurred outside his own peculiar sphere.

These things are again apparent when he at last gets
his hero north. He narrates Douglas's exploits in the
south, then goes on :—

> " And turn we to the noble King;
> That, with the folk of his leading,
> Toward the mounth has taken the way
> Right stoutly, in-to good array.
> Where Alexander Fraser him met,
> Also his brother, Simon het,
> With all the folk they with them had."

Then follows a full description of Bruce's adventures in
Aberdeenshire, ending up with the Battle of Inverurie
and the Herschip of Buchan, when Bruce

> " —— harried them in such manner,
> That after that for fifty year
> Men minded 'the Herschip of Bouchane."

Then, without a pause, he goes straight on—

> " The King then till his peace has ta'en
> The north countree that humbly
> Obeisit to his seignory ;
> So that benorth the mounth were none
> That they not were his men each one,
> His lordship wox ay mair and mair,
> Toward Angus then did he fare,
> And thought soon to make all free
> Upon north half the Scottish Sea."

Thereafter he makes Bruce proceed at once to the capture of Forfar, and thence to the siege and capture of Perth
—which latter event did not take place till 1313. Then,
Perth captured five years before its time, he goes on—

> " Upon north half the Scottish Sea
> Obeyed all to his Majesty
> Except the Lord of Lorn and they
> Of Argyle that would with him gae."

The foregoing extracts are the only references Barbour has to all the very important happenings in the north which we are now about to consider. He gives in great detail the events which befel in his own district of Aberdeen, but of Bruce's Highland campaigns—with the exception of that in Lorn at a later date—he has but the vaguest idea. Thus we see once again that while Barbour may be trusted when he describes events in detail, he is anything but a satisfactory guide when he writes in general terms, when, in a word, he ventures outside his own circumscribed limits. For the former, as he assures us repeatedly, he depends on the narratives either of actual participators in the events he describes, or of persons to whom these have related them. For the latter he has only his own vague knowledge or imagination to guide him, or stories of the usual legendary nature, which, of course, were current during the period when he wrote, that is some seventy years after the date at which we have now arrived.

The real turning-point in Bruce's fortunes was his northern campaigns of 1307 and 1308. Until he went north his cause had not made much headway outside the province of Moray, and nothing had been accomplished which held out any prospect of either an ultimate or a permanent triumph. The northern campaigns changed all that. In the course of a few months the whole north from Caithness to Aberdeen was solidly behind him. Of his two most powerful opponents, one, the Earl of Ross, had made complete surrender, becoming Bruce's friend and ally; the other, the Comyn Earl of Buchan, had been driven from the north never to return, leaving his territories devastated, his vassals dead or Bruce's men. There followed rapidly the subjugation of Argyll and the winning of all the country north of Forth, with the exception of Perth and Dundee. Then, and not till then, was real headway made in the south. It was with a following which, the Lanercost chronicler expressly tells us, came from the outer isles of Scotland, that Edward Bruce, Douglas, Robert Boyd, and Alexander Lindsay in

1308 invaded Galloway and "made nearly all that district subject to them"; while in 1311, when Bruce was again marching towards Galloway, the same authority says that Edward II sent the Earl of Cornwall "to the town of St. John (Perth), beyond the Scottish Sea, *in case Robert de Brus should go beyond the said sea to collect troops.*" These facts will suffice in the meantime to indicate the importance of the northern campaigns of 1307 and 1308.

The material which exists for a reconstruction of the events in the north in 1307 and 1308 is, as we have seen, unfortunately very scanty, and sometimes contradictory. The important Forfar letter of May 1307 we have already examined, and we have also noted Edward I's letter of 6th March in the same year concerning the "rebel" Bishop of Moray. We shall now consider the very important petition, or series of petitions already briefly referred to, addressed by the Earl of Ross and his son Hugh to Edward II in 1307.[1] There is, unfortunately, no date on any of the petitions, but they have been assigned by Mr. Bain to May 1308, and on that assumption certain theories have been based. This, however, is an impossible date, as the internal evidence shows.

The principal petition narrates that Sir Robert de Bruce had come towards the parts of Ross with such great power that the earl had not sufficient power to oppose him. He remained, it says, with three thousand men for a fortnight, at the earl's expense, on the borders of Ross, Sutherland, and Caithness, and had threatened to destroy these territories utterly unless the earl made a truce with him till Pentecost next (1st June 1308), "by which time we hope succour will arrive from the King, on whom all our hopes of safety depend. Be it known, Sire, that in no manner can we refuse to make truce with him, because the Guardian of Moray is absent, and his people will not assist us without his orders. We have therefore no hope of assistance but from the King."

Mr. Bain apparently assigned this letter to May 1308 for two reasons, (1) the reference to Pentecost next, and

1 Bain, iv. 399.

(2) because of a letter of thanks for his loyalty addressed by Edward II to the earl on 20th May 1308.   To take the latter first, Mr. Bain assumes that this letter is an acknowledgment of a sort of the earl's petition.   But it is nothing of the kind.   On 20th May Edward simply addressed formal letters of thanks to thirteen of his Scottish adherents,[1] those so addressed including the Earl of Athol, Sir David de Brechin, Sir Reginald le Chen, the Earl of March and his son, and the Earl of Ross and his son.   All the letters are couched in identical terms, and beyond indicating that the men to whom they were addressed were at that time numbered among the adherents of England, are of no value whatsoever.   It is perhaps ominous, however, that the "Scottish adherents" to whom they are addressed number thirteen !

The reference to "Pentecost next" is quite another matter.   Mr. Bain has here overlooked a very important point which, as I have before pointed out, must always be kept in view in reading these fourteenth century documents, that is the slowness of the means of communication, and the consequent allowance which must be made for the time which would elapse between the despatch of a letter and its arrival at its destination.   As we have already seen, it took in normal times about a month for a letter to be carried in the fourteenth century from Inverness to London.   Now, the Earl of Ross in the above petition expressly says that he hopes for succour from the king before the expiry of the truce.   If a letter took a month to reach the king, two months more, at the very lowest estimate, would elapse before a force could arrive in Ross-shire, and that even though orders were sent at once to the English commanders in Scotland to march to the earl's assistance.   Thus, even on a cursory examination, the earl's letter must have been written at the very least three months before Pentecost, and, as Pentecost in 1308 fell on 1st June, it could not, therefore, have been written later than the 1st March.   But the writer says that at the time of writing

[1] Foedera.

Bruce had been for a fortnight in his territories with three thousand men, which means that if the letter were written three months before Pentecost, Bruce must have been as far north as Inverness by the first week of February.

Now, as we shall see, not only was Bruce certainly not anywhere near Inverness in January or February 1308, but other reasons make it impossible to assign so late a date as the beginning of March to the earl's letter.   In the first place, it is not in the least likely that the Earl of Ross could have addressed to Edward II the appeal he did if only three months lay between him and the expiry of the truce.   For though it is just within the bounds of possibility that assistance might have been forthcoming within three months, it is so remote a possibility that it may at once be ruled out of the reckoning.   The Earl of Ross, at all events, would never have dreamt of such a possibility.   He had been, not so many years before, one of the leaders of the Scottish Army.   He had assisted in invasions of England; he had spent a long term of captivity in England; he had made the journey between London and Ross-shire; and he had acted for two years as one of the Lieutenants of England in the north.   He was, accordingly, acquainted with all the difficulties of communication with England, and with the character of the men who now ruled England and administered her affairs; and he was well versed in all the arts, and all the difficulties, of mediæval war.

In the second place, of what possible advantage could a truce of anything like three months, or less, have been to Bruce?   It would merely have tied his hands, compelling him either to remain in the neighbourhood of Ross till the truce expired, or, if he wished to attempt anything elsewhere, to leave Ross behind him in a state of slumbering hostility for a period too short to be of any value to him.   In other words, a short truce would simply have meant that the northern campaign had been a failure, that Bruce had been compelled to abandon it with his work half done, and that the task would have had to be undertaken again.   The terms of the earl's

letter and Bruce's subsequent actions are alike inconsistent
with any such view; while to suggest that Bruce merely
marched to Ross-shire and marched away south-east again
without accomplishing anything and leaving a potential
enemy in his rear, is to ascribe to him a lack of military
skill, which it is impossible to imagine in the man who
was the greatest military genius of his generation.

The question next arises, granting that a short truce
is on the face of it unlikely, is there any reason why
Bruce should have desired a long truce, or, indeed, any
truce at all? As we have just seen, a short truce with
the Earl of Ross would have made it impossible for Bruce
in the interval to carry out his plans elsewhere. The
next question, therefore, is, Had Bruce any such plans?
The fact that the Earl of Ross places Bruce's force at
three thousand men, shows that the neighbouring districts had, as the Forfar letter prophesied, rallied in no
uncertain way to Bruce's aid; as does also the further
fact that the earl, in spite of all the resources of the
earldoms of Ross and Sutherland, was unable to offer
any opposition to him. With Ross and Sutherland
owning the sway of the Earl of Ross,[1] it is, of course,
plain that the three thousand must have come mostly
from the province of Moray; and with that great province so whole-heartedly behind him, Bruce was clearly
in a strong position for striking either at the Earl of Ross
on the north or the Earl of Buchan on the east. If my
reading of the earl's letter to Edward is correct, then
Bruce struck first at the Earl of Ross, probably as the
less formidable foe; and, on rendering him innocuous
for a sufficient period, turned his attention to Buchan.
No doubt he could have reduced the Earl of Ross by
force if he had wished, but Bruce was sagacious in council
as well as skilful in war, and he knew that if he could
win the earl to his side by peaceful means, it would be
very much better for himself and his cause.

The Earl of Buchan was in quite different case. Be-

---

[1] The Earl of Sutherland was at the time a minor and under the
guardianship of the Earl of Ross.

tween him and Bruce there could never be peace or friendship. The blood of John Comyn on the one side and the blood of Bruce's three brothers on the other lay for ever between them. Only blood could wipe out these memories. So Bruce readily granted truce to the Earl of Ross, in order that his hands might be free to deal with Buchan. Then, with Ross and Sutherland neutral behind him, he would be able to advance through friendly Moray against his mortal foe. But for such a purpose a truce with the Earl of Ross of anything less than six months would be useless—and it may be said that Bruce frequently granted truces of similar or longer duration—and the idea of a truce for a short period, such as the dating of the Earl of Ross's letter in April or May, or even in March, would imply, must therefore, on this count also, be dismissed as impossible. That being so, the earl's letter cannot be assigned to a date later than the beginning of December 1307, which means that Bruce was in Moray in the autumn of that year.

No consideration of the very important matter of the truce between Bruce and the Earl of Ross would be complete which neglected the personal factor. Both Bruce and the Earl of Ross knew very well what manner of man Edward II was; and Bruce accordingly, in agreeing to the truce, must have felt fairly certain that there was little likelihood of the earl's ever obtaining help from England. Everything, therefore, would depend on the fortunes of the campaign against Buchan. If Bruce was successful the Earl of Ross would, willy nilly, have to throw in his lot with the patriots. If Buchan were successful, the earl was in as strong a position as ever. Thus, from the point of view of policy, a truce was clearly to the advantage of both Bruce and the earl. On Bruce's side, moreover, we may be sure that every possible precaution would be taken to secure that the earl observed the truce. As the dictator of terms Bruce would, of course, demand hostages according to the custom of the time, and it is improbable that he would be content with less than

a son or sons of the earl. As is well known, between
Edward Bruce and the family of the Earl of Ross
there grew a great affection, and it is possible that its
beginnings may be traced to this time. For in all
probability, Walter, one of the younger sons of the
earl, whose death at Bannockburn Edward Bruce so
bitterly lamented, was one of the hostages delivered
to Bruce as security for his father's good behaviour
during the truce of 1307–8.

This reading of the events of 1307 and 1308 is, to
modern students at least, entirely novel; but even if it
depended solely on the facts and arguments already
adduced, I find it difficult to conceive how the internal
evidence of the Earl of Ross's petition can be explained
away. Fortunately, however, there exists other evidence
of a corroborative nature, which confirms our deductions
so strikingly as to place their accuracy beyond question.

It was the custom of the English officials to endorse
on petitions notes explaining how they were dealt with.
The petition we have been considering bears upon it the
significant endorsement, "To this petition no answer
can be made without the king."[1] This is a most
unusual endorsement, and can only mean that for some
reason or other the king was for a time beyond the
reach of his officials and the affairs of State. It cannot
mean that the king was simply moving about the
country, that it was an ordinary absence from London
caused by the movements of the Court. In such circumstances letters and papers were always forwarded,
and the necessary business was transacted wherever the
king happened to be. A glance at any Calendar of
State Papers of the period will make this clear.

Now, in the year which succeeded Edward's return
to England in September 1307, after his abortive
Scottish expedition, there is only one possible period
to which such an endorsement of such a petition can
be assigned. That is the period of sixteen or seventeen
days during which he was absent in France, on the

[1] Bain, iv. 399.

occasion of his marriage to Isabella, the French king's daughter. He left London in the second week of January, to travel by way of Dover to Boulogne, where he was married on 25th January; and it may be mentioned, as bearing out what I have just said regarding the transaction of business wherever in his kingdom the king might happen to be, that while on this very journey orders were issued from Dover concerning certain Scottish prisoners. He sailed from Dover on Monday, 22nd January, returned to Dover on 7th February, and reached the Tower of London on 21st February.[1] From then until the middle of June Edward was never more than a few miles from London,[2] while during April and May he was in almost daily attendance at Westminster, where the Parliament was sitting which decreed the banishment of his favourite Piers Gaveston. It is quite plain, therefore, that the phrase "No answer can be made without the king," cannot refer to the period from the middle of February to the middle of June. Yet, if the petition were written in either April or May, as Mr. Bain suggests, or in January, February, or March, it must certainly have arrived when the king was in London, or, at the latest, in the last week of June, when he was no further away than Bristol. Clearly, therefore, it was not written in any of these months.

As Edward was also in London from the beginning of November until the middle of January,[3] the same argument holds good as to that period, and we are therefore forced to the conclusion that the Earl of Ross's appeal for aid could only have reached London about the end of January or the beginning of February 1308. Thus the accuracy of our deductions from the internal evidence of the petition itself seems to be clearly proved. For if a month were the normal time occupied in the transit of a letter from Inverness to London in

[1] For these dates see *Genesis of Lancaster*, i. 9, and authorities there quoted.
[2] See *Parliamentary Writs, Calendars of Documents*, &c., &c.
[3] *Ibid.*

T

summer, in the impetuous days of Edward I, two months to ten weeks is not too much to allow for a messenger carrying despatches from Ross-shire to London, in the depth of winter, in the troubled times of Edward II. But two months prior to the beginning of February carries us back to the beginning of December, the latest date at which, according to our previous deduction, the letter could have been written. As a matter of fact, it was probably written a week or two earlier, and, as the writer states that Bruce was on the marches of Ross a fortnight before he wrote, the arrival of the King of Scots in Ross-shire can, with tolerable certainty, be assigned to the third or fourth week of October. This means that he reached Moray not later than the beginning of October 1307, and Inverness not later than the end of the first or second week of the same month.

We have had already, in the course of this inquiry, remarkable evidence of the effect on the history of the War of Independence of the limited purview of the later Scottish historians. Their treatment of the period with which we are now dealing provides us with yet another forcible illustration of this. Fordun is generally regarded as the most trustworthy of the early Scottish writers on the fourteenth century, and Fordun thus narrates the story of the events of 1307. He tells us how Bruce returned to Carrick, and goes on : " As soon as he had reached that place, he sought out one of his castles, slew the inmates thereof, destroyed the castle, and shared the arms and other spoils among his men. Then being greatly gladdened by such a beginning after his long spell of ill-luck, he got together his men, who had been scattered far and wide ; and, crossing the hills with them in a body, he got as far as Inverness, took the castle thereof with a strong hand, slew its garrison, and levelled it with the ground. In this way dealt he with the rest of the castles and strongholds established in the north, as well as with their inmates, until he got with his army as far as Slenach " (*i.e.* Slivoch, about sixteen miles north-west of Inverurie and near his own castle of Kildrummy).

Bishop Leslie, writing in 1578, has a somewhat similar account, based no doubt on Fordun, while Hector Boece describes the northern campaign in graphic verse, which will bear quotation. After describing Bruce's descent on Carrick, he proceeds :

> " Soon after this that ye have heard me say,
>   To Inverness he passit on a day,
>   Where that the castle, as my author says,
>   With Englishmen was keepit in those days,
>   And in the town also were in great number
>   Over all those parts which they did so cumber.
>   This ilk castle he seized and he won,
>   Where he left living neither wife nor man
>   Within the house, and in the town also
>   He spared neither that time poor nor rich
>   Of English blood, and Scotsmen that were false
>   Some he gart head and some hang by the neck.
>   Suchlike he did in many sundry part :
>   Then some by force and some by subtle art,
>   The North of Scotland that time good and ill
>   He wielded all at his plesour and will."

Similarly, George Buchanan says that Bruce, striking north in September, surprised and captured the castle of Inverness, which, he explains, owing to its remote situation, was negligently guarded. Now, no doubt, the accounts of Leslie, Boece, and Buchanan are all founded on Fordun, but my point, meantime, is that such was the narrative of the course of events current in Scotland until at least the close of the sixteenth century. But the nineteenth-century historian, with his perverted outlook and his distrust of all the earlier historians, treated these statements with a snort of contempt. He had got it into his head that it was only the southern part of the country which really counted. Was not, therefore, the war supported entirely and won solely by the Lowlands ? The north had nothing to do with it. Therefore Bruce could not have gone to Inverness and Moray in the autumn of 1307. Therefore, further, he did not go. Accordingly, Fordun's account was cast contemptuously aside. The possibility of the Highlands having played any part in the war was ignored, and such dogmatic travesties of fact as "the War of Independence was won by the Lowland Scots, in origin mainly of English descent, fighting under the standards of leaders more or less Norman by blood," [1] were solemnly set down by historians of repute, and passed into the domain of sober history. Yet it is hardly necessary to point out to anyone who has read thus far how wild and inaccurate, how totally at variance with all the known facts, any such view is.

It will be observed how closely Fordun's narrative corresponds with the deductions which we have drawn from the Earl of Ross's letter. He makes Bruce go to Inverness, capture the castle, reduce the north, and then, and not till then, advance against the Earl of Buchan; and he explicitly says that these things occurred in 1307. At Slenach he causes him to be attacked by "the Earl of Buchan with many nobles both English and Scots," just as Barbour does; and as Barbour tells us expressly that this attack took place "after the Martinmas, when snow had covered all the land," we get a date, about the beginning of December, which fits in exactly with the course of events as we have thus far deduced it. So I do not think it can now be disputed that Bruce in the early autumn advanced to Inverness, drove the English faction out of Moray—the Earl of Ross, it will be remembered, says in his letter that the guardian of Moray was absent— brought the Earl of Ross to terms, and then marched to Aberdeenshire. Fordun's definite statement is confirmed by the Earl of Ross's letter, and our deductions from that letter are in their turn confirmed by Fordun's narrative.

It may be argued that if Bruce were in Galloway at the end of September there was no time for him to have accomplished all we say he did accomplish between then and his arrival at Slivoch in the beginning of December. But, in the first place, it is by no means certain that Bruce

[1] Andrew Lang's *History of Scotland*, i. Appendix.

was in Galloway at the end of September. The belief that he was rests on two English documents, one dated at Clipstone, near Nottingham, on 25th September,[1] and the other dated at Lenton on 30th September.[2] By the first the king commands Robert de Clifford to allow the men of Galloway feed their flocks and herds in Englewood Forest, "whither they have come to take refuge for fear of Robert de Brus and his accomplices," and by the second he commands certain of his officers and magnates to march into Galloway against Bruce as "he and his accomplices are burning and plundering and inciting and compelling the inhabitants to rebel." The date of the raid is fixed by the first document; and as Edward knew of it in Nottingham, a week distant from the Scottish border, on 25th September, it must obviously have occurred not later than 15th, and probably a week or so earlier. Accordingly, if Bruce left Galloway by 15th September, he could easily have been at Inverness by the first week in October, and in Ross by the third week. If he remained there no longer than the fortnight, which the Earl of Ross mentions, that would leave him fully three weeks to get to Slivoch before the beginning of December.

There is, however, another point to consider. It does not follow that Bruce personally took part in the raid on Galloway. The English documents mention Bruce and his accomplices; but just as in the Boer War, De Wet was frequently reported to be at the same time in two places, hundreds of miles apart, so a raid on Galloway by Bruce's followers would be presumed, even by the people raided, to be led by Bruce himself. Barbour, curiously enough, mentions no raid on Galloway at this time; but as he says that Bruce left Douglas behind him to carry on the war in the south-west, and as he further asserts that Douglas at this time performed many brilliant feats of arms, it is quite possible that the real leader of the attack on Galloway was Douglas not Bruce, that Bruce at an earlier date than has hitherto been believed may have been in the north.

The Lanercost chronicler, who from his close proximity to Galloway had pretty full knowledge of all that passed there, seems to bear this out. He says: "While all these affairs were being transacted" (*i.e.* Edward's dismissal of his father's trusted officials and his raising of Piers Gaveston to the highest place in the realm in the autumn of 1307), "Robert Bruce, with his brother Edward and many of his adherents, was moving through Scotland wherever he liked, in despite of the English guardians, and chiefly in Galloway, from which district he took tribute under agreement that it should be left in peace." This can only mean that it was not in Galloway alone that Bruce, or his adherents, was making his power felt, and almost necessarily implies that successful campaigns were being conducted in different parts of the country at the same time. Be that as it may, the point is not of great importance once it is grasped that between 15th September and the beginning of December there was plenty of time for Bruce to proceed to Inverness and Moray, bring the Earl of Ross to terms, and march with a strong force to Slivoch on the western border of Aberdeenshire.

CHAPTER XXVI

CAMPAIGN IN MORAY AND ROSS (1307)

BEFORE we can proceed to place in their true order and perspective all the facts relating to the northern campaigns of 1307 and 1308, there are one or two points yet to be considered. The most important of these is a somewhat perplexing reference to the Bishop of Moray in one of the petitions by the Earl of Ross above referred to.

It is, unfortunately, impossible to arrive at any conclusion as to the date of this petition, but, so far as the internal evidence indicates, it seems to have been drafted some time in the summer of 1307. It is a complaint addressed by the Earl of Ross to Edward II, and runs somewhat as follows: " Be it known that the Bishop of Moray was one year against the peace of your Scottish realm. And because he would not come to your peace we descended on his land, and on the lands of others who were also against your peace, and his land was wasted by us and our people ; *and because the said Bishop is now received to your peace* he addresses monitions to us that we should make restoration of the property destroyed and wasted by us and our people *at the time when he was against your peace.* Grant, dear sire, to command him to cease such monitions," &c.[1] The endorsement on this request runs: " Let a royal letter be sent to the Bishop of Moray that he cease from his monitions and threats in regard to the things which were done at the time when he was against the peace." [2]

The whole tenor of the letter, and especially the words which I have italicised, are a little difficult to

---

[1] The italics are mine.   [2] Bain, iv. 400.

reconcile with the other facts which we possess regarding the Bishop. As we saw, Edward I himself denounced him as a rebel on 6th March 1307. The above letter declares that he was for a year against the peace of the English king's Scottish realm. The Forfar letter of 15th May, with its reference to "false preachers" in the Bishop's own diocese, clearly indicates that he had not then come to Edward's peace. Bruce's advance to the north in September 1307, because of the success which was attending the efforts of his adherents in these parts, and the immediate rallying to his side of a force which the Earl of Ross estimates at 3000 men, is absolute proof both of the power of the "false preachers" and of the extent of the "rebellion" in Moray in the summer and autumn.

Nor is this all. On 13th December 1307 Edward II, "being about to set out for Boulogne," ordered letters to be addressed to the clergy of Scotland, begging them to keep the peace in that realm.[1] On the following day similar letters were addressed to many of the great magnates of the kingdom.[2] But none were sent either to the Bishop of Moray or to any ecclesiastic within the diocese. This omission cannot have been accidental. Among the bishops addressed are those of Aberdeen, Dunkeld, Ross, Brechin, and Caithness, none of whom were at that time in open antagonism to England. Beyond those bishops, no northern ecclesiastic is mentioned, though many abbots were made the recipients of Edward's commands, of whom the Abbots of Scone, Cupar, and Arbroath, and the Prior of St. Andrews, are the most northerly. The omission of the Bishop of Moray and of all the clergy within his diocese, some of whom, like the Abbot of Kinloss, for example, and the Priors of Pluscardyn, Beauly, and Inverness, were men of importance in the northern ecclesiastical world, must therefore have been deliberate; and the only possible conclusion is that the Bishop and clergy of Moray were not asked to assist in keeping the peace in Scotland because they were known

---

[1] Bain, iii. 29. [2] *Ibid.*

enemies of England, or, to put it negatively, because they were not reckoned among the friends of England. Our knowledge of the fact that Moray had been for several months before 13th December in open and dangerous rebellion confirms this in the fullest possible way.

We know also that in 1308 the Bishop of Moray was a close friend of Bruce. He is, as we have seen, the first witness to the deed by which, on 31st October 1308, the Earl of Ross and his sons made full and complete surrender to Bruce, receiving at his hands a new grant of all their lands and several signal marks of Bruce's favour. Then we have the Bishop's career prior to midsummer 1307 to consider; and bearing it in mind, and all he had ventured and suffered in the cause of freedom, it is impossible to believe that in 1307 he really abandoned Bruce and made his peace with England. Finally, though of course its absence is not conclusive evidence, there is no record of any sort in the English archives of the Bishop having come to Edward's peace or sworn fealty to England.

It is, of course, impossible to dogmatise on such a matter, but, in the face of all the evidence, what probably happened is this. The Bishop returned to Moray, and, for his own purposes, after the death of Edward I, patched up a sort of truce with Sir Reginald le Chen, the guardian of Moray. Sir Reginald le Chen was the Bishop's cousin; and, as the Forfar letter shows, he was, as early as April 1307, if not earlier, having a particularly trying time in the district which was his especial care. From his point of view things went rapidly from bad to worse, and in the circumstances it is quite probable that he came to some sort of arrangement with his cousin, the Bishop. Like the rest of his countrymen, his sympathies were no doubt divided; and as, like them, he knew the character of the new King of England, he may have thought it wise to guard against eventualities by having a friend in the Scottish king's camp. At all events, it is clear from the Earl of Ross's letter that the Bishop could not really have made his peace with

England, else why all his threatenings against one of England's chief lieutenants for having performed his duty to England by destroying the Bishop's property when he was a rebel and an outlaw? If any difficulty is presented by the fact that, on receipt of the Earl's complaint, it was directed that a royal letter should be sent to the Bishop, it must be remembered that one of Edward II's first acts was to remove all his father's advisers and trusted officials, and the newcomers must have been for some considerable time woefully ignorant of Scottish personalities and Scottish affairs. Nor is there any indication that the suggested letter was ever sent.

It must also be remarked that the Earl's statement is not in itself conclusive evidence that the Bishop ever came to Edward's peace, or even to an arrangement with Sir Reginald le Chen. The Earl, no doubt, believed he had, but, again, the threats to which he was subjected by the Bishop are not quite reconcilable with such a view.

Finally, it must never be forgotten that it was a time of strange ideas. Oaths sat lightly on princes of the Church as well as on other folk, and no Scottish bishop of that day would have hesitated to swear all manner of oaths to England with the full and deliberate intention of breaking them at the first favourable opportunity. Of that we have had abundant evidence. The Bishop of St. Andrews and the Bishop of Glasgow did this not once or twice but many times, and were fully persuaded that they were performing a sacred and patriotic duty in so doing. So it is quite within the bounds of possibility that the Bishop of Moray may, with the deliberate intention of being in a position to use to the full his position as bishop and the riches of his diocese in further- ing the national cause, have nominally come to Edward's peace in the spring or summer of 1307. But whichever of all the possible solutions of the Earl of Ross's state- ment is the true one, there cannot, in view of all the facts we have just been considering, be any doubt that the Bishop of Moray was all through 1307 one of Bruce's strongest and staunchest adherents.

The sequence of events in the north in 1307 is now fairly clear. Bruce's northern adherents, who, like himself, had been compelled to seek safety in flight in the latter half of 1306, returned to the province of Moray in the early spring of 1307, at precisely the same time as Bruce returned to Carrick. That they and Bruce were acting in concert is, therefore, almost as certain as any fact of the period can be. In Moray and the neighbouring districts the success of the renewed revolt was immediate, far transcending that which attended Bruce in the south-west, so much so that by the beginning of May it was officially reported to Edward that the people of these parts were "all ready at Bruce's will more entirely than ever." Thereafter we have no direct indication of the progress of events, though we know that in the succeeding months things went from bad to worse for England, till the whole of the wide district from the Beauly to the Spey was openly on the side of Bruce, Sir Reginald le Chen and the English officials being powerless to prevent the spread of the rising. By the end of April, at all events, Edward's writ had practically ceased to run in the whole province of Moray, and in the high country of Banff, Aberdeen, Kincardine, and Athol; and by the end of August the position of Bruce's party in these districts was so strong that Bruce, who of course had been kept informed of what was happening, decided deliberately to proceed forthwith to the north and place himself at the head of his adherents.

That Bruce should have taken this step is the best commentary on the measure of success which had attended the efforts of his northern adherents. For he was about to proceed to the near neighbourhood of his mortal foes, the Comyns, to a district which, unless things had been going particularly well for him in the surrounding localities, he would have carefully avoided. The Comyns, it must always be remembered, were no contemptible foes. They were the most powerful family of the time in Scotland, and in the very district to which Bruce was about to proceed they had lorded it for nigh a hundred years. With them, too, were other powerful friends of England, Sir David de Brechin and Sir John de Moubray among them; and Bruce must, therefore, have been very sure of finding in the north a strong force "all ready at his will" before he ventured to place himself within reach of the men who in all Scotland were his most implacable adversaries. As we know from the Earl of Ross's letter, Bruce did find in the north a very large number of men ready and eager to follow him; and in that fact, accordingly, lies the key to the whole secret of Bruce's northward advance and of his subsequent successes in Aberdeenshire.

Fordun, it will be remembered, makes Bruce himself capture the castle of Inverness, thereafter bring the whole north to his side, and then advance on Aberdeenshire. In all probability, however, the capture of Inverness should be ascribed to his northern adherents, of whose names and deeds Fordun was entirely ignorant. The Forfar letter shows that by the end of April the officers of England in Moray were completely demoralised, and the fact that in October Bruce was in Ross with a force estimated by the Earl of Ross at 3000 men suggests that between April and October the national cause in the north made very rapid headway. Now, at the head of that cause in the north were almost certainly Alexander Pilche and the Bishop of Moray, with those other knights whose names we have already elucidated. We have seen that in 1297 Alexander Pilche had been Andrew de Moray's chief lieutenant, when, without the aid of any of the magnates of the district, in face indeed of their open hostility, the northern patriots had been strong enough to capture some castles and attack others. Later, they had cleared the whole district of the English, and had gained possession, by surrender or assault, of all the castles held for England. From then until the seemingly final debacle in 1304, Alexander Pilche had been steadfast in his opposition to England, and he only came to Edward's peace when all hope of resistance appeared at an end. The fact that in 1305 he was appointed by Edward to the very important position of Constable of Inverness Castle is a striking proof of the place which he occupied in the eyes of the northern world, and of the estimation in which he was held by those who had been his opponents. But though Alexander Pilche, like many another Scot in like case, held the castle of Inverness for England so long as there seemed no hope of throwing off the English yoke, he was still ready to risk everything in another bid for freedom if the opportunity should offer. And so when Bruce struck the blow which transformed him into a patriot and a leader, Alexander Pilche early threw off his hated allegiance to England and hastened to Bruce's side.

It is, therefore, more than probable that the castle of Inverness was captured before Bruce went north, and may, indeed, have fallen early in the campaign of 1307. This, of course, does not in any way discredit Fordun's statement, for writers of the fourteenth century were not in the habit of distinguishing very particularly between Bruce and his adherents. On the contrary it rather strengthens it, for on the one hand it destroys that hyper-criticism which reads Fordun's statement to mean that the attack on Turnberry and the capture of Inverness by Bruce occurred within a few weeks of each other, and therefore dismisses Fordun's account of the events of 1307 as impossible; and on the other hand meets the possible objection that, granting Fordun is not to be read in that sense, too little time is left to Bruce for all the deeds ascribed to him between the time he did go north in September and his descent on Aberdeenshire in November.

This latter objection, however, is not so strong as at first sight it seems. Fordun's narrative reads that Bruce "got as far as Inverness, took the castle thereof with a strong hand, slew its garrison, and levelled it with the ground. In this way dealt he with the rest of the castles and strongholds established in the north, as well as with their inmates, until he got with his army as far as Slenach." At a cursory glance this seems a very great deal to have accomplished in so brief a period, but if all the facts we have elucidated thus far are kept in view, it will be seen that Fordun has simply lumped together a number of events which extended over a considerable time, and gives us the result in one short paragraph. For it is perfectly clear that a good deal must have been accomplished in the north before Bruce went thither in September, and that the 3000 who caused the Earl of Ross such trepidation in October did not spring full-armed from the ground in a single night.

It will be noticed that Fordun makes Bruce level Inverness Castle with the ground. This, of course, was in accordance with Bruce's usual practice. It was by means of the castles that England was able to maintain her hold upon Scotland; and Bruce, therefore, early made it his deliberate policy to destroy as many of these dangerous strongholds as was consistent with the well-being of the country. The point for us meantime, however, is that Fordun's statement is confirmed by the Charter of Novodamus of the earldom of Moray granted by Bruce to Randolph in 1324, wherein the "site" of the castle is specifically mentioned, and in such a way as to leave no doubt that it is the vacant site which is meant.

Before we resume our narrative it is necessary to dispose of another error, which owes its origin to Barbour, and upon which many false hypotheses have been based. Barbour tells us, in a passage already quoted, that Bruce "thought he would fare beyond the Mounth" to see "who his friends would be." He goes on:

> " In-to Sir Alexander the Fraser
> He trusted, for they cousins were,
> And his brother Simon, they two."

A little later, speaking of Bruce's arrival in the Mounth, he says:

> " Where Alexander Fraser him met,
> Also his brother, Simon het,
> With all the folk they with them had."

On these two passages all subsequent writers have relied, both as explaining Bruce's northward movement and as indicating who his principal northern adherents at that time were. In course of time Barbour's simple statement was, not unnaturally, expanded considerably, until at last we find two of our modern authorities asserting categorically that Bruce " must have been fully occupied in the northern and central parts of Scotland, with the assistance of his allies, Alexander and Simon Fraser, during the winter and spring of 1307–8, in holding his own against the English,"[1] and that "the national cause, which had been greatly strengthened in the north by the adhesion of Simon and Alexander Fraser, came near to ruin towards the end of 1307, by reason of the king's health breaking down."[2] It would be difficult to discover, in all that has been written on the War of Independence, two other sentences of similar length into which more inaccuracies and more misconceptions have been packed. Several of these are of course at once apparent to anyone who has followed our narrative thus far. The others will divulge themselves in due course.

The explanation of Barbour's error is perfectly simple. Let it be borne in mind, to begin with, that he wrote his poem seventy years after the events of 1307, and that he was Archdeacon of Aberdeen. Now, the Frasers were rewarded for their loyalty to Bruce by grants of land in Aberdeenshire; and Barbour, therefore, knew either themselves or their successors. He accordingly also knew that they had actually been with Bruce during his campaign in Aberdeenshire in 1307–8, but he did not know under what circumstances or in whose company they had joined him. Of all the northern events and personages, outside " Aberdeen and twal miles roun'," he was entirely ignorant, as we have already seen and as we shall still see. Accordingly, when he came to deal with Bruce's northward movement he knew neither the names of his chief adherents in the north nor the reasons

---

[1] Bain, iii. Introduction, p. xii.
[2] Maxwell's *Bruce*, pp. 175–6.

which dictated that movement. But he did know the names of two near neighbours of his own, who had certainly taken part in that campaign, and who subsequently became famous in the War of Independence. So, confusing their presence in Bruce's force in 1307–8 with their later greatness, he ascribed to them in 1307 a prominence to which they were certainly not entitled, even though they were fortunate enough, for their own fame, to hold lands at a later date in the neighbourhood of the poet's own town of Aberdeen.

As a matter of fact both the Frasers were in 1307 very young men, neither of them, in spite of Barbour's reference to "Sir Alexander," being knights until after 1312. In Bruce's later years they both rose to high position, and were known as stark fighters throughout the War of Independence. It was, therefore, quite natural for Barbour, writing seventy years after 1307, to allow his knowledge of their later greatness obscure his conception of their earlier years. But though in 1306, 1307, and 1308 they both fought manfully in the national cause, they were not then high in the councils of the leaders; and their names are not to be found in any contemporary document of the time in any manner which would suggest a contrary view. They had, moreover, at that period neither lands nor following in the Highlands. Their lands and interests lay in Fife and Stirling, and it is, therefore, on the face of it, impossible that they should, as young esquires of twenty or thereabouts, have played other than a subordinate part in the northern campaign of 1307.

The leaders of the northern rising were unquestionably the men whose names we have repeatedly met, and shall still meet, in the documents of the period, the men who, from the very first raising of Bruce's standard, had been the tried and proven friends of the new-crowned king and the cause of independence, men of assured position and power in the north, chief among whom were the Bishop of Moray, Alexander Pilche, Sir William Wiseman, Sir Walter de Berkeley, Sir John de Stirling,

and Sir Laurence de Strathbogie.   Incidentally, too, the
fact that Barbour can mention no person from the
neighbourhood of his own town of Aberdeen as being, at
the beginning of Bruce's Aberdeenshire campaign, of
Bruce's party, is a most striking indication of the extent
to which the great men of Aberdeenshire, with the Earl
of Buchan at their head, were opposed to Bruce; and
confirms in a very remarkable way the conclusions we
have drawn as to the part of the northern district which
made possible Bruce's northward movement and supplied
him with men and all manner of assistance.   It goes far
to explain, too, Barbour's ignorance of all that occurred
in the north outside his own county of Aberdeen.

CHAPTER XXVII

THE CAMPAIGN IN ABERDEENSHIRE (1307-8)

WE come now to the events which preceded and led to the battle of Inverurie and to that battle itself. Unfortunately the only two authorities upon whom we can place any reliance, Barbour and Fordun, differ in their account of the campaign in several important respects, and therefore caution is necessary in endeavouring to arrive at any conclusion upon the matters in dispute. Until within the past few years Barbour's account was almost universally accepted as the correct one, but when Mr. Bain published the third volume of his *Calendar* he discredited it on extremely flimsy grounds, and all subsequent writers have followed him blindly. But a very little consideration will show that, whatever the true facts may be, Mr. Bain's reasons for discarding Barbour are of no historical value whatsoever, and should have carried no weight. I quote them in full here, so that the reader may judge for himself.[1]

"Bruce," he says, "must have remained during that winter and spring in the neighbourhood of Buchan's territories, or somewhere in the central parts of the country. Fordun relates that they" (*i.e.*, Bruce and Buchan) "met in battle at Inverurie in 1308—it is said on Ascension Day (22nd May)—when Buchan's army was routed, and the victor committed the devastations in his earldom which Barbour graphically calls 'the Hership of Bowchane.'" In a note he adds, "The late Lord Saltoun believes that the battle of Inverurie was fought on Christmas Eve 1307, and his reasons are not without weight. But if it be the fact, as stated by

---

[1] Bain, iii. Introduction, p. xii.

Barbour, that Sir David of Brechin, who fought against Bruce there, came to terms soon after, and surrendered his castle of Brechin, where David, Earl of Athol, had besieged him on behalf of Bruce (as Barbour also relates), then the battle must have occurred during the year 13c8, as related by Fordun. *For on 20th May 1308, Edward II thanks David, Earl of Athol, David of Brechin, and other Scotsmen, for their faithful service, which clearly shows that they were of his party long after Christmas preceding."* (The italics are mine.)

Thus by putting aside Barbour's plain definite statement that the battle was fought on Christmas Eve, and by interpreting a vague general statement in the strictest possible sense, Mr. Bain arrives at the extraordinary conclusion that a plain assertion of Barbour must be wrong, because a later assertion, couched in general terms, may, on one interpretation, on an interpretation which it does not as a matter of fact bear, be read as casting doubt on the earlier assertion. In other words, because he makes Barbour say, what he does not say, that David de Brechin came to terms soon after Inverurie, therefore the battle could not have been fought on the date on which Barbour says it was fought, for the sole reason that Edward II on 20th May thanks de Brechin, five months after Inverurie, for his faithful service. This is a method of historical deduction which carries its own condemnation on the face of it.

As it happens, however, Barbour does not use the words " soon after," and even if he did it hardly requires to be pointed out that to a man writing seventy years later, " soon after " might mean anything from two weeks to two years. As a matter of fact, though Sir David de Brechin was an adherent of Bruce for some time prior to 15th June 1310, on which date he was received to Edward's peace [1]—it being expressly stated that he had been adhering to the king's enemies in Scotland—he appears in the English records as an adherent of England in July 1309,[2] so that the castle of Brechin must have

---

[1] Bain, iii. 121.   [2] *Ibid.*, p. 121.

fallen either shortly before that date or between then and the end of 1309. Accordingly, even accepting Mr. Bain's own " soon after," it is plain that it is impossible to interpret loose phrases of that sort as necessarily meaning so many days or weeks or months.

I have pointed out, however, that Barbour does not use the phrase ascribed to him by Mr. Bain, and it will be well therefore to quote his own words. He describes the defeat, and goes on :

> "Till England fled the Earl of Buchan,
> Sir John Mowbray is with him gone,
> And were resetted with the King.
> But they had both but short lasting,
> For they died soon after syne."

The Earl of Buchan was certainly dead by 3rd December, but Sir John Moubray lived for many years after 1308. The poem proceeds :

> " And Sir David of Brechyne
> Fled to Brechine, his own castle,
> And garnished it both fair and well,
> But the Earl of Atholl, Davy,
> His son that was in Kildrummy,
> Came syne, and him besieged there.
> And he, that would hold weyr no more,
> Nor bargain with the noble King,
> Came syne his man with good treating."

There is no word there of de Brechin's becoming Bruce's man "soon after" Inverurie. He fled after that battle, says Barbour, to his castle, which he had ample time to put in an excellent condition for defence. The Earl of Athol came " syne " and besieged him, and " syne " Sir David surrendered. But "syne," it has to be observed, does not in Barbour usually mean soon. It is one of the poet's favourite words, and its meaning is usually either " afterwards," " then," " next," or " at last." So to " syne " as meaning " soon " no significance in this context can possibly be attached. It may also be remarked that there is abundant evidence to show that from 1307 to 1312 the Earl of Athol was an active adherent of

England, and accordingly could not have captured Brechin for Bruce in 1308 or 1309.

Let us now see what Fordun says regarding the campaign in Aberdeenshire. "In the year 1307," he writes, "John Comyn, Earl of Buchan, with many nobles both English and Scots, hearing that Robert, King of Scotland, was with his army at Slenach, marched forward to meet him and give him battle. But when they saw the king with his men over against them ready for the fray, they halted; and on Christmas Day, overwhelmed with shame and confusion, they went back and asked for a truce, which the king kindly granted. After the truce had been granted the king abode there without fear for eight days; and he there fell into a sickness so severe that he was borne on a pallet whithersoever he had occasion to go.

"In the year 1308 John Comyn and Philip of Moubray, with a great many Scots and English, were again gathered at Inverurie. But when King Robert heard of this, though he had not yet got rid of his grievous sickness, he arose from his pallet, whereon he was always carried about, and commanded his men to arm him and set him on horseback. When this had been done, he, too, with a cheerful countenance, hastened with his army against the enemy to the battle-ground, although by reason of his great weakness he could not go upright save with the help of two men to prop him up. But when the opposing party saw him and his men ready for battle, at the mere sight of him they were all sore afraid and put to flight, and they were pursued as far as Fivy, twelve leagues off. So when the rout was over and the enemy were overthrown and scattered, King Robert ravaged the earldom of Buchan with fire; and of the people he killed whom he would, and to those whom he would have live he granted life and peace. . . . And from that day the king gained ground and became ever more hale himself, while the adverse party was daily growing less."

Now, it is surely obvious that the foregoing as an

account of the campaign is vague and unconvincing, though the account of the actual battle itself is on a different footing. Let anyone compare the account of the campaign with Barbour's very full, very detailed, and very graphic account of the same events, and no possible doubt can remain as to which is to be preferred. Fordun's account, moreover, if read literally, is historically really impossible. It is frankly not credible that Buchan and his allies behaved as he alleges; that Bruce, after " kindly " granting them a truce, lay for several months in their neighbourhood the while they gathered forces to over-whelm him; and that finally, when after months of preparation they plucked up courage to advance against him, Bruce routed them with the utmost ease at Inverurie. Not that Fordun's account is altogether erroneous. Confusing would be the better word, for confusing it undoubtedly is. It reads as if he had somehow succeeded in mixing up his facts, and that is what I believe really occurred. It seems to me that either Fordun himself or Bower, who compiled the narrative from Fordun's notes, simply confused the Earls of Ross and Buchan. Knowing nothing either of Bruce's campaign against the former or of the truce granted to him, but coming across references of some sort or other to these, he imagined they referred to the Earl of Buchan, and so incorporated them in his account of the campaign in Aberdeenshire. It must always be remembered, moreover, that the narrative of the period with which we are dealing was not actually written by Fordun himself, but was compiled by Bower from Fordun's notes twenty or thirty years after Fordun's death. And everybody who has ever had any experience of endeavouring to write up another man's notes knows what that means, and how easily confusion and error result.

Fordun's account of the Aberdeenshire campaign being, therefore, to put it at the lowest, not altogether reliable, we are compelled to fall back on Barbour; and Barbour, as I have already remarked, was almost universally accepted as an entirely safe guide to that campaign until Mr. Bain, on the flimsiest of grounds, threw doubt upon him, and was so blindly followed that it now appears in most Scottish histories as an apparently incontrovertible statement of fact that the battle of Inverurie was fought on Ascension Day, 22nd May 1308, which, by the way, it is worth remarking Fordun himself does not say. He merely says it was fought in 1308. Now, as I have repeatedly pointed out, Barbour has been proved over and over again, by the discovery of contemporary records, to be extraordinarily accurate when he relates events in detail. It is when he generalises or writes in outline that he is unreliable. The reason for that is, of course, obvious. When he writes in detail he has full knowledge of whatever it may be he is describing. When he generalises he is, as a rule, proceeding on surmise or on very scanty evidence. His narrative of the Aberdeenshire campaign most emphatically belongs to the former class, and is indeed told with a picturesqueness and wealth of detail which carry conviction on the face of them. When it is remembered that Barbour was born and brought up in Aberdeenshire and spent most of his life in a high position in the Church of Aberdeen, the marvel, indeed, would be if he did fall into any such egregious errors regarding the battle of Inverurie as Mr. Bain and his followers would have us believe. I would go further, and say that if his poem is worthy of credence at all it must surely be accepted as trustworthy in regard to events which occurred in the poet's own district, and many of the actors in which he must have known personally. To put it otherwise, if we cannot accept Barbour's account of the Aberdeenshire campaign, we may as well consign his whole poem to the rubbish heap, for if he cannot be trusted to describe accurately events which he had every opportunity of ascertaining fully and accurately, he is unworthy of belief when he writes of matters concerning which he could not have had anything like the same sources of information.

Barbour's graphic account of the Aberdeenshire cam-

paign is, unfortunately, too long to quote in full, but it
may be briefly summarised. He brings Bruce, as we have
already seen, to the Mounth, and then makes him " hold
straight the way to Inverurie " :

> " And there he took such a sickness
>   That put him to full hard distress,
>   That he forbare both drink and meat."

In these circumstances it was thought wise to remove the
sick king from the dangerous neighbourhood of the
Comyns to the greater security of Slivoch, which lies in
the parish of Drumblade about sixteen miles north-west
of Inverurie, near Bruce's own castle of Kildrummy. From
the fact that he was not taken to Kildrummy itself,
we may surmise either that the castle was still held for
England, or that it had not been repaired after its capture
in September 1306, when Nigel Bruce's surrender is
traditionally said to have been brought about by the
treacherous destruction by fire of the provisions in the
castle.

News of the king's illness and of his whereabouts
speedily reached the Earl of Buchan, and assembling a
" great company " he hastened to Slivoch with a force
which, Barbour says, outnumbered Bruce's by two to one.
" This was after the Martinmas, when snow had covered
all the land," adds the poet with one of those graphic
touches which distinguish him. Buchan's men advanced
against their foes with great confidence, but Bruce's men
" stood in array right closely " by the side of a wood. So
determined a front did they present, that Buchan did not
venture to attack them directly. Instead he sent forward
his archers " to bicker them " ; but Bruce also had archers,
and these replied " so sturdily " to Buchan's that " they of
the earl's party into their battle-array withdrawn were."

" Three days in this wise lay they there," and every
day the archers on both sides " bickered," but the bowmen of Buchan " the worse had ay." Bruce's men,
however, were in a precarious situation. Not only did
Buchan's force " wax more and more " each day, but the

provisions of Bruce's men gave out, and at last " they had nothing for to eat."

> " Therefore they took counsel in hy (haste)
> That they would there no longer lie,
> But hold their way where they might get
> Till them and theirs victual and meat."

So they made them ready, and

> " In a litter the king they lay,
> And readied them and took their way,
> That all their foes might them see : "

and so marched out and away in full view of the enemy,

> " Ilk man buskit in his degree,
> To fight if they assailed were."

The poet also tells how,

> " In midst of them the king they bear,
> And went about him closely."

But though, as he also says, they were compelled to go slowly, nevertheless when the earl saw how bold a front they presented and how " with so little fear they held forth with the king," all " ready to fight who would assail," the hearts of himself and his men

> " All began to fail,
> And in peace they let them pass their way,
> And till their houses home went they."

Several points of interest and importance may be gleamed from the foregoing narrative. In the first place, it is surely a very striking fact that Bruce's force was able to march away unmolested, and that although, as Barbour says, they were hampered by the litter in which the sick king was carried, and had to proceed slowly. It follows, therefore, that Bruce had either a very numerous force or a force which contained an unusually large proportion of well-armed men. Barbour's narrative distinctly indicates that the latter was the case, for not only does he say that

Buchan's force was twice as numerous, but the lines I have quoted imply the presence of many well-armed men on Bruce's side. " Ilk man buskit him to his degree," he says, and marching in close order round the king they presented so formidable an appearance that Buchan with his much stronger force dared not attack. And yet Buchan had with him all the chivalry of Buchan and Aberdeenshire, as well as a host of common men and archers.[1]

Who, then, composed Bruce's force? Again there is only one answer—the men of Moray and many of those other northern knights and warriors who, as we saw, followed him in 1306, the flower of the three thousand who had brought the Earl of Ross so swiftly to his knees. Barbour tells us that Bruce's companions on his northward journey were his brother Edward, Sir Gilbert de la Hay, the Earl of Lennox, " that with the king was everywhere," and Sir Robert Boyd. These, obviously, were not the cause of Buchan's discomfiture, of his three days' unsuccessful siege of Bruce's force, of his refusal to attack in the open, of his inglorious retreat. Even if we were still ignorant of all that we have elucidated regarding the events in the north, an intelligent reading of Barbour's narrative would compel us to realise that elementary fact, unless, that is, we were full of preconceived ideas and prejudices which forbade us to look facts in the face. As it is, Barbour's narrative makes it clear that all our previous deductions as to Bruce's northern campaign are accurate, and that it was the support which he obtained from the knights, the clergy, and the men of Moray that alone enabled him to carry the war into Aberdeenshire, maintain himself in safety there during his illness, and eventually not only sweep the Earl of Buchan and his allies from their own country, but accomplish that task with a rapidity and a crushing thoroughness which has no parallel in the whole history of the War of Independence.

Before we pass from this aspect of the Aberdeenshire

---

[1] Barbour, ix. 110-52.

campaign, it is necessary to remark that, by all the laws of war and of history, the whole story as told in Barbour and in the pages of the modern Scottish historians is, as it stands, absolutely impossible. It only becomes possible when the story of the preceding northern campaign is rescued from oblivion and placed in its true prospective. For observe what the modern historians, serving up a compound of Barbour and Fordun, do. They make Bruce go north with a small following; when he gets there they do not bring to his standard any recruits of importance; they make him remain, very ill and still with a small following yet practically unmolested, for anything from two to six months in the dangerous neighbourhood of his foes the Comyns; and finally they make him, still with a problematical force, rout at Inverurie a numerous, well-armed, well-led host, and devastate the territories of the powerful Earl of Buchan. They themselves are frankly perplexed by their own story. They cannot account for it, or rather they make no serious effort to account for it. And yet if they had studied aright the materials at their disposal, the whole of their perplexity would have disappeared. That they did not do so is at once their condemnation, and a justification of the criticisms to which they have been subjected in these pages. They could make nothing of the battle of Inverurie and the events which preceded it, because they completely misunderstood both the history of mediæval Scotland and the history of the War of Independence.

From Slivoch Bruce's force proceeded to Strathbogie, which, it will be remembered, owned as its lord a staunch adherent of Bruce in the person of Sir Lawrence de Strathbogie. But Strathbogie stands high, and on the approach of wintry weather the little army made its way to Inverurie again, another evidence of its strength and confidence. Barbour says that when it lay at Inverurie on this occasion it numbered 700 men, and he is, as a rule, reliable in his estimate of numbers. Now 700 men was in these days a pretty considerable force, and if among the 700 there was, as I have already suggested, a large portion of well-armed men, its strength was even greater than its numbers indicate. At all events 700 men of any sort was a large number for Bruce to have with him at Inverurie in the very middle of winter, and is another indication of the popularity of his cause in the counties to the north and west of Aberdeen.

Buchan, who had evidently full knowledge of the movements of his enemy, no sooner learned that Bruce was at Inverurie than he began to assemble a force for his destruction. Brechin, Moubray, and their men speedily joined him, and he soon had "a full great company of men arrayed handsomely." "A thousand, trow I well, they were," adds the poet. With this force Buchan advanced confidently to Old Meldrum, where he halted on the evening before Christmas Eve. On the morning of Christmas Eve Sir David de Brechin made a reconnaissance in force towards Inverurie, "to look if he in any wise might do skaith to his enemies." He succeeded in surprising Bruce's outposts, slaying some and dispersing the others. The latter "fled their way towards the king," who, "with the most of his gathering," was encamped beyond the town. At the tidings Bruce immediately called for his horse, ordered his men to arm themselves, and, in spite of the expostulations of his friends, announced his intention of leading them in person against the enemy. His friends had good reason for their anxiety, for both Barbour and Fordun tell us that he was not yet recovered from his illness, the latter adding that he was still confined to his litter. But to all expostulation Bruce made answer, "Their boast has made me hale and sound, for no medicine would so soon have cured me as they have done." And so, held on his horse by two men, says Fordun, he led his followers to battle with his mortal foe.

Buchan and his men were quite unprepared for so speedy an act of retaliation, and accordingly the tidings of the approach of Bruce's force was, in its turn, something of the nature of a surprise. "The discoverers," *i.e.*, the scouts, "saw them coming with banners waving to the wind," says Barbour :

> "And told it to their lord in hy (haste),
> Who caused arm his men hastily,
> And them arrayed for battle."

Behind them he placed the camp followers, "and made good appearance for the fight." But Bruce was not disturbed by their warlike array. Instead, he came on "with muckle might," and for a little it looked as if the two parties would meet in the clash of battle, for Buchan's knights and men-at-arms stood waiting until the foe was almost on them. At the last moment, however, their courage failed. For "when they saw the noble king come stoutly on without stinting, a little on bridle they them withdrew," and Bruce, knowing full well the importance of pressing hard upon an enemy that was showing signs of fear, "pressed on them with his banner, and they withdrew them more and more." Whereupon "the small folk," that is the foot-soldiers and bowmen, seeing the knights and mounted men behaving so shamefully, promptly "turned their backs all" and fled. The mounted men, in their turn, perceiving "their small folk were fleeing, and the king stoutly coming," turned their backs in like manner and rode off the field in a body. "A little while together they held" in their flight, adds Barbour, but soon they separated, and it became a case of every man for himself.

> "Fell never men so foul mischance
> After so sturdy countenance,"

comments the poet, and in truth he is right. With hardly a blow struck Buchan's force melted away at Bruce's first onset :

> "And when the king's company
> Saw that they fled so foully,
> They chased them with all their main,
> And some they took, and some were slain."

The survivors continued their flight ingloriously, but the pursuit was conducted so ardently that he "who had a good horse got best away." Then followed almost immediately the Herschip of Buchan which Barbour describes briefly but pungently. Bruce, he says,

> " . . . caused his men burn all Bouchane
> From end to end, and spared nane ;
> And harried them in such manner,
> That after that, full fifty year,
> Men minded 'the Herschip of Bouchane.'"

It will be noticed that between Barbour's graphic description of the battle, or rather of the rout, and Fordun's more general account there is a close resemblance. "When the opposing force saw him and his ready for battle," says the latter, "at the mere sight of him they were all sore afraid and put to flight, and they were pursued to Fivy, twelve leagues off. So when the rout was over, and the enemy were overthrown and scattered, King Robert ravaged the earldom of Buchan with fire ; and of the people he killed whom he would, and to those whom he would have live he granted life and peace."

A possible explanation, of course, is that Bower, who wrote up Fordun's notes, knew Barbour's poem. It is much more likely, however, that the resemblance is due to the fact that both Barbour and Fordun were Aberdonians, and that they were, therefore, simply giving the version of the story of the battle which was current in Aberdeen and in the district where the battle took place. Be that as it may, it certainly adds to the credibility of Barbour's description of the rout—a description which, for reasons already given, we should in any case accept as accurate—to find that Fordun agrees with it so strikingly. The importance of the manner of the rout, as described by Barbour, the reader has probably already gathered. Again we have unmistakable evidence of the presence with Bruce of a strong, well-armed force which included a considerable number of mounted mail-clad men, for there is no escaping from the conclusion that his following must have been of an unusually formidable description to make Buchan, de Brechin, Moubray,.and the chivalry of Aberdeenshire behave as they did.

CHAPTER XXVIII

THE HERSCHIP OF BUCHAN

In the months following the battle of Inverurie Bruce and his adherents were engaged in the task of reducing the castles and strong places in Aberdeen, Kincardine, and the neighbouring counties. Sir Thomas Gray tells us how his father at this time held the castle of Cupar-Fife for England, and in *Scalacronica* there is an interesting account of two desperate efforts made by Bruce's adherents to capture Gray. The first of these was made by Sir Walter de Bickerton, seigneur of Kilconquhar in Fife, who, as we have already seen, was one of the knights who joined Bruce immediately after his coronation, and the second by Alexander Fraser. As Gray's account of these attempts throws some light upon the chronology of the period and is of considerable interest and some importance otherwise, we shall consider it now.

"At this time," says the author of *Scalacronica*, "Thomas de Gray was warden of the castle of Cupar and Fife, and as he was travelling out of England from the king's coronation to the said castle, Walter de Bickerton, a knight of Scotland, who was an adherent of Robert de Bruce, having espied the return of the said Thomas, placed himself in ambush with more than four hundred men by the way the said Thomas intended to pass, whereof the said Thomas was warned when scarcely half a league from the ambush. He had not more than twenty-six men-at-arms with him, and perceived that he could not avoid an encounter. So, with the approval of his people, he took the road straight towards the ambush, having given his grooms a standard and ordered them to follow behind at not too short an interval.

"The enemy mounted their horses and formed for action, thinking that they [the English] could not escape from them. The said Thomas, with his people, who were very well mounted, struck spurs to his horse, and charged the enemy right in the centre of their column, bearing many to the ground in his course by the shock of his horse and lance. Then, turning rein, came back in the same manner and charged again, and once again returned through the thick of the troop, which so encouraged his people that they all followed him in like manner, whereby they overthrew many of the enemy, whose horses stampeded along the road. When they [the enemy] rose from the ground, they perceived the grooms of the said Thomas coming up in good order, and began to fly to a dry peat moss which was near, wherefore almost all [the others] began to fly to the moss, leaving their horses for their few assailants. The said Thomas and his men could not get near them on horseback, wherefore he caused their horses to be driven before them along the road to the said castle, where at night they had a booty of nine score saddled horses.

"Another time, on a market day, the town being full of people from the neighbourhood, Alexander Frisel [Fraser], who was an adherent of Robert Bruce, was ambushed with a hundred men-at-arms about half a league from the said castle, having sent others of his people to rifle a hamlet on the other side of the castle. The said Thomas, hearing the uproar, mounted a fine charger before his people could get ready, and went to see what was ado. The enemy spurred out from their ambush before the gates of the said castle, so doing because they well knew that he (Sir Thomas) had gone forth. The said Thomas, perceiving this, returned at a foot's pace through the town of Cupar, at the end whereof stood the castle, where he had to enter on horseback, and where they had occupied the whole street. When he came near them he struck spurs into his horse; of those who advanced against him, he struck down some with his spear, others with the shock of his horse, and, passing through them all, dismounted at the gate, drove his horse in, and slipped inside the barrier, where he found his people assembled."

These two incidents are eminently characteristic of the period, and enable us to realise far better than many pages of descriptive or argumentative writing what manner of contest was waged throughout Scotland from 1307 to 1314, and especially in the east country in the spring and summer of 1308. Let us note, too, the importance of the horse in the warfare of the period. To a well-mounted mail-clad man many things were possible, as the foregoing extracts very plainly show. For our present purpose, however, the narrative of these two attempts to capture Sir Thomas Gray has a more immediate importance. The first took place, says his son, when Sir Thomas was returning from the king's coronation. That event took place on 25th February 1308, and we may therefore confidently place the date of the ambush about the beginning of April. But if those who hold that the battle of Inverurie was fought in May 1308 are right, Bruce was in April lying somewhere among the hills of Aberdeenshire recovering his health. The Comyns, de Brechin, de Moubray, and the rest had, therefore, not yet been humbled, and the power of England in the east country was in consequence still unbroken. It is not likely, therefore, that Sir Walter Bickerton would be in a position to lay ambushes with 400 men in Fife, or that Alexander Fraser could make such an attack on Cupar as Sir Thomas Gray relates, even if we assume, what it is indeed well-nigh impossible to assume, that Bruce, sick and in the neighbourhood of his foes the Comyns, would take the risk of imperilling himself and his whole force by permitting so many of his followers to depart on a dangerous expedition to Fife.

On the other hand, Sir Thomas Gray's story describes exactly what we know did occur after the Herschip of

x

Buchan, that is, guerilla warfare on a large scale against
the English in the eastern counties, and a succession
of daring attacks on the castles held for England in the
same district.   Some writers realise this, but, obsessed
with the idea that the battle of Inverurie was fought in
May, fall into the stupid mistake of leaving no time for
the events to happen which they themselves say must
have happened.   Thus they are forced to commit themselves to the conclusion that the battle of Inverurie and
the Herschip of Buchan took place within a few days of
each other, and that Buchan, de Brechin, and the rest
either fled immediately or were driven out of Aberdeenshire and the neighbouring districts in an incredibly short
time.   That, of course, is nonsense.   The Comyns were
not poltroons; while the fame of Sir David de Brechin
among his contemporaries for skill and courage in war
was such that he was known by the proud name of
" The Flower of Chivalry."   Yet in June 1308 we find
Edward appointing Buchan, de Moubray, and Sir Ingram
de Umfraville to be wardens of Galloway, Annandale,
and Carrick, each with forty men-at-arms; Sir Alexander
de Abernethy, Sir Edmond de Hastings, and Sir John
de Fitz Marmaduke being at the same time appointed
wardens between the Forth and Orkney.[1]   This can only
mean that by June Edward had tidings of the expulsion
of Buchan and Moubray from Aberdeenshire, and as in
June Edward was never further north than London or
Bristol, the news must have been despatched from Scotland
not later than the end of May.   Accordingly, if Inverurie
was fought on Ascension Day, 22nd May, Bruce performed a feat of arms which bordered on the miracu-
lous if in eight short days the Comyns were driven in
headlong flight from Aberdeenshire, their castles captured,
their lands destroyed, and their vassals subdued.   The
thing, of course, is ridiculous.   The battle of Inverurie
must have been fought long before the end of May
1308, and as Barbour gives us both a definite date and
a detailed description of the events which preceded the

[1] Bain, iii. 47.

battle, and of the battle itself, his date, Christmas Eve 1307, must, in view of all we have elucidated, be accepted.

At the beginning of this chapter I stated that in the months following the battle of Inverurie Bruce and his adherents were engaged in the task of reducing the castles and strong places in Aberdeen, Kincardine, and the neighbouring counties. That, of course, was not accomplished in a day or a week or a month. The eastern counties were studded with castles, many of which were held by English garrisons or by the opponents of Bruce. In Aberdeenshire alone in 1308 the Comyns possessed the strong castles of Kinedar (nowadays corrupted into King Edward), Slains, Rattray, Dundarg, and Kelly; the Hastings were in Coull and Lumphannan; and the Chens in Ravenscraig; while the royal castles of Aberdeen, Aboyne, Fyvie, and Kintore were held by English garrisons. Nobody is foolish enough to imagine that either the battle of Inverurie or the Herschip of Buchan caused all these to fall into Bruce's hands without a blow being struck in their defence.

Barbour tells us that after Inverurie Comyn's defeated force was pursued to Fyvie. The fact that at Fyvie there was a royal castle with an English garrison provides the explanation of the halt of the pursuit at this point. Subsequently Edward Bruce followed the Earl of Buchan into his own country, and is traditionally said to have overthrown him finally at a place near the village of Old Deer called Aiky-Brae. On his way thither he is also said to have encamped on a hill two miles west of the village of New Deer, known to this day as Bruce Hill, and a glance at the map will show that Bruce Hill lies in close proximity to the route by which a pursuing force would advance from Fyvie to Old Deer.

Be these traditions literally accurate or be they not, however, they undoubtedly contain the key to what did happen. In Buchan the Comyns were in their own country, amid their own vassals, and with four strongly fortified places in which to defend themselves. It is not to be supposed, therefore, that they gave up the contest without a fierce struggle, and it is to that fact that the Herschip of Buchan was mainly due. It has too long been supposed that the sweeping devastation of Buchan's territories was merely an act of savage vengeance on the part of Bruce, difficult though such a deed is to reconcile with all that is known of his conduct and character. For it must not be forgotten that in an age notorious for its cruelty in warfare, Bruce was distinguished for his humanity, as even the English chroniclers admit. But the Herschip of Buchan, as we shall presently see, was not a simple act of vengeance. It was forced on Bruce, or his brother Edward, partly by necessity and partly by policy.

Let us consider the situation. Almost a year had now elapsed since Bruce's return to Scotland, but his foes were still numerous, dangerous, and implacable, and he had not yet made much real headway in his struggle for a kingdom. At the end of a year of constant warfare he had behind him only the province of Moray, part of Athol and Lennox, and a number of desperate men, outlaws for his sake from their own lands elsewhere. To the north of the province of Moray lay Ross, Sutherland, and Caithness, almost wholly under the sway of the Earl of Ross. For the time being, because of a truce extorted from the Earl, they were neutral, but if disaster fell upon Bruce there could be little doubt as to what course the Earl of Ross would pursue. West and south of Moray lay Argyll, but though certain of the barons of Argyll were Bruce's men, Alexander of Argyll was his deadly foe. South of the Forth and Clyde, Lothian had as yet taken no part in the struggle, and outside Lothian Galloway was fiercely hostile, while in the rest of the south-west Douglas was maintaining what was at best only a guerilla war. In the east country, north of the Forth, his cause had made little or no progress of a material kind. Certain adventurous knights and a number of other gallant spirits had joined him, but though the people were sympathetic, were in fact " all ready at his will," all the castles and strong places from Fife to Buchan were in the hands either of English knights or Bruce's Scottish foes. Accordingly, however eager for the success of Bruce the population might be, they had as yet been unable to declare themselves openly, and so long as the castles were in the hands of his enemies, it was unlikely that they would do so.

Thus, in the weeks preceding and succeeding the battle of Inverurie, Bruce's fate was trembling in the balance. The tide in his affairs had come, and if he failed to take it disaster irretrievable would probably overtake him. The Comyns were not only his mortal foes. They stood for all that was hostile to him or his claims in Scotland and England, and according as fate decided between them and him now, so would the future of his cause be. Their humiliation meant the rallying to his side of all the east country from Spey to Tay, and the removal of all danger from the Earl of Ross. Their victory meant the failure of his entire northern campaign, and with it, in all probability, the ruin of his hopes. This it is which explains his eagerness to come to grips with the Earl of Buchan, his determination to fight him at all costs, and the vigour and determination with which the advantage gained at Inverurie was followed up. The personal equation no doubt also played its part. But the personal equation was not the impelling motive in the Aberdeenshire campaign, though it gave an added fierceness to the spirit in which it was conducted on both sides.

Now it is essential to bear in mind that the campaign which succeeded the battle of Inverurie was conducted for the most part in the country of the Comyns. It has long been the fashion to hold the Comyns up to all manner of ignominy because they fought against Bruce, and therefore, in the long run, against the cause of freedom. Only within the past few years has it been realised that the Comyns had, as a matter of fact, proved themselves quite as good patriots as the Bruces, and that it was only Bruce's murder of the Red Comyn which ranged them amongst those who, because of the course which events afterwards took, are remembered chiefly as the enemies of Scotland. But the Comyns bore themselves bravely in the wars of 1296 and 1298 to 1304, while, as we have seen, the murdered "Red Comyn" had been one of the guardians of Scotland from 1298 to 1304, and the Earl of Buchan one of the Scots ambassadors to France in 1303, when strenuous efforts were made to get the French king to support Scotland against England. It was the Red Comyn, moreover, who inflicted the great defeat on the English at Roslin in 1303; and it was only after his attempt to prevent the capture of Stirling Castle had failed that he surrendered to Edward in February 1304. In 1306, 1307, and 1308 the Comyns were fighting not against Scotland but against a man whom they regarded with justice as the sacrilegious murderer of their kinsman, against a man who had long been their public and private enemy, and against a man who, when they were fighting for the independence of Scotland, had fought on the side of England. By the irony of fate the fortunes of war reversed their positions, and the man who had fought against his country became the champion of that country's freedom, while the men who had borne the burden and heat of their country's earlier struggles found themselves in arms in a cause which eventually became the cause of her enemies. But that is no reason why less than justice should be done to the Comyns. On the contrary, it is a very strong reason for rescuing their memory from the ignominy which has undeservedly been cast upon it.

In Aberdeenshire the Comyns had been great lords for nearly a century, and for more than fifty years they had been the most powerful family in Scotland. The earldom of Buchan was theirs by virtue of the marriage of William Comyn, in or before 1214, to the daughter and heiress of the last Celtic earl; and the Earl of Buchan who in 1308 opposed Bruce was the grandson of that union.[1] The Comyns were not, therefore, overlords of Buchan by conquest. They were in the eyes of the Celtic population—and Buchan in 1308 was almost wholly Celtic—the rightful lords of Buchan, and all the evidence we possess goes to show that they were so regarded by their tenants and vassals. Accordingly when Bruce, or his brother—for according to tradition the campaign in Buchan was conducted by Edward Bruce, the king himself not having recovered sufficiently to undertake it—invaded Buchan, Bruce's army found that the whole population was ranged against them, for the blood-feud of Comyn was the blood-feud of his people, and between the vassals of the Comyns and the Bruces, as between their masters, there had never been any love lost.

The fact that the population of Buchan was at that time Celtic intensified their loyalty to the Comyns and their hostility to Bruce. For, as every student of Celtic history knows, the Celts were ever noted for their devotion to the ties of family and blood. To the man of Buchan in the year 1308, therefore, the war in which he was engaged was not in any sense a war in favour of England or a war against Scotland. It was simply a righteous war against the bloody enemy of his chief, and therefore of himself. It was far different in Badenoch, of which district the murdered Comyn had been lord. There the Comyns were in no sense the recognised chiefs of the Celtic family which had formerly ruled in Badenoch. They had become lords of Badenoch less than eighty years before by suppressing for the Scottish king a rising in that district, and had risen to power on the ruins of the old Celtic family. There was, therefore, no personal or family tie between them and the warlike men of Badenoch, and their ascendency was at best endured simply because it could not be overborne. The murder of the Red Comyn, accordingly, did not rouse in his

[1] See B. P. under Buchan and Badenoch for the Comyns and their connections.

vassals in Badenoch any desire for vengeance. Their sympathies, on the contrary, would be rather with those who were in arms against the order of things for which he had stood. At all events they exhibited no hostility to Bruce, and throughout his wanderings in the Highlands there is no indication anywhere that he was ever in danger from the men of Badenoch. This point is of some importance if we are ever to understand the history of the period. The Earl of Ross was a formidable opponent because, as head of the Celtic House of Ross, he could bring into the field the whole array of Ross and Sutherland. Alexander of Argyll, as we shall see, was able as Lord of Argyll to range against Bruce all who owed him allegiance. Already, at Dalry, had Bruce tasted the quality of the men of Argyll, and at the Pass of Brandir he was to taste it, though with better result, once again. Similarly the Macdowalls of Galloway, from chief to herd-boy, were his bitter foes. The Earl of Buchan was in exactly similar case to these. Like them he was the recognised and legitimate chief of the Celtic territory, of which he was the titular head ; and that his kinsman, John Comyn of Badenoch, had never been. So just as the men of Argyll and Galloway followed their lords, so the men of Buchan followed their earl in his quarrel with Bruce, and made it their own.

Unfortunately we possess no trustworthy account of the campaign in Buchan. But, and this is the important point, it must have been prolonged and fiercely contested else there would have been no Herschip of Buchan. That is a plain and simple conclusion, which it is surprising has been so long overlooked. If we adopt the traditional narrative, and there is no reason for not doing so, Buchan's force retreated from Fyvie, and was pursued by Edward Bruce to Old Deer, where it was overtaken and utterly routed. Open resistance in the field was then at an end, but there still remained the Comyn castles of Kinedar, Slains, Kelly, Rattray, and Dundarg, which would have to be reduced before the overthrow of the Comyns could be regarded as complete. Now, in mediæval warfare, the castles played a very important part. By them, as we have seen, a country was held ; and Bruce impressed that fact on the history of Scotland by systematically destroying practically every castle that fell into his hands. But just because they were of such importance, the castles were places of great strength, and their capture a matter of great difficulty. They might be taken by surprise. They were seldom taken by direct assault. As a general rule, they only fell after a long siege had starved the garrison into surrender.

An example or two will make this clear. In 1304 Stirling Castle, with a garrison of less than 200 men, defied for three months the whole might of England, though Edward I, fresh from his triumphant progress through Scotland, himself directed the siege, and had to aid him all the engines of war known to the soldier of the period.[1] In the end Stirling succumbed to famine ; and the records of the war are full of other sieges with similar results. In 1298 and 1299, for example, Bothwell Castle was defended by its English warden, as he himself reports,[2] "against the power of Scotland for a year and nine weeks, to his great loss and misfortune, as all his companions died in the castle except himself and those with him who were taken by famine and by assault." Numerous other instances could be cited, but these will suffice to show that an attempt to capture a mediæval castle was like to be a long and difficult business.

In Buchan, accordingly, Edward Bruce could have had no easy task. He had at least four castles to capture, he was operating in the midst of an unfriendly population, he had no siege engines, his force was comparatively small, and there was always the danger of attack from the rear. In these circumstances it is not surprising that he wasted Buchan with fire and sword. It was, in fact, a matter of necessity, the mediæval way of carrying out what the British in South Africa accomplished by means of concentration camps. But it was

[1] See various entries. Bain, ii.   [2] Bain, ii. 1867.

also in part a matter of policy. The demonstration of Bruce's strength which the overthrow of the Comyns gave to all Scotland gained a hundredfold by the harrying of their territories. Its moral effect was enormous. Here was the district of Bruce's most powerful foes, a district which might well hope to defy him with every prospect of success; yet, in the result, its castles were captured, its lands were laid waste, its people were slaughtered or dispersed, its lords were driven out, and all with a terrible completeness, which carried its lesson plain upon the face of it. The personal factor no doubt entered in to make the devastation worse than it might otherwise have been. Bruce had the blood of his slaughtered brothers to avenge, and full well he knew that if he himself fell into the hands of his enemies short would be his shrift. But when all allowance is made, it is clear that this of itself would not have caused the Herschip of Buchan. Policy alone, to say nothing else, would have prevented it, had there been no motive for it save revenge. The Herschip of Buchan was the direct and natural outcome of a combination of circumstances—the resistance of the Earl and his people, the desperate nature of the situation in which Bruce was placed, the bitter personal enmity existing between the contestants, the necessity of Bruce's destroying the power of the Comyns once and for all, and the need of his impressing on the minds of his contemporaries that he had the will and the power to exact a great price from those who were his enemies, and to protect those who were his friends. But though all these played their part, the really impelling circumstance was the resistance offered by the Earl and his people, a resistance which must have been determined and have given every promise of being prolonged.

How or when the castles of the Comyns fell we have no means of ascertaining; but by the end of March Sir Walter de Bickerton was free to attempt the capture of Cupar-Fife; by at latest the end of May news of the total downfall of the Comyn power in Buchan had been despatched to Edward[1]; and by the first or the second week in June the castle of Aberdeen was closely invested.[2] It is a fair inference, therefore, that by the middle of March Buchan had been devastated and most of the Comyn strongholds captured. Some time in June or July Aberdeen Castle also fell, the citizens, according to Hector Boece, aiding Bruce in a successful assault upon it, and by the end of the summer the only castle remaining to England in Aberdeenshire and all the country to the west and north was Banff.[3] The royal castles of Fyvie, Aboyne, and Kintore must, therefore, all have fallen in the spring or summer of 1308—Fyvie possibly before Edward Bruce resumed his pursuit of the Comyns in December 1307 or January 1308—and in no long time thereafter the strongholds of the few adherents of England still remaining in Aberdeenshire must also have fallen, the Hastings castles of Coull and Lumphannan and the le Chen castle of Ravenscraig among them.

The results of the overthrow of the Comyns and the Herschip of Buchan are, therefore, the best justification of these events. Prior to them, from the shires of Aberdeen, Kincardine, and Forfar only a few adventurous spirits had dared to join Bruce, for the power of England and of the adherents of England was heavy upon the land. But the collapse of the Comyns, and the circumstances which attended it, removed all obstacles from the path of those whose sympathies were with Bruce, and from that moment his cause never looked back. Recruits of all sorts and conditions flocked to his standard; with hardly an exception every burgh and hamlet from Spey to Tay ranged itself openly on his side; by the end of 1308 almost every castle in the same district had fallen into the hands of himself or his adherents; and long before the close of 1308 his strength was such that, in the beginning of August, he was able to advance to the west in an endeavour to bring to terms the other great branch of the

[1] Bain, iii. 47.   [2] *Rotuli Scotiae*, i. 55.   [3] *Ibid.*, p. 63.

Red Comyn's kinsfolk, the Macdowalls of Argyll and Lorn. Behind him he left a number of eager young warriors, whose interests lay in Forfar and Fife, to harass the English in these parts, and throughout the autumn and winter the game of winning castles went merrily on. By the middle of 1309, in all Scotland north of Tay, only Dundee and Banff remained to England, while between Tay and the Firths of Forth and Clyde only Stirling, Perth, and Kirkintilloch were in English hands. Of these Dundee and Banff owed their immunity from capture to their position on the sea-coast, whereby they were revictualled and reinforced by the English fleet again and again[1]; while Kirkintilloch, in the southmost corner of Stirlingshire, belonged to the Comyns, and was in a district to which the arms of Bruce had not yet penetrated. Perth and Stirling were of such great strength that their capture had not yet been seriously attempted; while the former, in addition to its strength, was constantly receiving supplies and reinforcements from the English fleet, which from 1308 to 1312 was seldom away from the Scottish coast for any length of time, and is frequently mentioned as carrying men and provisions to Perth.[2]

[1] *Rotuli Scotiae*, i. 63, 79, 80.
[2] See various entries in Bain, *Rotuli Scotiae*, i. 80, and chapters *infra* for particulars regarding these towns and castles.

CHAPTER XXIX

THE CONQUEST OF ARGYLL (1308)

BARBOUR tells us how the castle of Forfar fell, but though the way in which he runs his tale together makes it appear as if it were captured very soon after the Herschip of Buchan, it could not have fallen before the second week of November 1308, as on 3rd December orders were issued by Edward in England for its revictualling and reinforcement.[1] This is its last appearance in the English records, so its capture may confidently be placed in the winter of 1308–9. Says Barbour :

> "The castle of Forfar was then
> Stuffit all with Englishmen,
> But Philip the Forster of Platan
> Has of his friends with him tane,
> And with ladders all privily
> To the castle he did him hie,
> And climbed out o'er the wall of stane
> And this way has the castle ta'en,
> Through fault of watch, with little pain.
> And then all that he found has slain :
> Then yields the castle to the king.
> That made him right good rewarding,
> And syne did break down the wall,
> And spoiled the well and castle all."

This description is interesting as showing by what manner of feats many of the castles were taken, and when read along with Sir Thomas Gray's tale, above quoted, of his father's adventures as Constable of Cupar-Fife, gives us an excellent idea of the sort of warfare that was waged in the intervals of battle and invasion, and of the means by which the country was freed of the

---

[1] *Rotuli Scotiae*, i. 61.

English. It will be noticed, too, that Forfar Castle was destroyed by Bruce in the same way as Inverness, Aberdeen, and many another. Of other east country castles, Cupar-Fife probably fell in the summer or autumn of 1308, for not only is there no reference to it in English records when succour is being sent to other castles in 1308,[1] but it does not appear in the list to which provisions and help were twice ordered to be sent in 1309.[2] What is perhaps of even more significance, however, is that Sir Thomas Gray has nothing further to say about the exploits of its constable, his father, after his escape from Alexander Fraser's ambuscade, which seems to have occurred in the summer of 1308. Brechin must also have fallen in 1308 or early in 1309, for it, too, does not appear in the list of castles to which aid was sent. Moreover, Sir David de Brechin was for some time at least, prior to 15th June 1310, an adherent of Bruce, for on that date, as we have already seen, he was received by Alexander de Abernethy to Edward's peace, it being expressly stated that he had been adhering to the king's enemies in Scotland.[3] As Sir David was a nephew of the Earl of Buchan, it is not surprising that he did not long remain attached to Bruce's party, which he in all probability joined after the fall of Brechin.

The most striking evidence of the magnitude of the change in Bruce's fortunes which the year 1308 witnessed is afforded by the very document in which, in June 1308, the Earl of Buchan is appointed one of the wardens of Galloway, Annandale, and Carrick. Instructions are given for the victualling of the king's castles in Scotland, and the document then proceeds [4] : " The king to take no sufferance or truce from Robert de Bruce, but the Guardians of Scotland may take such as long as possible, as they have done hitherto of their own power or by commission, on condition that the king, however, may furnish his castles with men and victuals." An endorsement on

---

[1] *Rotuli Scotiae*, i. 55–61.   [2] *Ibid.*, p. 63.
[3] *Ibid.*, p. 82.   [4] Bain, iii. 47.

the document adds that letters are to be written to the Guardians of Scotland, "that it is the king's pleasure that they take truce from Robert de Bruce, as from themselves, as long as they can, but not beyond the month of Easter . . .; and the king to victual and garrison his castles during the truce; and that he may break the truce at pleasure, if the others will yield this point; but if they will not the truce to be made without it." Little more than six months before Bruce seemed in desperate case. Now the king of England was directing his officers to make truce with him. A more significant tribute to the growing power of the king of Scots, and the remarkable results which had flowed from his northern campaigns, could hardly be forthcoming.

There is considerable difficulty in arriving at anything like a final conclusion in regard to the order of events during the year which succeeded the Herschip of Buchan. Fordun tells us in the most definite way that within a week after the Assumption of the Blessed Virgin, that is to say in the third week of August, Bruce overcame the men of Argyll in the middle of Argyll, and subdued the whole land to himself, and soon after captured the castle of Dunstaffnage, the chief seat of Alexander of Argyll. Barbour tells the story of the same campaign at length and with a wealth of picturesque detail, but makes no mention of any date. On 11th March 1309 John of Lorn, son and heir of Alexander of Argyll, received letters from Edward II, and in reply thereto sent a long report to the king,[1] in which he says that he had been for half a year on a sick-bed at the date (11th March) when the letters arrived, that Robert de Bruce had approached his territories (when he does not say) with a force which was said to number 10,000 or 15,000 men, and that Bruce had asked for a truce "which he granted for a short space, and received the like till the king send him succour." He adds that the barons of Argyll gave him no aid, and that "he has three castles to guard, and a lake twenty-four leagues

[1] Bain, iii. 80.

long (Loch Awe probably) on which he has vessels properly manned, but is not sure of his neighbours."

To complicate matters still further the name of John of Lorn's father, Alexander of Argyll, appears on the record of Bruce's famous Parliament held at St. Andrews on 16th March of the same year,[1] 1309, at which also the barons of Argyll and Inchegall were present, while fourteen months later, on 16th June 1310, both Alexander of Argyll and John of Lorn are on record as having been "with other loyal Scots" at a Council of the English king at Westminster.[2]   Finally, as we have seen, Bruce himself in person received the surrender and the homage of the Earl of Ross at Auldearn, near Nairn, on 31st October 1308, while Barbour seems to make Edward Bruce invade and conquer Galloway about the same time, ascribes the capture of Thomas Randolph by Douglas to the same year, and gives to Douglas a prominent part in the campaign in Argyll.   Out of such a tangle it is difficult to evolve a narrative which we can accept without hesitation as unquestionably accurate, but we may, I think, succeed in reconstructing the course of events from the material at our disposal in such a way as to arrive at certain conclusions which cannot be very far wide of the mark.

Accepting Fordun's very definite statement as to the date of the battle at the Pass of Brandir, Bruce must have set out from the eastern counties before the end of July 1308.   John of Lorn's statement as to the strength of his force is, of course, a manifest exaggeration, but that it was a very strong force is quite clear.   That it was composed very largely of Highlanders Barbour's account, as we shall see, also makes clear; but this we should naturally expect, as Bruce's route lay through the heart of great Highland territories friendly to him, and his recent successes had been gained by means of the adherence to his cause of Moray and other Highland districts.

[1] Acts of Parl., i. 99.
[2] Bain, iii. 95, and Note p. 609 as to date.

Alexander of Argyll was now an old man, and the active leader of the men of Argyll was his son John of Lorn, that Lord of Lorn whose name is so familiar to, and has been held in so much despite by many generations of Scotsmen. As in the case of the Comyns, however, this is quite undeserved. Alexander of Argyll was uncle of the murdered Comyn, and John of Lorn was, therefore, his cousin; and in that age it would have been strange indeed if they had been other than Bruce's mortal foes. But as it fared with the Comyns, so with the Argylls. The cause of Bruce became the cause of Scottish freedom, and the Argylls, who, like the Comyns, had in their day struck stout blows for Scotland, found themselves in the end, by the irresistible course of events, ranged among the foes of their country. But the essential thing to remember is that neither the Argylls nor the Comyns nor the Macdowalls of Galloway were in any sense traitors to Scotland. They were moved neither by loyalty to England nor hostility to Scotland. Their sole motive was enmity to Bruce, in whom it is not to be wondered at that they failed to recognise either the rightful king of Scots or the champion of their country's freedom.

John of Lorn, Barbour tells us, had early notice of Bruce's approach, and made every possible preparation to meet him. As soon as it became clear that Bruce must advance by the Pass of Brandir, Lorn sent 2000 men "for to stop the way." The way "was in an evil place," so straight and narrow that in some parts "two men together might not ride." The lower side of the pass was particularly perilous, for there "a sheer crag, high and hideous," descended abruptly from the pass to the sea. On the other side Ben Cruachan rose so steeply "that it was hard to pass that way." It formed, therefore, an ideal place for an ambush, and there, accordingly, John of Lorn placed his men, concealing them on the mountain-side above the pass, while he himself with his galleys lay on the loch below. But he had to deal with a skilful adversary. Bruce, either fearing or being

Y

informed of an ambush, made plans for ambushing any possible ambuscaders. He divided his force into two, sending the archers, under Douglas, to climb the hill and come on the ambush from above. With Douglas he sent Sir William Wiseman, "a good knight"; "Sir Alexander Fraser, the wicht"; and "good Sir Andrew Gray," all three of whom, it is of importance to note, were of Scotland north of the Forth.

The mention of Sir William Wiseman is of special interest, for he is the only one of Bruce's Moray adherents named by Barbour. As we have already seen, he was one of those who on Bruce's first appearance in 1306 had thrown off their allegiance to England, and, though he himself had escaped after the debacle at Methven, his wife had been captured with Bruce's queen and consigned to an English prison. He was a very prominent personality in Moray, his name frequently appearing in the documents of the period, and in 1305 he had been appointed by Edward I Sheriff of Elgin, while Alexander Wiseman, in all probability his brother, was appointed Sheriff of Nairn.

Douglas's detachment climbed the hill so quickly and quietly that they seized "the height above their foes" without being perceived, from which it is clear that the men whom Douglas led must have been Highlanders. Bruce and the rest of his force meanwhile held their way towards the pass, and presently entered it. Immediately, with a shout of triumph, Lorn's men rose from their ambush, assailed them with flight upon flight of arrows, and hurled stones, "right great and heavy," down upon them. "But they harmed not greatly the king, for he had in his following men that light and nimble were and light armed." These "stoutly climbed the hill and prevented their foes from fulfilling the most part of their felony." At almost the same moment Douglas and his men came on them from above, and, giving a great shout, poured a hail of arrows upon the surprised ambush, and charged down upon it with waving swords. For a moment or two the men of Lorn defended themselves manfully; then, perceiving they were taken in front and rear, they broke and fled headlong. Bruce's men followed eagerly, and so ardent was the pursuit and so complete the rout that all resistance in the open was soon at an end. From his ships John of Lorn in angry amazement viewed the discomfiture of his men, and, unable either to assist them or to attack Bruce, could only rage furiously. But worse was to follow. Bruce gave his foes neither time nor opportunity to rally. His army overran the land, taking great spoil, and appearing at last suddenly before Dunstaffnage itself compelled it in a very short time to surrender.

We come now to the chief difficulty in connection with the Argyllshire campaign. Both Barbour and Fordun make the capture of Dunstaffnage occur very soon after the battle at the Pass of Brandir, Barbour adding that Alexander of Argyll thereupon surrendered and came to Bruce's peace, "but John of Lorn, his son, yet was a rebel, as he was wont to be, and fled with ships to the sea." Fordun says that though the castle was surrendered, Alexander refused to do homage, and was allowed to depart with his friends to England. John of Lorn's letter, already quoted, written after 11th March 1309, with its reference to his having three castles to guard, further complicates matters. But the record of Bruce's Parliament at St. Andrews on 16th March 1309 proves that at that time Alexander of Argyll was with Bruce, while his presence along with John of Lorn at an English Council in June 1310 shows that subsequently he did refuse to acknowledge Bruce, and did retire to England. Neither Barbour's nor Fordun's account, therefore, is inaccurate, nor do they contradict each other, as at a first glance they seem to do. Alexander of Argyll did come to Bruce's peace for a time, in how full a sense of the meaning of that phrase matters not, and he did eventually retire to England, as Fordun relates.

We are still left, however, with one real difficulty, the date of the campaign, though the realisation that

Barbour and Fordun do not nullify each other helps us towards a solution. Fordun, as we have seen, specifically places its beginning in August 1308. John of Lorn's letter seems, at first sight, to render that date impossible. But at the very time when that letter was written Alexander of Argyll was with Bruce at St. Andrews, while Lorn himself states that, at some date unmentioned, he had made truce with Bruce. The only questions which remain, therefore, are—When was the truce made, and had Dunstaffnage fallen some months before the date of John of Lorn's letter?

We have seen, from Edward's instructions to the Guardians of Scotland, above quoted, that in June 1308 they were authorised to take truce from Bruce for any length of period up to Easter 1309, on such terms as he was willing to grant. We have also seen that about a year prior to September 1308 Bruce had entered into a long truce with the Earl of Ross. It is, therefore, impossible to argue either that the possibility of a truce between Bruce and the Argylls is out of the question— even if we leave John of Lorn's own admission out of the reckoning, or that, if agreed to, it could not have been granted as far back as September 1308.

A further matter for consideration is that, in his letter to Edward, John of Lorn says that on 11th March he had been on a sick-bed for half a year. But if Barbour is correct in saying that John of Lorn was present with his galleys on Loch Awe when the battle at the Pass of Brandir was fought, then half a year carries us back to just about the date when Fordun says it was fought, the third week of August 1308, unless we assume, as Mr. Mackenzie in a note in his edition of *The Bruce* suggests, that Lorn's presence in a galley on Loch Awe, instead of with his men in the ambush, was due to his illness. This is, of course, a possible explanation, but the words used in the letter do not seem to me to admit of such a construction. They are quite specific. Lorn acknowledges receiving Edward's letters on 11th March, and goes on: " He was on sick-bed at their reaching him, and had been for half a year. Robert de Bruce had approached his territories with 10,000 or 15,000 men, it was said, both by land and sea," and so on. Not only does he not say that Bruce arrived when he was on sick-bed, but this expression itself seems to imply that he was tied to his bed in a way which would not have permitted him to take any part, even in a galley, in a campaign of any sort. Perhaps it would not be far wrong to suggest that his illness was caused by wounds received or hardships endured in the defence of his territories against Bruce. Moreover, the tenor of Lorn's letter leaves the impression that Edward's letters, to which it was an answer, referred to Bruce's invasion of Argyll; and it is more than possible that they were sent in reply to an appeal by Lorn for aid when Bruce first approached his territories.

In the next place it is difficult to resist the conclusion that the true explanation of Alexander of Argyll's presence with Bruce at St. Andrews on 16th March 1309, is that he was in reality a hostage in Bruce's hands for the observance of the truce and for the good behaviour of his son and the men of Argyll. Buchan, remember, had already been devastated when Bruce descended on Argyll with an army which must have been very large, though Lorn's 10,000 or 15,000 is a manifest exaggeration. Moreover, Lorn's neighbours, the barons of Argyll and the Isles, gave him no aid, as he himself tells Edward, and as the record of the St. Andrews Parliament bears out. Accordingly, after the battle at the Pass of Brandir and the spoiling of the country, the Argylls may well have considered that it would be wise to make a temporary surrender in the hope that Edward would soon carry out his long-promised intention of invading Scotland in force and dispose of Bruce once and for all. Meanwhile they knew that they were outnumbered, out-fought, and out-generalled, and they had the example of their kinsmen of Buchan to remind them of what they might expect if they fought the quarrel out to the end. So when Dunstaffnage was besieged they surrendered on terms. A truce was granted them for a specified period, as it had been granted to the Earl of Ross, and on its expiry they would have to make their final choice of peace or war. Meanwhile Bruce took Alexander of Argyll with him as a hostage; a faithful adherent of the king, according to Barbour, was placed in command of Dunstaffnage Castle with a strong garrison and a supply of provisions so ample "that he there a long time might be in spite of them all of that country"; and Bruce marched away north with his army to come to a final reckoning with the Earl of Ross. John of Lorn, meanwhile, departed in his ships to one of his other castles, for, as he himself says, he was included in the truce, while the men of Argyll on the mainland "were to the king all obedient and he their homage all has taken."

That this version of what occurred in Argyll is as near to the truth as is possible for us now to get seems to be borne out by Bruce's dealings with the Earl of Ross. If it be argued that it is unlikely that Bruce would have made truce with the Argylls and then marched away with the possibility of having to do his work over again, we reply that he had already pursued successfully an exactly similar course with the Earl of Ross. And, after all, the risk in the case of the Argylls was not great. They had more cause than the Earl of Ross for not playing Bruce false, for Bruce had in the immediately preceding months given signal proof of his power, and there was always the memory of Buchan to keep them in the paths of rectitude did Alexander of Argyll in Bruce's hands and a garrison in Dunstaffnage not suffice. At all events we know that Bruce did pursue with the Earl of Ross the course which the few facts we possess seem to indicate he pursued with the Argylls, and that is, at least, strongly corroborative evidence in favour of our reading of the tangled tale. The fact, too, that, if our reading is correct, Bruce proceeded at once from Argyll to Moray in order to receive the final surrender of the Earl of Ross, is a further point in our favour. For not only was Bruce to meet the Earl of Ross with all the glamour of the success of the campaign in Argyll fresh upon him, but if Alexander of Argyll were with him the latter could hardly fail to be impressed by the acknowledgment of Bruce's sovereignty by the northern magnate.

This brings us to our next point. Bruce received the final surrender of the Earl of Ross at Auldearn in Moray on 31st October 1308, when an imposing array of knights and other notables accompanied the Scottish king. Accordingly, if the Argyll campaign had not been concluded before the middle of October it could not have been begun earlier than the third week of November, and must have been finished before the end of February. But it is exceedingly unlikely that Bruce would have undertaken a Highland campaign during the winter months, especially a campaign which entailed his marching with a large force through the very heart of the Highlands. The question of commissariat, to say nothing of other things, would have been sufficient to give him pause. Again, it is a fact well known to every student of Highland history that Highland warfare was usually conducted in the summer and autumn. One reason for this is that only then were the rivers likely to be easily fordable and the country fairly dry ; while another is that questions of food supply caused little trouble, the invading force simply living on the country. Barbour's account of the Argyll campaign suggests the latter strongly, for he tells us that Bruce "seized the prey of all the land, where men might see so great abundance . . . that it were wonder to behold," which can only mean that the campaign took place about the time of harvest. His statement, too, about the great provisioning of Dunstaffnage suggests the same thing, and there is something grimly humorous in the idea of the castle which was to hold the district in awe being rendered impervious to starvation by the spoil of that same district. Then, again, John of Lorn informs Edward that Bruce approached his territories " both by land and sea," which also seems to indicate a fine-weather campaign.

In October or early in November 1308, moreover, the castle of Rutherglen was being besieged by the Scots,[1] and was in such imminent danger that on 3rd December Edward, at Westminster, issued peremptory orders for the despatch of a strong force to its rescue.[2] But Bruce was at Auldearn on 31st October, and accordingly could not have been at Rutherglen early in November. On the other hand, as we shall presently see, Edward Bruce, Douglas, and others were in Galloway during the winter of 1308-9. Moreover, the names of Edward Bruce, Douglas, and their companions are conspicuous by their absence from the deed which sets forth the surrender of the Earl of Ross. Accordingly, it seems clear that after the close of the campaign in Argyll Bruce divided his forces, he himself going north, and Douglas going south to rejoin Edward Bruce. As Barbour expressly assigns the capture of Rutherglen to Edward Bruce, and as the entry of 3rd October 1308 is the last reference to it in the English records, there can be little doubt that Edward Bruce was engaged in besieging it in the autumn of 1308. After its fall he returned to Galloway, and accordingly he, like Bruce himself, could not have been in Argyll in the winter of 1308-9.

There remains one other matter which we must examine before we pass from our consideration of the date of the campaign. Barbour tells us that Thomas Randolph, Bruce's nephew, was captured on the Water of Lyne, near Peebles, by James Douglas just prior to the expedition to Argyll. After his capture at Methven in June 1306 Randolph had made his peace with Edward I, and in 1307 and 1308 fought on the side of England. When captured by Douglas, he was with an English force, and Douglas straightway carried him to Bruce. Towards his royal uncle Randolph exhibited anything but a friendly spirit, and his only reply to Bruce's suggestion that he should rejoin the national party was a taunt regarding Bruce's method of conducting the war. Where-

[1] Foedera. [2] *Ibid.*

upon he was sent " to be in firm keeping " until he should come to a better frame of mind.

Now, on 4th March 1309,[1] Edward, at Westminster, granted to Adam de Gordon the manor of "Stichill in Scotland forfeited by the rebellion of Thomas Randolph," which means that the news that Randolph had made his peace with Bruce had reached Adam de Gordon or Edward's officials in Scotland not later than the end of January 1309, and probably a good deal earlier. It is a fair inference, accordingly, that the reconciliation had actually taken place some weeks at least before word of it came to the ears of the English faction in Scotland, and as Randolph spent some time in durance before he made up his mind to cast in his lot with Bruce, we are carried back to a date for his capture which can hardly be later, and may be considerably earlier, than August 1308. It all depends on how long Randolph was " in firm keeping," and that, of course, we have no means of knowing, though Barbour's words imply that it was for some time. An entry in the English records may, perhaps, refer to the episode which resulted in the capture of Randolph. On 6th December 1308 Richard Galoun " lately captured," whilst in the company of the Sheriff of Roxburgh, " in a conflict between the king's men and the Scottish rebels," states that he was released on a promise to pay a ransom and deliver to them one of the Scots prisoners in his place.[2] He accordingly petitions for such a prisoner, and an exchange is arranged. As his petition is dated 6th December, his capture must have taken place some considerable time, probably three or four months, before, which would carry us back to the very time when Randolph appears to have been captured. Moreover, as Richard Galoun was captured about the same place as Randolph is said to have been captured, and as Randolph was only one of several prisoners then taken, it is more than probable that Richard Galoun was taken at the same time, and that his petition, accordingly, confirms the date which Barbour's narrative suggests for the capture of

---

[1] Bain, iii. 76. [2] Close Rolls, Ed. II., p. 86.

Randolph, namely about July or August 1308. The few facts we possess, therefore, all point to July or August 1308 as the date of Randolph's capture, and fit in with our reading of the course of events in the latter half of 1308.

One or two other matters of some importance to our narrative require attention before we pass from the expedition to Argyll. As we have already seen, the men who ambushed the ambush at the Pass of Brandir must have been Highlanders. It is equally plain that the men whom Bruce led into the defile were also Highlanders. It is impossible to imagine that such nimble climbers were anything else. For "men that light and nimble were, and light arming had on them," says Barbour, "so that they stoutly climbed the hill," and met the men of Argyll on the brae-face.

Then there is John of Lorn's statement of Bruce's approach "by land and sea." This can only mean that Bruce's island allies with Angus Og and the men of Kintyre were with him once again. There remains John of Lorn's letter. It must, of course, be remembered that it is the letter of a defeated man putting the best face he can upon things to his royal master. His remark that Bruce had "10,000 or 15,000 men, it was said," condemns itself by its studied vagueness and the careful "it was said." Similarly his statement that he himself had only 800 men is an effort to minimise his own want of success. But if he had only 800 men then our whole argument as to the probability of Bruce's having granted him a truce and marched away is vastly strengthened. For if that were all his strength there was nothing to fear from him, and the barons of Argyll and the Isles could safely be trusted to keep a vigilant and sufficient watch upon him. As to Bruce's force, we may safely place it at 5000 at the outside, if indeed it numbered even one-half of that.

We may sum up our observations on the Argyllshire campaign as follows. It was almost certainly begun in August, and concluded late in September or early in

October 1308, the men of Argyll being routed at the
Pass of Brandir, Dunstaffnage Castle being captured and
garrisoned, and Alexander of Argyll and John of Lorn
agreeing to a truce with Bruce, in terms of which the
former either did homage to Bruce as king of Scots or
surrendered himself as a hostage. The army with which
Bruce achieved this success was a Highland army, and, as
in his previous campaigns, the knights and men-at-arms
who accompanied it were drawn almost entirely from
Scotland north of the Forth and Clyde, and largely from
the province of Moray. It follows, therefore, that the
strong position in which Bruce found himself at the close
of 1308 was entirely due to the support which had been
accorded him in Scotland north of the Forth and Clyde.
Galloway and the south-west were as yet either openly
hostile or uncommitted to the national cause, while
Lothian, as Barbour in an illuminating line at the conclusion of his account of the Argyllshire campaign tells
us, thus confirming unexpectedly the conclusions at which
we have arrived, "still was him against." With Scotland
north of the Forth and Clyde at his back Bruce was soon
to embark on a sustained and successful effort to make
the rest of Scotland his own.

CHAPTER XXX

WE have seen that on the conclusion of the Argyll campaign Bruce returned to the province of Moray, where, on 31st October 1308, he received at Auldearn the surrender and homage of William, Earl of Ross. "Because," says the Earl in the deed wherein the submission is recorded, "the magnificent prince, Sir Robert, by the grace of God, king of the Scots, my lord, out of his natural goodness, desire, clemency, and special grace has forgiven me sincerely the rancour of his mind, and relaxed and condoned to me all transgressions or offences against him and his by me and mine . . . and has graciously granted me my lands and tenements, and has caused me also to be heritably infeft in the lands of Dingwall and Ferncrosky in the sheriffdom of Sutherland of his benign liberality : I taking heed of the great benevolence of such a prince and because of so many gracious deeds to me . . . surrender and bind me and my heirs and all my men to the said lord my king . . . and we will be of a surety faithful to him and his heirs, and we will render him faithful service, assistance, and counsel . . . against all men and women who may live or die. And in token of this I, William, for myself, my heirs, and all my men to the said lord my king, have made homage freely and have sworn on the evangel of God." [1]

I quote this document almost verbatim, as it affords an excellent example of Bruce's methods of dealing with those who from being his enemies became, either of their own will or by force of circumstances, his adherents.

[1] Acts of Parl., i. 477.

He could be a fierce enemy, but he was always a generous friend; and he ever preferred to win men to his side by peaceful means rather than by the sword. It was, of course, policy so to do. Men who have been compelled to allegiance by conquest make, as a rule, uncomfortable subjects. Bruce's treatment of the Earl of Ross, at all events, bore splendid fruit. He and his amply fulfilled their bond to Bruce and his, and, as we have already seen, between the Earl's family and Edward Bruce there grew a great affection. Henceforward Bruce could safely number the Earl of Ross among his faithful adherents, and as the Earl was guardian of the youthful Earl of Sutherland, that meant that all Scotland north of the Tay, with the exception of the town of Banff and one or two castles in Forfar, was solidly on his side.

The names of the witnesses to the Earl of Ross's submission are of both interest and importance. First come "the venerable Fathers in God, David and Thomas, by the grace of God bishops of Moray and Ross." Then follow Sir Bernard, Chancellor of the king; Sir William de Hay, a one-time Sheriff of Inverness; Sir John de Stirling, a knight of Moray, who had been appointed Sheriff of Inverness for England in September 1305; Sir William Wiseman, who had been made Sheriff of Elgin at the same time; Sir John de Fenton of Beaufort; Sir David de Berkeley, who had held the lands of Avoch before he joined Bruce in 1306 [1]; Sir Walter de Berkeley, who had been appointed Sheriff of Banff for England in September 1305, and who had been one of the gallant band of knights who, with the Red Comyn, had held out against Edward I until forced to surrender in February 1304; Master Walter Heroc, Dean of the Bishopric of Moray, a well-known churchman in his day; Master William de Crewsel, precentor of the same diocese; and "many other nobles, clerics, and laity, assembled at same time and place." All of these names are already familiar to us, and I only mention them here

[1] Bain, iv. 400.

in order to show of whom the force was composed which accompanied Bruce from Argyll to Moray, and in order to emphasize again the strength of his following in Moray and the neighbouring districts.

From Auldearn Bruce proceeded east and south again. We have, unfortunately, no exact knowledge of his movements at this time, but one or two other facts which we do possess may throw some light upon them. But before we consider them, we must glance at a suggestion sometimes made that during the winter of 1308–9 Bruce was engaged either in the siege of Dunstaffnage or in a second invasion of Argyll, which resulted in the capture of the castle. It is possible that on the expiry of the truce, which must have been subsequent to March 1309, as John of Lorn's letter shows, Bruce made another expedition to Argyll to bring Alexander of Argyll and John of Lorn finally to terms, just as he had previously done with the Earl of Ross. But if that is so, then it could not have taken place earlier than the summer of 1309, for, as we have seen, the Parliament at St. Andrews was held on 16th March, and either then or later John of Lorn was writing to Edward from one of his castles in Argyll. The impossibility of either the first expedition or the siege of Dunstaffnage having taken place between 31st October 1308 and 16th March 1309 we have already observed. Of course any conclusion on the whole question is in the circumstances largely a matter of surmise, but looking to Alexander of Argyll's presence at St. Andrews in March 1309, and the appearance of himself and his son in June 1310 at a Council of the English king at Westminster, it is, I think, reasonable to suggest that some time in the summer or autumn of 1309 Bruce either conducted a second expedition to Argyll, as a result of which Alexander and John retired to England, or on the expiry of the truce he gave them the choice of becoming his men, as the Earl of Ross had done, or of leaving Scotland.

The latter possibility is not so improbable as it may seem, for by the middle of 1309 Argyll was hemmed

about with adversaries.   Alexander of the Isles, Argyll's
kinsman and ally, had been captured in 1308 or early in
1309.   His lands had been forfeited and conferred on
his brother Angus Og, who as Lord of Kintyre had been
one of Bruce's earliest and staunchest adherents, and who
now as Lord of the Isles was the most powerful man in
all the west.[1]   Another faithful adherent of Bruce, Sir
Neil Campbell, one of the barons of Argyll, was in
Lochow on the shores of Loch Awe, of which territory
and of Ardskeonish he was king's bailie,[2] while, as we
have seen, all the other barons of Argyll and Innisgail
were openly on Bruce's side.   Moreover, the hoped-for
aid from England had not been forthcoming.   No English
army had marched into Scotland to the succour of
Edward's Scottish adherents; victory everywhere was
shining on Bruce's arms; the Macdowalls of Galloway
had been humbled, as we shall presently see, and a large
part of their country had come to Bruce's peace; while
of all the great Comyn connection the Argylls alone had
not yet been driven to the final choice of surrender or
open enmity.   But at last their hour, too, came, and
in all the circumstances it may well be that, threatened
with the choice of absolute surrender or another invasion which could only have one end, they thought
discretion the better part of valour, and, unable to bring
themselves to bow the knee to Bruce, retired to England, there to wait for what they hoped might be happier
times.

This conclusion, drawn quite fairly from all the facts
we have been considering, gathers probability when we
recollect that it fits in with what Fordun actually says
did happen, namely that Alexander of Argyll refused to
do homage, and was allowed a safe conduct for himself
and his friends to England.   At all events to England,
either in 1309 or 1310,[3] the Argylls did retire, and their
lands in Scotland knew them no more, Alexander dying
in Ireland in December 1310, and John of Lorn serving

[1] See *Clan Donald;* and B. P., under Lord of the Isles.
[2] B. P., Argyll.   [3] Bain, iii. 95, 121, 132.

Edward faithfully as his Admiral of the Western Isles [1] until his death in 1317.[2] A single quotation from the English records will suffice to show how complete was their severance from Argyll. In July 1310 Edward granted to John of Argyll and his brothers [3] the lands of Knapdale "if they are able to take them from the hands of the Scots." With that final evidence of the completeness of their downfall we may dismiss Alexander of Argyll and John of Lorn from our narrative.

In tracing the fortunes of the Argylls to the end we have outrun our narrative somewhat; but it was necessary to make clear that if there was a second expedition to Argyll it could not have taken place between 31st October 1308 and the end of March 1309. Let us now consider the other facts which seem to give us a little further light on the events of the winter and spring of 1308-9. We saw that on 3rd December 1308 orders were issued in England for provisions and reinforcements to be sent to the castle of Forfar. We may deduce from this that the castle was early in November in some danger, and, as we have already suggested, it probably fell in no long time thereafter. At the same time, as we have also seen, Rutherglen was in even greater danger. Accordingly in November 1308 we find Bruce himself in Moray, one strong Scottish force, almost certainly under Edward Bruce and Douglas, at Rutherglen, and another operating in the neighbourhood of Forfar.

In the next place there is the important fact that Bruce was able to hold a Parliament at St. Andrews on 16th March 1309. This he could only have done if his position in Fife was by then fairly secure, for it is impossible to assume either that the Parliament was held at a moment's notice, or that Bruce marched hastily from the north-east, and his brother Edward hurried from Galloway with Alexander Lindsay and James Douglas in order to attend it. Common sense makes it clear either that Bruce and his principal adherents were for some

---

[1] Bain, iii. 191, 203, &c. &c.   [2] *Ibid.*, 912.
[3] *Rotuli Scotiae*, i. 90.

cause or another in Fife in February and March 1309, or that at some date considerably anterior to 16th March he summoned them from far and near to meet him there. If the latter be the case, common sense again tells us that if Bruce were in Argyll or the north in the winter of 1308-9, he would not have appointed a place so far away, and of such doubtful security, as St. Andrews for a gathering of his adherents.

On the other hand the fact that the Parliament was held at St. Andrews, and that, as its record shows, it was attended by most of Bruce's principal supporters, implies either that Bruce himself was in Fife early in 1309, or that many of his leading followers were. But Edward Bruce and many others were at that very time in Galloway, so we are driven back to the conclusion that Bruce himself must have been in Fife or its neighbourhood early in 1309. For let it be remembered that the Parliament was held in the month of March, that the period was the beginning of the fourteenth century, that travelling was slow and communication difficult, and then consider whether it is credible that Bruce, at a long distance from St. Andrews in the middle of the winter of 1308-9, summoned his adherents from Galloway and the Isles to meet him at a place far away from him and them, at a place, too, which, if he himself were not in its near neighbourhood, he could not be sure would be in his power on any specified date. For St. Andrews lay on the east coast, easily open to attack by the English fleet, while the castle of Dundee, strongly held for England, was not very far away. And, as we have seen, the English fleet was frequently in these waters at that time, and was in constant communication with Perth, Dundee, and Banff.

Bruce's movements in the winter of 1308 and 1309, accordingly, now seem fairly clear. On 31st October he was at Auldearn, and thence moved by easy stages east and south. Some of his force he probably left at Banff to keep an eye on the English garrison, while he himself continued his march south by way of Aberdeen and

z

Forfar.   Looking to the period of the year his southward progress must have been slow ; and, in addition, he
would probably make some stay in each of the towns
through which he passed, in order to receive the homage
of the people, to hold courts of justice, and generally to
perform all the duties which at that time fell to the lot
of a feudal monarch.   Policy, if nothing else, would
dictate such a course, for it was essential that Bruce
should impress on the country that he was king in fact
as well as in name, and that he should make sure of the
affection and loyalty of his new subjects.   The march
from Auldearn to St. Andrews was, therefore, a royal
progress, the purpose of which was as much political as
military.   It brought the people into contact with their
new sovereign, it enabled him to sweep up any dregs of
opposition which might yet remain in districts which had
belonged to adherents of England, and, above all, it
impressed the whole country through which he passed
with a sense of his power, with a knowledge that his star
was in the ascendant, and that the day of English
domination was really over.

We may, accordingly, take it as certain that Bruce
did not reach Forfar much before Christmas.   By that
time, as we have seen, the castle may have fallen, though
it was still holding out in the second week of November.
Brechin, too, may have fallen about the same time, and
perhaps it was Bruce's presence in the neighbourhood
which caused Sir David de Brechin to cast in his lot with
Bruce, as we have seen that for a period he did.   At all
events, according to Barbour, Philip the Forester, who
captured Forfar, handed it over to Bruce, who " made
him right good rewarding," and straightway " broke
down the wall and destroyed the well and castle all,"
which can only mean that Bruce was in the neighbourhood either at the time of its capture or very soon
thereafter.

The opening weeks of 1309 must have found Bruce
in Fife.   There, as we have seen, he had many adherents,
but such scanty evidence as we possess gives no indication

that prior to the winter of 1308-9 much actual success had been achieved in that district. By the end of January 1309, however, Bruce's position in Fife was such that he was able to send summonses to his adherents to assemble at St. Andrews on 16th March, there to meet him in the first Parliament of his reign. That simple fact is sufficient of itself to prove that practically the whole of Fife had by the end of January come to his peace, and that he himself was by that date, at latest, present in force in the county of Fife.

We have thus elucidated the probable order of events in the latter half of 1308 and the opening months of 1309. The invasion of Argyll took place in August, and the campaign was over by the first or second week of October. Bruce himself, with the northern portion of his army, then returned to Moray, while Edward Bruce, Douglas, Alexander Lindsay, and a force composed mainly of West Highlanders and Islemen, besieged Rutherglen and thereafter proceeded to another invasion of Galloway. In the east country about Forfar and Fife others of Bruce's adherents maintained the war against the English, besieging and capturing castles, among them the castles of Forfar and Brechin, and giving their enemies no respite. From Moray, Bruce, in November and December, advanced slowly east and south, consolidating his position and bringing help to his more southern adherents, until at last, by January 1309, in all Scotland north of the Forth, only Perth, Dundee, and Banff were held for England, and the Scottish king was strong enough to summon his friends to come to meet him at St. Andrews on 16th March. Scotland north of the Forth and Clyde, the ancient Celtic kingdom, had thus been recovered by war from the hands of the English, and by its aid Galloway, as we shall now see, was, before the St. Andrews Parliament met, compelled to throw off its allegiance to the English king.

CHAPTER XXXI

THERE are many difficulties connected with the invasion of Galloway by Edward Bruce, Douglas, and Alexander Lindsay in 1308, but most of them are of no more than local importance, and therefore need not detain us here. The passage in which Fordun describes the invasion, however, requires some consideration. He there tells us that on 29th June 1308 "Donald of the Isles gathered together an imposing host of foot and marched up to the river Dee. He was met by Edward Bruce, who overcame all the Galwegians. In this struggle he slew a certain knight named Roland, with many of the nobles of Galloway, and arrested their leader, the said Donald, who had taken to flight. After this he burnt up the island."

The minor difficulties connected with this passage we need not go into meanwhile. It is sufficient to observe that Donald of the Isles should be Alexander of the Isles, who, as we have seen, was closely related by marriage to the family of Lorn. In 1296 or 1297 he was Admiral of the Western Isles for England,[1] and when Bruce threw off his allegiance to Edward he made himself very active as a supporter of the English interest.[2] He is said to have escaped from Edward Bruce's hands to Castle Swen, in North Knapdale, and there to have been captured by Bruce, and sent to Dundonald Castle in Kintyre, where he died.[3] At all events he disappeared from history about 1308 or 1309, and his lands were conferred on his brother, Angus Og, Bruce's faithful friend, who became Lord of the Isles and Chief of Clan Donald.[4]

[1] Stevenson, ii. 101.   [2] B. P., v. 35.   [3] *Ibid.*   [4] *Ibid.*, p. 36.

The real difficulty of the passage quoted, however, lies in the fact that the actual conquest of Galloway did not take place till early in 1309, as we shall see presently, and that between Fordun's date of 29th June 1308 and the beginning of 1309 the invasion of Argyll took place. Now the Lanercost chronicler tells us that "taking advantage of the dispute between the king of England and the barons" (that is the dispute about Piers Gaveston) "Edward de Brus, brother of the oft-mentioned Robert, and Alexander de Lindsay and Robert Boyd and James de Douglas, knights, with their following which they had from the Outer Isles of Scotland, invaded the people of Galloway," and so on. He mentions no date, but the context makes clear that the summer of 1308 is meant. He thus confirms Fordun, and, accordingly, Fordun's definite date must be accepted. But Barbour tells us that Edward Bruce remained for a year in Galloway, during which time he subjugated the country and captured thirteen castles; while we have already noted that in June Edward appointed the Earl of Buchan, de Moubray, and Sir Ingelram de Umfraville to be wardens of Galloway, Annandale, and Carrick, and that by the beginning of August Douglas had captured Randolph and carried him north to Bruce. From all these facts it is possible, I think, to piece the true tale together.

After the expulsion of the Comyns from Aberdeenshire, which, as we saw, must have been accomplished by the end of May, Bruce determined to proceed immediately against the other two strongholds of their influence, Galloway and Argyll, and thus complete, if possible, the overthrow of the House which was the most formidable rival to him and his claims. Accordingly Edward Bruce was sent south with Lindsay, Boyd, and Douglas to attack Galloway, while Bruce himself made ready for the task of reducing Argyll. On 29th June 1308 Edward Bruce defeated the Galwegians, as recorded by Fordun, but that victory by no means completed the subjugation of Galloway. For at least the greater part of the next seven or eight months he remained in Galloway performing the exploits so graphically related by Barbour, and eventually, as we shall see, succeeded in reducing to his obedience the whole district, with the exception of a few of the stronger castles. The fighting, however, was not confined to Galloway, as we know from the document, already quoted, relating to the capture of Richard Galoun when on service with the Sheriff of Roxburgh.[1]

Accordingly we may reconstruct the story of these months as follows. After Edward Bruce's victory on 29th June 1308 the war in the south-west was carried on over a wide district. Douglas naturally devoted himself to recovering his own territories, and while engaged in this congenial work captured Thomas Randolph, Bruce's nephew. With his prize he hurried north to Bruce ; partly, no doubt, because he regarded Randolph's capture as a matter on which the king himself ought to be consulted ; partly, probably, in order to give Bruce full information as to the progress of events in the south ; and partly, perhaps, with the hope or intention of taking part in the invasion of Argyll. At all events he arrived in time to take part in that invasion, and on its conclusion went south again to rejoin Edward Bruce.

Now we have seen that the castle of Rutherglen was being besieged by a strong Scottish force as early as the beginning of November 1308, and probably some time earlier. A glance at the map will show that Rutherglen lies directly on the route which a force marching from Argyll to the south-west would follow, and as the date of the siege in 1308 corresponds exactly with the date of Bruce's meeting with the Earl of Ross at Auldearn after the expedition to Argyll, it is difficult to resist the conclusion that Rutherglen was besieged and captured as a result of the junction of the forces of Douglas and Edward Bruce at the close of the Argyll expedition.

Immediately after the capture of Rutherglen, Edward Bruce, now greatly strengthened by the force which Douglas had brought with him, returned to Galloway. According to Barbour, the leaders of the force defeated

[1] Close Rolls, Ed. II, p. 86.

by Edward Bruce on 29th June had found refuge in the castle of Buittle, and thence one of them, St. John, had ridden by and by to England for help. He " purchased there of armed men a great company," and with them hastened back to Galloway.[1] Now obviously that could not have been accomplished in a day. Three months at the very least, and more probably six, must have elapsed between the defeat of 29th June and the return of St. John with his reinforcements, a fact which explains Edward Bruce's presence before Rutherglen at the beginning of November. For if St. John had not returned by then Edward Bruce, who of course would have no knowledge of the fact that St. John was raising men in England, would have Galloway sufficiently at his mercy to justify him in advancing against Rutherglen, while, on the other hand, if St. John had returned with strong reinforcements by the beginning of October, which is hardly likely, Edward Bruce may have thought it wise to obtain reinforcements for himself before meeting him in battle. If that were so he might well have marched north in order to obtain these from his brother, and seized the opportunity thus offered to attempt the capture of Rutherglen.

There is, however, a third possibility. Though Barbour does not mention him as taking part in the Argyll campaign, he may quite well have done so. He defeated the English in Galloway on 29th June. The battle of the Pass of Brandir was not fought till seven weeks later, and there would therefore have been ample time for him to have joined forces with his brother in his expedition against the third branch of the Comyn kin. The siege of Rutherglen would then have followed quite naturally on his return towards the south after the close of the campaign in Argyll. But whichever of these explanations is the true one is immaterial so long as it is realised that it was possible, and easy, for Edward Bruce to have been engaged in the siege of Rutherglen in November 1308.

---

[1] Barbour, ix. 541, &c.

St. John's return must have been the cause of Edward Bruce's second campaign in Galloway, the campaign which resulted in his real conquest of the district. It was then he accomplished his famous defeat of the 1500 by the fifty, an exploit to which we shall have to direct our attention in a moment or two. The date of the campaign is fixed by two documents in the English archives dated respectively 1st[1] and 8th April 1309,[2] and by the record of Edward Bruce's presence at his brother's Parliament at St. Andrews on 16th March of the same year. By the English documents the manor of Temple-Couston in Yorkshire is conferred on Sir Dougald Macdowall as a residence for his wife and family, it being expressly stated that they were unable to dwell in Scotland owing to the rancour and ill-will conceived by the king's enemies to the said Sir Dougald, which is simply a diplomatic way of saying that Sir Dougald's lands were no longer in his own possession, but in that of the Scots. Sir Dougald himself, however, did not reside at Temple-Couston. It was given him for his wife and family, while he remained in command of the castle of Dumfries, which ultimately he was compelled to surrender to the Scots on 7th February 1313.[3]

The campaign of 1308-9, however, it is necessary to remark, did not result in the complete subjugation of Galloway. The inhabitants were compelled to submit to Edward Bruce, the smaller castles were captured, and the English were completely overthrown in the open. But they still held the strong castles of Dumfries, Caerlaverock, Dalswinton, Thybres, Lochmaben, and Buittle, and continued to hold them till at least the closing months of 1312.[4] Until these were captured the conquest of Galloway could hardly be regarded as complete. We have already seen that the Lanercost chronicler says quite plainly and definitely that the force led by Edward Bruce and his followers was composed of men from the Outer Isles—that is to say of men from

---

[1] Bain, iii. 83.
[2] *Ibid.*, 84.
[3] *Ibid.*, iii. 304.
[4] See below, Chapter XXXVI.

Scotland north of the Forth and Clyde. Barbour's tale of Edward Bruce's defeat of the 1500 horse by the fifty confirms this. He tells us how Edward Bruce left his infantry in camp, while with his cavalry he conducted a reconnaissance. A heavy mist came down, and when it lifted suddenly the little body of Scots found themselves less than a bow-shot away from the foe for whom they were searching. But Edward Bruce did not hesitate a single moment, though the odds were so great. Calling on his men to follow him, he rode furiously down on the English, and ere the latter had recovered from their surprise, the whole company of the Scots was upon them. The shock of their charge carried them right through the English, but as soon as they had gained the other side they turned their horses' heads and again charged their surprised and bewildered foes. A few moments of hard fighting and they had cut their way clean through the English ranks once more, leaving a broad trail of dead and dying behind them. Then again Edward Bruce ordered his men to turn their horses' heads, and for the third time they bore down on their now confused and broken enemy. But two of those fierce onsets had been enough.* As the Scottish horsemen, ardent and triumphant, came on in their third charge the English wavered, then broke, and, before their eager foes could reach them, scattered in desperate flight. The third Scottish charge became a pursuit, and when the chase was ended the victory of the small body of Scots was as complete as it well could be.

From this tale two facts of importance emerge—First, the very small number of horsemen Edward Bruce had with him during his campaign in Galloway, for Barbour expressly says that he took on this reconnaissance all his mounted men; and second, the presence in Edward Bruce's force of a body of infantry. Now Galloway was not conquered by fifty horsemen and a few foot soldiers, and it is, therefore, quite clear that the latter must have constituted very much the greater part of the force, which is exactly what the Lanercost chronicler, an English authority be it observed, says it was composed of, namely men from the Outer Isles of Scotland, who, with possibly one or two exceptions, were, of course, all foot soldiers. Thus once again the extremely important part which Scotland north of the Forth and Clyde played in the War of Independence is evident. Even the invasion of distant Galloway could not be undertaken without its aid.

CHAPTER XXXII

BRUCE'S FIRST PARLIAMENT (*March* 1309)

We must now give some consideration to the Parliament which met at St. Andrews on 16th March 1309, and of which we have made such frequent mention. For some reason or other doubts have been expressed as to the genuineness of the record of this Parliament, but it seems to me that the mere recital of the names contained in it is sufficient to demonstrate its authenticity.[1]

Twenty-four names appear in the record, along with that of Bruce himself, "and the barons of the whole of Argyll and Innisgall, and the inhabitants of the whole kingdom of Scotland." Three of the Celtic earls were present in person, the Earls of Ross, Lennox, and Sutherland, while the *communitates* of the other Celtic earldoms of Fife, Menteith, Mar, and Buchan, and the earldom of Caithness, whose heirs, the record states, were in ward, were represented, as were also the *communitates* of the other earldoms of the whole kingdom of Scotland. The names of these other earldoms follow, but the manuscript at this point is undecipherable, and the only name which can be distinguished is Dunbar. The Earls of Ross, Lennox, and Sutherland were, of course, all adherents of Bruce; the Earl of Mar, a boy of tender years, was Bruce's nephew; the young Earl of Caithness was in ward to the Earl of Ross; the earldom of Buchan was in Bruce's hands, though its youthful head was in England, and the same was the case with the earldom of Fife; while John de Menteith, the real though not the nominal head of the earldom of Menteith, the heir being a child, had by 1309 thrown in his

---

[1] Acts of Parl., i. 99.

lot with Bruce. Of the remaining earldoms, the Earls of Angus, Stratherne, Athol, and Dunbar were at the time actively engaged on the side of England, while the earldom of Carrick was, of course, vested in Bruce himself. Thus the record, so far as the earldoms are concerned, is absolutely in accord with the situation as it existed in March 1309, a fact which goes a long way to prove its genuineness.

Following the eight earldoms come the names of Edward Bruce, James the Steward, Donald of Isla, Gilbert de Haye, Robert de Keith, Thomas Randolph, James Douglas, Alexander de Lindsay, William Wiseman, David de Berkeley, and Robert Boyd. With two exceptions every one of these names is familiar to the reader of these pages as having been, before March 1309, and most of them long before then, staunch adherents of Bruce. The two exceptions are Donald of Isla and Robert de Keith. The former is quite clearly a mere clerical error for Alexander of Isla. The Lords of the Isles were always " Donald " to the rest of Scotland, an error which is quite understandable when it is remembered that they were Chiefs of Clan Donald. The error is of frequent occurrence, and need create no difficulty. That Bruce's faithful friend, Angus Og, was by March 1309 Lord of the Isles and Chief of Clan Donald, we have already seen.

Robert de Keith we have hitherto come across only casually. He was head of the Lothian family of that name,[1] who were the hereditary Marischals of Scotland, and down at least to May 1308 was an adherent of England.[2] But a document in the English archives tells us that he joined Bruce at Christmas 1308, so that in his case, too, the record is in accordance with the facts. He it was who commanded the Scottish cavalry at Bannockburn.

Three other names complete the record as it exists to-day. These are Alexander of Argyll; "Hugh, son and heir of the Earl of . . .," the manuscript unfortun-

---

[1] Bain, iii. 44.   [2] *Ibid.*, p. 245.

ately becoming undecipherable at this point; and John de Menteith. We have already considered all the facts relating to Alexander of Argyll, including the probability of his presence at the St. Andrews Parliament, so his name need not detain us. "Hugh, son and heir of the Earl of . . .," is certainly that son of the Earl of Ross whom we have so frequently met in the course of our narrative, for his seal is attached to the original deed, as is also that of John de Menteith, the one-time ardent supporter of England, who by August 1309 was so high in the councils of Bruce that he was one of the two envoys appointed by the Scottish king to treat with the Earl of Ulster in regard to a proposed peace, his companion on that occasion being the patriotic and faithful Sir Nigel Campbell.

In addition to these names, however, six other adherents of Bruce are on record as having attended the St. Andrews Parliament. In the manuscript as it exists to-day there is a large gap, and in it their names doubtless appeared. At all events they attached their seals to the manuscript, and that is sufficient. They are Donald, Nigel, and Thomas Campbell, Edward de Keith, Gillespie Maclachlan, and Alexander Fraser. Thomas Campbell was probably a brother of Nigel, as Donald certainly was [1]; Edward de Keith was a brother of Sir Robert, whom he succeeded as Marischal on the latter's death in 1346 [2]; Gillespie Maclachlan was head of the West Highland family of that name, and obtained a grant of lands from Bruce for his services [3]; and Alexander Fraser we have met already.

Thus we see that the record of the St. Andrews Parliament stands the test of the most exacting of all examinations. If it were not a genuine record it would be impossible for it to be so extraordinarily accurate in the names it contains. Not only is there not a single name in it upon which any reasonable doubt can be cast, but the names are for the most part those of the men who

<hr />

[1] Balfour Paul, i. 320. [2] *Ibid.*, vi. 32, &c.
[3] *Registrum Magni Sigilli*, p. 554, No. 654.

bore the burden and heat of Bruce's earliest struggles for
a Crown and a kingdom.   More than that, it contains
the names of men who do not figure in the pages of
Scottish histories as among the companions of Bruce,
though, as a matter of fact, they are more deserving of
mention than many whose names make frequent appearance.   Save for a passing reference in Barbour, the name
of Sir William Wiseman, for example, appears in no
history of Scotland or of the War of Independence for
nearly six hundred years, while the same is almost literally
true of the Earl of Ross and his son Hugh, the Earl of
Sutherland, and John de Menteith.   These latter, it is
true, are mentioned, but almost always as enemies of
Bruce, not as men who rendered him welcome and
powerful aid.   To put the whole matter shortly, the
record must be genuine, for the simple reason that at no
period during the last six hundred years has anyone
possessed sufficient knowledge to forge so remarkably
accurate a document.

Let us now see how the record of the St. Andrews
Parliament bears out, or otherwise, the conclusions we
have thus far reached.   It must be obvious, even at a
cursory glance, that it confirms them to a striking degree.
Excluding Bruce himself and the barons of Argyll and
Innisgall, twenty-eight names are specifically mentioned.
Of these no fewer than twenty belong to Scotland north
of the Forth and Clyde, viz. the Earls of Ross, Lennox,
and Sutherland, the earldoms of Fife, Menteith, Mar,
Buchan, and Caithness, Donald of Isla, Gilbert de Haye,
William Wiseman, David de Berkeley (who, as we saw,
held the lands of Avoch in Ross-shire), Alexander of
Argyll, Hugh, son and heir of the Earl of Ross, John
de Menteith, Donald, Nigel, and Thomas Campbell,
Gillespie Maclachlan, and Alexander Fraser.   Between
them these names not only include men who in 1309
were powerful knights or magnates, but they embrace
practically all Scotland north of the Forth and Clyde.
If we exclude Alexander of Argyll from the reckoning,
as being present not of his own will, the barons of

Argyll and Innisgall are sufficient to cover most of the west to the north of that line and to the south of the territories of the Earl of Ross.

We are thus left with eight names for the representatives at Bruce's first Parliament of Scotland south of the Forth and Clyde. How striking a contrast they present to those of the north, both in numbers and in influence. Edward Bruce was the king's own brother, and owned not an acre of land beyond that which he had just conquered by the aid of the men from the Isles. Thomas Randolph was Bruce's nephew, and only the accident of his capture by Douglas had brought him but a short time prior to March 1309 to throw in his lot with Bruce. He was as yet of neither influence nor importance in the kingdom of Scotland, his possessions being but small and his fame yet to win. There remain James Douglas, James the Steward, Robert and Edward de Keith, Alexander de Lindsay, and Robert Boyd. Of these, James the Steward and Alexander de Lindsay were, in 1309, the only two representatives from the south of any importance, but their territorial possessions could not compare with those of the northern representatives. Of the others, James Douglas was a young landless man, who was rapidly climbing to fame as a warrior of courage and skill, though he was not yet a knight; Robert de Keith, though Marischal of Scotland, was not a great landholder, and had but recently joined Bruce; Robert Boyd had been an obscure Ayrshire landholder before he threw in his lot with Bruce; and Edward de Keith was still a young man with his spurs to win. Where, we may well ask, were all the knighthood and nobility of Scotland south of the Forth and Clyde on the day when Bruce held that historic Parliament at St. Andrews? Assuredly they were not there, else had their names appeared on the record. The reason of their absence is plain. They were not yet adherents of the man who for three years now had been striving manfully to free Scotland from the English yoke.

At the risk of repetition I must again point out how

emphatically the record of the St Andrews Parliament,
thus critically examined, conforms to the view which I
have advanced so frequently and so strongly in these
pages. It is necessary so to do, for it is difficult to
convince some people that the theories of centuries may
be wrong. But the St. Andrews record is there to speak
for itself, and plain upon its surface it bears that in
March 1309, after three years of gallant and unwavering
endeavour, Scotland north of the Forth and Clyde—
high and low, rich and poor, great magnate, small
knight, burgess, landholder, and simple man—was almost
solidly on the side of Bruce, and alone was sustaining
the burden of the struggle, while Scotland south of the
Forth and Clyde was still making no effort to throw off
the English yoke. That in Bruce's first Parliament
Scotland south of the Forth and Clyde was represented
only by the king's brother, the king's nephew, and six
warriors of adventurous or heroic spirit, is a fact sufficient to dispose once and for all of the long-cherished
legend that the freedom of Scotland was won by that
part of Scotland which lies to the south of the old Celtic
kingdom of the Scots.

The principal business of the St. Andrews Parliament
was the framing of a letter to the king of France setting
forth in explicit terms that Bruce was now not only
king of Scotland, but was recognised as such by the
prelates, magnates, and community of the kingdom.
This letter was the result of negotiations which, at the
instigation of the king of France, had been begun between Edward and the Scots. On 29th November 1308
the French king had sent his son Louis to Edward asking
him to grant a truce to the Scots,[1] and Edward, "at the
request of the said king," appointed the Earl of Angus,
John de Crombewell, John Wogan, and John le Benstede,[2]
with full powers, "to treat in our name . . . with the
people of Scotland for truce, or take sufferance between
us . . . on the one part, and them and their allies and
abettors on the other." It is thus clear that in 1308

---

[1] Foedera R., ii. 63.   [2] *Ibid.*

Bruce had sent ambassadors to the Court of France in order to endeavour to obtain assistance of some kind from the French king.

One of the great factors in Bruce's success was, of course, the long quarrel between Edward II and his chief barons.   So absorbed were both parties in this quarrel, which raged in the early years of Bruce's reign round the person of Edward's favourite Piers Gaveston, that little real attention was devoted to affairs in Scotland, and Bruce in consequence was able to make much greater and much more rapid progress than might have been the case had things been otherwise.   But Edward's struggle with his barons had a direct as well as an indirect influence on Bruce's fortunes.   It not only prevented Edward from pouring men into Scotland, and from sending speedy aid to his hard-pressed adherents in the northern kingdom, but it led him more than once to endeavour to come to terms with Bruce in order that he might be able to concentrate all his energies on crushing his enemies in England.   This it was which led Edward to lend so ready an ear to the French king's proposal of 29th November 1308, and caused him to open negotiations with the Scots early in 1309.

On 4th March 1309 Edward granted a safe conduct to Oliver de Roches, messenger of Philip, king of France,[1] "going into Scotland to the Bishop of St. Andrews and Robert Bruce."   The fact that the messenger of the French king is accredited to the Bishop of St. Andrews as well as to Bruce, and that the Bishop's name comes first, is of both interest and importance.   The Bishop of St. Andrews was still that William Lamberton who had so often set a higher value on the freedom of his country than on the sacredness of his plighted word to her enemies.   Consigned to an English prison by the first Edward in July 1306, he had been released two years later by Edward II, though under a strict bond and on the condition that he remained within certain bounds in England.   Subsequently he seems to have acted as an

[1] Foedera R., ii. 63.

2 A

intermediary between Edward and Bruce, and he is found sometimes in Scotland and sometimes in England.[1] The tenor of the safe conduct shows that in the early part of 1309 he was in Scotland, and it may be that Edward had permitted him to leave England in the hope that he might bring Bruce to terms.

This brings us to the next point. The safe conduct is made out to the Bishop and Robert Bruce, not, be it observed, to the Bishop and the King of Scots. Further, as we have seen, the main business of the St. Andrews Parliament was the framing of a letter to the king of France stating in plain terms that Bruce was now king of Scotland. The conclusion is clear. Edward was prepared to purchase freedom from the Scottish sore, which was so seriously sapping his strength, by making certain concessions to Bruce; but he was not prepared to go the length of recognising him as king of Scotland. Later events bring this out even more forcibly. On 3rd August 1309 Edward wrote to Philip of France[2] complaining that his messenger had letters addressed to Robert de Bruce, in which he is styled King of Scotland, while in those produced to the king of England he is styled Earl of Carrick. The king of France and his advisers were plainly men of considerable astuteness!

The negotiations begun in the spring of 1309, however, came to nothing; and on 30th July we find Edward writing to Philip regretting that the meeting which they had arranged must be interrupted on account of the state of affairs in Scotland,[3] while on the same date writs of military summons were issued for the assembling of an army at Newcastle-on-Tyne to march against the Scots.[4]

In the meantime, however, Edward had taken advantage of the negotiations to order, on 12th May 1309, provisions to be sent to certain of the castles and towns of Scotland still held for England; while on 20th May special orders were issued for the provisioning and fortifying of the castles of Banff and Ayr. The castles and

---

[1] See various entries, Bain, ii. and iii.   [2] Foedera R., ii. 63.
[3] *Ibid.*, p. 79.   [4] *Ibid.*

towns thus named are of some interest. They were, on 12th May, the castle and town of Berwick, the castles of Roxburgh, Stirling, Linlithgow, Edinburgh, Banff, Dundee, Dumfries, and Caerlaverock, and the town of Perth.[1] It will be noticed that, with the exception of Stirling, Banff, Dundee, and Perth, all these are in Scotland south of the Forth and Clyde. It is also curious to observe that orders regarding Banff Castle were issued twice within nine days, viz. on 12th and 20th May.[2] From this it would seem as if Banff were in special danger, but if it were it did not fall into the hands of the Scots until at least six months later, for on 15th December 1309 it appears in a list of places then held for England. This is its last appearance in the English documents of the period, so it is safe to conclude that it fell sometime in the winter of 1309–10.

Edward's preparation for the renewal of the war at the beginning of August 1309 did not, however, put an end to his efforts to patch up a truce or peace of some sort. Negotiations were reopened, on some other basis probably, and on 21st August a commission was issued to Richard de Burgh, Earl of Ulster, empowering him to treat with Bruce for peace.[3] On the same date a safe conduct was issued in favour of " John de Menteith and Nigel Campbell, knights, the Scottish envoys coming to treat with the Earl of Ulster." [4] The choice of the Earl of Ulster as the English commissioner is an indication of how anxious Edward was to come to terms with Bruce, for the Earl was the Scottish king's brother-in-law. But the negotiations came to naught. Nothing short of the recognition of Bruce as king of an independent Scotland would satisfy the Scottish envoys, and that Edward was not yet prepared to grant. So negotiations were broken off, and by the end of October the war appears to have been renewed on both sides, for on the 26th of that month ships were being prepared at Great Yarmouth for carrying provisions and assistance to the town of Perth,[5]

---

[1] *Rotuli Scotiae*, i. 63. [2] *Ibid.*, pp. 63, 64. [3] Foedera.
[4] *Ibid.* [5] *Rotuli Scotiae*, i. 79, 80.

while on 15th December 1309 orders were again issued
for the garrisoning, fortifying, and provisioning of certain
towns and castles held for England.[1] The list of places
to which such aid was sent is of great interest, as it shows
very clearly in what parts of Scotland the power of
England was still in the ascendant. In all twenty places
are mentioned, but to these may be added seven more
which we know from other documents to have been in
1309, and most of them for several years longer, in the
possession of England.

Of these twenty-seven no fewer than thirteen are in
Lothian or its borders, that is to say in the old English
kingdom of that name, which included roughly the
whole of the modern counties of Edinburgh, Haddington,
and Berwick, the eastern half of Roxburgh, the eastern
corner of Selkirk, the eastern bounds of Peebles, and the
greater part of Linlithgow. The places in Lothian to
which aid was ordered to be sent on 15th December
1309 [2] were Edinburgh, Linlithgow, Roxburgh, Jedburgh,
Dunbar, Dirleton, and Selkirk, while the other towns
and castles in the same district which we know to have
been then held for England were Berwick, Haddington,
Livingstone, Yester, Luffenok, and Cavers.[3] A glance
at the map will show that these not only covered between
them the whole of Lothian, but included every place of
any importance in the old English kingdom. It is,
therefore, perfectly clear that up to the end of 1309 all
that extensive district was still in the hands of those who
were opposed to Bruce and the cause of Scottish independence. Lothian, plainly, had not yet played any
part in securing for Bruce a kingdom and for Scotland
her independence, and that though nearly four years had
elapsed since Bruce had been crowned at Scone.

There remain fourteen strong places in all the rest
of Scotland which are known to have been held for
England at the end of 1309. Of these six were in
Dumfries and Galloway, the country of Bruce's mortal

[1] *Rotuli Scotiae*, i. 80.   [2] *Ibid*.
[3] Bain, iii. Various entries.

foes, the Comyns and their kin.   They were [1] Dumfries, Caerlaverock, Dalswinton, Thybres, Lochmaben, and Buittle, strongly fortified places all, which only a pro- longed siege or a successful surprise could reduce.   Of the eight others Ayr, Bothwell,[2] and Lanark [3] were isolated strongholds, strongly held and strongly fortified ; Kirkin- tilloch,[4] in the southmost corner of Stirling, was the one remaining Comyn stronghold in all Scotland outside Dumfries and Galloway; while Perth, Stirling, Dundee, and Banff were, besides Kirkintilloch, all that remained to England in Scotland north of the Forth and Clyde.[5]   The reduction of these last was only a question of time.   So far their strength and their position had made it im- possible for Bruce to capture them.   Dundee, Perth, and Banff were all easily accessible by sea, and their capture was in consequence an extremely difficult task, for men and provisions were repeatedly thrown into them, and any attempt to reduce them by starvation was accordingly almost impossible.   Stirling, of course, was the most strongly fortified and the most powerfully garrisoned place in Scotland, and, as we have seen, Edward I himself was only able to effect its capture by starvation, though he besieged it with all the might of England and with every engine known to the military science of the age.

It was in this last-mentioned arm that Bruce was weak.   Men and arms and horses he had, but in siege material he was woefully deficient, and, accordingly, the siege of any strongly-fortified place imposed a great strain on his resources, and in the early years of his reign was indeed a task almost beyond his powers.   Many castles, of course, he did capture during these years, but these were either starved into surrender after a comparatively short siege, or were taken by assault or a *coup de main*, or were given up by their defenders because they were only half-hearted in their allegiance to England.   Places like Perth, Dundee, and Stirling in the north, and

[1] *Rotuli Scotiae*, i. 80.   [2] *Ibid.*   [3] Bain, iii. 176, 218, 221.
[4] *Rotuli Scotiae*, i. 80.   [5] *Ibid.*

Edinburgh, Roxburgh, Berwick, Dumfries, Ayr, Bothwell, Lochmaben, and many others in the south were too strongly fortified, too strongly garrisoned, and too well provisioned to be taken save by a prolonged siege or by surprise, and the first of these Bruce, in the first five or six years of his reign, was not able to attempt. It must always be remembered, too, that in the early years of his reign his armies were composed very largely of Highlanders and Islemen, and these never, at any period in history, had the peculiar qualities necessary for the conduct of a long siege. In time Bruce overcame to a considerable extent these difficulties, but it must be patent to anyone who knows Scottish history that the Scots as a whole never proved themselves besiegers of the first class. Bruce, therefore, had not only to contend with the great difficulty of mediæval warfare, the practical impregnability of mediæval castles, but he had to contend with it without many of the contrivances and without the kind of force which experience had proved to be necessary. Even with these things the reduction of a mediæval stronghold was usually an undertaking of great magnitude. Without them it was a task which promised little hope of success.

It is easy to understand now why in Scotland north of the Forth and Clyde, Perth, Dundee, Stirling, and Banff were still in English hands at the close of 1309, though the whole of the districts in which they stood had long been on Bruce's side. In the end, however, they fell. Perth, after apparently being besieged unsuccessfully several times, was captured by surprise; Dundee, alone among the northern strengths of which we have knowledge, was starved into surrender after a long siege; Banff fell no man knows how; and Stirling was surrendered as a result of Bannockburn. When at last Bruce was strong enough to endeavour to wrest Lothian from England a similar tale falls to be told. Edinburgh, Roxburgh, and Linlithgow were all captured by stratagem, and of all the castles in the south of whose fall any recollection survives, Dumfries alone was reduced by siege and starvation.   With the exception of Banff, which probably fell in 1310, all these captures took place two or three years later than the period which we have now reached, but I mention them here to show to how very large an extent Bruce's success in dealing with fortified places was due not to successful siege operations, but to the military genius of himself and his principal lieutenants, and the dash and gallantry of themselves and the men whom they led.

CHAPTER XXXIII

EDWARD II INVADES SCOTLAND (1310–11)

On the failure of the renewed negotiations with the Scots writs of military summons were issued by Edward for 29th September 1309.[1] But the quarrel between the king and his barons caused their repeated postponement, though certain preparations were actually made for the renewal of the war. These took the form of preparing a fleet at Great Yarmouth, at the end of October, for bearing succour to Perth,[2] while two separate forces, under the command respectively of Sir John de Segrave and of the Earl of Hereford, Sir Robert de Clifford and Sir John de Cromwell, were sent to Berwick and Carlisle to keep the east and west marches.[3] These barons, however, were not in mood for renewing the war just then, and accordingly, about the end of November, they concluded a truce with Bruce to last till 14th January 1310,[4] subject to the consent of the king of England being obtained. Sir Robert de Clifford, the Lanercost chronicler tells us, "went to the king to ascertain his pleasure. On his return he agreed to a further truce with the Scots until the first Sunday in Lent (8th March 1310), and afterwards the truce was prolonged till summer"; for, adds the chronicler, "the English do not willingly enter Scotland to wage war before summer, chiefly because earlier in the year they find no food for their horses."

The Lanercost chronicler is confirmed by a document in the English archives, by which, on 16th February 1310, Bishop Lamberton and certain others are commissioned

<hr/>

[1] *Parl. Writs*, ii. 1, 381.
[3] *Ibid.*, pp. 76-8.
[2] *Rotuli Scotiae*, i. 78.
[4] Lanercost.

by Edward to treat with the Scots for a truce.[1] The Lanercost narrative thus fills in the blanks for us in a manner which admits of no doubt as to its general accuracy, and explains, moreover, the reason for the absence in the records of any sign of hostilities between 15th December 1309 and June 1310. On the former date, it will be remembered, orders were issued for the provisioning and garrisoning of various castles and strong places in Scotland held by the English, while in the latter month great preparations were begun for an invasion of Scotland.[2]

The truce was welcome to both parties. It enabled Edward to concentrate all his attention for a time on the domestic affairs of his kingdom, which were in a parlous state owing to his quarrel with his barons and his favouritism for Piers Gaveston ; while to Bruce it gave a very welcome period of relief from the anxieties of war. We have no actual knowledge of how Bruce spent those six months of peace, but there are indications that they were utilised in setting the affairs of the kingdom on a proper basis, in consolidating Bruce's position, and in making every possible preparation for the renewal of the struggle.[3]

The only event of importance which we know to have occurred in Scotland during these months was the holding of a great assembly of the Scottish Church at Dundee on 24th February 1310,[4] at which " the bishops, abbots, priors, and the rest of the clergy of Scotland " solemnly recognised Bruce as " the true heir to the throne," and pledged themselves to support him to the uttermost. As we have already seen the conquest of Scotland meant the subordination of the Scottish Church to the English hierarchy, and that no Scottish cleric worthy the name would tolerate. So throughout the long struggle priest and bishop, monk and friar, were in the forefront of the resistance to England, and we have repeatedly seen in the course of these pages how

---

[1] Foedera.
[3] Acts of Parl., i. 100.
[2] *Rotuli Scotiae*, i. 82, &c.
[4] *Ibid.*, pp. 100-1.

powerful an influence they exerted. It is indeed not too much to say that Scotland owed her independence to the Catholic clergy of the thirteenth and fourteenth centuries more than to any other class or body of men in the kingdom. We have seen how William Lamberton, Bishop of St. Andrews, and Wishart, Bishop of Glasgow, counted no oath as sacred, no bond as binding, which came between them and the cause of Scottish freedom, and how again and again they were either the instigators or in the forefront of every attempt to throw off the yoke of England. We have seen, too, how the Bishop of Moray proved himself a prince among patriots, how by example and by exhortation he encouraged the flock of his bishopric to rebel, how, when all seemed lost, he continued in the field, and how he responded to every call to any effort however desperate which was aimed against the hated domination of England. We have seen, too, how in the hour of his direst need the Church stood by Bruce, how the fact that the blood of sacri- legious murder was red on his hands counted with them as nothing, and how when all the terrors of excommuni- cation were flung at him and them by an outraged Pope, they wavered not in their ardent support of him and his cause. We have seen, too, how they used the knowledge and the power which were theirs, proud bishop, parish priest, cloistered monk, and humble friar, to preach a Holy War against England and the English, and, in spite of the pains and penalties of excommunication, to promise the holiest blessing of Mother Church to those who took up arms against the hated southerner. Com- plained the indignant Edward to the Pope concerning the Bishop of Moray : "He told them they were not less deserving of merit who rebelled with Sir Robert to help him against the king of England and his men, and took the part of the said Robert, than if they should fight in the Holy Land against pagans and Saracens."

And as it was in the beginning of Bruce's struggle so it was to the end. Neither the terrors of this world nor fears for the next—and the Pope promised them

many horrible tortures hereafter—deterred Bruce's adherents, whether churchmen or laymen, from following
the path they had chosen.   In the course of 1309
Bruce had been excommunicated once again for "damnably persevering in iniquity," but excommunication
had long lost its terrors for Bruce and his adherents.
Excommunication, indeed, but spurred them to greater
efforts, and so it is that in the assembly at Dundee on
24th February 1310 we may see the defiant answer
of the clergy of Scotland to the papal fulminations of
the previous year.   Bruce and all who should dare to
continue to aid him had been excommunicated for "damnably persevering in iniquity."   The clergy of Scotland
gave defiant answer that they would continue damnably
to persevere in iniquity, preferring clearly to take the risk
of going to his own place with Bruce rather than share
the joys apparently reserved by the Pope for the king and
the Church of their hated enemies of England.   Anyway
"damnably persevere" in the path they had chosen they
did, and by so doing, by following to the end the difficult and hazardous way on which they had first embarked
ten years before Bruce was crowned at Scone, they won
through to the goal of their desire—a Church, a throne,
and a kingdom, each free of English domination, and
each as independent as any known to the world of the
Middle Ages.

The Lanercost chronicler tells us that "the English do
not willingly enter Scotland to wage war before summer,
chiefly because earlier in the year they find no food for
their horses."   He states here a commonplace of mediae-
val warfare, which every student of the period must
keep in mind, for it explains much in the history of the
long wars between Scotland and England.   And now,
in the year 1310, with the coming of summer, England
began to make preparations to enter Scotland to wage
war once more.[1]   On this occasion, moreover, it was to
be an invasion in force.   Three years had gone since
Edward II, barely two months after his father's death,

---

[1] *Rotuli Scotiae*, i. 82, &c.

had conducted in person the last invasion on a great scale. In the interval England had seen her conquests in Scotland wrested one by one from her, and though several expeditions had been sent to endeavour to stem the tide of disaster, no invasion, in the whole-hearted manner of the first Edward, had since been attempted. Yet by some such invasion alone could England hope to stay the progress of Bruce, and since 1307 England's adherents in Scotland had never ceased to beg for it. Hitherto they had been put off by promises and by the noise of preparations which came to naught; but in 1310 Edward at last made up his mind to embark on a great Scottish campaign.

The decision once made, Edward seems, contrary to his usual custom, to have acted with considerable energy. On 15th June ships and men were sent to Perth, and the Scottish Rolls contain many pages of orders issued during June and July for the assembling of troops and the conduct of the campaign.[1] At the same time special power was given to the Earl of Ulster (on 18th June to be exact) to receive Scots to the king's peace,[2] from which it appears as if Edward looked forward to the campaign with high hopes.

By the beginning of August preparations were well advanced, and on the 2nd of that month orders were issued to the Mayor of Dover and the mayors of no less than forty-one other ports to provide ships for the coming expedition.[3] A week or two later Edward himself went north, and after lying some time at Berwick, where fresh dissensions with his barons broke out,[4] he crossed the border in the third week of September 1310, reaching Roxburgh on the 20th of the month.[5] Thence, after visiting St. Boswells and Roxburgh, he advanced to Biggar, on the border of Lanark and Peebles, where he remained from the 1st to the 14th October.[6] While at Biggar news reached him that Bruce was encamped on

---

[1] *Rotuli Scotiae*, i. 82–96.
[3] Foedera R., ii. 114.
[5] Bain, iii. 162.

[2] *Ibid.*, p. 84.
[4] Lanercost.
[6] *Ibid.*, p. 171.

a moor near Stirling,[1] and this may account for his
further advance northwards, though winter was now
rapidly approaching. At all events he led his army to
Lanark and Renfrew, and thence across country to Linlithgow, where he lay from the 23rd to the 28th October.[2] If he hoped by this march to bring Bruce to
battle, as the Lanercost chronicler says, he was disappointed. For Bruce wisely refused to run the desperate
risk of a pitched battle; " wherefore they (the English)
returned to Berwick," and there prepared to spend the
winter. " But as soon as they had retired," adds the
chronicler, " Robert and his people invaded Lothian,
and inflicted much damage upon those who were in
the king of England's peace."

This last quotation is of special interest, for it contains two points of importance. It contains the first
recorded appearance of Bruce in any part of Scotland
south of the Forth after his advance to the north in
September 1307, and it speaks of Lothian in terms
which can only mean that in November 1310 it was still
regarded as adhering to England. It hardly requires to
be pointed out that both of these are in exact accordance
with the facts which we have thus far elucidated in the
course of our narrative.

In *Vita Edwardi Secundi* there is a graphic account
of the manner in which Bruce avoided a pitched battle
during this campaign, and at the same time harassed
the English greatly. On one occasion his men surprised
a foraging party composed of English and Welsh foot
and a number of horsemen. The latter fled and roused
the main army, but before they could reach the spot the
foragers had been overwhelmed and 300 men slain.
The Scots had vanished, and the English had to return
to camp ingloriously.[3]

On tidings of Bruce's invasion of Lothian reaching
Edward he at once set out with a small force to endeavour again to bring Bruce to battle; but again he
was disappointed, and had to return to Berwick empty-

[1] Bain, iii. 166.   [2] *Ibid.*, p. 171.   [3] *Chronicles*, ii. 165-6.

handed.[1] Then he seems to have begun to realise that the re-conquest of Scotland was a very much greater task than he had imagined. At all events he entered into negotiations of some sort with Bruce, and at Christmas Bruce himself met two envoys of the English king at Selkirk.[2] This meeting apparently seemed to promise well, for another meeting was arranged, this time at Melrose. But Bruce was warned that the English intended treachery, and the negotiations were therefore promptly broken off.[3] A week or two later we hear of Bruce leading a force towards Galloway,[4] probably with the intention of creating a diversion by invading England by the western marches—at a later date a favourite device of his—and it is difficult to avoid the conclusion that this raid, whether it actually eventuated or not, was an act of reprisal for the contemplated treachery at Melrose.

The Lanercost chronicler, who is our authority for this march towards Galloway, places it in the first week of February 1311, and adds the very interesting and important piece of information that Edward sent the Earl of Cornwall, Piers Gaveston, "with 200 men-at-arms, to the town of St. John (*i.e.* Perth), beyond the Scottish sea,[5] in case Robert de Brus, who was then marching towards Galloway, *should go beyond the said sea to collect troops.*" (The italics are mine.) This, be it observed, was in February 1311, and the importance of the remark, as confirming all that we have hitherto deduced, cannot be gainsaid. For it shows conclusively that the Lanercost chronicler, who lived too close to the Scottish border for his comfort, and who writes, moreover, with unquestioned authority of the events of the war in the border counties, knew that as late as the beginning of 1311 the troops on whom Bruce depended were drawn from beyond the Forth.

---

[1] Lanercost. [2] Bain, iii. 197. [3] *Ibid.* [4] Lanercost.
[5] A statement which is confirmed by documents in Bain. See iii. 201, 202, 204, &c. In 204 his force is given as 500 men-at-arms.

Two other events of this period fall to be recorded before we follow the course of the war in 1311. As we have noted Edward was accompanied on his invasion of Scotland by a great fleet, in this following the example of his father who well knew the advantage of sea power in his wars with Scotland. But the Scots were not unduly terrified by the multitude of ships, for on 9th November 1310 we find Edward writing to the Count of Flanders requesting him "to give no shelter to the pretended exiles from Scotland who harass the English fleet." [1] An illuminating sidelight this on the part played in the war by the merchant-traders and seamen of the East of Scotland.

The other matter is of equal interest. On 15th December 1310, while Edward with his mighty army was lying at Berwick, news reached him that the foe, who ought to have been living in fear of the force which was arrayed against him, was actually fitting out a fleet to proceed against the Isle of Man. [2] Whereupon Edward, in hot haste, ordered aid to be sent forthwith to the threatened island. Here again we have evidence both of the military genius of Bruce and the confidence of the Scots. Bruce saw that, in order to feed his troops on the east coast, Edward had denuded the west of ships, and straightway he sent the bold mariners of the Isles, the men who already had aided him so powerfully, to attack the Isle of Man. What measure of success they met with we know not, but less than two years later Bruce himself marched through Cumberland, thence crossed over to the Isle of Man, and conquered it once more for Scotland.

---

[1] Foedera R., ii. 118.   [2] *Ibid.*

CHAPTER XXXIV

WE saw that Piers Gaveston, Earl of Cornwall, was sent
to Perth in February 1311. There he remained, with
the empty title of Warden beyond the Forth, till April,[1]
when he rejoined Edward at Berwick, and in July the
English king returned to London without having accomplished anything in all his ten months' campaign against
the Scots. But it was impossible for him to tarry longer
in the north. The quarrel with his barons had broken
out fiercely again, and Edward was compelled to summon
the Parliament they demanded and proceed to London
to meet it. We can well believe the Lanercost chronicler
when he says that he went "unwillingly enough," for
the principal act of the Parliament was to pass a sentence
of perpetual banishment on Piers Gaveston, while the
Archbishop of Canterbury solemnly excommunicated all
"who should receive, defend, or entertain him in England." Piers Gaveston was in very truth at this time
Scotland's best ally, for so hated was he in England that
the quarrel with the king concerning him occupied the
mind of Parliament to the exclusion of all else, and
brought the kingdom to the verge of civil war.

England's absorption in her domestic troubles was
Scotland's opportunity, and Bruce was quick to take
advantage of it. "The said Robert," says the Lanercost
chronicler, "taking note that the king and all the nobles
of the realm were in such distant parts, and in such dis-
cord about the said accursed individual (*i.e.* Piers
Gaveston), having collected a large army invaded England by the Solway on Thursday before the Feast of the

[1] Bain, iii. 201, 202.

Assumption of the Glorious Virgin, and burnt all the land of the Lord of Gillsland, and the town of Halt-whistle and a great part of Tynedale, and after eight days returned into Scotland, taking with him a very large booty in cattle. But he killed few men besides those who offered resistance." As the Thursday before the Feast of the Assumption fell, in 1311, on 12th August, this means that the raid took place very soon after Edward's departure from Berwick, a fact that shows not only that Bruce was kept well informed of Edward's movements and Edward's troubles, but that the Scottish king had throughout the summer of 1311 a considerable force in the field.

Bruce was hardly back in Scotland before he was over the border again, this time entering Northumberland by the eastern march, and penetrating, by way of Harbottle, Holystone, and Redesdale as far as Corbridge, "burning the district and destroying everything, and causing more men to be killed than on the former occasion."[1] Thence he "turned into the valleys of North and South Tyne, laying waste those parts which he had previously spared, and returned into Scotland after fifteen days; nor could the wardens whom the king of England had stationed on the marches oppose so great a force of Scots as he brought with him."

The date of this raid is "about the Feast of the Nativity of the Blessed Virgin," that is about 8th Sep-tember, and the chronicler's words indicate clearly that Bruce's force was much larger than on the former occa-sion. This probably means that Bruce, when under-taking the first raid with the force then at his disposal, had sent summonses to others of his adherents to join him on a more extended invasion at a slightly later date. At all events the Northumbrian raid partook more of the nature of an invasion than of a raid, and it was concluded by the Northumbrians, in the words of the Lanercost chronicler, sending "envoys to him to negotiate a temporary truce, and they agreed with him

[1] Lanercost.

that they would pay £2000 for an exceedingly short truce—to wit until the Purification of the Blessed Virgin," that is until 2nd February 1312. As a matter of fact, however, the truce was only granted till Christmas 1311, and was afterwards extended to the later date.

The page of the *Chronicle* which contains the last quotation also contains the following statement, not quoted, so far as I am aware, by any Scottish historian. It comes directly after the sentence last quoted. "Also those of the county of Dunbar," it runs, "next to Berwick in Scotland, who were still in the king of England's place, were very heavily taxed for a truce until the said date," a striking proof of the part which that part of Lothian at least had played thus far in the wars of Bruce.

These two raids are of more than passing importance, for they mark a new phase in the history of the War of Independence. Hitherto Bruce had been engaged in the strenuous task of winning Scotland itself, slowly, and step by step, from the hands of the English. His energies had been confined for several years to the country north of the Forth and Clyde, and he had not been able either to make much headway in the district to the south thereof or to create a diversion by carrying the war into the enemy's country. Now all that was changed. He began now, in a word, openly to take the offensive on a large scale. A systematic attempt was made to wrest the south from England; the war was carried into England, her people made to suffer something of what Scotland had suffered, her riches seized to help the Scots to bear the strain of the war, and the great castles and fortified towns in Scotland which were still held for England were made the object of determined siege and assault. The whole character of the war, in short, was changed. Henceforward Scotland was boldly aggressive, while England was compelled to act almost wholly on the defensive.

It is just at the time when the war enters on this new phase that the Lanercost chronicler makes an observation which has frequently been quoted, and has indeed already appeared in these pages. But it will bear repetition. He has just brought his narrative down to the conclusion of the two raids on the North of England which we have been considering, and continues: "In all these aforesaid campaigns the Scots were so divided among themselves that sometimes the father was on the Scottish side and the son on the English, and vice versa; also one brother might be with the Scots and another with the English; yea, even the same individual be first with one party and then with another. But all those who were with the English were merely feigning, either because it was the stronger party, or in order to save the lands they possessed in England; for their hearts were always with their own people, although their persons might not be so."

Commenting on this passage, Mr. Joseph Bain, in his *Edwards in Scotland*, says: "There is not a little truth in the Friar's words. The records prove beyond doubt that many of his own countrymen and even near neighbours in Annandale were long hostile to the king of Scots. Names generally associated with the cause of independence, *e.g.* Baillie, Cathcart, Craigie, Gordon, Graham, Kirkpatrick, Maxwell, Napier, Ramsay, Seton, Sinclair, Stewart of Bonkhill, Torthorald, and others are found years after the death of Edward I ranged under the banner of England. Though Bannockburn recalled not a few to their country's cause, many remained partisans of England. Whatever the reason the fact is beyond question." Exactly! The War of Independence was neither sustained nor won by Scotland to the south of the Forth and Clyde, nor by the men who are "generally associated with the cause of independence." It was sustained and won by that part of Scotland which for centuries has been ignored by partisan historians, and it was sustained and won by men whose names, unlike those of the supposed patriots of the south, are not found during the critical years from 1307 to 1312 enrolled among the adherents of England.

The success which had attended Bruce's arms in the autumn of 1311 had been great and inspiring, but it was soon eclipsed by the remarkable series of triumphs which distinguished the year 1312. Early in the year a strong Scottish force, apparently commanded by Edward Bruce, was engaged in the siege of Dundee, and the constable, Sir William de Montfichet, by and by found himself in such straits that he agreed to surrender, within a stipulated time, both the castle and the Scottish prisoners whom he had in his keeping.[1] Word of this was brought to Edward as he lay at York, and he immediately sent orders to Montfichet, on 2nd March 1312, to break the agreement and hold the castle to the last on pain of confiscation and death.[2] The bearer of Montfichet's message to Edward was perhaps Sir David de Brechin, who had been a member of Dundee garrison during the winter,[3] and is on record as having been at York on 3rd February 1312.[4] At all events he was appointed, on 21st March, Joint Warden of Dundee along with Montfichet,[5] though he does not seem to have taken up his command, for we find him on 20th April[6] at New-castle with Edward, on which date he was appointed Warden of Berwick-on-Tweed by the English monarch, and ordered, by word of mouth, to send reinforcements of horse and foot to Dundee.[7] This is the last mention of Dundee in the English records, and we may therefore conclude that it surrendered to Edward Bruce, who Barbour tells us was its captor, before the middle of July 1312, for about the end of June Bruce held a Parliament at Ayr, at which his brother Edward was present, and at which a plan of campaign for the succeeding months was agreed upon.[8]

The capture of Dundee was an event of considerable importance. It was one of the two strongholds remaining to England in all Scotland north of the Forth, and was both strongly garrisoned and strongly fortified.[9] Its

[1] *Rotuli Scotiae*, i. 108.   [2] *Ibid.*   [3] Bain, iii. 238.
[4] *Ibid.*, p. 283.   [5] *Rotuli Scotiae*, i. 109.
[6] Bain, iii. 267.   [7] *Ibid.*, pp. 267, 268.
[8] *Ibid.*, p. 279.   [9] For roll of garrison see Bain, iii. 427–31.

situation on the Tay, moreover, made it easily accessible by sea, and it was, of course, by sea that communication with England was maintained and reinforcements, such as those sent from Berwick, were received. Its fall, therefore, was an event of profound significance, for it meant not only that the Scots were now strong enough to undertake successfully the siege of a strongly-defended fortress, but that England was no longer able to give the attention to the Scottish war which was necessary if she were to retain any hold on the country. We can probably trace to the fall of Dundee the plan of campaign which Bruce adopted a few weeks later, and carried out so successfully in the months which followed.

Edward's mad affection for Piers Gaveston, which already had proved so valuable an aid to Scotland, was still Scotland's best ally. Early in 1312 Gaveston returned to England in defiance of the Parliament's decree of banishment, and Edward immediately proceeded north with him in order to keep him out of the hands of the lords ordainers, the earls and barons who were banded together against him. On 27th January 1312 we find Edward at York, and there he remained till at least 5th April. On 12th April he is at Newcastle, on 29th May he is back at York, and there we still find him on 26th June.[1] During all these months a state of civil war existed in England, the lords ordainers, with the Earl of Lancaster at their head, marching north in pursuit of the king and his favourite, and resting not till they had captured the latter at Scarborough, and beheaded him on 19th June. The execution of his favourite naturally intensified the anger of the king against the lords ordainers, and for many months thereafter all his energies were devoted to his feud with them. Scotland accordingly was left to look after herself, with what results we shall presently see.

" Now, while the aforesaid things were being done with Piers," says the Lanercost chronicler writing of the events of the first half of 1312, " the march of England

[1] See various entries, Bain, iii.

had no defender against the Scots," which defines the situation tritely and truly. "Wherefore," he adds, " they rendered tribute to Robert in order to have peace for a while." Before then, however, Edward himself endeavoured to come to terms with Bruce in order that he might be free to deal with the lords ordainers. On 26th January 1312 he appointed commissioners to treat with Bruce[1]; all the commissioners, it is interesting to observe, being Scotsmen, viz. the Bishop of St. Andrews, the Earls of Athol and March, Sir Alexander de Abernethy, and Sir Adam de Gordon.[2] But Bruce refused the terms offered, and the war went on, under conditions now exceedingly favourable to the Scots.

In the preceding September, it will be remembered, the northern English counties had purchased a truce from the Scots until Christmas, which was afterwards extended to 2nd February 1312. The truce had hardly expired when the Scots were over the border again, and sometime in the early part of 1312 attacked the castle of Norham, burned the town, and carried away many prisoners and cattle.[3] This they did, says the Lanercost chronicler, " because the castle did them great injury." It was apparently after this raid that the northern counties paid tribute to Bruce " in order to have peace for a while." At all events they seem to have enjoyed a short period of immunity, for nearly six months elapse before we hear of the Scots being over the border again. In the interval, as we have seen, Dundee fell, and with its fall Bruce was in a position to plan a campaign on a larger scale than he had ever before attempted.

On 14th July 1312 we find some unknown person on the English side writing to Edward from Dumfries.[4] He informs the king that, since he left him at York, " Sir Robert de Bruce had held a Parliament at Ayr, and intended to send Sir Edward his brother, with the greater part of his forces, into England, while he himself

---

[1] *Rotuli Scotiae*, i. 108.   [2] *Ibid.*   [3] Lanercost.
[4] Bain, iii. 279. The writer was probably Sir Dugald Macdowall, who was constable of the castle. See also Bain, iv. 1839.

attacked the castles of Dumfries, Buittle, and Caerlaverock, remaining there, and sending his light troops to plunder the north for their support." The writer of the letter, whoever he was, was certainly very accurately informed of Bruce's intentions, intentions which, as we shall see, he carried out very completely. But meanwhile we shall consider some other points which the letter suggests.

In the first place the date of the letter makes it clear that the Parliament was held not later than 7th or 8th July, and probably a week or two earlier. In the next place it gives us an insight into the care and the skill with which Bruce formed his plans, and the manner in which he conducted his campaigns. In the third place it shows us how great was the confidence of the Scots when they could plan and carry out a campaign of such magnitude, with its invasion of England and its siege of three of the strongest castles in the south of Scotland. And in the fourth place it tells us that Ayr was, by the middle of 1312, in the hands of Bruce.

We have frequently had cause to mention Ayr in the course of these pages. It was one of the four Scottish towns—the others being Perth, Dundee, and Banff—which down to the close of 1309 figure in every list of places in Scotland to which aid was sent from time to time. In May 1309 it appears as the " New Castle in Ayr in Scotland." On other occasions it appears along with Perth, Dundee, and Banff as a town as distinct from a castle, which probably means that both town and castle were fortified and held for England. Its last appearance as a fortified place held for England is on 15th December 1309, and as it does not occur among the places mentioned as being in English hands on 25th June 1311,[1] it is plain that it must have fallen between December 1309 and June 1311. Now, the places which are specifically mentioned as being in English hands on the latter date are Dunbar, Yester, Luffenok, Dirleton, Kirkintilloch, Stirling, Selkirk, Jedburgh, Cavres, Loch-

---

[1] Bain, iii. 218.

maben, Buittle, Dalswinton, and Dumfries,[1] while Perth, too, was still held for England, as were also Berwick, Roxburgh, Edinburgh, Bothwell, Livingstone, and Linlithgow.[2]   All these, with the exception of Kirkintilloch, Stirling, Perth, and Bothwell, are in Lothian and its borders, or in the country of the Comyns and their kin in the extreme south-west.

Bruce lost no time in putting into operation the plan of campaign agreed upon at the Parliament, or Council, at Ayr.   With what the Lanercost chronicler describes as "a great army" he crossed the border about 15th August, lay at Lanercost Priory, sixteen miles northeast of Carlisle, for three days "doing an infinity of injury," and thence marching on Hexham and Corbridge burnt these towns and the surrounding districts, and took much spoil and prisoners; "nor was there anyone who dared resist," adds the chronicler plaintively.   He then fixed his headquarters near Corbridge, and from there despatched part of his army under his brother Edward and Douglas on a daring raid into the county of Durham.

Pushing forward with great rapidity the Scots succeeded in surprising the town of Chester-le-Street, six miles to the north of the city of Durham, and thence pressing on furiously surprised Durham itself.   "They came on it by night," says Hemingburgh; "they arrived there suddenly on market day," says the Lanercost chronicler; the truth probably being that it was Chester-le-Street they came on by night, and pressing on from there reached Durham early in the morning before news of their seizure of Chester-le-Street could reach the city. However that may be, surprise Durham they did, and falling upon it with great fury destroyed it with fire and sword, carrying off a great booty, killing all who resisted them, and reducing a great part of the town to ashes. "But they scarcely attacked the castle and abbey," says the Lanercost chronicler, which, too strong to be carried by assault, could only look on helplessly while the town

---

[1] Bain, ii. 218.   [2] *Ibid.*   Various entries.

was destroyed and the country for miles round laid waste.

Durham sacked, Edward Bruce made his headquarters at Chester-le-Street, while Douglas swept on as far as Hartlepool like a destroying angel, wasting the country far and wide and seizing and sacking Hartlepool itself. Then with a great booty and a large number of prisoners, mostly douce English burgesses and their wives, he returned to Edward Bruce at Chester-le-Street.[1]

The effect of this inroad was great and instantaneous. Not for many years had the inhabitants of the county and bishopric of Durham suffered from the ravages of the Scots, and now the enemy whom they had come to regard as innocuous had descended on them in overwhelming force, had swept the country bare of cattle and corn, had slain all who resisted them, and had burned and sacked their principal towns, including the proud and wealthy city of Durham. Terror-stricken they begged for a truce, " fearing more mischief from them and despairing of help from the king." [2] But the Scots were now in a position to dictate what terms they pleased, and accordingly when the people of Durham offered to pay as the price of a truce for ten months, namely until 24th June 1313, a sum of £2000, " the Scots refused to accept it save on condition that they might have free access and retreat through the land of the bishopric whensoever they wished to make a raid into England," to which humiliating condition the bishopric of Durham had perforce to agree.[3]

The unhappy experience of Durham struck terror into the rest of the northern counties. Above all things they now dreaded a visit from the all-conquering Scots, and so hastened to send envoys to them to endeavour to get themselves included in the truce. The Scots were willing—at a price. And so the Northumbrians paid £2000 to have the truce extended to them ; " and the people of Westmoreland, Copland, and Cumberland redeemed themselves in a similar way ; and as they had

<hr/>

[1] Hemingburgh. [2] Lanercost. [3] *Ibid.*

not so much money in hand as would pay them, they paid a part, and gave as hostages for the rest the sons of the chief lords of the country."[1] Thus did Bruce make war pay for war, and avenge some of the wrongs which England had inflicted on his unhappy country.

Flushed with the success which had attended the invasion, the Scottish army on its return northward attempted to capture Carlisle. But the garrison was on the alert, and though the Scots delivered a determined assault upon it, they were repulsed with considerable loss.[2] It was no part of Bruce's policy to waste time in the siege of strong fortresses on the English side of the border, so, the attempt to take Carlisle by assault having failed, the Scottish army did not sit down before it, but continued its march to Scotland, there to carry out the rest of the plan of campaign which had been evolved at Ayr.

That plan, it will be remembered, was to send Edward Bruce, with the greater part of the Scottish king's forces, into England, "while he himself attacked the castles of Dumfries, Buittle, and Caerlaverock, remaining there, and sending his light troops to plunder the north for their support." If the Lanercost chronicler is right this plan was altered in so far that Bruce himself accompanied his army as far as Corbridge, though it is quite possible that on this occasion, as on others, the chronicler failed to distinguish between Bruce and his brother. Be that as it may, however, there can be no doubt that the castles of Dumfries, Buittle, and Dalswinton, and probably also Caerlaverock, were besieged about this time, for Fordun places the capture of the first three in the year which ended on 31st March 1313, a statement which is confirmed by a contemporary document in the English archives, which records the surrender of Dumfries to the Scots on 7th February 1313.[3]

The extraordinary success which had attended the invasion of England, however, caused Bruce to alter his plans in several important particulars. It was now no longer

[1] Lanercost.   [2] Hemingburgh.   [3] Bain, iii. 304.

necessary to send his light troops "to plunder the north for their support" while the castles in the south-west were being besieged, nor was any danger to be apprehended from England for many months to come. For not only had the whole north of England purchased a truce till the 24th of the following June, and given hostages for its observance, and not only was the season fast approaching when it was next to impossible for the English to invade Scotland, but Edward was far too busily engaged in the south, and the domestic affairs of England were in a much too critical state, for him to devote either attention or energy to what was passing in Scotland, or even in the northern parts of his own kingdom. In the phrase used by the Lanercost chronicler to describe the attitude of the English monarch towards the northern counties on the expiry of their truce with Bruce in June 1313, "he was engaged in distant parts of England, seeming not to give them a thought."

Bruce, accordingly, found himself in the latter half of 1312, and all through 1313, in a situation as favourable to him and his schemes as it could well be. The campaign in England, which began with the crossing of the border in the middle of August, must have been over by, at latest, the middle of September. Bruce was then in a position which was, for the time, absolutely unassailable. Attack from the direction of England was well-nigh impossible, and it was in the highest degree unlikely that the English garrisons in Lothian would seek to interfere with him. For one thing they had quite enough to do to maintain themselves, while for another most of them were only half-hearted in their allegiance to England. So Bruce was free to proceed undisturbed with his campaign against the castles in the south-west, and to pursue whatever plans he might desire. Most important of all, it was no longer necessary for him either to keep the greater part of his forces in the south, or to remain to direct operations himself, both of which, when the Parliament of Ayr broke up, he had apparently intended, if the report of the English spy is to be believed.

Accordingly he quickly decided on a change of plans, or rather on an extension of his original plans. Messengers had come to him from the king of Norway desiring him to meet envoys of the Norwegian monarch in order to settle certain matters in dispute between the two countries. By going north to meet these envoys at Inverness he could accomplish several other matters of importance as well. He could dispense justice and stimulate the loyalty and enthusiasm of the districts through which he passed; he could look into various affairs of moment in the north-east; he could recruit his forces; and he could, if the opportunity offered, attempt the capture of Perth. So, leaving Edward Bruce and Douglas in charge of the operations in the south, he proceeded north with a force which included Randolph and the Earl of Athol, and came to Inverness in the last week of October 1312.

CHAPTER XXXV

THE INVERNESS PARLIAMENT (*October* 1312)

THE business transacted by Bruce at his Inverness Parliament need not detain us. Suffice it to say that, so far as the record which survives bears, it was concerned mainly with the settlement of various matters in dispute between the kingdoms of Scotland and Norway. The important things for us are—first, its date, viz. 29th October 1312; and second, the names of those on record as being present.[1] These latter are the Bishops of Aberdeen, Moray, Ross, and Caithness, and " William, David, and Thomas Randolph, Earls of Ross, Athol, and Moray."

The two names last mentioned require some consideration. Thomas Randolph, it will be remembered, had fought on the side of England for about two years after the battle of Methven. Captured by Douglas in the late summer or early autumn of 1308, he had remained some time in durance before making up his mind to throw in his lot again with Bruce, his uncle. His decision once made, however, he had never wavered in his allegiance, and during the three and a half years which had elapsed between his final adherence to Bruce in the early part of 1309, and his coming to Inverness with his royal uncle in the autumn of 1312, he had taken rank with Edward Bruce and Douglas as one of the most trusted and most daring of Bruce's lieutenants. He now received a signal mark of Bruce's confidence by the re-creation in his favour of the long dormant earldom of Moray, and the bestowal upon him of a vast domain which included the greater part of the ancient province of that name. On 12th April 1312 he appears on record

---

[1] Acts of Parl., i. 101.

by the name and title of Sir Thomas Randolph,[1] and as the first mention of him as Earl of Moray occurs in the record of the Inverness Parliament, it is, I think, a fair conclusion that the earldom was conferred upon him during Bruce's visit to Moray in October 1312. By this creation Bruce gave to the warlike men of Moray, to whom he owed so much, a leader of their own, and that leader his own nephew. Henceforward it was the banner of Randolph the men of Moray followed in war; and it was with the men of Moray Randolph performed those exploits which have endeared him to the heart of every Scot.

We have already had occasion to consider the case of the Earl of Athol, but it will bear a little further consideration. Down to January 1312 he appears repeatedly in the English records as an adherent of England, and in December 1311, not in December 1312 as has been too hastily assumed from the misdating of an undated entry in Bain's *Calendar*,[2] he attended a Parliament in England, along with several others of Edward's Scottish adherents, in order to consult " on the affairs of Scotland." As a result he, Sir Alexander Abernethy, the Bishop of St. Andrews, the Earl of March, and Sir Adam de Gordon were, on 26th January 1312, appointed commissioners to treat with the Scots, he and Sir Alexander Abernethy being on the same date also specially authorised to make a truce with the Scots.[3] These negotiations, as we have seen, came to nothing, and thereafter there is no mention of Athol in the English records till 8th October 1314, on which date Edward grants him certain manors in Norfolk " till he recovers his Scottish possessions."[4] About the same time, as we know from Scottish sources, his lands in Scotland were forfeited and conferred on Sir Nigel Campbell.[5] Barbour, however, tells us that he fought on the English side at Bannockburn, and that on the night before the battle, that is on the evening of the day which saw the dis-

---

[1] B. P., vi. 292.　　[2] Bain, iii. 303.　　[3] *Rotuli Scotiae*, i. 108.
[4] Bain, iii. 396.　　[5] Robertson's *Index*, p. 26, and B. P.

comfiture of Clifford and the slaying of de Bohun, he made a successful attack on the Scottish king's supplies which lay at Cambuskenneth under the charge of Sir William Airth. Barbour rather implies that the attack was a treacherous one, and tells us that because of it " he was banished, and all his lands were seized and forfeit to the king, that did thereof according to his liking." As Bannockburn was fought on 24th June, and Athol was a landless fugitive in England by 8th October, Barbour's story is supported by the dates.

Between 26th January 1312 and 23rd June 1314, therefore, Athol appears nowhere as an adherent of England. But on 29th October 1312 he was present at Bruce's Parliament at Inverness, he shortly afterwards appears on record as Constable of Scotland, he is stated by Gray, in *Scalacronica*, to have taken part in the capture of Perth on 8th January 1313, and early in the same year he appears as a witness to charters by Bruce in favour of the Abbey of Arbroath.[1] Now, David, Earl of Athol, was the son of that John, Earl of Athol, who had paid for his devotion to Bruce by having ·his head struck off on Tower Hill in 1307, and he might, therefore, have been expected to inherit a tradition of loyalty to the cause of Scottish freedom. But his wife was a daughter of the murdered Red Comyn,[2] and her husband, accordingly, was involved in the blood feud between Bruce and the Comyns. These facts probably explain his behaviour down to the beginning of 1312, and make it easier to understand his conduct in the light of subsequent events.

The fact that the Earl of Athol was one of Bruce's companions on his northward journey in the autumn of 1912 suggests that he was by that time high in the favour of the king. It seems probable, therefore, that he had joined Bruce some considerable time previously, and my reading of the riddle is that his negotiations in the spring of 1312 having brought him into close contact with Bruce, and having enabled him to form a fair estimate of the Scot-

tish king's prospects, he, on the failure of these negotiations, threw in his lot with the cause to which his birth
and his instincts inclined him. To that cause and to
Bruce he seems to have remained faithful until shortly
before Bannockburn, when a family quarrel led him to
range himself on the side of Bruce's enemies once more.
Barbour, who is our authority for the story, says that
Edward Bruce, who was married to Athol's sister, Isabel,
transferred his affections to a daughter of the Earl of
Ross, and came to hold his own wife in great dislike.
He and Athol quarrelled fiercely over the matter, " and
so great distance fell between him and the Earl Davy,"
that, on the eve of Bannockburn, Athol went over to the
English. There is nothing improbable in the story, for
Athol certainly did abandon Bruce about this time, re-
maining an active adherent of England till his death in
January 1327; while Edward Bruce was married to
Athol's sister and did have an intrigue with a daughter
of the Earl of Ross, for he received, in June 1317, a papal
dispensation for the marriage which he had contracted
with " Isabella, daughter of William, Earl of Ross." [1]

Among the other persons mentioned as present at the
Inverness Parliament we may note David de Moravia,
Bishop of Moray, the tried and proven friend of the
cause of Scottish freedom; and as it was in 1313 that
his project of sending four poor scholars from his diocese
to study at Paris first took shape,[2] it is more than probable that the idea had its origin in the Inverness Parliament of 1312, and that the real foundation of the Scots
College may accordingly be placed in that year. We
may also note that, in the record of this Parliament, no
name occurs which is not connected with Scotland north
of the Forth, Thomas Randolph, the only possible exception, being present not as a young southern knight
but as the newly-created chieftain of the loyal, hard-
fighting province of Moray.

While Bruce was thus engaged in the north, his lieutenants were eagerly carrying on the war of liberation in

---

[1] *Calendar Papal Registers*, ii. 156.　　[2] *Scot. Hist. Rev.*, iv. 399.

the south. The castles of Dumfries, Buittle, Dalswinton, and Caerlaverock were being besieged, and one or more of the last three may have fallen before the end of November, for on 6th December a well-planned attempt was made to take Berwick by surprise. The Lanercost chronicler, who tells the tale at length, and whose account I shall presently quote, ascribes the attempt to Bruce himself, but this is clearly impossible. For if Bruce were at Inverness on 29th October 1312, and captured Perth, after a siege, on 8th January 1313, it is exceedingly unlikely—it is, in fact, not possible—that he marched from Inverness to Berwick in less than five weeks in the month of November, and returned north to Perth, besieged it and captured it, within four weeks thereafter. The Lanercost chronicler, who apparently was in Berwick at the time of the attempted surprise, of course could not know who led the Scots, and it was only natural for him in the circumstances to imagine that the leader was Bruce himself. The probable course of events in the winter of 1312-13 is that Bruce marched from Inverness to the siege of Perth, and that his followers in the south, led probably by Douglas, for the scheme has a ring of Douglas about it, varied their sieges of the castles by attempting to take Berwick by surprise. How nearly the attempt succeeded let the Lanercost chronicler tell.

"Now the oft-mentioned Robert, seeing that thus he had the whole march of England under tribute, applied all his thoughts to getting possession of the town of Berwick, which was in the king of England's hands," he begins, thus showing clearly that he had no idea that Bruce ever left the border counties after his return from his successful invasion in August and September. "Coming unexpectedly to the castle on the night of St. Nicholas," he continues, that is on 6th December 1312, "he laid ladders against the walls and began to scale them; and had not a dog betrayed the approach of the Scots by loud barking, it is believed that he would quickly have taken the castle, and, in consequence, the town.

"Now these ladders which they placed against the

walls were of wonderful construction, as I myself, who write these lines, beheld with mine own eyes. For the Scots had made two strong ropes as long as the height of the wall, making a knot at one end of each cord. They had made a wooden board also, about two feet and a half long and half a foot broad, strong enough to carry a man, and in the two extremities of the board they had made two holes, through which the two ropes could be passed; then the cords, having been passed through as far as the knots, they had made two other knots in the ropes one foot and a half higher, and above these knots they placed another log or board, and so on to the end of the ropes. They had also made an iron hook, measuring at least one foot along one limb, and this was to lie over the wall; but the other limb, being of the same length, hung downwards towards the ground, having at its end a round hole wherein the point of a lance could be inserted, and two rings on the two sides wherein the said ropes could be knotted.

"Having fitted them together in this manner, they took a strong spear as long as the height of the wall, placing the point thereof in the iron hole, and two men lifted the ropes and boards with that spear, and placed the iron hook (which was not a round one) over the wall. They then were able to climb up by those wooden steps, just as one usually climbs ordinary ladders, and the greater the weight of the climber the more firmly the iron hook clung over the wall. But lest the ropes should lie too close to the wall and hinder the ascent, they had made fenders round every third step which thrust the ropes off the wall. When, therefore, they had placed two ladders upon the wall, the dog betrayed them, as I have said, and they left the ladders there, which our people next day hung upon a pillory to put them to shame. And thus a dog saved the town on that occasion, just as of old geese saved Rome by their gobble."

CHAPTER XXXVI

1313—THE ALL-CONQUERING SCOTS

THE capture of Perth on the night of 8th January 1313 was a brilliant feat of arms. Perth had long been a thorn in the side of the Scots, and eagerly they desired its capture. It was, with the possible exception of Berwick, the most strongly fortified town in Scotland, and a large garrison was constantly maintained there. Its situation on the Tay made communication with England by sea a matter of ease, and we have frequently noticed, in the course of our narrative, the issue of orders for its provisioning and defence, and the despatch of troops to it. In 1312 it was under the command of Sir William Oliphant,[1] the same Scottish knight who had made so gallant a defence of Stirling Castle against Edward I in 1304. In July 1312 the garrison consisted of 120 mounted men, besides archers and foot-soldiers,[2] and as mounted men, as a general rule, formed only a small proportion of a fourteenth-century garrison or army, it is clear that Perth was very strongly held.

The fortifications of the town, moreover, had been well looked after. In 1306, for example, they had been strengthened by the erection of a tower and the digging of a deep ditch,[3] while in 1311–12 the rents of the burgh were spent in still further " enclosing " the town.[4] From the very beginning of the War of Independence Perth, in fact, had been regarded by the English as second in importance only to Berwick, and they had made of it a very strong place indeed. Its strategic value is, of course, self-evident. So long as England held Perth, so long could she menace the whole central

---

[1] Bain, iii. 247, 264, 425.   [2] *Ibid.*, pp. 425–7.
[3] *Ibid.*, p. 268.   [4] *Ibid.*, p. 433.

part of Scotland, and so long had she a magnet in the very heart of Scotland to attract her armies. Throughout the War of Independence the truth of this was manifested time and again. Only eighteen months before the date at which we have now arrived, on the occasion of Edward II's invasion in 1310–11, English troops passed repeatedly between Berwick and Perth, the Earl of Cornwall on one occasion proceeding to the town with a force which one contemporary letter-writer describes as "a great rout," [1] and another says included no less than 500 men-at-arms.[2] So Perth was plainly a place which it was extremely important for England to hold, and a place, accordingly, which it was even more important for the Scots to capture. It was, moreover, the last strong place left to England in all Scotland north of the Forth.

Several fourteenth-century narratives of the siege and capture of Perth are in existence, but as Barbour's is the most detailed and picturesque, and does not differ in essentials from the others, we shall follow it. The town was captured, he tells us, seven weeks after the commencement of the siege, and as the date of its capture is either 8th or 10th January 1313,[3] this carries us back to the last week of November for the date of the beginning of the siege. This date fits in exactly with our previous conclusion that Bruce proceeded to the siege of Perth direct from Inverness, where he was on 29th October.

To our knowledge from official sources Barbour adds the information that the wall which surrounded Perth was of stone, and that it was surmounted with several towers, details which other chroniclers confirm. Strongly fortified, strongly garrisoned, and well provisioned, it was therefore a hard nut for Bruce to crack, and after a siege of six weeks he found himself no nearer achieving its capture than he had been at the outset. But Bruce was ever fertile in resource, and when ordinary methods failed he resorted to stratagem. During the siege he carefully examined the state of the defences,

[1] Bain, iii. 246. [2] *Ibid.*, 204. [3] Lanercost ; Fordun.

paying particular attention to the height of the walls and to the moat, which was broad and deep. By assiduous sounding he by and by discovered a place " where men might to their shoulders wade," and laid his plans accordingly. Then, about the end of December, he gave orders for the raising of the siege, and on or about 1st January he broke up his camp, and marched away in full view of the enemy, " as if he would there do nothing more."

Barbour tells us, with a graphic touch, that when those within the town saw the besieging host retiring " they shouted at them and scorning made." But Bruce and his men held on their way as if they had " no will again to turn," and Perth in a few hours realised that the enemy had indeed disappeared. At first, no doubt, Sir William Oliphant, skilful soldier and gallant knight, suspected a trick, and kept firm watch and ward. But as the days went past and there was no sign of the Scots, and no whisper of an attempted surprise, his suspicions were quietened, and by the time a week had gone the garrison were lulled into a sense of security once more. For five years they had defied Bruce and his men, and they might well believe there was nothing to fear from them now.

Bruce meanwhile was quietly making his preparations and awaiting his opportunity. He had halted his army in a secret place at a safe distance from Perth, and there set them to work to construct ladders of a length suffi- cient to reach to the top of Perth wall. Then when eight days had passed, and he rightly judged that the garrison would have ceased to be on the alert, he set out " on a mirk night " for the sleeping town. Horses and servants were left behind, and on foot, carrying their ladders, the Scots approached their goal:

> " They heard no watchers speak or cry
> For they that were within, ma fall,
> As men that dread nought, sleepit all.
> They had no dread then of the king,
> For they of him heard no tiding
> All these three days before and mair:
> Therefore secure and trusting they were."

And so the Scots, with their king at their head, came to the moat.

When Bruce saw that their approach had been un-observed, that there was no stir in the town, " he was blithe upon great manner," and seizing a ladder lowered himself in full armour into the water. Then with his ladder in one hand and his spear in the other he began to wade boldly across, testing the depth with his spear as he went. The water deepened rapidly, and presently reached to his neck, but he held on and in a moment or two had gained the other side, and placed his ladder against the wall. Fired by his example, his men pressed hastily after him, and on that dark, cold January night pushed their way through the deep water of the moat to the further side. So quickly indeed did they follow Bruce that though his ladder was first against the wall, he was not the first to scale it, another ardent Scot beat-ing his king in the race for that honour. But though not first, Bruce was second in the scramble for the top of the wall, and there he in a very few moments found himself surrounded by an eager and ever-increasing crowd, who, Barbour tells us, kept " coming over in full great haste, yet raised neither noise nor cry." Hastily he divided them into two detachments, the larger being sent to scour the town in all directions, while Bruce himself with a chosen band stood vigilantly on guard, " so that he might be prepared to defend if he were assailed."

Then was the silence of the night suddenly and terribly broken. Through the sleeping town rushed the eager Scots, scattering in all directions as they ran, and " putting soon to great confusion their foes that in their beds were, or scattered fleeing here and there." The surprise was complete, and resistance there was little or none. " But there were few slain ; for the king had given them commands, on great pain, they should slay none who, except with great trouble, might be taken. That they were kin to the country he knew, and had for them pity."

In this last statement both Fordun and the Lanercost chronicler differ from Barbour, the former having it that the treacherous folk, both Scots and English, were slain, and the latter declaring that on the day after the capture Bruce " caused those citizens of the better class who were of the Scottish nation to be killed, but the English were allowed to go free." Of the three statements Barbour's is the most likely to be true, for it was never Bruce's policy to slay his prisoners, and especially not prisoners who were Scotsmen. As we have before remarked, he was noted for his humane treatment of his enemies, and the contemporary records, as well as the chronicles, are full of evidences of the truth of this.

The Lanercost chronicler states that Sir William Oliphant " was bound and sent far away to the Isles," which is to a certain extent borne out by Barbour's remark that the " prisoners whom there took he, he sent where they might holden be." However that may be, Sir William Oliphant was not detained a prisoner long, for a few months later he was in England,[1] whither perhaps he had been allowed to go to arrange for his ransom, a method of treating prisoners of rank which was not uncommon with Bruce.

Perth itself shared the fate common to all the strong places which Bruce captured, and which in its case was particularly necessary. Save Berwick it was the only stone-walled town in Scotland, and next to Berwick was of all the fortresses in Scotland the most important to a would-be conqueror. So, in the words of the Lanercost chronicler, it was " utterly destroyed." Its walls, towers, and fortifications were levelled with the ground, not one stone being left upon another; its ditches were filled up; and, according to Fordun, everything else was burned. Its very strength was its ruin. Bruce was determined that it should not again provide even a semblance of temptation to his enemies of England.

We cannot pass from the siege of Perth without recounting a picturesque tale which Barbour tells of a

[1] Bain, iii. xviii.

French knight who was with Bruce on the night of the surprise. When the Frenchman saw Bruce in the water, "and with him take his ladder so boldly," he was overcome with admiration. "Ah, Lord!" exclaimed he, "what shall we say of our lords of France, that always with good food fill their stomachs, and will but eat and drink and dance, when so right worthy a knight as this has, through his chivalry, put himself in such jeopardy to win a wretched hamlet?" With those words he ran to the ditch, and, jumping in, "over after the king he won." The tale, like the whole story of the siege and capture of Perth, brings the real Bruce vividly before us, and gives us a glimpse of the personality which won for him the devoted service which was his in such abundance. That is why I have thought it well to re-tell the whole graphic tale of the siege and capture of Perth. For in it we see Bruce the leader, Bruce the strategist, and Bruce the man, as we have not yet seen him in all our study of the War of Independence.

Perth fell on 8th or 10th January 1313. A month later, on 7th February, the strong castle of Dumfries, commanded by Bruce's inveterate enemy, Sir Dougald Macdowall, surrendered to the Scots.[1] It is usually stated that the surrender was made to Bruce in person, but there is no real warrant for this. The only contemporary reference to the surrender is a note on the margin of the account-book of Edward's receiver at Carlisle,[2] which runs: "Memorandum—That the castle of Dumfries was surrendered on 7th February of this 6th year to Sir Robert de Bruys by Sir Dungal M'Douwile." As we have already remarked, such a reference does not necessarily imply that Bruce himself was actually present in person, though he may quite well have been, but the point is really not of much importance. What is important is that the strongest castle in the country of Bruce's mortal foes was now in the hands of the king of Scots.

Dumfries was almost certainly starved into surrender.

---

[1] Bain, iii. 304. [2] *Ibid.*

As early as the beginning of July 1312 Sir Dougald Macdowall had complained to the English king that the keeper of the stores at Carlisle had failed to keep him properly supplied with provisions, and that as a result many of his men had deserted.[1] Edward immediately sent orders to Carlisle commanding the keeper of the stores to supply victuals to the garrison of Dumfries forthwith, but as these orders could not reach Carlisle before the end of August,[2] it is extremely unlikely that they were ever carried out. For, as we have seen, the Scottish invasion of the North of England was by then in full swing, and Dumfries itself was probably by that time in a state of siege. At all events surrender it did on 7th February 1313, and as it was clearly a surrender and not a capture by force, there can be little doubt that the weakness in men and provisions disclosed by its constable in July had not been made good.

It is more than likely that Caerlaverock and Dalswinton, both of which are within a few miles of Dumfries, fell about the same time as the latter. Fordun states quite definitely that Dalswinton and Buittle, at all events, fell before 31st March 1313, and so far as the evidence goes Caerlaverock seems also to have fallen about this time. Now, whether or not Bruce was actually at the surrender of Dumfries, a strong Scottish army was unquestionably engaged in the siege, and we know that Bruce himself must have been in the south-west in force a few weeks later, as early in May he set out from Galloway to invade the Isle of Man. It is, accordingly, a fair conclusion that the fall of those castles, which were situated in the very district in which a powerful Scottish army was operating, occurred in the early months of 1313.

The Isle of Man had become part of the kingdom of Scotland in 1266, when the king of Norway had ceded the Sudreys, including the Isle of Man, to the Scots for the sum of 4000 merks. Scottish dominion, however,

---

[1] Bain, iii. p. 281.
[2] They are dated at Dover on 8th August.—Bain, iii. No. 281, p. 56.

did not become firmly established till 1275, when the Manx were defeated in a decisive battle at Ronaldshay.[1] With the outbreak of the War of Independence Edward I asserted his dominion over the island, and in England's hands it remained till 1313.

We saw that as early as December 1310 Bruce was credited in England with designs on the Isle of Man, and preparations were made to resist him if he should attempt to carry out his reported intention of despatching all his navy to the island "for the purpose of destroying it and establishing a retreat there." After that, however, we hear nothing further concerning it until May 1313, when the *Chronicle of Man* tells us that, "on 18th May Lord Robert, king of Scotland, put in at Ramsay with a large number of ships, and on the following Sunday went to the nunnery at Douglas, where he spent the night, and on Monday laid siege to the castle of Rushen."[2] The constable of the castle was Duncan Macdowall, who may or may not have been the same person as the Sir Dugald Macdowall who had surrendered Dumfries on 7th February.[3] It is usually asserted that the two were one and the same, but the evidence is inconclusive. At all events if the defender of Rushen were the same as the defender of Dumfries, he had the unwelcome experience of having to surrender two castles to his mortal enemy within the short space of five months, for on "the Tuesday after the Feast of St. Barnabas the Apostle," that is on the first Tuesday after 11th June, Rushen Castle fell into the hands of the Scots.

The Isle of Man was thus recovered for Scotland, and a few months later, on 20th December 1313, Bruce conferred it, in free regality, on his nephew, Thomas Randolph, Earl of Moray.[4] He kept, however, the patronage of the bishopric in his own hands, while Randolph for his new lands had to pay yearly 100 merks at Inverness, and find "six ships each of twenty-

---

[1] A. W. Moore in *Scottish Historical Review*, July 1906.
[2] *Ibid.*   [3] *Ibid.*   [4] *Ibid.*

six oars." Mr. Arthur W. Moore, to whose article on "The Connection between Scotland and Man," in the *Scottish Historical Review* for July 1906, I am indebted for much of my information, adds : "This mention of Inverness as the place of payment is very interesting, because it seems to indicate that the government of the Isles centred in that town." This may well be so, but it also indicates that Randolph's interests now were regarded as centring at Inverness, that he was in actual fact, as well as in name, head of the province of Moray.

Before we leave the subject of the Isle of Man we may glance briefly at its subsequent history. In the summer or autumn of 1314 it was reconquered for England by Bruce's old enemy, John of Argyll,[1] who had been, since his expulsion from Scotland, in the service of England with the rank of Admiral of the Western Seas of England, Wales, Ireland, and the Isles of Scotland. Throughout 1316 there was constant fighting between the Scots and English in Man, with what result is uncertain. Eventually, however, the Scots were triumphant, for although there is little or no evidence to go upon for several years after 1317, we find in July of that year that Thomas Randolph was preparing to attack the island,[2] and three months later that he was on the point of setting out for it.[3] But whatever happened the Isle of Man was recovered by Scotland and remained a Scottish possession till 1333. For some years thereafter it was a sort of shuttlecock between the two kingdoms, but it finally passed from the possession of the Scots, and after 1346 no formidable attempt was ever again made to recover the island for Scotland.[4]

The truce which the northern counties of England had been glad to purchase from Bruce at so great a price in the autumn of 1312 expired on 24th June 1313, and, as soon as he had returned from the Isle of Man, Bruce threatened to invade England in

[1] A. W. Moore in *Scottish Historical Review*, July 1906 ; and Bain, iii. 420.
[2] *Ibid.*, p. 2 ; and Bain, iii. 562.   [3] *Scottish Historical Review*.
[4] *Ibid.*

what the Lanercost chronicler calls his "usual manner."
That is to say he would still make war pay for war.
But, adds the chronicler, "the people of Northumberland, Westmoreland, and Cumberland, and other bor-
derers, apprehending this, and neither having nor hoping
for any defence or help from their king (seeing that he
was engaged in distant parts of England, seeming not to
give them a thought), offered to the said Robert no
small sum of money, indeed a very large one, for a
truce to last till the Feast of St. Michael in the following
year," that is to say until 29th September 1314. This
offer was made in July 1313, and Bruce readily accepted
it. He thus received without any effort a large and
welcome accession to his exchequer, and was free to
devote all his energies, throughout the rest of 1313
and the early months of 1314, to completing the task
so well begun in the previous winter—the task, namely,
of wresting from the hands of the English the few
strongholds which yet remained to them in Scotland.

CHAPTER XXXVII

THE RECOVERY OF LOTHIAN (1313-14)

It is hardly necessary now to point out to the reader of these articles that Lothian, down to the very eve of Bannockburn, took no part in Bruce's struggle for the freedom of Scotland. As we shall presently see, a few knights and men of Lothian did, from time to time, throw in their lot with Bruce, and the sympathies of the population as a whole were doubtless with Bruce, but it remains, none the less, an incontrovertible historical fact that Lothian had neither lot nor part in the burden and heat of the critical years which won for Bruce a kingdom and for Scotland her freedom. From the very outset of Bruce's revolt in the beginning of 1306 down to the close of 1313 Lothian was held for England, and that in the fullest sense of the meaning which the phrase implies. Not only were her castles and her strong places held by English garrisons or by Scottish adherents of England, but her natural leaders were active on the side of England, her affairs were administered by English officials, her revenues were drawn by England, and her population accepted English rule and English administration, though probably not with a very good grace.

It will, perhaps, be well to remind ourselves what districts are included under the term Lothian. They are all the modern counties of Edinburgh, Haddington, and Berwick, the eastern half of Roxburgh, the eastern corner of Selkirk, the eastern confines of Peebles, and the southern and eastern portions of Linlithgow. A roll of revenues of the sheriffdoms of Scotland, collected by England during the years 1311-12,[1] shows that the

---

[1] Bain, iii. 393-434.

sheriffdoms of Berwick, Roxburgh, Edinburgh, Haddington, and Linlithgow, that is to say all the counties of Lothian, were then being actively administered by English officials. The only other sheriffdoms on the roll are Stirling and Perth, and the towns of Stirling and Perth were then, as we know, held by English garrisons.

In June 1312 there were English garrisons in Berwick, Roxburgh, Edinburgh, Linlithgow, Livingstone, Dunbar, Yester, Luffenok, Dirleton, Selkirk, Jedburgh, Cavers, Stirling, Bothwell, Kirkintilloch, Perth, Lochmaben, Buittle, Dalswinton, Caerlaverock, and Dumfries.[1] By June of the following year, 1313, Perth, Buittle, Dalswinton, and Dumfries had fallen; Kirkintilloch, Lochmaben, and Caerlaverock had almost certainly shared a similar fate; and Selkirk was perhaps also in the hands of the Scots. The other thirteen were still held for England, and of these thirteen two only, Stirling and Bothwell, were outside Lothian. Thus by the middle of 1313 it only remained for Bruce to wrest Lothian from England, in order to make all Scotland his own, for Stirling and Bothwell were now simply isolated strongholds, whose capture was only a question of time.

Towards the end of 1308 Bruce had received a number of welcome recruits from Lothian, chief among them being Sir Robert Keith,[2] whom he afterwards made Earl Marshal, and who commanded the Scottish Horse at Bannockburn. With Keith there went to Bruce's banner his neighbours, Sir Thomas de la Hay and Godfrey Broun,[3] both of whom held lands in Lothian, while a few months earlier Geoffrey de Fressingleye of Wester Duddingstown likewise threw in his lot with Bruce.[4] Early in 1310 Sir Edmond de Ramsay of Upper Cockpen followed the example of Sir Robert Keith,[5] and at Martinmas in the same year, during an invasion of Lothian by Bruce, Peter de Pontekin, who held the lands of that name in the barony of Mussel-

---

[1] See numerous entries in Bain and *Rotuli Scotiae;* also foregoing chapters.
[2] Bain, iii. 245.　　　[3] *Ibid.*　　　[4] *Ibid.*　　　[5] *Ibid.*

burgh, and Adomar de Haudene of Uckeston, also decided to join their fortunes to those of Bruce.[1] The example of these patriots was not, however, followed by the other men of Lothian, and their names are recorded as practically the only known exceptions to the rule which Lothian, as a whole, elected to follow.

We have already seen that after the inglorious failure of Edward II's invasion of Scotland in 1310 the lot of Lothian was not a happy one. As soon as Edward retired to Berwick on that occasion, Bruce invaded Lothian, and, in the words of the Lanercost chronicler, "inflicted much damage upon those who were in the king of England's peace." On subsequent occasions parts of Lothian were glad to purchase, in common with the northern counties of England, short periods of truce from the Scottish king; and long before the date at which we have now arrived the inhabitants must have begun to feel that Lothian would be wise to throw in her lot with Bruce and the rest of Scotland. But so long as her castles were all held for England, and so long as powerful magnates like Sir Patrick Dunbar, Earl of March, and Sir Adam de Gordon, Justiciar of Lothian, were active in the king of England's interest, the people of Lothian preferred to bear the ills they had rather than fly to others that they knew not of.

This state of affairs, however, could not last for ever, and throughout the summer and autumn of 1313 it gradually became apparent to some of the English offi-cials that Lothian was seething with disaffection. And, indeed, it was no wonder. The truce which, in common with the English counties, the southern parts of Lothian —including the counties of Haddington, Berwick, and Roxburgh, and perhaps Edinburgh—had purchased in 1312, expired on 24th June,[2] and in a few weeks there-after Bruce was in their midst again. Some of the in-habitants in the neighbourhood of Berwick thereupon purchased a temporary truce of fifteen days,[3] and a little later all the counties purchased a truce till Martinmas at

---

[1] Bain, iii. 245.   [2] See Petition quoted *infra*.   [3] *Ibid.*

the price of 1000 quarters of corn.[1] The document in which these and many other facts are recorded is so full of interest, and casts so vivid a light on the condition of the south-eastern counties at the time, that I quote it in full:[2]

"*Petition to the King from the people of Scotland, by their envoys Sir Patrick de Dunbar earl of March and Sir Adam de Gordon.*

"(1) Since his departure from Scotland at the 'Gule' of August three years ago, they have suffered losses by their enemies to the amount of £20,000. Matters are daily getting worse, and for the 'suffraunce' they have till this Martinmas, they had to give 1000 qrs. of corn. Yet their live stock is plundered, partly by the enemy and partly by the garrisons of Berwick and Roxburgh, especially by Gilbert de Medilton and Thomas de Pencaitlande, and their company at Berwick.

"(2) When 'upplaunde' people go to buy their 'vivers' in Berwick, the garrison spy out and seize them, confining some in houses, and carrying off others to Northumberland, holding them in concealment and 'duresce' there till they get a ransom—and the Scots are fined in Northumberland for resetting them. They took from the Bishop of St. Andrews 8 tuns of wine, and when he was commanded by the K. to go to Berwick on his business, he was so rudely received and menaced in life and limb by the garrison, that he dared not come.

"(3) Some of them, at the end of the 'suffraunce' at midsummer, purchased from Sir Robert de Bruys, at his late coming, a truce of fifteen days, and on his retreat, after they had returned to their houses, the next morning the warden and whole garrison of Berwick came and took their people in their beds, carrying them off dead and alive to Berwick, and held them to ransom, viz. on this foray within the bounds in the earldom of Dunbar, both gentlemen and others, to the number of 30. Also 300 fat beasts, 4000 sheep, besides horses and dead stock.

[1] See Petition quoted *infra*. [2] Bain, iii. 337.

"(4) Some of the Berwick garrison, with Thomas de Pencaitland as 'Guyde,' carried off some of the poor people to Berwick. Those who had wherewithal were ransomed; those who had nothing were killed, and thrown into the Water of Tweed.

"(5) During the truce till Midsummer [la St. John], which the K. had ordered his servants to observe in all points, came Sir William de Felyng, constable of Roxburgh, and took certain people, for whose deliverance they had to pay him 80 marks, and also to the enemy 160 marks, as a fine for his breach of the truce.

"(6) The Roxburgh garrison also, instead of protecting his lieges, plunder and imprison the merchants who come there.

"(7) When the aldermen and commune of Roxburgh, at the request of Master John de Weston, the K.'s chamberlain, came to make complaint to the constable of their treatment and losses, he appointed them to meet him next morning, when he would do reason. When they came, he at once arrested Sir Adam de Gordon and imprisoned him against all manner of justice, which arrest has astonished all his good people of Scotland, and they pray the K. for redress."

One of the most important points in this petition is the evidence it affords of the suspicion with which all the inhabitants of Lothian, high and low, rich and poor, had come to be regarded by the English officials in the summer and autumn of 1313. The treatment of Sir Adam Gordon is especially significant. Ever since Bruce had first taken up arms he had been a staunch and active adherent of England, and had repeatedly rendered her signal service.[1] From Edward II he had received many marks of favour, and in 1313 had been for several years Justiciar of Lothian.[2] Yet in August or September of that year he was regarded by his old comrades-in-arms with such suspicion that he was arrested, and placed under heavy security to appear before the king and not to

---

[1] Bain, iii., numerous entries. [2] *Ibid.*, pp. 181, 211, 403.

2 D

injure the castle of Roxburgh. It may be said here that he lost little time in conveying himself, and the petition of which he was the bearer, to London, where he surrendered to his security on the 13th of October, whereupon he and those who had gone security for him were released from their obligations.[1] Nevertheless the suspicions of the men on the spot were justified, for before many months had passed Adam de Gordon had openly become an adherent of Bruce,[2] and there is some ground for believing that for several years prior to 1314 he had had one foot in the Scottish camp.

For the rest, the petition makes clear that while the south-eastern counties were regarded with suspicion by the English garrisons, they were also regarded as hostile by the Scots, and had in consequence to endure many things at the hands of both. As Adam de Gordon was in London on 13th October, the deeds of which the petition complains must have been committed in August or September, that is to say, probably a little before the first great Scottish success in Lothian, the capture of Linlithgow, though it is possible that the high-handed act of the Constable of Roxburgh in arresting Sir Adam Gordon was due to the confirmation of his suspicions which he found in the unexpected news of the fall of Linlithgow by means which must have savoured to him of treachery.

Edward's answer to the petition is interesting. He promised redress, urged his petitioners to be of good courage, and informed them that he was to lead an army to their relief at the following midsummer.[3] As this reply is dated 28th November, it suggests very strongly that he had before that date received news of de Moubray's compact with Edward Bruce in regard to the surrender of Stirling Castle.

The situation in Lothian in 1313 being thus made clear, we must now retrace our steps a little. According to Barbour, Edward Bruce began the siege of Stirling Castle in Lent 1313, and made his famous compact

---

[1] Bain, iii. 344.   [2] B. P., iv. 511-2.   [3] *Rotuli Scotiae*, i. 114.

with its Constable, Moubray, at midsummer, in terms of which the Castle was to be surrendered unless relieved by 24th June 1314. The *Chronicle of Lanercost*, however, makes the siege commence after the capture of Roxburgh and Edinburgh, as does also the contemporary writer of *Vita Edwardi Secundi*. But Roxburgh did not fall until 27th or 28th February 1314, and Edinburgh until the middle of March, by which time Edward was already making great preparations for the coming campaign.[1]

There is, however, a simple explanation of this apparent discrepancy. The Lanercost chronicler has it: "Having accomplished this success" (*i.e.* the capture of Edinburgh), "they marched to Stirling and besieged that castle with their army."

Now the castle had to be relieved by 24th June 1314,[2] and as the English army might appear long before that date the Scots would have to be on the alert as soon as weather favourable for campaigning set in. Moreover, they would be certain to have knowledge that Edward had begun his preparations early in March, but they could hardly know whether he might be expected in April, May, or June. Accordingly the Scottish army would be summoned to assemble at the beginning of April, in order to bar the way to Stirling; and we know, as a matter of fact, from an English document that it was certainly in position by the beginning of May. For on 27th May, Edward writes to the Sheriff of York [3] informing him that he has received intelligence that the Scots are assembling in great numbers "in strong and marshy places (where access for horses will be difficult) between us and our castle of Stirling." The Lanercost chronicler is therefore right in stating that Randolph and his followers proceeded from Edinburgh to Stirling.

[1] *Rotuli Scotiae*, i. 114, &c. Mr. Mackenzie says, pp. 21–22, that these preparations were for an Easter campaign which did not come off. One or two of the writs do mention Easter, but the majority, issued at the same time, viz. about 10th March, say the Feast of St. John the Baptist, that is, 24th June, so the point is by no means clear.
[2] Foedera, 27th May 1314.   [3] Foedera.

But they did not proceed to the siege of Stirling. They went to join the rest of Bruce's forces which were assembling in order to endeavour to prevent the relief of the castle before 24th June.

The English version of the siege of Stirling may now present no difficulty. Chronologically it is impossible: historically it confuses two separate events—the actual siege of the castle in 1313 and the assembling of the Scottish army to oppose the expected English invasion at Easter 1314. It must not be overlooked, moreover, that unexpected confirmation of Barbour's version is forthcoming from the pages of *Scalacronica*. It is there stated that after the capture of Perth, Bruce "marched in force before the castle of Stirling, where Philip de Moubray, knight, having command of the said castle for the king of England, made terms with the said Robert de Bruce to surrender the said castle, which he had besieged, unless he should be relieved; that is, unless the English army came within three leagues of the said castle within eight days of St. John's Day (24th June) in the summer next to come, he would surrender the said castle." This account not only confirms Barbour, but fits in exactly with the chronology of the period as we have ascertained it. Perth fell on 8th or 10th January 1313, Dumfries on 7th February, and Dalswinton, Buittle, and Caerlaverock probably about the same time, while by the middle of May, Bruce was in the Isle of Man. Now Stirling lies directly on the route which Bruce would take in passing from Perth to Galloway, and as Barbour says the siege lasted from Lent to midsummer, he and Gray are practically at one as to the date of its commencement. Accordingly we may take it as certain that the siege of Stirling followed directly on, was indeed the first result of, the fall of Perth. To Stirling, Bruce led his army fresh from the capture of Perth, and leaving part of it there under the command of his brother, he himself proceeded to Galloway, and thence, in due course, to the Isle of Man.

Edward Bruce's chivalrous treaty with the Constable

of Stirling Castle was in reality an act of chivalrous folly, and well did it merit the wrath with which Bruce heard the news on his return from the Isle of Man. Whatever the motive which actuated Edward Bruce may have been, such a treaty, in that age, was a challenge to the whole might of England, a challenge which could not be ignored. As the event proved, it was a fortunate challenge for Scotland, but in the summer of 1313 the issue was still on the knees of the gods, and all Bruce knew was that his brother's action had saved Stirling Castle to England, and had made an English invasion of Scotland within twelve months a matter of certainty.

The expectation of coming invasion had, however, no effect on the spirit and determination of the Scots, save perhaps to inspire them to even greater efforts than ever during the autumn and winter of 1313-14. During these months their attention was devoted to Lothian, and some notable captures were made. In September 1313, during the harvest, a farmer of West Lothian, William Bunnock by name, effected the capture of Linlithgow Peel by the daring stratagem of hiding armed men in a waggon of hay, and cutting the traces when the waggon was in the middle of the gateway and directly under the portcullis. The gate in consequence could not be shut, nor could the portcullis fall, and with the assistance of the men who had been hidden under the hay, Bunnock held the entrance until a strong force, which had been lying in ambush not far away, was able to come up. Taken completely by surprise the garrison were unable to make much resistance, and so Linlithgow Peel passed into the hands of the Scots.

The Peel of Linlithgow had been built by Edward I in 1301-02,[1] and as late as August 1313 orders were being issued in England for munitions for it and Edinburgh.[2] The Constable of Edinburgh Castle, Sir Peter de Loubaud, was also warden of Linlithgow Peel,[3] but in 1311-12 the knight in actual command of Linlithgow, though responsible to de Loubaud, was Sir Archibald

---

[1] Bain, ii. 1321, 1324.   [2] *Ibid.*, iii. 330.   [3] *Ibid.*

Livingstone,[1] de Loubaud's headquarters being of course at Edinburgh. Like his superior, Livingstone was also responsible for the safe keeping of two strongholds, his own Peel of Livingstone, distant but a short way from Linlithgow, being also under his charge.[2] With Sir Archibald Livingstone in Linlithgow were eighty-seven men-at-arms, many of them bearing well-known Lothian names.[3] On its capture by the Scots, Linlithgow Peel shared the fate of the other captured strengths. It was levelled with the ground; of its garrison some were slain, some captured, and some escaped to Edinburgh.

A few months after the capture of Linlithgow came the turn of Roxburgh. Every Scotsman knows how in the gathering dusk of a spring evening James Douglas and his men crawled to the foot of the wall in the guise of cattle, black mantles covering their armour; how they placed cunningly-contrived ladders against the wall, and so climbed up and over; and how, surprising and overcoming the guard, they broke in on the feasting garrison and made the castle their own. But alongside that tale we may place two less well-known English versions of the capture.

Says the Lanercost chronicler: "At the beginning of Lent the Scots cunningly entered the castle of Roxburgh at night by ladders, and captured all the castle except one tower, wherein the warder of the castle, Sir William Fiennes, a knight of Gascony, had taken refuge with difficulty, and his people with him; but the Scots got possession of that tower soon afterwards. And they razed to the ground the whole of that beautiful castle, just as they did other castles which they succeeded in taking, lest the English should ever hereafter be able to lord it over the land through holding the castles." And Sir Thomas Gray, soldier and knight, in *Scalacronica*: "Roxburgh was in charge of William Fiennes, a knight of Burgundy, from whom James de Douglas captured the castle upon the night of Shrove Tuesday, the said William being slain by an arrow as he was defending the great tower."

---

[1] Bain, p. 411.   [2] *Ibid.*   [3] *Ibid.*

The fate of Roxburgh Castle and its gallant constable is thus clear. It was this same constable, Sir William Fiennes or Fillinge,[1] who, a few months previously, had treated so cavalierly Sir Adam de Gordon, the Bishop of St. Andrews, and the inhabitants of the parts of Lothian near to him. His garrison in 1311–12 consisted, so far as we can gather, of between 150 and 200 regular soldiers—that is to say, men-at-arms, archers, and cross-bowmen.[2] It included a considerable number of men of Lothian, and a fair proportion of Englishmen.[3] The date of its capture is 27th or 28th February 1314.[4]

Thomas Randolph, Earl of Moray, had meantime been engaged in the siege of Edinburgh Castle. Its constable was Sir Peter Loubaud,[5] whom we have already met. He was also Sheriff of Edinburgh and Linlithgow,[6] and in 1311–12 had acted in a similar capacity in Haddington.[7] Yet, according to Barbour, he was only prevented by force from betraying Edinburgh Castle to Randolph. In 1311–12 his garrison in the castle consisted of about 200, made up of men-at-arms, cross-bowmen, and archers.[8]

There are several versions of the well-known tale of Randolph's daring capture of Edinburgh Castle, but they all agree on the main points. According to Barbour, the tidings of the taking of Roxburgh fired Randolph with a determination to attempt the capture of Edinburgh by a like *coup-de-main*, for the siege had now lasted some time, and he saw little chance of bringing it to an end by the ordinary methods so long as "they within had men and meat." At all events the bold taking of Roxburgh probably inspired him with the idea that the rock on which Edinburgh Castle was situated might likewise be climbed, especially as the

---

[1] Bain, iii. 406, 419, Nos. 332, 351.
[2] *Ibid.*, pp. 405–7.   [3] *Ibid.*
[4] Barbour, Fordun, and *Scalacronica* all have 27th February, Lanercost 28th. It certainly fell between January and May. Bain, iii. 352, 358, 894.
[5] Bain, iii. 254, &c.   [6] *Ibid.*
[7] *Ibid.*, p. 432.   [8] *Ibid.*, pp. 408–11.

besieging force was composed for the most part of his own tried and proven warriors from the Province of Moray, men used to climbing in steep and perilous places. If the rock were climbable at all they would climb it. So he caused inquiry to be made carefully and secretly, promising a rich reward to anyone who would discover to him a possible way of ascent.

By and by one William Francis was brought to him, a man who in his youth had served in the castle. While there he had had a love affair with a girl in the town, and, love finding out a way, he had visited her by descending the castle rock, returning by the same perilous path when other means of egress and ingress were forbidden. He now offered to put the experience then gained to other use, saying that he would lead a party up the rock to a place at the foot of the castle wall where it could be scaled by a twelve-foot ladder. But he himself "would foremost be of all," he insisted; "and if," he added to Randolph, "you think you will essay to pass up after me that way, up to the wall I shall you bring, if God keep us from being perceived by them that watch on the wall." To this proposition Randolph joyfully assented, and preparations for the daring attempt were set afoot forthwith.

Thirty men were chosen for the perilous attack, men, we may be sure, in whose climbing powers Randolph had confidence, and "on a mirk night" they assembled secretly at the foot of the north side of the castle rock. Randolph himself was of the company, for he was not of the type to send his men into a peril which he himself would not share ; and so, following close behind William Francis, he faced all the dangers of the way. "The crag was high and hideous and the climbing right perilous," says Barbour, and that nobody who looks at the castle rock to-day requires to be told. We can well believe, moreover, that in the darkness of that March night the climb was only accomplished "with meikle pain."

When half-way up, the party were so "breathless

and weary" that they crouched for a few minutes'
breathing-space on "a broad place" under the shelter
of the overhanging rock.   Then it was that the dramatic
incident, so often narrated, occurred.   Right above them
on the wall the officers of the watch going their rounds
came to a stop, and peered down into the darkness.
Well might Barbour exclaim :

> "Now help them, God, that all things may!
> For in full great peril are they.
> For, might they see them, they should nane
> Escape out of that place unslain."

But wondrous dark was the night, he adds, and so they
were not perceived, though one of the watch, either
thinking to alarm his comrades, or perchance having
heard some unwonted sound, suddenly "swappit down
a stone," and cried out, "Away! I see you well."   The
stone came hurtling down the rock ; in grim silence the
gallant thirty crouched as closely as possible to the
towering crag; and as, striking an overhanging piece of
rock above them, the missile went flying out over their
heads into the darkness, they dared not even breathe a
sigh of relief.   They could but "sit still, lurking each
one."   For a moment the officers of the watch stood
listening, but no sound floated upwards through the
black darkness, and presently, all unsuspicious, they took
themselves away.

The thirty lost no time in resuming their ascent,
and, dragging their ladder after them, "towards the wall
climbed hastily."   Presently, after "great peril and
pain" they reached their goal, and without more ado
placed the ladder against the wall at a point where it
was nigh twelve feet high.   Still keeping the perilous
place of honour which was his so justly, William Francis
was the first to mount the ladder, and hard behind him
followed Sir Andrew Gray and Randolph himself.   And,
adds Barbour, when Randolph's men saw their lord
climbing the wall so boldly, they climbed after him like
men who were mad.   But before they had all got up
the watch heard sounds of "both stirring and speaking

and also the clanking of armour." Shouting an alarm
they dashed for the wall, and in a twinkling fierce
hand-to-hand fighting was in progress. Then in the
darkness of the night, with a sheer drop of 200 feet
below them, men fought, and shouted, and struggled on
the top of the wall, while within the castle itself cries of
" Treason! Treason!" arose, and wild confusion reigned.
The constable, clad in full armour and followed by
many of his men, rushed out while the fight on the wall
was still raging, but ere he could fling himself into it
Randolph and his men had driven back their assailants
and gained the firm ground within the wall. But they
were still in great danger, for they were far outnumbered
and " the constable and his company met him and his
right sturdily."

The Lanercost Chronicle has it that " in the evening
one day the besiegers of that castle delivered an assault
in force upon the south gate, because owing to the
position of the castle there was no other quarter where an
assault could be made. Those within gathered together
at the gate and offered a stout resistance ; but meanwhile
other Scots climbed the rock on the north side, which
was very high and fell away steeply from the foot of the
wall. There they had laid ladders to the wall, and
climbed up in such numbers that those within could not
withstand them ; and then they threw open the gates,
admitted their comrades, got possession of the whole
castle, and killed the English."

This account, I think, may be taken as filling in the
gaps in Barbour's narrative, and certainly explains the
speedy appearance *in full armour* of the constable, " and
with him many hardy and stout," for armour in mediæval
times was certainly not put on in a moment. It also
has the merit of probability to commend it. Randolph
may well have thought to absorb the attention of the
enemy by an attack in force on the south gate. At all
events when the constable and his company met Randolph
and his men there ensued a brief period of fierce fighting,
during which the Scots were hard put to it to hold their

own against a numerically superior foe.   But presently
the constable was slain in the midst of the mêlée, and
with his fall the heart went out of his men.   The Scots
pressed home their advantage, the English broke, and a
sauve qui peut followed.   All resistance was soon at an
end, and Edinburgh Castle was once again in the possession
of the Scots.[1]

The date of the capture is some time in March 1314.
Fordun gives it as the 14th of the month, which is
probably right, and in any case is as near the real date as
it is possible now to get.   Immediately after its capture
the castle, in accordance with Bruce's invariable practice,
was destroyed, and for many years it remained a mere
tumbled ruin, as an English force which endeavoured to
take refuge in it in the next reign discovered to its cost.
Other castles in Lothian fell into the hands of the Scots
during the autumn and winter of 1313–14, though of
their capture no record remains.   But when, a bare three
months after the fall of Edinburgh, Edward II led his
mighty army into Scotland, of all the castles which at
the beginning of his reign seven years before had owned
his sway, Berwick, Bothwell, Stirling, Jedburgh, and
Dunbar alone remained in precarious allegiance to him.
Lothian had at last, to all intents and purposes, been
recovered by war from the hands of the English.

As soon as the destruction of Edinburgh Castle was
complete, Randolph, as we have seen, marched away with
his men towards Stirling, to join the rest of the Scottish
army which was assembling in the Torwood in expectation
of the coming of the English.   Thus Edinburgh Castle
is the last of the Scottish strongholds known to have
fallen into the hands of the Scots prior to the battle of
Bannockburn, and its capture is therefore a fitting climax
to the first phase of Bruce's struggle for the freedom of
Scotland, and a fitting prelude to Bannockburn itself.

---

[1] Sir Thomas Gray, who wrote his narrative while a prisoner in
Edinburgh Castle, says simply : " Peres Lebaud, a Gascon knight, was
Sheriff of Edinburgh, from whom the people of Thomas Randolph, Earl
of Moray, who had besieged the said castle, took it at the highest part of
the rock, where he suspected no danger."

Moreover, its capture, alike in the daring of its conception and the gallantry of its execution, comes as a final example of the qualities and the spirit which had sustained the Scots through so many years of varying war, and were soon to lead them to overwhelming triumph on the field of Bannockburn.

CHAPTER XXXVIII

THE PRELUDE TO BANNOCKBURN

Our study of the War of Independence has now brought us to the eve of the greatest event in that war, to the eve of the most famous episode in the whole history of Scotland—the battle of Bannockburn. Fortunately it is not necessary for us to attempt to solve the many problems in connection with the battle, which, for nearly six hundred years, have baffled and misled historians, for the most of these have been solved, once and for all, within the last few months by another Highland writer, Mr. W. M. Mackenzie.[1] It is sufficient to say here that Mr. Mackenzie's conclusions are, in the main, incontrovertible; that his account of the battle, which is based on the only dependable authorities, is the only feasible account which has ever been written; that his views have been accepted by the few modern authorities competent to form a critical opinion of any value, especially by the greatest of English authorities on the period, Professor Tout; and that his facts and conclusions fit in with the history of the war prior to June 1314 as we have elucidated it. Our account of the battle, accordingly, is based on Mr. Mackenzie's book and Professor Tout's criticisms thereon, though in some matters of detail conclusions are come to which differ from those of Mr. Mackenzie, for reasons which will be made clear in their place, while certain questions are discussed which Mr. Mackenzie either passes by or only touches on in cursory fashion.

We have seen that by the beginning of May at latest, and probably some weeks earlier, the Scots had begun to assemble in force in the Torwood, that is in the wooded

[1] *The Battle of Bannockburn*, by W. M. Mackenzie. (Maclehose.)

country to the south of the Bannock Burn.   Thus Bruce
had ample time in which to make his dispositions and
prepare his men for the ordeal which lay before them.
The steadiness and discipline displayed by the Scots on
the day of Bannockburn show that the opportunity thus
afforded was not wasted.   Bruce knew, none better, the
long odds against which his men were presently to be
matched, and he would not have been the fine soldier he
was had he not appreciated the immense value of training and discipline in such a contest.   Bannockburn
stands out from all the battles which the Scots ever fought
as the single one in which the " perfervidum ingenium
Scotorum " was suitably restrained, in which the whole
Scottish army moved at the bidding of one consummate
tactician, at which the chances of victory were not im-
perilled by over-eagerness or rashness.

We come now to the very interesting and thorny
question of the numbers engaged at Bannockburn.
Many good Scotsmen regard it as tantamount almost
to an act of treason to suggest that the English army
numbered a single man less than 100,000 or the Scots a
single man more than 30,000.   But it may at once be
said that both these figures are altogether out of the
question.   They are but figments of too patriotic imagi-
nations, the fact being that no civilised country in the
Middle Ages could have put into the field a force approaching anything like 100,000 men.   It was the
fashion of mediæval chroniclers to indulge in tall talk
where numbers were concerned ; and it has been proved
times without number that they were utterly without
sense of proportion in such matters, and altogether
untrustworthy and misleading.   One fact alone will
suffice to make this clear.   The population of England
at the close of the thirteenth century numbered at most
only 2,000,000, while that of Scotland probably did
not exceed 400,000.

Mr. Mackenzie estimates the English strength at
Bannockburn at about 20,000 all told, and the Scots at
7000.   It may at once be said that, whether he is right

or not, he cannot be very far wrong. We know from the English official documents of the time that the actual number of foot soldiers ordered to be levied in England and Wales for the Bannockburn campaign was 21,540. We also know that the total number levied never, on any occasion, assembled. Contemporary official documents leave no room for doubt on that point. But the documents which would have given the actual strength of the English army at Bannockburn perished with much else on that fateful day. So we are compelled to fall back on other data in order to arrive at some conclusion as to what proportion of the men levied responded to the summons. Certain figures of Edward I's reign provide us with a basis, and on examining them we find that, as a rule, not more than fifty per cent. of the foot soldiers levied could be depended on to answer the call. If, in the special circumstances of the Bannockburn campaign, we assume that about two-thirds would respond— and that would be a large proportion—we get 14,000 English and Welsh foot soldiers. Four thousand archers and foot were also ordered from Ireland, and as they had longer notice, and as some of them were also probably part of the permanently embodied army of occupation, 3000 of them may actually have been at Bannockburn. That gives us a total of 17,000 foot.

The number of horsemen next arises. We have seen frequently in the course of these articles that the number of mounted men in an invading army, in a garrison, or on an expedition, was never large. Their strength consisted not in their numbers, but in their armour, horses, and equipment. Even Barbour, who gives Bruce 30,000 men at Bannockburn, gives him only 500 horsemen, while we know from numerous contemporary documents that in point of numbers the cavalry always formed a small proportion of a mediæval army. For example, in July 1297, Hugh de Cressingham reported to Edward that the army which he was about to lead into Scotland numbered 300 covered horse and 10,000 foot.[1] As it

[1] Stevenson, ii. 202.

happens there is no official record in existence to enable us to form an estimate of the cavalry at Bannockburn, but the facts just cited show that they must have numbered very much less than the foot. A contemporary English chronicler [1] places them at 2000, while a contemporary Scottish churchman—Abbot Bernard of Arbroath—who wrote a poem in celebration of the battle, makes them 3100. Neither of these estimates can be very far from the truth, and if we split the difference and place the cavalry arm of the English army at 2500 we are probably very near the real figure.

We thus arrive at 17,000 foot—English, Welsh, and Irish—and 2500 horse, a total of, in round numbers, 20,000. To these we have to add, however, men from the French provinces, as well as a certain number of Scots, which latter Barbour terms "a great party," a phrase which may mean anything. When all is said and done, however, the English army at the very outside could not have numbered more than 22,000 men, of whom 3000 at the most were mounted. Mr. Mackenzie is not disposed to place it at more than 20,000, but it is of course impossible to dogmatise on such a point. The most that can be said is that it could not have numbered more than 22,000, and is unlikely to have numbered less than 15,000, and that either of those figures would, at that time, have meant an army of extraordinary strength.

When we come to consider the question of the size of the Scottish army, we find ourselves confronted with a problem of much greater difficulty, for we have no official documents to go upon, and, indeed, no contemporary record of any value whatsoever. We have, however, one plain, undoubted fact to help us, the fact that the English army very greatly outnumbered the Scottish. Barbour, who puts the English strength at 100,000 "and more," gives the Scots 30,000 "and more." This means that the English outnumbered the Scots by more than three to one, and Mr. Mackenzie suggests that we should

[1] *Vita Edwardi Secundi.*

adopt this proportion, which all accounts of the battle make clear cannot be greatly, if at all, exaggerated, and apply it in light of the ascertained facts regarding the English army. On this basis he places the Scottish army at 7000 men, and though he does not pursue the matter further, it may be said that this estimate, small though it may seem, not only cannot be very far wrong, but may even err on the side of magnitude.

We have already remarked that at the close of the thirteenth century it is unlikely that the population of Scotland numbered more than 400,000. Five hundred years later, in 1801, when the first census was taken, it was only 1,608,000. By the date of the battle of Bannockburn, however, the fighting strength of even that population of 400,000 must have been greatly reduced, for there had been twenty years of almost incessant warfare. Moreover, all the fighting population was not on Bruce's side. So that, on the broad facts of the case, the Scottish army at Bannockburn could not have been large.

Unexpected confirmation of this general conclusion is to be found in the pages of Barbour, as an examination of his narrative will demonstrate. The Scottish army, he tells us, was divided into four divisions or battles. Of these the first, the vanguard, was assigned to Randolph. Mr. Mackenzie, too hastily interpreting a phrase of Barbour, says that with Randolph was "the general mass of men of higher rank." This is quite erroneous. The general mass of men of higher rank, so far as they formed a separate entity, made up the cavalry division under Sir Robert Keith. Barbour, describing the assembling of the Scottish troops, tells how "the Earl of Moray, with his men arrayed well, came also there in good condition for to fight"; and, when he comes to describe the arrangement of the Scottish army, says, to him Bruce "gave the vaward in leading; for in his noble governing and in his high chivalry they relied right sovereignly. And for to maintain his banner, lords, that

2 E

of great worship were, were assigned with their men into his battle for to be."

Now, these two extracts read together can have only one meaning. Randolph and his own men—that is the men of the earldom of Moray—formed the vanguard, and certain knights and nobles, who were not his vassals, were likewise placed under his command along with their followings. Randolph's own men were, of course, the knights, landholders, and free tenants of the famous fighting province who had fought so sturdily for Bruce through all the many years of the war, and to whom Bruce had, two years before, given a leader of their own in the person of his nephew. Nobody who has read these pages thus far can have any doubt on that point. The unnamed "lords, that of great worship were," were, very probably, those knights and nobles from Moray and the surrounding districts whose overlord Randolph was not, but who had fought in Bruce's early campaigns, and both before and after Randolph's elevation to the earldom, side by side with the men who now acknowledged Randolph as their overlord. For it was part of Bruce's carefully-devised scheme that the Scots at Bannockburn fought under their own proven leaders. Edward Bruce and James Douglas, as we shall see, led into action, in their divisions, the men whom they had led in so many a dashing exploit and on so many a daring raid. That is to say they led not only their own feudal vassals, as we should of course expect, but also the men —knights, squires, landholders, burgesses, free tenants, and the like—who had been in the habit of fighting under their command during the war. And as it was with Edward Bruce and James Douglas, so it was with Randolph.

Now, the strength of the vanguard, as Barbour lets us know in indirect but unmistakable fashion, was 500 men, and Sir Thomas Gray's account of the skirmish between it and Clifford's cavalry on the eve of Bannockburn bears this out. Barbour, besides definitely placing Randolph's force which opposed Clifford at 500, gives

Clifford 800, and remarks elsewhere that Randolph's foes "were more than he." Sir Thomas Gray, whose father fought by Clifford's side, and was captured by the Scots, says the English numbered 300, and states most explicitly that Randolph led his division—not, be it noted, a part of it—against them. As to this, indeed, there is no room for doubt, and no suggestion to the contrary has, so far as I am aware, ever been made. But it is well to have it made clear that both Barbour and Gray agree on this point.

Accordingly we find an English cavalry force, intent on the relief of Stirling Castle, and numbering at least 300 and at most 800 men, waiting, after they had passed Randolph, and when no barrier lay between them and their objective, for the Scots to come up with them. Plainly, therefore, the advancing Scots could not have been of great strength, and Barbour's emphatic statement that they numbered " 500, no more," cannot, in consequence, be controverted, and that whether Sir Thomas Gray's figure or the Scottish poet's be accepted for Clifford's force. If the former, then 500 is clearly the highest possible figure for Randolph's men ; if the latter, then we have Barbour's definite statement as to their number, his further statement that the English out-numbered them, and the undoubted fact that the English cavalry turned deliberately from their course in order, as they thought, to win easy honour for themselves, and perform a feat of arms, by routing them.

Five hundred men may seem, at a first glance, so surprisingly small a number for the Scottish van that it may prove hard of belief to some. But readers of these articles will have noticed that all through the war the numbers engaged on both sides were very much smaller than has for centuries been popularly believed. When we turn back to Barbour's account of Bruce's campaign against the Comyns in Aberdeenshire in the winter of 1307, we find that he places Bruce's force at only 700 men. But, as we have seen, Bruce had by then, by the aid of the men of Moray, humbled the Earl of Ross and compelled him to agree to a long truce. Accordingly, when he turned from Ross to Aberdeen, and, marching through Moray, descended on the Comyn country, he had behind him practically the full fighting strength of the patriotic province, as well as a number of adherents from elsewhere. Yet his total force was only 700 men, a figure which, when allowance is made for the ravages of war, corresponds very strikingly to the number which Barbour assigns to Randolph's division at Bannockburn, a division composed of the very men who had formed the bulk of Bruce's northern force in 1307.

There can be little doubt, therefore, that the first of the four divisions of the Scottish army at Bannockburn consisted of, in round figures, 500 men. Like the other three divisions, the van fought on foot, and it is worthy of remark that, at that period, as for many centuries previously, the vast majority of the men north of the Forth who owed military service fought not on horse but on foot. The great magnates and the knights were horsemen, but there were not many of these in all the great district which lay north of the Spey, while even they were in the habit of fighting on foot just as frequently as on horseback. But the general body of landholders and free tenants were foot-soldiers pure and simple, their service being of the kind known as Scottish service. In any northern levy it was they who formed the bulk and the backbone. It must be understood, moreover, that they were not of the class known as the " small folk." The landholders comprised chiefs, thanes, lairds, and so on, while the free tenants corresponded to the tacksmen and farmers of a later generation.

In the province of Moray, as we have already seen, these landholders and free tenants occupied a particularly favourable place, holding their lands direct from the king, and following a banner of their own, the banner of Moray. With them must also be reckoned the burgesses, each burgh having to supply a quota of fighting men to the royal army. The burghs owing military service to Randolph were Elgin, Forres, and Nairn, while the burgesses of Inverness, though not vassals of Randolph, would also fight under his banner. The number of burgesses, however, would be small, probably not more than eighty or a hundred in all from the four burghs. It was over these men then—the knights, landholders, burgesses, and free tenants of Moray—that Randolph had been set as their feudal leader; and in choosing them to form the van of his army, Bruce was choosing men who had been trained from their earliest days to fight on foot, and men, moreover, in whose fighting capacity he had every reason to feel the highest confidence. It was, however, assuredly not simply because they were good fighting men that Bruce assigned to the men of Moray the place of honour in the Scottish army. The giving to them of that honour was a recognition of the great part they had played in Bruce's struggle for a kingdom, as well as a proof that Bruce had extraordinary faith in their valour and their steadfastness.

This brings us to another point. Why is it that at Bannockburn the Scottish army fought on foot, the cavalry playing only a subsidiary, though important, part? Barbour tells us the latter numbered " 500 armed well in steel, that on light horses were horsed well," and their special duty was to disperse the English archers. Now mediæval cavalry was of two kinds, heavy and light. The former were fully armed knights and men-at-arms mounted on " covered," that is armour-protected, horses, and in a Scottish army were never numerous. The latter were knights and men-at-arms, more or less fully armed, mounted on unarmoured horses. The Scottish cavalry at Bannockburn was clearly of the latter type, and, accordingly, would be at a serious disadvantage in close hand-to-hand fighting, either with heavy cavalry or with footmen armed with spears. Barbour puts words into Bruce's mouth, which show that the disadvantage was well understood. He makes him announce to his men his intention of meeting the English on foot, "for if we attempt to fight on horse, then our foes are more of might and better horsed than are we; we should in great peril be." The words, of course, are apocryphal, but they none the less convey the truth so far as the comparative strength of the Scottish and English cavalry is concerned, though they are wrong in so far as they suggest that this was the real reason why the Scots at Bannockburn fought on foot.

Bruce's army fought on foot for two reasons. In the first place, it was the manner in which Scottish armies nearly always fought; and, in the second place, the army itself was composed almost entirely of foot-soldiers, and foot-soldiers of a type very different from the prevailing type of infantry in England and in other countries where the cult of the fully-armed horseman predominated. In Scotland the foot-soldier had largely preserved his identity and his importance. He was not regarded as a mere auxiliary to the mounted men-at-arms, for the simple reason that in Scotland there never was a very large body of the class perhaps best described by the modern term feudal chivalry. It was the Scottish infantry which won Stirling Bridge, it was the Scottish infantry which went down before the English archers at Falkirk, it was the Scottish infantry which, two hundred years later, formed the grim impenetrable ring which died round James IV at Flodden.

At Bannockburn, moreover, Bruce was weaker in the cavalry arm than any Scottish king had been for two centuries, for he had no heavy cavalry whatsoever to oppose to the mailclad knights and men-at-arms of England. War-horses, that is horses of the peculiar strength and breed which alone could carry effectively the weight of a fully-armed knight and his horse-armour, were always valuable commodities, as the official documents of the time very clearly show. In Scotland, by the time of Bannockburn, they were few and far between, twenty years of warfare having almost wiped out whatever stock there had been, and the same cause preventing the importation of more from England or the Continent. That is why the 500 " armed well in steel " are described by Barbour as mounted on light horses, and that is why their share in the actual fighting was limited to dispersing the English archers.

We thus see that the Scottish army at Bannockburn fought on foot because it was the way in which Scottish armies were accustomed to fight, and because, in the special circumstances of Bannockburn, it could, even it would, have fought in no other way. In fighting on foot, moreover, the knights and magnates who fought side by side in the schiltroms with Randolph, Edward Bruce, Douglas, and their men were not fighting in a manner to which they were unaccustomed, or in a manner deemed unworthy of their knighthood, as would have been the case in England. They were but fighting as they and their ancestors had often fought, and as their successors were often yet to fight. So the Scottish army at Bannockburn was an army of infantry, an army of skilled, disciplined, veteran infantry, supported by a single division of cavalry, and light cavalry at that.[1]

The second division of the Scottish army was commanded by Edward Bruce, and Barbour tells us that he came to the place of assembly " with a full great company of good men, armed well and dicht, hardy and strong for the fight." Now, Edward Bruce had, ever since the battle of Inverurie on Christmas Eve 1307, commanded a force of his own with which he had performed many doughty exploits, including the conquest of Galloway. He had also, as readers will remember, led Bruce's army in the campaign in Aberdeenshire which followed the battle of Inverurie, proceeding thereafter, in the middle of 1308, to Galloway with a force which included, among others, as the Lanercost chronicler tells us, men from the Isles. It is probable that that force also included a number of the Aberdeenshire men who had fought under his banner

---

[1] It is a remarkable fact, too often overlooked, that the Scottish fighting man has almost invariably been a foot-soldier. The Scottish mercenaries who in the seventeenth century carried the martial fame of the Scots to every country in Europe were foot-soldiers. The Scottish armies from Bannockburn to Culloden were almost entirely composed of foot-soldiers. The men who have made the name of Scotland world-famous by their exploits in the British army have been, with hardly an exception, foot-soldiers.

in the early part of 1308, and it certainly contained some knights from the south-west, of whom we know Sir Alan Cathcart to have been one.[1] James Douglas and Walter Stewart, who commanded the third division, had taken little leading part in any of the northern campaigns, Douglas's energies being confined to the districts which lay in the neighbourhood of his own country, that is in and about Roxburgh, Selkirk, Peebles, Lanark, and Dumfries ; while Walter Stewart was, at the date of Bannockburn, but a mere youth. It is, accordingly, highly probable that the men from Aberdeen and the neighbouring counties fought in Edward Bruce's division at Bannockburn, and that the rest of his command was composed of such of the men of Galloway as had acknowledged his overlordship and fought under his banner prior to the summer of 1314, with, of course, the addition of knights like Sir Alan Cathcart, who had been in the habit of fighting under his command.

The third division, though nominally led by Walter Stewart, was really under the command of James Douglas, and Barbour leaves no doubt as to who formed its backbone. Douglas, he tells us, brought with him, as we should have expected, " men that were well used to fighting," who feared no odds and were not likely to give way to panic, no matter how many their foes might be. Walter Stewart, he likewise says, " came with a rout of noble men," which means probably that he was accompanied by the knights and others who owed him feudal service as the lord of broad lands in Renfrewshire. At all events it is clear that Douglas's men were the men whom he had led so frequently into England, the hard-bitten, war-inured warriors so well described in the pages of Froissart, the forerunners of the moss-troopers of the borders. They came chiefly from Douglas's own country and its neighbourhood, the district which we may describe as the Middle South lying between Galloway on the one hand and Lothian on the other.

Bruce himself led the fourth division, which formed

[1] Barbour.

the reserve, and was posted in a position which would enable it to advance easily and quickly to the aid of any division which might stand in need of assistance. It, Barbour tells us explicitly, was composed of " the men of Carrick all wholly, and of Argyll and of Kintyre, and of the Isles, whereof was Sir Angus of the Isles, and Bute " ; while " of the plain-land he had also a mekill rout." But in which division were the men of Lennox, Menteith, and the neighbouring districts, those gallant warriors who had served Bruce so well? Unhappily, Barbour gives no hint of any kind to guide us, but looking to the great part which Edward Bruce had played throughout the war, and to the fact that many of his exploits were performed in the district between Clyde and Forth and the country immediately north and south thereof—the capture of Dundee and Rutherglen, for example—I am inclined to think that they were in his division, especially as Barbour does not say they were in Bruce's own division, in which we might have expected to find the Lennox men.

Now at first sight it would seem as if Bruce's division must have been extremely strong in numbers. But the total strength which Alexander of the Isles and his son, John of Lorn, had at their call in 1309 was 800 men,[1] and that though they had 500 men in their pay and were allied with Alexander of the Isles. That John of Lorn was not under-estimating his strength when he put it at this figure a record of 1307 shows, for he then received pay for 22 men-at-arms and 800 foot from Argyll engaged in the pursuit of Bruce in Galloway.[2] Accordingly, the whole available force of Argyll and the Isles in 1314 must be numbered by hundreds, not by thousands. And so with the men of Kintyre and Bute. When Bruce landed in Carrick in 1307 his following was composed mainly of men from Kintyre and the Isles ; yet his total force did not exceed 300 all told.

Again, in 1303 Edward I summoned the young Earl of Carrick, the future king, to join him with the men of

---

[1] Bain, iii. 80. [2] *Ibid.*, ii. 520.

Kyle, Cunningham, Cumnock, and Carrick to the number of 1000.[1] At the same time 1000 foot were summoned from Galloway.[2] Thus the fighting strength of the whole of the modern counties of Ayr, Dumfries, Kirkcudbright, and Wigtown was, in 1303, reckoned at about 2000 foot, besides men-at-arms, who were comparatively few, probably considerably under 100 altogether. If we suppose that the same number of foot-soldiers was available in 1314, which is exceedingly unlikely, we find that half of the 2000 would be in the division of Edward Bruce, now Lord of Galloway, and that of the remaining half the men of Carrick formed only a part. Similarly the men of Bute could only have been few, while the "mekill rout" from the "plain-land" could not have numbered more than a few hundred at most. They were probably drawn in part from Kyle and Cunningham, and in part from the borders of Lothian, the latter probably men whose lords were dead or still on the side of England.

There is, moreover, another point. Not all of the men from Moray and Ross, from Mar, Aberdeen, Angus, and the Mearns, from Menteith and Lennox, from Galloway, Renfrew, and the Middle South, from Argyll and the Isles, from Kintyre and Bute, who assembled in the Torwood fought in the four divisions which formed the ordered array of the Scottish army at Bannockburn. Only the well-armed men were there. The rest, as we shall see presently, were with the misnamed "campfollowers," who by their timely appearance created so great a panic in the ranks of the disheartened English. Thus Bruce's division, which was clearly the strongest division, did not number, on a liberal estimate, more than 2000 men, and if we allow 1000 to each of the divisions of Edward Bruce and James Douglas, which seeing that Randolph had only 500 is rather an over than an under estimate, we have 4000 to add to the 500 of Randolph and the 500 cavalry—a total of 5000 men of all ranks. If it be objected that 1000 seems small for Edward Bruce, seeing that he was Lord of Galloway, a district which in

---

[1] Stevenson, ii. 178; Bain, ii. 1049. [2] *Ibid.*

1297 could of itself put 1000 foot in the field, it must be remembered that a great part of Galloway was in spirit still hostile to Bruce; and that Edward Bruce, though its nominal lord, could not, even if he would, have compelled the fighting men of these districts to follow him. Mr. Mackenzie draws attention to two facts which go to show that this estimate of the size of the Scottish army is not far out. After Randolph had repulsed Clifford, on the afternoon of the day before the battle, almost all the fighting men of the Scottish army crowded round to congratulate him, and were addressed on the spot by Bruce himself—both obvious impossibilities had the army been large.

Several other facts may be mentioned, which indicate the comparative smallness of the Scottish army. Bruce sent out James Douglas and Sir Robert Keith with a number of "well-horsed men" to observe the advance of the English army. They were so greatly impressed with what they saw that they told the king of it privately, and received orders to spread a report to the contrary effect, and to represent the enemy as discouraged and confused, lest the spirits of the Scots should sink at the thought of the long odds against them. Again, after Randolph's defeat of Clifford's cavalry, and the repulse of the English advance-guard with the death of de Bohun, Bruce addressed his army, and put it to them whether they had done enough for honour and should now retire, or whether they would remain where they were and fight on the morrow. Finally, there is Sir Thomas Gray's story, which he must have had from his father, who was at that moment a prisoner in the Scottish camp, that in the evening of the day which had witnessed Clifford's defeat and de Bohun's death, the Scots "thought they had done well enough for the day, and were on the point of decamping in order to march during the night into the Lennox, a stronger country," when an English traitor came to Bruce with news of the discouragement into which the events of the day had thrown the English, and decided him to stake all on a battle the following morning.

I have remarked, however, that the four divisions of the Scottish army did not comprise all the fighting men who had flocked to join Bruce in the Torwood. These divisions, it must again be emphasized, were composed, as Barbour makes clear, of picked men, that is of well-armed soldiers, knights, landholders, free tenants, burgesses, and the like, the tried and proven warriors whom Bruce and his lieutenants had led to victory so often, and whom the stern experience of war and the genius of their leaders had welded into fighting material of the highest class. But there was a host of others besides these, the men who are famous in the story of Bannockburn as "the gillies," a name which has caused a great deal of misunderstanding, and which is, in fact, a complete misnomer.

Barbour in describing Bruce's arrangements tells us that, after he had formed his four battles, "all the small folk and pouerale he sent with harness and victual into the park," where they concealed themselves in a valley. When he comes to speak of their dramatic appearance at the moment when the English ranks were breaking he describes them as "yeomen, swains, and poueraill, that in the park to guard the victual were left." Now it has always been assumed that the men so described were camp-followers and nothing else. But Barbour most explicitly says that this was not so—and he is the only authority. He divides them in the clearest possible way into small folk and "pouerale," the last mentioned, literally "poor folk," being the actual camp-followers. The rest were, as he says, "small folk," that is, as he also says, "yeomen and swains." They were men who had come to fight, but men whom Bruce did not consider sufficiently well armed or disciplined to take their place with the picked men in the schiltroms upon whose fighting effectiveness and disciplined valour he was staking all his hopes of victory.

Now, as it happens, Barbour elsewhere uses the phrase "small folk" in a manner which leaves no possible doubt as to his meaning, and shows, moreover, that it was a perfectly well understood term. If we turn back to our account of the battle of Inverurie we may read there how when Bruce advanced against Buchan and his friends at Old Meldrum, "a little on bridle rein they them withdrew," and Bruce, seeing this, "pressed on them with his banner." Whereupon "they withdrew them more and more. And when the small folk they had there saw their lords withdraw them so, they turned their backs all and fled. . . . The lords, that yet together were, saw that their small folk were fleeing, and saw the king stoutly coming. They were each one so dismayed that they their backs turned and fled." There cannot be the slightest doubt as to what "small folk" means there. They were fighting men similar to those whom Barbour, in his account of the battle at the Pass of Brandir, describes as "men who light and nimble were, and light arming had on them." They were, in a word, the light troops of a mediæval Scottish army.

It is important, moreover, to observe that Bannockburn differed in one very important respect from almost every other battle on a large scale which the Scots ever fought. The fierce charges of Highlanders and Galwegians were conspicuous by their absence, and the battle was fought and won by steady well-ordered infantry. In an Act of the Scottish Parliament, passed only four years after Bannockburn, we have that infantry described. It was then ordained [1] that "every landed man having ten pounds in goods shall have for his body and for defence of the Realm, one sufficient Acton (a padded leather jacket), one basnet (a steel head-covering), and gloves of plate with a spear and a sword. Who has not an Acton and basnet, he shall have one good habirgeon (a chain neck-covering) and one good iron jack (back and breast pieces) for his body; and a hat of iron and gloves of plate." So here, beyond question, we have the Scottish infantry who won Bannockburn, men protected by steel head-pieces, body armour, and gloves of mail, and carrying each a spear and sword—the heavy-armed infantry as

[1] Acts of Parl., i. 113.

opposed to the "small folk," the folk who, not having "ten pounds in goods," were only required to provide themselves with "a good spear or a good bow with a sheaf of twenty-four arrows."

Barbour places the number of small folk and camp-followers who were sent to the valley at 20,000, and later tells us that 15,000 of them formed the company whose sudden appearance completed the discomfiture of the disheartened English. These figures are, of course, exaggerated, but not to the same extent as those of the army proper. For many of the knights and landholders, and especially those from the Highlands, must have been accompanied by a considerable following of ill-armed men, whose only weapons were bows, axes, swords, spears, dirks, or knives. It was these men who formed the bulk of the force sent to the valley, a conclusion which Barbour bears out still further when he says that the reason for their hastening to take part in the fight was their seeing " their lords " giving such a good account of themselves against the English. In fact there can be no question that the men who appeared so dramatically when the ranks of England were breaking, were for the most part the rank and file of the clans, those ardent fighters of Bruce's Argyll campaign, "who light and nimble were, and light arming had on them."

That Bruce acted wisely in sending these impetuous warriors to lie in a valley well to his rear, until such time as he could use them with advantage, no student of Scottish history can question. Time and again in their wars against the English the Scots flung away, by their own undisciplined valour, sometimes the chance of victory, sometimes a victory already more than half won. The Battle of the Standard two centuries before Bannockburn, and Cromwell's battle at Dunbar three centuries after, tell the same tale, with many another in the centuries between. Accordingly, in sending far to the rear the impetuous Highlanders and Galwegians of the rank and file, and the ill-armed yeoman and country folk, Bruce was putting into effect two principles of mediæval warfare which his countrymen never learned to understand. The one was the folly of pitting ill-armed men, whatever their valour, against mail-clad men—a fact which Harlaw a century later impressed for all time on Highland history—and the other was the truth that numbers are not everything, that the disciplined few are better than the undisciplined many.

There remains, however, another point before we dismiss the men in the valley from our consideration. Mr. Mackenzie finds himself regretting that he knows of nothing which will enable him to say that the dramatic appearance of these men at the critical moment of the battle was part of Bruce's plan, a regret which many have shared. But is that regret well - founded? I venture to think it is not, for it seems to me impossible to doubt that their appearance was part of Bruce's plan. Consider the situation. Bruce deliberately sent these men to the rear because he knew that their presence in the ordered ranks of his army would be a danger rather than a help. But he also knew that they were fierce and gallant fighters, and that in certain circumstances they would be of the utmost value. Against an unbroken and well-ordered mediæval army they would be of no avail, but against an army which had become dispirited, or had lost its order and its cohesion, they would be of great service. Moreover, is it in the least likely that these ardent warriors would have retired quietly to lie perdu in a valley, when there was stark fighting forward, unless they had been promised their full share in due time? And, finally, there is the plain fact that they appeared at the very moment when their appearance was most advantageous to the Scottish army.

Now, Bruce was the most skilful soldier and tactician of his time, and eight years of continuous warfare had made him acquainted with the uses and the quality of all the available fighting material in Scotland. Long experience had taught him when to use and when not to use men of the type which he sent to the valley, and the mere fact that, on the eve of the battle, he placed these latter where he did is proof positive that the question of what should be done with them on that occasion had received serious consideration. Accordingly, if he decided deliberately not to utilise them in one phase of the approaching battle, it is impossible to imagine that in coming to that decision he gave no consideration to the other side of the case. That is to say, in deciding not to utilise them in circumstances unfavourable for their use, he could hardly have lost sight of the possibility of circumstances arising which might be favourable for their use. We are, therefore, forced to the conclusion that, when Bruce sent the small folk and camp-followers of the Scottish army to lie hidden in a valley to his rear, he, to put it at its lowest, contemplated the possibility of an occasion arising in which they might be useful. That the occasion did arise, and that prompt advantage was taken of it, seems to prove, in view of all the circumstances, that the sudden appearance of the undisciplined and ill-armed portion of the Scottish army was part of a deliberate plan.

We may, therefore, state Bruce's final dispositions in the Torwood as follows. In the van was Randolph with the men of Moray and the neighbouring districts. In the rear was Bruce himself in command of the reserve, consisting of the men of Carrick, Kintyre, Argyll, Bute, and the Islands, and a number of men from " the plainland." Between Bruce and Randolph, and parallel to each other, were the divisions of Edward Bruce and Douglas, composed, the former probably of men from Aberdeenshire, Perthshire, Lennox, and the neighbouring counties, and such men from Galloway as had accepted Edward Bruce as their lord, and the latter of Douglas's own hard-bitten veterans of the Middle South, along with Walter Stewart's men from Renfrew and its borders. In addition there was the 500 cavalry whose final position would be determined by the position of the English archers, and a host of several thousand light-armed Highlanders and country folk, who would be brought into action as opportunity should offer. In such wise did the Scots await in the Torwood the coming of their powerful enemy throughout the lengthening June days of 1314.

Note.—In arriving at the foregoing estimate of 5000 men as the number of Scots who formed the ordered array of the Scottish army at Bannockburn, I am considerably below Mr. Mackenzie's estimate of 7000, which, however, he is careful to point out, is only a rough and ready reckoning arrived at by allowing the Scots one-third of the 20,000 which he regards as the outside figure for the English army. On the eve of passing these pages for press, however, I have read a lecture delivered recently by Sir James Ramsay and printed in the *English Historical Review* for April 1914, in which he discusses the whole question of the numerical strength of mediæval armies. He places the armies at Bannockburn at 14,000 or 15,000 on the English side, " of whom 1000 might be lances," that is, mounted, mail-clad men, and at 3000 to 4000 on the Scottish side. As, however, he only allows the Scots three divisions, whereas there can be little doubt that there were four, and as the basis of his estimate is an allowance of 1000 to 1500 men for each division, there is not really much difference between us. He points out, too, that the nature and extent of the ground would not permit of a much larger figure, and though he makes that remark with the old accepted site of the battle in view, it is even more true of the real site. He also points out that an army of 15,000 on the English side would have been considered extremely large at the time.—E. M. B., 14th *May* 1914.

CHAPTER XXXIX

BANNOCKBURN: THE FIRST PHASE

In the Torwood the Scots lay until Saturday, the 22nd June 1314, on which day Bruce's scouts brought him word that the English had lain at Edinburgh the previous night. Whereupon he forthwith led his army northwards across the Bannock Burn,[1] and, in accordance with the plan already decided upon, took up his position on the undulating ground between Stirling Castle and the burn.[2] He had thus the Bannock Burn immediately in front of him to the south, and behind him, about two miles away, Stirling Castle and the Forth. On the east the Bannock Burn, about a mile from his position, turned sharply to the north, and fell into the Forth, about $2\frac{1}{2}$ miles to the north-east of the Scottish army. Thus the English, if they wished to give battle or reach Stirling, would be compelled to cross the Bannock Burn, and fight on ground bounded on three sides by the Forth and the Bannock, on ground, moreover, which was broken and marshy, and covered in places with wood.

There were two easy routes across the Bannock Burn to Stirling, and Bruce had to provide against an approach by either or both of these. The direct way was by the road which crossed the Bannock directly to the south of Bruce's position, and held straight through the New Park to Stirling. The other was by the level plain to the east of Bruce's position, where the banks of the Bannock were so low as to prove almost no obstacle to mounted men. The former was the natural way of approach, but it had one disadvantage. It ran for some

---

[1] Barbour, xi., line 356, &c.   [2] *Ibid.*, 281, &c.

distance through a wood, and, accordingly, was not
favourable for cavalry, whose ordered ranks would be
broken by the trees. But once clear of the trees the
road emerged on "ane playne field," on which the
English cavalry would have plenty of room to operate.
So to prevent this, Bruce on the Saturday set his men
to work on the famous pots, and by Sunday morning
the "plain field" for a considerable distance on each side of
the road was honeycombed with these concealed traps.
Bruce's flanks were thus protected, while at the same
time if the English horse attempted to deploy and ride
down the Scots by sheer weight of numbers they would
come to grief.

Early on the morning of Sunday, 23rd June, Bruce
himself inspected the pots, and expressed himself well
satisfied. Then he ordered his men to arm, "and when
they all assembled were, he arrayed them for the fight,"
and commanded that

> "Whosoever he was that found
> His heart not steadfast for to stand,
> To win all or die with honour,"

should "take his way betimes," and that

> "None should dwell with him but they
> That would stand with him to the end,
> And take the fate that God would send."

But there was no faint heart in the Scottish ranks. "All
answered with a shout" that they would fight to the
end. And in this high spirit the final dispositions were
made.

First of all the small folk and camp followers were
sent to a valley well to the rear of the Scottish position.
Then the Earl of Moray with the vanguard was posted
on a tree-covered slope beside St. Ninian's Kirk, which
lay at the extreme north of the Scottish position. His
division was thus the nearest to Stirling, and it was his
duty to guard the eastward approach to the castle, the
way over the shallows of the Bannock Burn and the level
plain. Bruce himself undertook to keep "the entry,"

as the regular road across the burn and through the wood
was called, and took up his position on the pot-protected
ground.   Between himself and Randolph he placed the
division of his brother Edward and that of Douglas and
Walter Stewart, with orders that they should lend assistance to whichever of the other two might require it.
The cavalry meantime were assigned no particular place.
Their position would be determined whenever the position of the English archers was disclosed.   It will be evident that by these dispositions the terms, vanguard and
rearguard, cease to have any significance.   Either Bruce
or Randolph might find himself commanding the van or
the rear, according as the English advanced by "the
entry" or the level plain.

As it drew towards midday on Sunday, 23rd June,
the waiting Scots got their first glimpse of the approaching
enemy.   Soon all eyes were riveted on the great host,
the largest and most magnificent array of armed men
that any there had ever looked upon.   Straight along
the road towards "the entry" it came, and so intent
were the Scots on watching it that no one observed the
body of horse under Sir Robert Clifford and Sir Henry
Beaumont, which had been detached from the main
army, and, under cover of the trees, had made a detour
towards the level plain to the east.   The eyes of Randolph
and his men, like the eyes of all others, were directed
towards the entry, and so it was that a rose fell from
Randolph's chaplet.   He had been set to guard the
passage by the plain, and, lo! already Clifford's force
had nearly passed it.

Right nobly did Randolph make amends for his
carelessness.   When he first saw the English horse they
were almost directly below his position, and his own
force was but infantry.   Yet not a moment did he
hesitate.   Out of the wood and down the slope he
rushed his men "in great haste,"[1] and marched them
rapidly across the level open ground towards the enemy.[2]
The English evidently were unaware of the presence

[1] Barbour.   [2] *Scalacronica.*

THE BATTLE OF BANNOCKBURN

FIRST PHASE

Sunday, 23rd June 1314

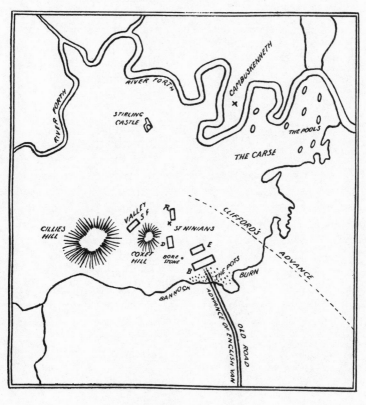

B—BRUCE.
E—EDWARD BRUCE.
D—DOUGLAS.
R—RANDOLPH.
SF—THE SMALL FOLK.

of the force by St. Ninian's Kirk, and certainly never dreamt that foot-soldiers would dare to attack cavalry. Moreover the way was now clear before them to Stirling, and as they were mounted they could, if they would, reach it without striking a blow. But as soon as Beaumont saw the advancing Scots [1]—

"Let us retire a little," he called to his men. "Let them come on. Give them room!"

"Sir," said Sir Thomas Gray, the narrative of whose son we are quoting, "I doubt that whatever you give them now, they will have all too soon."

"Very well," retorted Beaumont, "if you are afraid, be off!"

"Sir," answered Gray, "it is not from fear that I shall fly this day." So saying he spurred in between him and Sir William Deyncourt, and charged into the thick of the enemy. Deyncourt was killed, Gray was taken prisoner, his horse being killed on the pikes, and he himself carried off with the Scots on foot, when they marched away, "having utterly routed the squadron of the said two lords."

Thus the English version. Barbour gives us some further details. Randolph's men were in schiltrom, a formation similar to the modern British square, save that it was oval-shaped and bristled with spears. Against these spears, the spears of the men of Moray, the English horse rode in vain. The schiltrom was "environed all about"; the English raged round it like the French cavalry round the British squares at Waterloo, and "assailed it on ilka side," but the stubborn northern spearmen held their ground. Again and again the English tried to break that impenetrable ring, and failed. Then they took to casting spears and knives, and at last even swords and maces, at their foes, but the only result was that within the Scottish ring "a mountain was of weapons that were cast there." So the fight went on. The day was hot and the ground dry, and soon on both sides men were warm and weary, while

[1] *Scalacronica.*

from the field rose a great cloud of dust. Nevertheless, eager Scots rushed here and there from the schiltrom, and directing their spears at the horses, brought horse and rider crashing to the ground.

Douglas, watching the struggle from afar, grew anxious, and at last obtained Bruce's leave to go to Randolph's help. But as he drew near he saw the English were giving way, and so halted his men that Randolph and his gallant company might have all the honour. It was Douglas's approach, however, which gave Randolph the opportunity of turning a repulse into a rout. In vain had the English dashed themselves on his spears, but though they had failed to break the Scottish ring they were not yet broken themselves. But at the sight of Douglas hurrying to the rescue, " they gave way and made an opening." Whereupon Randolph, seeing his chance, at once rushed his men into the gap, " and pressed them so wondrous fast with hard strokes that at last they fled and durst not bide no more." Nor was their flight an orderly one. They rode away "in full great haste, not all together but separately," and they that were overtaken were slain. The rest went to their host, " of their loss sorry and woe."

That this is not a fanciful description, Sir Thomas Gray, whose father, a prisoner in the Scottish schiltrom, saw the whole affair, makes certain. The English were utterly routed,[1] he says, and " some of them fled to the castle and others to the king's army," thus confirming Barbour's statement that Randolph drove his exulting schiltrom into a gap in the English ranks. And so first blood was to the Scots. But, more important than that, their infantry had proved themselves superior to the dreaded English cavalry. Not only had they repulsed a fierce and prolonged attack of mounted knights and men-at-arms, but they had broken and scattered them and driven them in headlong flight from the field. More, the marvel had been witnessed of mounted mail-clad men fleeing from the pursuit of foot-soldiers. The

[1] *Scalacronica.*

moral effect of Randolph's victory was, therefore, tremendous. The sight of the English horsemen fleeing in wild disorder before the footmen from the North was worth 10,000 men to Bruce. It filled every man in his army with elation and ardour, and inspired all with the confidence which commands success. "From that moment," says the English chronicler of Lanercost, "began a panic among the English, and the Scots grew bolder."

Meanwhile, at the other end of the Scottish position, events of moment were taking place. The main body of the English had halted a mile or so to the south of the Bannock Burn in order "to take counsel"[1] as to their course. The advance guard, however, led by the Earls of Gloucester and Hereford, and full of overweening confidence, pressed hastily along the road towards the entry, at the very time, according to Barbour, when Douglas was hurrying off to the aid of Randolph. As they came out of the wood on to "the playne field," they saw Bruce, mounted on a small palfrey, marshalling his men. Henry de Bohun, Hereford's nephew, who was riding in front of the English van, perceived that the Scots were prepared, and were too strongly posted for the van alone to attack them. So he gave the signal for retiral, and as he did so Bruce rode forward as if to challenge him to single combat. De Bohun hesitated not a moment. Laying his lance in rest, he charged furiously down on the Scottish king, missed him, and went thundering past. But as he passed, Bruce, who carried only a battle-axe, rose in his stirrups and with one smashing blow cleft his head in twain. De Bohun tumbled in a heap to the ground, and ere the English had time to recover from the surprise and confusion caused by his fall, the Scots, fired to fierce ardour by their king's action, were advancing boldly upon them. Still confused by De Bohun's fall, the whole English van began to retreat, whereupon the Scots gave a great shout, and pressed hard after them. Sir Edward Bruce promptly brought up his men in support, but the English declined

[1] Barbour. See also *Scalacronica*, &c.

to give battle, and hastily fell back on the main body, leaving a number of dead behind them. With their retreat the first day's fighting ended, and full of confidence the Scots awaited the coming of the morrow.[1]

Elated though the Scots were by the events of 23rd June, it seems certain that Bruce contemplated retiring during the night to the wilds of the Lennox. No one was better able than he to judge the strength of the odds which his army would have to face on the morrow, and he may well have considered that enough had been done for honour. As a leader of experience and skill, he knew that great though the effect of the day's happenings on the morale of his men might be, they had after all only repulsed two small sections of the English army, and the circumstances would be very different when they were face to face with the whole strength of their foes, whose numbers and capacity he had now had good opportunity of estimating. It had, of course, always been his strategy to avoid a pitched battle in the open when the odds were against him, and never certainly had the odds been so great as those with which he was now confronted. Humanly speaking, his chances of success were infinitesimal, and it behoved him as a good leader to look at the situation from every point of view. The responsibility on his shoulders was enormous. Was he to stake all that he had striven for through so many years, as well as the lives and the fortunes of those who had followed him so loyally, on the issue of a single battle against an immensely superior force?

Barbour tells us that after Clifford's force had fled in confusion before Randolph and his men, the latter retired, either to their old position or to the main body of the army, and there were surrounded by their comrades, eager to congratulate them. Bruce, seeing his fighting-men all thus assembled, took the opportunity

---

[1] This account is taken from *Vita Edwardi Secundi*. Some people will have it that the story is fiction pure and simple. Yet it is confirmed by *Scalacronica*, and Barbour—which is sufficient for any intelligent person.

of placing the situation fairly before them. " If you think we should fight, we shall fight," he concluded ; "and if you think we should leave, we shall leave. I shall consent to whatever you desire. Therefore declare your will plainly." Whereupon, " with one voice," they demanded to be led against the English the following morning.

Compare this with Sir Thomas Gray's story.[1] " The Scots in the wood," he says, " thought they had done well enough for the day, and were on the point of decamping in order to march during the night into the Lennox, a stronger country, when Alexander de Seton, who was in the service of England and had come thither with the king, secretly left the English army, went to Robert de Bruce in the wood, and said to him, ' Sir, this is the time if ever you intend to undertake to reconquer Scotland. The English have lost heart and are discouraged, and expect nothing but a sudden, open attack.' Then he described their condition, and pledged his head, on pain of being hanged and drawn, that if Bruce would attack them on the morrow he would defeat them easily without much loss. At whose instigation they resolved to fight, and at sunrise on the morrow marched out of the wood in three divisions of infantry."

Accordingly, we may conclude that Bruce had resolved not to face the risk of a pitched battle, but that on hearing of the demoralised condition of the English army, and, possibly, on perceiving that they had been so foolish as to cross the Bannock near to its junction with the Forth, and entangle themselves in marshy and broken ground surrounded on three sides by water, he changed his plans so far as to submit the question of fighting or not fighting to the decision of his followers. If Barbour is to be believed he gave it as his own opinion that the condition of the English army was such as to give the Scots every chance of victory, adding, however, that they were not to take that as

[1] *Scalacronica.*

meaning that it was his wish that they should decide in favour of fighting. The decision was to be theirs, and theirs alone. All of which is a pleasing commentary on the relationship in which Bruce stood to his followers, a relationship which, in feudal times, was exceedingly uncommon. As we have seen, the decision of the Scots was instant and emphatic. They would fight, and they would not fail.

The effect on the English army of the rout of Clifford and the repulse of the advance guard was extraordinary. English writers like Gray and the Lanercost chronicler agree with Barbour in stating that they were so much discouraged as to be almost demoralised. Says Gray, they proceeded to encamp, "having sadly lost confidence and being too much disaffected by the events of the day"; while later he makes Seton describe them as having lost heart and being discouraged, and expecting nothing but a sudden, open attack. The Lanercost chronicler tells us that from the moment of Clifford's defeat there "began a panic among the English, and the Scots grew bolder," while Barbour adds their discouragement was so great that heralds were sent throughout the host to allay their fears. The events of the day were not the sole cause of this depression in the English ranks, though they put the final touch to it. The army had little faith in its leaders. The character of Edward II was too well known to inspire confidence, while it would have been strange indeed had it not been known that divided counsels prevailed among the king's advisers. The troops, moreover, were tired and hungry.[1] On the Saturday they had marched more than twenty miles from Edinburgh to Falkirk, an exceptionally long march for a mediæval army, and on the Sunday morning they had done eight more. So they were in a tired, depressed, grumbling mood, and it required only a slight set-back to complete their demoralisation.

We saw that the main body of the English halted a mile or so from the Bannock Burn in order that their

[1] *Vita Edwardi Secundi.*

leaders might take counsel together, and it was during this pause that the advance guard rode forward to its repulse at the entry, and Clifford and Beaumont to their rout at the hands of Randolph. The reason of the halt seems to have been the arrival of the Constable of Stirling Castle, Sir Philip de Moubray, who, Gray tells us,[1] met the army advancing to his relief, "three miles from the castle, on Sunday, the vigil of St. John, and told him (Edward) that there was no occasion for him to approach any nearer, for he considered himself as relieved. Then he told him how the enemy had blocked the narrow roads in the forest," as the advance guard were even then finding to their cost.

This last sentence of Gray's is important, for it explains the decision of the English king to lead his army across the Bannock, well to the east of Bruce's position, and encamp for the night in the Carse, that is, in the triangle of ground bounded on three sides by the Forth and the Bannock, and open only towards the west, towards the Scottish position. The repulse of Clifford and of the English van doubtless helped the decision, for this not only proved Moubray's information to be correct, but probably led the English to suppose that "the narrow roads in the forest" were more completely blocked, and the Scots stronger in numbers and position than was actually the case. Thus the Scottish successes on the Sunday afternoon had the double effect of discouraging the English army and causing the English leaders to commit a grave tactical error. So instead of pressing forward in force towards the entry, or proceeding by the route Clifford had taken, the English army turned sharply to the right, and, marching for two miles away from the Scots, crossed the Bannock Burn, and found themselves ordered to encamp in what Gray describes with perfect truth as "an evil, deep, wet marsh." There in profound discomfort, with the Forth and the Bannock on three sides of them, on marshy ground covered in places with broad pools of water and intersected with small water-

[1] *Scalacronica.*

courses, the English army spent the night of 23rd June. Nor could they seek respite from their discomforts in sleep.[1] They were in hourly expectation of attack, and so the whole night through they remained under arms, with even their horses bitted.[2] No wonder that the last remnants of spirit in the disheartened host oozed slowly away amid the mud and dank of that "evil, deep, wet marsh," and the discomfort and weariness of the slow-moving night.

It was far otherwise with the Scots. Full of ardour and elation they looked forward to the coming battle, with all the zest of men about to fight in an inspiring and sacred cause. As soon as day broke on the 24th June, they gathered together to hear mass, then partook of some food and made themselves ready for the fight. Very soon every man was at his post, and when the four battles were fully arrayed, James Douglas, Walter Stewart, and a number of others were knighted by Bruce in view of the whole army. Then the order to advance was given, and out from the cover of the wood and down the slope to the plain below marched the Scottish army, the divisions of Edward Bruce, Randolph, and James Douglas leading, while Bruce himself brought up the rear with the reserve. "They directed their course boldly upon the English army," says Gray,[3] whose father, an unwilling spectator, watched the day's events from the Scottish camp. In spite of their anxious forebodings of the night the English were taken by surprise. They had feared a Scottish attack in the half-darkness of the June night, but they did not expect a bold, ordered advance in the full light of the early sun-lit morning.[4] So "they mounted in great alarm"—again it is an English chronicler who speaks [5]—"for they were not accustomed to fight on foot; whereas the Scots had taken a lesson from the Flemings, who before that had at Courtrai defeated on foot the power of France."

---

[1] *Scalacronica.*   [2] *Ibid.*   [3] *Scalacronica.*
[4] *Ibid.* Gray says the Scots marched out from the wood at sunrise.
[5] *Scalacronica.*

"And when the King of England saw the Scots thus take on hand to take the hard field so openly and upon foot, he had wonder and said, 'What! Will yon Scots fight?' 'Yea, certainly, sir,' then said a knight, Sir Ingram de Umfraville,"[1] who, himself a Scot, knew his countrymen well, for he straightway advised Edward to abandon his camp and pretend to retreat, when the Scots would almost certainly break those steadily advancing serried lines in order to plunder the English camp. But Edward, confident in his numbers and still despising his foe, would have none of it. "No man shall say that I eschewed battle and withdrew for such a rabble," he answered haughtily.

The Scots meanwhile drew steadily nearer, but when they were still some distance from the English lines they halted, and with one accord "full devoutly knelt all down to God to pray; and a short prayer they made to God to help them in that fight."[2] The English king was amazed. Not so was he wont to go into battle. "They kneel to ask mercy," he exclaimed triumphantly to Sir Ingram de Umfraville. "You say sooth now," was the reply. "They ask mercy, but not of you. These men will win or die." "Be it so," said the king, still scornful, and straightway ordered the trumpets to sound the advance.

The whole of this episode, which occupies a niche all its own in Scottish story, has so fine and romantic a flavour about it, that many people are inclined to regard it as wholly imaginative. So it is well to give a dry English version of it, the version of a contemporary chronicler who had no love for the Scots.[3] "Now when the two armies had approached very near each other," says he, "all the Scots fell on their knees to repeat a *Pater Noster*, commending themselves to God and seeking help from Heaven; after which they advanced boldly against the English." And so that reverent act of the Scottish army must be regarded as a fact of sober history, and we may, as historical students, read in it

---

[1] Barbour.   [2] *Ibid.*   [3] Lanercost.

the influence of those bishops and priests of the Church of Scotland who had made of the war a Holy War and had preached so untiringly, so ardently, and so boldly the sacred duty of resistance to England.

CHAPTER XL

Now, before the armies meet in the clash of battle, let us pause for a moment to examine the position and the tactics of the opposing forces. The English army, as we have seen, had placed itself in the rough triangle formed by the Forth and the Bannock. Its front lay towards the base of the triangle, its only outlet, and that base was, at a point midway between the Scottish and the English camps, barely a mile wide. Accordingly, unless the English could get beyond that point, they would be jammed between the Forth and the Bannock, and would in consequence be unable either to extend or to bring more than a mere fraction of their men into the fighting line. They would, moreover, be unable to out-flank their opponents, and, in addition, would be compelled to fight over an extremely narrow front. There are only 1760 yards in a mile, and as a yard to each man is rather under than over the allowance necessary for a mediæval fighting man, it is obvious that if the front were thus restricted and no flanking movement was possible, not more than 1700 men could be in action effectively at once. If, however, the English could get beyond the loop of the Forth which contained them on the right, their right would have the whole of the plain between that point and Stirling on which to operate, and, if the Scots advanced on to the plain, would be able to envelop them. Bruce, therefore, had two alternatives, once he had decided to fight. He could remain in his position on the crest of the wooded slope, and thus compel the English to advance uphill through the trees if they wished to attack him, or he could take the offensive and endeavour to prevent the English getting out of the triangle by flinging his schiltroms into the gap between the Forth and the Bannock. If he adopted the latter course and were successful in his initial movements, then he had the whole English host penned in between the two streams in such a position that their whole advantage of numbers would not only be gone, but would be a positive source of danger to themselves. Whatever his original intentions may have been, Bruce does not seem to have considered the first alternative after the decision not to retreat had been made. The choice was between retreat and attack, and, in view of all the circumstances, attack was decided upon.

This view of the battle of Bannockburn is, of course, entirely different from every other given by modern historians prior to Mr. Mackenzie. There cannot be any doubt, however, that Mr. Mackenzie's view is right, and I trust that readers of these pages will turn to his book and examine for themselves the evidence which he adduces. It is sufficient to say here that that evidence is overwhelming in its completeness, and makes one marvel that so much that was erroneous should have found its way into the pages of modern historians. Perhaps, however, we need not marvel. We have had only too many opportunities in the course of these pages of observing how superficial has been the attention devoted by modern historical writers to the period of the War of Independence.

I have already observed that Mr. Mackenzie's view of the battle is accepted by the greatest living authority for the English history of the period, Professor Tout,[1] and that though, as he says himself, "the acceptance of Mr. Mackenzie's views will compel me to recast more than one version of the battle that I have already published." Only on one point does he differ from Mr. Mackenzie, and there the difference does not seem to be so great as he imagines. "It is the hardest of all Mr. Mackenzie's doctrines to believe that the Scottish foot was the attacking force," he says, though he

[1] *Scot. Hist. Review*, Oct. 1913.

qualifies this a little later when he remarks, "but it may be conceded that there was substantially an attack when the Scots ranged themselves facing eastwards on the plain of the Carse, and provoked the English to battle." But Mr. Mackenzie nowhere contends that the Scots hurled themselves on the waiting English, as Professor Tout seems to imply. On the other hand there can be no doubt that they would have done so had the English been foolish enough to wait for them. Mr. Mackenzie's contention, in his own words, is that "the Scots took the initiative in forcing the battle," as Professor Tout himself admits, and as every reliable fourteenth-century account of the battle makes clear. Professor Tout adds: "There was, therefore, a little more of the Waterloo in it than Mr. Mackenzie admits, but it was a Waterloo in which the weaker force compelled the enemy to fight by going so near him that any other course was impossible."

It is plain, therefore, that the difference between Mr. Mackenzie and Professor Tout is exceedingly slight, and amounts really to a difference as to the precise moment at which the English horse charged the advancing Scots. All that need be said is this. The Scots marched out of the wood and down the slope *before the English horsemen were even mounted*;[1] they held steadily across the plain towards the English, pausing only for a moment to kneel in prayer,[2] "after which they advanced boldly against the English"; their right division was then, and not till then, charged by the English van; and by then, as the whole subsequent course of the battle shows, the Scots had achieved their purpose of closing the gap between the Forth and the Bannock. Indeed in *Vita Edwardi Secundi*, another English authority be it observed, it is stated that the leading Scottish schiltroms fiercely attacked the division under Gloucester (*aciem comitis G. acriter invasit*), that is the English van. There is no suggestion there of even the English van attacking the Scots.

[1] *Scalacronica.*   [2] Lanercost; Barbour.

2 G

In order to clinch the matter, we may quote two of our recognised fourteenth-century English authorities. Says Gray : "The aforesaid Scots came in line of schiltroms *and attacked the English columns*, which were jammed together and could not operate against them (the Scots), so direfully were their horses impaled on the spears. The troops in the English rear fell back upon the ditch of Bannockburn, tumbling one over the other." And the Lanercost chronicler, after describing how the Scots said their Pater Noster, and "thereafter advanced boldly against the English," goes on, "of a truth when both armies engaged each other, and the great horses of the English charged the spears of the Scots, as it were into a dense forest, there arose a great and terrible crash of spears broken, and of destriers wounded to the death. And so they remained without movement for a while. Now the English in the rear could not reach the Scots because the leading divisions were in the way, nor could they do anything to help themselves, wherefore there was nothing for it but to take to flight." Then he adds : "This account I heard from a trustworthy person who was present as eye-witness." It is sufficient to remark that there is not much of Waterloo about either of those descriptions.

We may now resume our narrative at the point at which we broke off. Their Pater Noster said, the Scots rose from their knees and continued their steady advance. Edward Bruce's division was on the right, Randolph's seems to have been in the centre, and Douglas's and the Steward's on the left.[1] The advance may, as is sometimes stated, have been in echelon, but this is by no means clear.[2] At all events the English van was on the left front of the English line, and therefore nearest to Edward Bruce's division,[3] while the other nine divisions of the English army were so jammed together by the restricted nature of the ground, that they were crowded into one vast mass.[4] At last, when the Scots were very

[1] Barbour.
[2] Lanercost.
[3] Barbour ; *Vita Edwardi Secundi.*
[4] *Scalacronica;* Lanercost.

THE BATTLE OF BANNOCKBURN

SECOND PHASE—THE SCOTTISH ADVANCE

Monday, 24th June 1314

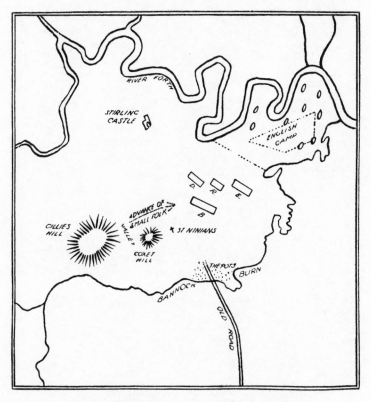

The dotted line represents the probable point where
the armies met.
Position of English archers uncertain, so not marked.
Position of Scottish cavalry probably such as to take
archers on flank.

near, the English van charged, choosing as their objective the division nearest to them, that of Edward Bruce. But Edward Bruce's men met them "right hardily,"[1] and against the terrible Scottish spears the English horsemen could make no headway.[2] As always, the Scottish spearmen directed their weapons against the horses of their foes, and horse and rider came crashing to the ground.[3] If the rider were lucky enough to rise, which owing to his heavy armour was well-nigh impossible, even had there been no mêlée raging round and over him, it would only be to find himself horseless, and therefore useless. The wounded horses, moreover, added another element of confusion to the scene, for many of them in their terror rushed headlong into the crowded English ranks.

Randolph, seeing the right division engaged and giving a good account of itself, held straight on for the main body of the English, and was met by some of the English horse,[4] who "came pricking as if they would o'er-ride the Earl and his company. But they met them so sturdily that many of them to earth they bore. For many a horse was steekit there, and many good men fell underfoot that had no power to rise again," a graphic description of the way the Scots used their spears, and the effect which the fall of his horse had on its rider. So fiercely did Randolph and the men of Moray fight, moreover, that the attacking horsemen began to give way before them, and the Scots, winning more and more ground, were presently pressing right into the main body of the enemy, "so that it seemed that they were lost among so great many as if they were plunged in the sea."[5] While Randolph and his men were thus engaged, Douglas and the Steward came up with their division, and in no long time the three Scottish battles "were all side by side fighting well near."[6]

It was probably during the advance of the Scots that the English archers came into play. Barbour, though

---

[1] Barbour.   [2] *Scalacronica*; Lanercost; Barbour.   [3] *Ibid.*
[4] Barbour.   [5] *Ibid.*   [6] *Ibid.*

obscure on the point, seems to indicate this,[1] while the Lanercost chronicler says that "when both sides had made ready for battle the English archers were thrown forward before the line, and the Scottish archers engaged them, a few being killed and wounded on each side ; but the king of England's archers quickly put the others to flight." Bruce, however, had held Sir Robert Keith and the cavalry in readiness for this emergency, and they, charging forward, took them in the flank and routed them utterly.[2] So overcome with panic, indeed, were the archers that they fled hither and thither, and many of them rushing blindly towards the English main body caused some confusion in the English ranks, and were struck down in anger by their own countrymen.[3] When the Scottish archers saw the fate which had overtaken their adversaries, they advanced boldly, and "with all their might shot eagerly among the horsemen,"[4] with disastrous results to the English.[5]

The day was now going well for Scotland. The dreaded English archers had been dispersed, the English van had been held in check and was plainly having the worst of the argument, Randolph had driven back the English horse opposed to him and was carving his way into the heart of the English host, and Douglas and the Steward were following his example at another part of the English line. Bruce, watching the progress of the struggle with eager and skilful eye, judged the moment for bringing up the reserve had come, and promptly led his division against, apparently, the English right wing.[6] His men were fresh and full of ardour, and they fell upon the English so stoutly "that at their coming their

---

[1] Book xiii., line 61, &c. [2] Barbour.
[3] Barbour, xiii. 100, &c. [4] Barbour.
[5] Mr. Mackenzie cites, from Dr. Bryce's *Grey Friars*, a contemporary story which illustrates the use which the Scottish archers made of their opportunities. A Gascon knight, vowed to St. Francis, when the battle was at its height and the Scottish arrows flying thick and fast, called on the saint, who appeared in the habit of his order and personally diverted the arrows. The knight's horse was horribly wounded by the Scottish pikes, which, as Mr. Mackenzie says, indicates their method of dealing with the mounted men. Page 79 *note*.
[6] Barbour.

foes were driven back a great bit." [1] Bruce himself, however, probably took no part in the actual fighting at this stage. With a chosen company, perhaps the cavalry, who, having dispersed the archers, seem thereafter to have been inactive till near the end of the battle, he remained apart from the mêlée, keeping an eagle eye on all parts of the field.[2]

The whole of the Scottish infantry was now engaged. The English were so crowded together that they could offer no effective resistance. Those within reach of the Scots had not sufficient room to wield their arms aright, those beyond reach could get no nearer because of the press. And ever the steadily advancing Scots were forcing the front rank of their foes back on the chafing crowd behind, while the uneven and marshy nature of the ground impeded still further the heavily armed men of England and caused not a few of them to stumble. Presently the English van was driven back, completely shattered, on the main body,[3] followed closely by Edward Bruce's eager, triumphant men; while Randolph's fierce warriors pressed further and further into the English ranks with such desperate valour that wherever they came their foes fled before them.[4] Hitherto the Scots had fought in grim and deadly silence, but now, as everywhere the English ranks began to reel, a great shout of victory went up: " On them ! On them ! On them ! They fail." [5] The shout was the signal for an even fiercer onset, while the Scottish archers plied their bows on the crowded mass more lustily than ever. It was at this juncture that there suddenly appeared advancing down the slope to the plain a great crowd of men, marching in military order, with banners waving in the wind.[6] To the jaded and already well-nigh broken English it looked as if a fresh army were coming against them, and signs of panic began to appear amongst them.[7] Bruce was quick to perceive the symptoms, and, shouting his war-cry, he flung himself and all his company upon them.[8]

---

[1] Barbour.   [2] This is implied by Barbour in xiii. 267–71.
[3] Barbour.   [4] *Ibid.*   [5] *Ibid.*   [6] *Ibid.*   [7] *Ibid.*   [8] *Ibid.*

It was the final blow. Men began to flee,[1] more and
more joined in the rout, and the Scots, realising that
their foes had actually begun to fly, " fell on them with
all their might." [2] The panic spread rapidly, men fled
openly in all directions, only a few men of might and
honour still maintained the fight.[3] Then the English
leaders saw that the day was lost, and seizing the king's
bridle rein, Aymer de Valence and Sir Giles de Argentine
led him off the field [4] with 500 men behind him.[5]
Their going was the signal for a *sauve qui peut*. The
battle of Bannockburn was over, and a kingdom had
been lost and won.

Edward rode from the battlefield not a moment too
soon. Already daring Scots were penetrating through the
broken squadrons and laying eager hands on the very
horse which the English king bestrode.[6] Says Gray:
" The English squadrons, being thrown into confusion by
the thrust of the spears upon the horses, began to fly.
Those who were appointed to attend upon the king's
rein, perceiving the disaster, led the king by the rein off
the field towards the castle, and off he went, though
much against the grain. As the Scottish knights, who
were on foot, laid hold of the housing of the king's
charger in order to stop him, he struck out so vigorously
behind him with a mace that there was none whom he
touched whom he did not fell to the ground. As those
who had the king's reins were thus drawing him always
forward, one of them, Giles de Argentin, a famous knight
who had lately come over sea from the wars of the
Emperor Henry of Luxembourg, said to the king: ' Sire,
your rein was committed to me ; you are now in safety ;
there is your castle where your person may be safe. I
am not accustomed to fly, nor am I going to begin now.
I commend you to God.' Then, setting spurs to his
horse, he returned into the mellay, where he was slain."
Barbour, on the Scottish side, tells substantially the same
tale, confirming both Gray's statement as to Edward

---

[1] Barbour.   [2] *Ibid.*   [3] *Ibid.*
[4] *Scalacronica.*   [5] Barbour.   [6] *Scalacronica.*

being led unwillingly off the field, and his story of Argentin's gallant death. So Edward II for once rose above the cowardice which was commonly ascribed to him by his own subjects; and his unwillingness to leave the stricken field and the quixotic courage and death of Argentin must both be regarded as belonging to the realm of history.

Little now remains to be told. Sir Philip Moubray refused to admit Edward to Stirling Castle, pointing out that in terms of his agreement with the Scots he would now be compelled to yield it forthwith.[1] So, " guided by a certain knight of Scotland who knew through what districts they could escape,[2] they rode round the rear of the Scottish army, keeping well to the west and out of sight of the Scots, and so round the Torwood and through the plains of Lothian to Dunbar,[3] whence Edward and some of his followers escaped by sea to England,[4] and the others rode furiously to safe refuge behind the walls of Berwick.[5] That headlong ride of the English king and his 500 armed and mounted followers was not, however, accomplished without unpleasant attentions from the Scots.[6] Douglas was speedily made aware of Edward's flight, and with but sixty horsemen he rode boldly in pursuit of the 500. Barbour tells in graphic language how with his small force Douglas kept the flying English on the run; how, unable by his weakness in numbers to attack them, he yet pressed hard on them, now but a stone-throw behind them, now but a hundred or two yards away on their flank; how, when they halted and dismounted to bait their wearied horses, he did the same " beside them near "; how, meeting the Scot, Sir Laurence de Abernethy, hastening with eighty men to the aid of England, he persuaded him to transfer his allegiance and join him in the chase of his

---

[1] Barbour; *Vita Edwardi Secundi*; *Scalacronica* likewise implies this.

[2] Lanercost. *Vita Edwardi* also says that a Scottish knight acted as guide.

[3] *Scalacronica*; Lanercost.　　　　[4] Lanercost.

[5] Barbour.　　　　[6] *Ibid.*

erstwhile master; how in this wise they "convoyed" Edward to Dunbar, picking up many a straggler from his company on the way; and how, finally, they pursued the remainder of the English king's companions to the border, only abandoning their "convoy" when the grey walls of Berwick received the fugitives. It makes a stirring bit of reading for anyone in whose veins Scottish blood flows.

Meanwhile, on the field of Bannockburn the flight of the English king had been followed by a panic to which there is no parallel in the history of either England or Scotland. Hemmed in on three sides by the Forth and the Bannock, and on the fourth by the triumphant Scots, the English, horse and foot alike, noble, knight, and squire, as well as humble archer and foot-soldier, were seized with one common terror-stricken desire to escape at all costs.[1] Arms and armour were flung away; men of all ranks fled in all directions; horsemen and footmen mingled in inextricable confusion;[1] the dangers of the Forth and the Bannock were ignored, men plunged in headlong fear into the waters, and, losing their footing in the treacherous bottom, or being thrown down by their terrified comrades, fell to perish miserably in the water or the slime;[1] while both on the field and in the pursuit the triumphant Scots, joined now by the "small folk" and the camp-followers, took a terrible toll from all the broken host.[1]

Barbour may complete the picture. "They were," he says, "to say sooth all aghast, and fled so, right terrified, that of them a full great party fled to the water of Forth, and there the most part of them were drowned. And Bannock Burn, betwixt the braes, of horses and men so charged was, that upon drowned horses and men, men might pass dry over it."[2]

Such of the English and Welsh foot as succeeded in escaping over the Bannock Burn fled towards the south, making blindly for the border. Comparatively few of them reached it. They were pursued for many miles by the victorious Scots, while great numbers of them were

---

[1] Lanercost; *Scalacronica;* Barbour; *Vita Edwardi Secundi*, &c., &c.
[2] Lanercost and *Scalacronica* confirm this.

captured or slain by the country folk.[1]   Let the Lanercost chronicler tell what befell another body of fugitives
who escaped towards the west.   " In like manner," he
says, " as the king and his following fled in one direction
to Berwick, so the Earl of Hereford, the Earl of Angus,
Sir John de Segrave, Sir Antony de Lucy, and Sir
Ingelram de Umfraville, with a great crowd of knights,
600 other mounted men, and 1000 foot, fled in another
direction towards Carlisle."   That is to say, they
fled west and south.   " The Earl of Pembroke," he
goes on, the Earl of Pembroke being our old friend
Aymer de Valence, " left the army on foot and saved
himself with the fugitive Welsh ; but the aforesaid Earls
and others, who had fled towards Carlisle, were captured
on the way to Bothwell Castle," which, it will be remembered, was one of the very few castles still in the hands
of the English.   " For the sheriff, the warden of the
castle, who had held the castle down to that time for
the king of England, perceiving that his countrymen had
won the battle, allowed the chief men who came thither
to enter the castle," to the number of fifty, Barbour
says, " in the belief that they would find a safe refuge,
and when they had entered he took them prisoners,
thereby treacherously deceiving them.   Many, also, were
taken wandering round the castle, and hither and thither
in the country, and many were killed ; it was said, also,
that certain knights were captured by women, nor did
any of them get back to England save in abject confusion.   The Earl of Hereford, the Earl of Angus, Sir
John de Segrave, Sir Anthony de Lucy, Sir Ingelram de
Umfraville, and other nobles who were in the castle were
brought before Robert de Bruce and sent into captivity,
and after a lengthy imprisonment were ransomed for
much money."   It is sufficient to say that this account
is singularly accurate, as ample contemporary evidence
makes clear.[2]   Hereford, however, was not ransomed in

---

[1] Barbour.
[2] *Chronicles of Edward I and II*, iii. 231 ; Barbour ; Fordun ; and
later, Baker, Walsingham, &c.

money. Fifteen Scottish captives of the highest rank, who had languished for years in England, including Bruce's queen and daughter and the venerable Bishop of Glasgow, were exchanged for him.[1]

Another body of fugitives from the battle gave Bruce a little trouble, and, according to Barbour, " this was the cause wherefore the king of England escaped home to his land." As we saw the English right rested on the Forth, and Stirling Castle was in consequence not very far from it. A great number of the English, accordingly, made for the castle when the day was lost, in this following the example of their king. It was the only place which seemed to offer any hope of safety. But the castle gates remained inexorably closed against them, and in despair they took refuge on the crags below the walls, where there were " so many that it was wonder for to see. For the crags all covered were about the castle, here and there, of them that for the strength of that place thither for refuge flew." [2] They were so numerous, indeed, that " King Robert, that was witty, kept all his good men " near by, for fear lest the fugitives should recover from their panic and attack him when the bulk of his men were engaged in making an end of resistance, pursuing the flying English, and plundering their camp. As soon as the first frenzy of the victory was over, however, and the field bare of foes, Bruce assembled his men, and sent a " great company " to attack the English on the crags. But the heart had gone out of the fugitives, they had no fight left in them, and surrendered at discretion.[3] Then the Scots gave up the rest of the day to " spoiling and riches taking," [4] and so great was the loot that an English chronicler of the period,[5] a trustworthy authority for all that pertains to the battle, estimated its value in money at £200,000, which is equal to nearly £3,000,000 of our day. No wonder Barbour says, " So great riches there they found that many a man was mighty made of the riches that they there had."

[1] *Vita Edwardi Secundi;* and Bain, iii. 393.   [2] Barbour.
[3] *Ibid.*   [4] *Ibid.*   [5] *Vita Edwardi Secundi.*

The English loss was enormous, though it is, of course, impossible to state it in numbers with any certainty. Barbour, however, tells us that on the battlefield alone 200 golden spurs, that is the spurs of knighthood, were taken from the bodies of dead knights, and when we turn to the English authorities we find that this must be very near the truth. Besides these at least 500 men of rank, nobles, knights, and squires were captured and held to ransom,[1] and when we recollect that the total strength of the English cavalry is estimated at from 2000 to 2500, it will be seen that, even on this the lowest reckoning, their loss was very great. It must be remembered, moreover, that not all the cavalry were men of rank, and that even of these not all were knights, so that the number of knights slain in the actual battle, as distinct from the pursuit, was, in proportion to their numbers, extremely large. No estimate can be formed of the number of the foot slain and captured, but, as the accounts of the battle and the pursuit which we have quoted show, and as every other account indicates, it too must have been exceedingly large. But whatever the number of slain and captured of the whole English army may have been, the outstanding fact is that the greatest armed host which had ever invaded Scotland had been utterly destroyed. The king of England had ridden in headlong flight from the field; with hardly an exception all his chief lieutenants had been killed or captured; 200 of the flower of his knighthood had been slain, and hundreds more made prisoners; his army had been scattered in terror-stricken flight; and the whole of his camp, his equipment, and his baggage had fallen into the hands of the victorious Scots. If Bannockburn was the greatest victory the Scots ever won, it may with equal truth be described

---

[1] Anything like the exact number it is impossible to state, but that 500 is the lowest possible figure a comparison of the authorities—*Chronicles*, *Vita Edwardi Secundi*, Lanercost, Baker, Fordun, Walsingham, Capgrave, &c., &c.—puts beyond question.

as the greatest military disaster which the arms of England ever suffered.

The losses of the Scots seem to have been comparatively small, but no numbers are given by any contemporary authority. Barbour, however, who is extraordinarily accurate in such names as he gives of those captured or slain on the English side, says that on the Scottish side "two worthy knights" were slain, Sir William de Vepont and Sir Walter de Ross; while a third, Sir William de Airth, was killed on the night before the battle when in charge of Bruce's baggage, which lay at Cambuskenneth, just across the Forth from the English encampment in the Carse. The Earl of Athol, who had deserted Bruce, was responsible for this mishap, he taking Sir William Airth by surprise, and slaying him and many of his men. Mr. Mackenzie suggests that Sir Walter de Ross is identical with an esquire of that name who was in English service in Linlithgow in 1312, but in this he is certainly in error. The Sir Walter de Ross slain at Bannockburn was the son of the Earl of Ross, while the Linlithgow esquire probably belonged to the family of Hamelake, on the borders.[1] The fact that these are the only Scots who are mentioned as having fallen at Bannockburn is a strong indication that the Scottish losses were very small, a conclusion to which the whole course of the battle would in any case lead us.

The immediate result of Bannockburn was the surrender of Stirling Castle; Sir Philip Moubray, its gallant constable, yielding it on the morning after the battle. Him Bruce treated with great courtesy, and he very soon transferred his allegiance to the Scottish

---

[1] Barbour states explicitly that Edward Bruce loved Sir Walter's sister *par amours*, and that that was the cause of his affection for Sir Walter. Now Edward Bruce did so love Isabella, a daughter of the Earl of Ross, and afterwards married her. In 1317 he received a papal dispensation for the marriage, which at the date of the dispensation, June 1317, had been for some considerable time an accomplished fact. In the dispensation she is described as "daughter of William, Earl of Ross" (*Calendar of Papal Registers*, ii. 156), and as that Earl had a son Walter the evidence is conclusive.

king, as did many another Scot who had hitherto stood aloof or been in arms against the slayer of the Red Comyn. For, as the Lanercost chronicler succinctly puts it : " After the aforesaid victory Robert de Bruce was commonly called king of Scotland by all men, because he had acquired Scotland by force of arms." Stirling shared the fate of the other Scottish castles. It was cast down, and remained in ruins till 1336, when it was rebuilt during Edward III's temporary occupation of the south and centre of Scotland.

Another immediate result of the battle was, of course, the enrichment of the impoverished kingdom by the spoil taken on the field and the ransom of the captives. So rich and varied was that spoil that there was hardly a house of any consequence in Scotland which did not possess for many a year some tangible token of the great day of Bannockburn. Then, as we have seen, there was the release of the Scottish captives who had so long languished in England. Among them, in addition to those already mentioned, we may note the youthful Andrew de Moray, the son of the hero of Stirling Bridge.[1] Born in 1298, he had been carried captive to England at the tender age of five, but, though the impressionable years from five to sixteen were spent at the English Court, he remained a Scot of the Scots, and in the years to come was, like his father before him, to lead his countrymen in yet another great struggle against the ambitious designs of England, and spend his life in the cause of his country's freedom.

[1] Bain, iii. 402.

CHAPTER XLI

THE END OF THE WAR

IT is unnecessary for us to pursue this study of the War of Independence beyond the battle of Bannockburn, and that for two reasons. In the first place, the problems with which we have been particularly concerned are peculiar to the period before Bannockburn, and after that battle neither the events nor the progress of the war present any difficulties of real importance. In the second place, the battle of Bannockburn, though it did not end the war, really marked the culminating point in the Scots' long struggle for freedom. From that day forward the issue was never in doubt, though many years were to pass, and many doughty deeds of war were yet to be performed, before the recognition of Robert Bruce as the independent king of an independent Scotland was to be wrung from a reluctant England. But Bannockburn made that recognition sooner or later inevitable, as it also made the conquest of Scotland by England for ever impossible. Henceforward Scotland might be overrun by the armies of England, as time and again she was overrun; her armies might be shattered, the flower of her leaders and her manhood cut off, as time and again these were shattered and cut off; the kingdom might be divided against herself, and treachery might be rife in her innermost councils, as time and again she was divided, as time and again such treachery was rife; but in the darkest hour her people never forgot that once before their freedom had been won by force of arms from England, and the pretensions of that arrogant kingdom shattered in open battle on the field of Bannockburn. The battle of Bannockburn, in a word, gave to Scotland an unconquerable confidence in her ability to hold her own at all times, and under any conditions, against the whole might of England. That confidence, it is true, often led to strange results, and to many bloody defeats—from the fields of Dupplin Moor[1] and Halidon Hill,[2] but three and four years after Bruce had been laid in his grave, to Flodden, Pinkie, and Dunbar; but it none the less was a possession of inestimable value to Scotland. We have but to look at the decade which followed Bruce's death to realise the truth of this. For had there been no memory of Bannockburn to lighten the gloom of that, perhaps the gloomiest period in the history of Scotland, and to keep alive in her people the spirit of resistance and the determination to be free, she might well have ceased to exist as an independent kingdom.

Like the good general that he was Bruce did not rest on his laurels after Bannockburn. The English invaders had been routed and driven in headlong flight from Scotland, but the long war was not yet over, the independence of Scotland was not yet recognised by her beaten and humiliated but still arrogant foe. So, in the August following Bannockburn, Bruce sent his brother Edward and Sir James Douglas to carry the war into the enemy's country, and for many years thereafter Scottish invasions of England were of constant occurrence. The boot was now on the other foot with a vengeance, and England endured something of the sufferings she had inflicted on Scotland. But whereas England had inflicted untold miseries on Scotland in order to gratify the unholy ambitions of a masterful king whose consuming passion was a lust for dominion and conquest, Scotland, in the years which followed Bannockburn, was inspired solely by the desire to wring from her beaten oppressor the acknowledgment of her freedom and a reasonable assurance that she would not again suffer from the evil ambitions of her poweful neighbour.

An English writer, whose name has escaped my memory, betrays a sad lack of perspective and knowledge,

[1] 12th August 1332.   [2] 19th July 1333.

to say nothing of humour and imagination, when he solemnly asserts that these Scottish invasions of England were a mistake because they annoyed the English so much that they filled them with the belief that there could never be peace till Scotland was subjugated! Which is very English and very foolish. For twenty years England had tried in vain to conquer Scotland. Bannockburn for a time put an end to her efforts, but it did not put an end to her desires. For thirteen years thereafter she obstinately refused to recognise the freedom of Scotland, and that though she was reduced time and again to the position of having to sue for peace or truce, and though she suffered defeats and humiliations innumerable. Her people desired peace, the Scots and their king were eager for peace, but the false pride of the English king and his barons would not permit them to concede the only terms on which the Scots would agree to peace. Only when thirteen years of ignominious warfare had taught the English that the Scots were their equals, if not their superiors, in both the art and the practice of war, did they reluctantly abandon their pretensions and concede all that the Scots had fought for through thirty-two long and bitter years.

But before the Treaty of Northampton, which brought to Scotland peace with honour, was signed, many things happened which need not be set down here. One episode, however, cannot on any account be omitted. Defeated in the field, the English invoked and obtained the aid of the Pope. But excommunication and interdict held no terrors for the Scots. One notable result, and one only, had the papal intervention. It drew from the nobility and community of Scotland, in Parliament assembled, that famous letter to the Pope, which placed on record for all time the spirit which animated the Scots in their long struggle for freedom.[1]

" We enjoyed peace and liberty, with the protection of the Papal See," it runs, " until Edward, the late king of England, in the guise of a friend and ally, invaded and

[1] Acts of Parl., i.

oppressed our nation, at that time without a head,
unpractised in war, and suspecting no evil. The wrongs
which we suffered under the tyranny of Edward are
beyond description, and, indeed, they would appear
incredible to all but those who actually felt them. He
wasted our country, imprisoned our prelates, burnt our
religious places, spoiled our ecclesiastics, and slew our
people, without discrimination of age, sex, or rank.
Through favour of Him who woundeth and maketh
whole, we have been freed from so great and unbearable
calamities by the valour of our lord and king, Robert.
He, like another Joshua or Judas Maccabeus, gladly
endured toils, distresses, the extremity of want, and
every peril, to rescue his people and inheritance out of
the hands of the enemy. Divine Providence, that legal
succession which we will constantly maintain, and our
due and unanimous consent, have made him our Chief
and King. To him, in defence of our liberty, we are
bound to adhere, as well of right as by reason of his
deserts ; and to him we will in all things adhere, for
through him salvation has been wrought to all our
people." Then follows this clarion note. " *But should he
abandon our cause, or aim at reducing us or our kingdom
under the dominion of the English, we will instantly try to
expel him as a common enemy, the subverter of our rights
and his own, and we will choose another king to rule
and protect us ; for while a hundred of us exist we will
never submit to England. We fight not for glory, wealth,
or honour, but for that liberty which no virtuous man can
survive.*"

Two other extracts from this memorable letter will
suffice. "Wherefore, we most earnestly beseech your
Holiness," runs the first, "that you behold with a
fatherly eye the tribulations and distresses brought upon
us by the English, and that you admonish Edward to
content himself with his own dominions, esteemed in
former times enough for seven kings, and allow us
Scotsmen, who dwell in a poor and remote corner, and
who seek for nought but our own, to remain in peace.

In order to procure that peace we are ready to do anything that is consistent with our national interests."
And the conclusion, with its clear note of determination,
defiance, and high courage: "Should you, however, give
too credulous an ear to the reports of our enemies,
distrust the sincerity of our professions, and persist in
favouring the English to our destruction, then we hold
you guilty, in the sight of the Most High, of the loss of
lives, the perdition of souls, and all the other miserable
consequences which may ensue from war between the two
contending nations. Ever ready, like dutiful children,
to yield all fit obedience to you as God's Vicegerent, we
commit our cause to the Supreme King and Judge; we
cast our cares on Him, and we steadily trust that He
will inspire us with valour and bring our enemies to
nought." [1]

Is there in the archives of any nation a more inspiring
national document than this; and are we to believe that
the Parliament which, on 6th April 1320, despatched
that ringing message to the titular head of Christendom
represented a people who twenty-five years before were
without any sense of nationality, were devoid of national
consciousness, national sentiment, and national cohesion?
Set alongside it the message of those two heroic young
Scotsmen, Andrew de Moray and William Wallace, to
the Mayor and Commons of Lubeck and Hamburg,
on 11th October 1297, and you have your answer—if
an answer is still necessary. Writing as "leaders of the
army of the kingdom of Scotland, and the community of
the said kingdom," they say: "We have learned from
trustworthy merchants of the said kingdom of Scotland
that you, of your own goodwill, lend your counsel, aid,
and favour in all matters and transactions touching us
and the said merchants, although we on our part have
previously done nothing to deserve such good offices;
and all the more on that account are we bound to tender
you our thanks and to make a worthy return. To do so
we willingly engage ourselves to you, requesting that you

---

[1] From Sir Herbert Maxwell's translation. *Bruce*, 272-4.

will make it known among your merchants that they can have safe access to all the ports of the kingdom of Scotland with their merchandise, *for the kingdom of Scotland, thanks be to God, has been recovered by war from the power of the English.*"

The spirit which animates these two documents, the one at the beginning, the other towards the end of the War of Independence, is the same, the unconquerable determination of a free nation to remain free ; and eight years after the despatch of the letter to the Pope that determination achieved its reward. In the autumn of 1327 Bruce was engaged in the siege of Norham Castle, when a messenger arrived from the English Parliament, then sitting at Lincoln, with proposals for the marriage of the child sister of the young Edward III to Bruce's son and heir David. This was a very long step in advance of any former overtures, and negotiations were at once entered upon. Commissioners were appointed by both parties to conduct these, and on 23rd November 1327, at Newcastle, preliminary terms of peace were arranged. On 1st March following, the commissioners again met at Newcastle in order to adjust the final terms, and on that day Edward III, or his advisers acting for him, agreed to a condition which the Scots insisted upon as a preliminary to any further proceedings. It was embodied on the same day in a proclamation by which the king of England announced his recognition of " our dear friend and ally Robert, by the Grace of God king of the Scots," and declared that such recognition was granted " by the assent and consent of the prelates, earls, barons, and commonalty in Parliament," and in order to put an end to the countless wars brought upon both nations by the attempts of former kings of England to establish rights of overlordship over Scotland. Edward then "willed and consented that the said kingdom, according to its ancient boundaries observed, in the days of Alexander III, should remain unto Robert king of Scots, his heirs and successors, free and divided from the kingdom of England, without any subjection, right of service, claim or demand whatever; and that all writings which might have been executed at any time to the contrary should be held as void and of no effect." [1]

Thus all that the Scots had contended for through thirty-two years of fierce and constant war was conceded at last, and once that was conceded the rest was easy. Terms of peace were speedily adjusted, and after they had been approved in that same month of March by the Scottish Parliament sitting in Edinburgh, they were submitted to the English Parliament which met at Northampton in May. The English Parliament in its turn ratified the conditions, which were thereupon embodied in a treaty, known as the Treaty of Northampton, to which the seal of the young king of England was affixed on 4th May 1328. The War of Independence was over. Scotland had been recovered by war from the power of the English; her independence had been recognised in the fullest and most solemn way by her would-be conquerors; and the right of her king to the Crown and the kingdom of Scotland had at last been admitted. Andrew de Moray and William Wallace and Simon Fraser, and a multitude of lesser but not less gallant men, had not laid down their lives in vain. They had fought and died "not for glory, wealth, or honour, but for that liberty which no virtuous man shall survive," and because of their gallant lives and their glorious deaths their successors had been able to make their country free.

[1] Foedera; Ramsay's *Dawn of the Constitution,* p. 196; Hailes's *Annals,* ii. 157–8 and *note.*

CHAPTER XLII

CONCLUSION

LITTLE now remains to be said. The facts which have been adduced in the foregoing pages are there to speak for themselves, but it may be well, perhaps, before I close, to repeat briefly the main conclusions which I claim to have proved.

These may be summarised as follows. (1) Scotland was a much more homogeneous kingdom at the death of Alexander III than is generally believed. (2) It was, moreover, still a Celtic kingdom; that is to say its kings sat on the throne by virtue of their Celtic descent; its people were for the most part Celtic; its language, outside English-speaking Lothian, which had become part of the kingdom of the Scots by conquest, was almost entirely Celtic, and throughout the whole kingdom, with the exception of Lothian, the ancient Celtic traditions and sentiments were still a potent force. (3) There was a very much stronger sense of nationality than has hitherto been believed. (4) It was those Celtic traditions and sentiments and that sense of nationality which were at the root of the resistance to England. (5) It was in the ancient Celtic kingdom of the Scots— roughly Scotland north of a line drawn from Renfrew on the Clyde to Bo'ness on the Forth, including the portions of Argyll and Kintyre which geographically are south of that line—in that kingdom which, by the conquest of Lothian and the annexation of Strathclyde, had made all Scotland its own, that the backbone of the resistance to England lay. (6) It was in Scotland north of the Forth and Clyde that the spirit of resistance to England first made itself felt, and it was in Scotland north of the Forth and Clyde that the general uprising of 1297 first assumed formidable dimensions. (7) It was in Scotland north of the Forth and Clyde alone that, under a northern leader, the revolt was maintained in the summer of 1297 when it had collapsed everywhere else, and it was in Scotland north of the Forth and Clyde that the successful campaign was conducted which resulted in Stirling Bridge and the first expulsion of the English. (8) It was with an army drawn very largely from Scotland north of the Forth and Clyde that the war was maintained from 1298 to 1304, under leaders who belonged to Scotland north of the Forth and Clyde. (9) It was to Scotland north of the Forth and Clyde that Bruce appealed when he raised the standard of revolt in 1306. (10) It was in Scotland north of the Forth and Clyde that Bruce conducted his first campaign, and it was in Scotland north of the Forth and Clyde that he obtained by far the greater and more influential part of his adherents in 1306, and on his return in 1307. (11) It was by the support accorded Bruce in Scotland north of the Forth and Clyde in 1307 that he was able to make his first real headway in his struggle for the Crown. (12) It was Bruce's northern campaign of 1307–8 which, like Andrew de Moray's northern campaign of 1297, changed the whole course of the war and made possible his ultimate victory. (13) It was when, and only when, Bruce had the north solidly behind him that his cause began to make real progress in the south. (14) Of all the south it was in the Celtic part alone that he found whole-hearted support prior to 1314. (15) It was with armies drawn mainly from Scotland north of the Forth and Clyde, and partly from the Celtic south, that the conquest of Galloway was achieved. (16) It was with armies drawn entirely from the same quarters that the invasions of England prior to 1314 were conducted. (17) It was with forces drawn almost entirely from Scotland north of the Forth and Clyde that Dundee, Perth, Edinburgh, and other strongholds held for England were captured. (18) It was with forces drawn from the Celtic north and the Celtic south that Roxburgh, Dumfries, and other southern castles were captured. (19) In the eighteen years of war which preceded Bannockburn English-speaking Lothian had neither lot nor part. (20) At the battle of Bannockburn the Scottish army was drawn almost entirely from the Celtic north and the Celtic south, the north supplying much the greater proportion, and English-speaking Lothian being practically unrepresented. (21) The War of Independence, accordingly, was made possible by, was sustained by, and was won by Scotland north of the Forth and Clyde, assisted latterly by Celtic Scotland south of the Clyde; and to Scotland north of the Forth and Clyde, the ancient Celtic kingdom of the Scots, the winning of the freedom of Scotland is therefore due.

In support of these conclusions two facts, not hitherto noticed, may be mentioned. In Robertson's *Index of Missing Charters* the first entry consists of a "Roll marked with the letter A, and having written on the back, Rob. I, A." The roll is a "Table of the Infeftments and Charters in the Rolls of Robert the First," &c. None of the deeds are dated, but the fact of their appearing on a roll marked "Rob. I, A," indicates that they are the earliest charters granted by Bruce. There are sixty charters on the roll. Of these one only is of lands south of the Forth and Clyde. All the others are of lands in the northern counties— Cromarty, Inverness, Nairn, Elgin, Banff, Aberdeen, Forfar, and Kincardine being those specifically mentioned. That is to say they are grants of lands in the districts in which Bruce found his earliest and most devoted adherents. Moreover, most of the grants are to men whom we know to have been in the early years of the struggle prominent among Bruce's supporters. Gilbert de la Haye, Walter de Berkeley, Hugh de Berkeley, Angus of the Isles, Hugh son and heir of the Earl of Ross, John son of the Earl of Ross, Gilbert Wiseman, Alexander Fraser, Robert de Keith, Patrick de Monte Alto, Alexander Stewart, Patrick de Ogilvie, Simon

Fraser, William de Strathbogie, the abbey of Deer, the abbey of Kinloss, and the burgh of Aberdeen, are among those mentioned. Accordingly the fact that no less than fifty-nine out of the first sixty charters known to have been granted by Bruce were grants of lands in the north to those who had aided him in the north, confirms in the fullest and most remarkable way the conclusions which we have drawn as to the part played by the north in the struggle for the freedom of Scotland.

The second fact is this. In the succeeding reign, when Scotland again suffered many things at the hands of England and came very near to destruction, it was to the north her leaders looked for men wherewith to meet the armies of England. And the most successful of all her leaders during these years was Sir Andrew de Moray of Petty, Avoch, and Bothwell, son of the hero of Stirling Bridge.

This brings us to another point. We have seen that from the very beginning of the war the Province of Moray fought ardently and whole-heartedly for the freedom of Scotland. No other part of the kingdom can show anything like its record during the years from 1297 to 1314. It was in the forefront of every attempt to throw off the yoke of England; it maintained the struggle, as in 1297 and 1304, when it had been abandoned in every other quarter; it responded to every call to arms, no matter how forlorn the hope or how desperate the prospect—1297, 1306, 1307, each tells the same tale; and its warriors, the gallant men of Moray, were the heroes of many of the most notable exploits of the war—the northern campaign of 1297, the Battle of Stirling Bridge, the defence of Urquhart Castle in 1303–4, Bruce's campaign of 1306 and 1307, the Battle of Inverurie, the expulsion of the Comyns, the conquest of Argyll, the capture of Perth, the capture of Edinburgh, and the rout of Clifford on the eve of Bannockburn. Moreover, it is a striking fact that the chief men of Moray, David de Moray, Bishop of Moray; Alexander Pilche, Sir William Wiseman, Sir Walter de Berkeley,

Sir John de Stirling, Sir Laurence de Strathbogie, and Sir John de Fenton, to mention only a few, are, unlike their compeers elsewhere, never found on the side of England at any time when the war is actually in progress during all these eighteen years. Some of them may, when all seemed lost, have come for a time to Edward's peace, but the moment the war was renewed, not only are they not to be found on the side of England, but almost every one of them appears on record as among the active enemies of England.

The consistency, no less than the ardour and the courage, of the men of Moray, high and low, rich and poor, throughout the whole period of the War of Independence is, therefore, a notable and an extremely important fact. To what that consistency is to be ascribed it is hardly necessary here to point out. But Bruce relied on it when he made his bid for the throne in 1306, and when he renewed his attempt in 1307; to it Wallace owes the great place in history which is his; and because of it the War of Independence ran the course it did. If to any one man more than another the credit for this is due, it is to Andrew de Moray, the true hero of the early stages of the War of Independence, the too-long-forgotten patriot who really laid the foundation of Scotland's success in her struggle against the ambitious designs of England. And when Andrew de Moray fell, covered with wounds and glory, his uncle, David de Moray, Bishop of Moray, took up his work, and carried it on with a thoroughness, a devotion, a courage, and a singleness of purpose, to which there is no parallel in the history of the War of Independence. But Andrew de Moray and David de Moray were Celts, members of an ancient Celtic house. William Wallace, too, was a Celt, while Robert Bruce was more Celtic than anything else. What need to point the moral? The War of Independence was the achievement of Celtic Scotland. It was inspired by Celtic tradition, Celtic sentiment, and Celtic fervour; it was sustained and won by the Northern Scots, in origin almost wholly of Celtic descent, fighting under the standards of leaders almost wholly Celtic by blood.[1]

Two observations of a general nature and I have done. The first is this. May I venture to express the hope that ardent patriots of the ultra-Scottish type will not leap to to the conclusion that in these pages I have sought to pluck a rose from the chaplet of Wallace? If I have done anything, I may claim, on the contrary, to have resuscitated the memory of another patriot whose name is worthy to rank with the immortal name of Wallace in Scottish hearts, and to have added another hero to the gallery of heroes in the national Valhalla. It was Andrew de Moray's fate to die young and to die unsung. But that is no reason why the historian should not accord him his due place in the history of his country, or why the most ardent worshipper of Wallace should begrudge him the fame which is justly his.

The second observation is one which applies just as truly to the whole history of Scotland as it does to the history of the War of Independence. It is that the history of Scotland has too long been written from a far too narrow standpoint, from the standpoint that is of the southern Lowlands, and from that standpoint alone. So far as the War of Independence is concerned we have had in the foregoing pages abundant demonstration of the truth of this, and it is only necessary to say that there is ample evidence to prove that the same is true, to a greater or lesser degree, of the whole history of Scotland. Meantime, however, I have succeeded in restoring Celtic Scotland, and especially the northern part of Celtic Scotland, to its true place in the history of the War of Independence, and with that, for the time being, I am content. But the time has surely come when it should be possible for the history of Scotland to be treated as the history of the whole land and people instead of as the history of the counties which lie nearest to the English border, of the counties which became, by conquest or annexation, part of the kingdom of the Scots.

[1] Compare Mr. Andrew Lang—"The War of Independence was won by the Lowland Scots (in origin mainly of English descent) fighting under the standards of leaders more or less Norman by blood." *Hist. of Scot.*, i. 495, in Appendix headed "The Celts in the War of Independence"!

INDEX

ABERDEEN, Flemings in, 5, 6; English stronghold, 323, 331
— Bishop of. *See* Chen, Henry le
Aberdeenshire, rising against Edward I, 22, 28, 59, 60, 61; Bruce's campaign of 1307 in, 306–318
Abernethy, Sir Alexander, 143, 144, 241, 242, 265, 398
Aboyne, English stronghold, 323; fall of, 331
Aiky-Brae, overthrow of Comyn at, 323, 328
Aird, John of the, 54, 58
Airth, Sir William de, 376
Alban, Celtic kingdom of, 212, 215
Alexander II, settlement of crown on Bruce, Lord of Annandale, 106, 108
Alexander III, death of, 11, 106, 113
Anglo-Norman element in Scotland, 9, 10
Angus, Earl of, one of Balliol's auditors, 109, 111; renews homage to Edward I on Balliol's resignation, 116; hostility to Bruce, 221, 364; flight from Bannockburn, 473
Angus, Lawrence de, 229
Angus Og, later Lord of the Isles, adherent of Bruce, 135, 223, 247, 273, 276, 346, 351, 356, 364, 465
Argyll, Alexander of, Bruce's foe, 20, 109, 111, 324, 328, 337; truce with Bruce, 335, 339, 340, 347; at St. Andrews Parliament, 336, 339, 350, 364; retiral to England, 339, 350, 351, 352
Argyll, John of, reconquers Isle of Man for England, 411
Argyllshire, rising against Edward I, 19, 20; conquest by Bruce, 333–347, 488
Athol, Countess of, 15
Athol, David, Earl of, takes Brechin Castle, 307, 308; hostility to Bruce, 364; becomes adherent of Bruce and accompanies him to Inverness, 396, 399; at Parliament of Edward II, 398; quarrel with Edward Bruce, 400; desertion of Bruce on eve of Battle of Bannockburn, 400, 476
— John, Earl of, father of above, adherent of Bruce, 66, 109, 110, 214, 215, 222, 228, 235, 245; petition to Edward I, 196; capture and execution, 246, 255, 267
Ayr Castle, English stronghold, besieged by Bruce, 143, 262, 277, 374; fall of, 373, 374

BAA, William de, 226
Bain, tentative dates of documents relating to Bruce discussed, 124. *Also many footnotes*
Balconie Castle, siege of, 41
Balkasky, Thomas de, 231
Balliol, Alexander de, 43
Balliol, John, declared King of Scotland by Edward I as overlord, 93, 107; cancels Treaty of Brigham, 94; renounces fealty to Edward I, 94; table showing descent, 105; auditors of, 109; refusal of Bruces to acknowledge, 114, 116, 117; resignation, 119; his party supported by the Comyns, 141, 142, 144, 188
Banff, 190, 332, 353, 370, 371, 373; fall of, 374, 375
Bannockburn, battle of, prelude to, 429–449; numbers engaged at, 430–436; divisions of the Scottish army at, 437–449; first phase of the battle, 450–462; second phase, 463–477; position and tactics of English army, 463; loot collected by the Scots, 474, 477; English losses, 475; Scottish losses, 476
Barbour quoted, 16, 236, 244, 248, 270, 279, 280–281, 302, 307, 308, 333, 335, 336, 339, 354, 357, 361, 398, 399, 400, 404, 405, 408, 418, 420, 423, 425, 426, 431, 433, 434, 435, 437, 440, 441, 444, 445, 446, 453, 456, 457, 458, 461, 466, 467, 468, 469, 470, 471, 472, 474, 475, 476
Barclay of Cairns, David. *See* Berkeley
Bartholomew, Roger, case of, 95
Beaumont, Sir Henry, 453
Berkeley, Sir David de, adherent of Bruce, 215, 222, 244, 268, 349, 364
— Hugh de, adherent of Bruce, 487
— Walter de, Sheriff of Banff, adherent of Bruce, 210, 304, 349, 487, 488
— Sir William de, adherent of Bruce, 229, 235, 268
Berwick, English stronghold, 1, 9, 370, 371, 372, 374, 392, 414, 416, 427; siege by Edward I, 1; attempted surprise by Bruce's army, 401–402
Berwick Burgess, case of appeal of, 93, 94
Bethune, James, Archbishop of Glasgow, his foundation for Scots scholars in Paris, 202

491